Who Are Koreans?

Who Are Koreans?

Hong Sah-myung

다옹

Preface and Acknowledgements

My gray hairs are honored by having a daunting research published in a book. This research project is one of a few attempts to characterize the identity of Koreans in terms of their behavioral and attitudinal tendencies. Nearly three decades have elapsed since the conception of this project and its completion. The age at which this research was undertaken increased the loneliness of an author for a theme with limited empirical and conceptual base. Aware that I am a captive of my own culture, I endeavored to hone the pre-conceptualized self image against the perceived image of Korea and Koreans. By reducing the perception gap, I trust that I can come down to a true image of them.

The self-identity is an undeniable component of the human experience and the quest for the national identity is given urgency as we move toward a globalized world in which each person feels the pressure to embrace a multi-cultural identity. Man will lose the self in a sea of diversity. Without the cognitive map to show the way of life, our life is merely a puzzling labyrinth. The sense of national identity was the vital force in the rebirth of Korea after its identity had been blurred by colonial rule. Globalization, on the other hand, obscures a people's sense of the past, and this global trend compels us to be more concerned about national identity as the departure point in a daunting journey into a future of uncertainty.

Geo-political factors, among others, are the most influential shapers of national identity. Korea shaped its unique character as it lived as a weakling surrounded by mighty continental powers. The resulting ethnic solidarity amounts to much as a high point of Korean history, but the professed ethnic consciousness belies a strong tendency toward factionalism. While Koreans are held together by ethnic and cultural homogeneity and the centralized governing system, Korean history attests to an impossible coexistence of ethnic solidarity and factional division. In centralized political systems and homogeneous culture, grouping is artificial; it is more often an opportunistic matter for access to power whenever Korea basked in spells of stability. Korean political factions rarely group into larger assemblies around a creed, ideology or class.

The most remarkable Korean values are hierarchical and collective consciousness on which the democratic ideals of equality and freedom were grafted. Hierarchical consciousness generates a strong vertical pressure to obscure one's horizontal perspectives. Seniority still marks each step up a hierarchical ladder. Average Koreans still subscribe to relatively closed social groupings and strong personal connections. Koreans' sense of belonging, being cared for, and dependence on the protective embrace of a group is strong. In the last few decades, liberal democracy elevated the importance of equality and freedom against the backdrop of the traditional values. These concepts are an effective guide to public life but have not been well internalized in the private domain where hierarchy and collectivity still dominate popular consciousness.

Globalization sharpens the clash of particular values against universalism. It is not Korea alone that experiences value conflicts. As globalization awakens people to new perspectives on life, an objective understanding of the self is as much important as an antidote for a fallible self-image. The parallel experiences of others, therefore, become a frame of reference to compare oneself with. With these in mind, reference to other countries is made a repeated refrain in the following chapters. Comparing Koreans with other ethnic groups, it is fair to say that Koreans are marked by a certain ethnic and cultural homogeneity. While national identity is a matter of history, culture and ethnicity, Koreans lack shared ideology, religion and sets of institutions holding together the mosaic society of diversity.

Globalization declares ethnic nationalism as anathematic to social advance. Still, many Koreans consider one ethnic patch as the touchstone of the state's legitimacy. Ethnic consciousness is one of the most revealing traits of Koreans. This study attempts to address questions such as: How did ethnic consciousness shape the unique traits of Koreans"; Are traditional values compatible with universal values?; Is the partial replacement of old values with new ones possible or must Koreans sew a new value tapestry?; and Is liberal democracy based on equality and freedom feasible in today's Korea?

The identity of Koreans has a limited validity because my focus on South Korea gave a short shrift to North Korea. Despite the professed ethnic and cultural homogeneity, the seeds of hatred and distrust remain fertile in the radicalism of ideological confrontation. The sentiment of brotherhood resounds with the call for the reunification of scattered families. But a forbidden gulf between the two Korean states not only in political and institutional but psychological and emotional structures create almost insurmountable obstacles to reunification. In the North, wrecks of traditional values lay scattered in the wake of ruthless iconoclasm while South Koreans struggle with value conflicts. The quest for the identity of Koreans, therefore, will remain incomplete unless justice can be done to the Northern half of the peninsula. The true profile of North Korea is hobbled by a wide gap between the contrived and real images of its identity.

Readers may see in the following pages "Korea" frequently substitute for "South Korea." I very often fail to distinguish between the two, in large part, due to the fact that South Korea is more visible than the north on the world stage. It has become customary to interchange the two words not only among Koreans but among foreigners. South Koreans may be baffled, if not incensed, by a question, "what part of Korea are you from," reproaching the questioner's ignorance of the contemporary situation of Korea. South Koreans tend to flatter their own ego to the denigration of its northern partner, and I often find myself susceptible to this bias. Should there be errors that mislead readers, I offers apologies for them in advance.

In creating this book, there are various groups of people to whom author owes his gratitude. In the first place, author is grateful to the faculty at the Hankuk University of Foreign Studies that endorsed the creation of a course on the identity of Koreans for graduate students. Dr. Ahn Byung-man, then the President of the University master-minded the creation of area studies of which this course was a component. Above all, Dr. David W. Strangway, the former President of the University of British Columbia was the first scholar to review the manuscript and gave encouragement and support throughout the research project. Despite the fact that his major was earth science, he was deeply concerned for areas studies and was credited with the creation of Korean studies at the University. Professor James Larsen lowered himself to be a student in author's class and placed at disposal his unpublished paper, enabling me to fill a grievous gap. Professor Gustav Rosen, the University of Stockholm provided me with an opportunity to teach the course on foreign students. This teaching experience abroad was of great help to objectify my own perspectives on Korea and Koreans.

My special thanks go to Professor Keith Howard, the School of Oriental and African Studies, the University of London, and Professor Edward Shultz, the University of Hawaii. They gave a thorough review of the manuscript and each line of the book is the reminder of my indebtedness to these scholars. Besides, Georg Neumann, my German colleague, showed a keen interest in my project and made available a German Government (DAAD: Deuscher Akademischer Austauschdienst) scholarship that enabled me to enrich my research. Professor Werner Sasse, Hamburg University, made his office available to do my research in Germany. I would like also to thank my students and friends who helped me, without reward, with specific tasks in creating this book. This book is not the result of my own efforts; it is the product of all who made their share of contribution. I now offer the results of this endeavor to readers, trusting that they find in it some perspectives to stimulate new thoughts about their own countries and people.

What is it about the Koreans?

How can one reflect on seeing, first hand, how Korea has developed from a colonial underdog into a divided peninsula of two competing states at the opposite ends of the political spectrum? How can one account for the way that ashes left by a civil war which marked the point when the Cold War turned hot were swept up to underpin one of the most cutting-edge digital economies in today's world? What does it mean to have lived through the miracle in which South Korea has hauled itself from a distant and largely unknown poverty-stricken economic basket case to a global superpower? These are the questions that Hong Sah-myung seeks to answer in the following pages.

Looking at Korea today, whether at the cosmopolitan modernity of Seoul or at the isolated strangeness of Pyongyang, we are apt to forget recent history, and to ignore what people on both sides of the DMZ have stood witness to. The remarkable changes experienced in the lifetimes of contemporary Koreans are, simply remarkable. Viewed from a distance, change is a fact, something we teach about but engage with from our own, different, experience. Close up, though, that change has an aura. While the aura can be diluted, distanced, and lost in modern mechanical reproduction (to take from Walter Benjamin's famous essay), it has a visceral quality to those who have lived within as well as through it. It smells, it sounds, it is seen. As an ethnomusicologist, I subscribe to Fran Tonkiss's observation that where the visual is action and spectacle, sound is atmosphere. By activating the senses, memories are ingrained within a temporal frame.

Radical change is best experienced when lived in, and there is, then, much that Koreans with grey hairs can tell us. Hong was born at the end of the colonial occupation. His country was divided when World War II ended, not by his compatriots but as part of a distant agreement between Roosevelt and Churchill to which Stalin acceded, and a division that was then inscribed on a map by two desk officers in Washington. He has had to find ways to understand both the tragedy of that division and its legacy, while learning to deal with the remarkable changes which have come during his lifetime. For any Korean, this is no easy task, and in any lived-in understanding we can expect to find selective appeals to tradition as well as modernity, understandings of race and ethnicity that challenge political correctness, and disturbing mixes of the dystopian and the utopian. Selection could be considered a mark of nostalgia, but to reduce it to this would be in just to those who have lived in rather than through recent history: nostalgia comes from the luxury of being elsewhere, in a different time and place, with time to reflect. The pace of change in Korea has, ultimately, been too fast, accelerating exponentially the processes of industrialization and modernization, individualism and democracy, and condensing change into a few short decades. Justification of the approach, though, makes reference to a more distant history, reference that is not unreasonable given the long dynastic history that tells of 'Korea' as a relatively unified entity, and which interprets Korean peculiarity into philosophical, ethical and behavioural traditions that emerged in antiquity. The distinction of history allows understandings that judiciously select from Western experience, and which may be reluctant to embrace Enlightenment discourse full-on. The story will, inevitably, expose clashes between East and West.

Are Koreans that special to be singled out? Within the discourse of Korea as a nation driven by *han* sits the belief that Koreans are shrimps between whales. The story is familiar: centuries of Chinese suzerainty ended with court meanderings in the face of external challenges as foreign navies looked for coaling stations, trading ports, and influence; the Sino-Japanese and Russian-Japanese wars fought over Korea led to Japanese colonial occupation; Japan's defeat at the end of World War II led to the division of Korea; the Korean War left two opposing states; Korean modernization is often seen in terms of Americanization, and a loss of identity. Koreans, though, have found ways to balance Arjun Appadurai's notion of deterritorialization, where shared technology and imaging removes distance to make the local global, with something of John Tomlinson's discussion of reterritorialization; the impetus towards globalization has been counterpointed by localizing forces which Anthony Giddens would describes as a weighing of anchors to conjoin proximity and distance. Be this through family and lineage, through language, aesthetics, or in the elevation of cultural production as icons of Intangible Cultural Heritage, Koreanness is a given. But, international acceptance, as much as the discourse within Korea, is hindered because of another aspect of history: there has been a long Western involvement with China and Japan, and this is witnessed in the abundance of accounts, whether academic or popular in orientation, that interpret 'East Asia' through either or both a Chinese or Japanese lens. Korea for too long remained largely unknown, and is as a result falsely seen as being in some way an orphan cast off by its powerful neighbours. One example from my own academic discipline is the still common assertion that Korean music has Chinese origins, despite the two central importations of Chinese instruments and repertoires having occurred in 1114 and 1116, within 50 years of those pesky Viking offshoots, the Normans, invading and taking over England. Koreans still need to defend their identity, and to position themselves within the aura of place: I am Korean, because I breathe Korean air, I drink Korean water, I eat Korean food.

Parts of a Korean account of modernity and change will not make comfortable reading. Walter Benjamin, after all, as he explored European cities in the 1920s and 1930s, found ugliness 'as the true reservoir of beauty, better than any treasure cast, a jagged mountain with all the inner gold of beauty gleaming from the wrinkles, glances, features'. Critical of the industrial detritus that surrounded him in Marseilles, as Graeme Gilloch puts it, he wrote imagistic miniatures that captured the vivid colours, dense impressions and abundant stimuli of the cityscape: the aura, writ large. The peculiarity of a Korean account hides sorrow, the in expungible tragedy of millions of lost family members that stands testament to that unjustified territorial division, to the migrations and repatriations caused as troops trampled north and south over the peninsula during the first year of the Korean War, and the consequence of the more recent escapes of refugees from North Korea.

Still, though, a Korean account must reconcile change that was once unimaginable, change that was both welcomed and difficult. My personal experience of Republic of Korea is far too limited. It only goes back four decades. In the 1980s, the countryside remained a different world – with dirt tracks rather than paved roads, with a single wind-up phone serving each village that required raising an operator to connect with neighbouring villages let alone the world outside, and with dodgy electrical supplies prone not just to failure but to short-circuiting and potential disaster. Into the 1970s, poverty still stalked the streets of Seoul. Few South Koreans had TVs; at the beginning of the 1980s, colour broadcasting arrived, but TV sets were expensive, and I recall only too well the fist-fight between my changgo drum teacher and my landlord, an Episcopalian priest, over a colour TV set that I won in 1981 as part of the top prize at the Korea Herald/KBS annual performance contest for foreigners. By the 1990s, high tech replaced heavy industrial production, and the dense packing of millions of citizens into rapidly expanding cityscapes meant Koreans were ready to embrace the Internet before almost anyone else. I have seen remarkable change in these few decades. But, step back further in time, and one reaches a point where those Koreans with white hairs today were forced to adopt Japanese names and experience, as Janet Poole puts it in her discussion of late 1930s' literature, the entangled realm of an everyday life lived under colonial facism. These are memories that inhabit the current volume.

Hong Sah-myung has for many years served as a friend and adviser to foreigners seeking to understand Korea. He has patiently listened to our misinterpretations and naivety, and has cautiously introduced us to the aura of Korea as a lived-in place. Many of us have struggled to live with the changing Korea, to smell, see, and hear it. As an interlocutor, he has served in a number of roles, most importantly steering the Korea Research Foundation in the 1980s and 1990s. Many of us will likely have sensory memories of the Foundation, at the time occupying a building on the site of the former Seoul National University: who recalls the thin mattresses that hardly softened the solid wooden beds, and the French Toast in the restaurant? Hong liaised with Korean officialdom as well as with

American, European, and Asian agencies, representing Korea but also championing Korean Studies. He arranged sponsorship, assisting with the birth of many publications, including translations of Korean scholarship into English. The result is that the names of many scholars and diplomats who have worked with Korea, both departed and living, will be found in this volume. Some stand witness to mutually enlightening discussions as much as to Hong Sah-myung's efforts to sponsor research, although erudition demands a broader reading, and here enables the author to blend his long-term engagement with Europe and America with his intimate knowledge of more local academic discourse. Many of us who practice Korean Studies have heard elements of his account, but here it is, complete.

Keith Howard, Professor Emeritus, SOAS, University of London

Table of Contents

Chapter One — Who Are Koreans? 17

Chapter Two — The Historical Identity of Koreans 47

Introduction

Korea looks like a mere blob precariously attached to the Asian landmass. Koreans have inhabited the peninsular for millennia and shaped over time the character of Koreans as distinct from those of its neighbors. Its land, roughly the size of Great Britain, borders on China and the Eastern maritime provinces of Russia in the north and is cradled, across the sea, by the Japanese archipelago. Korea has long served as a land bridge for the flow of continental cultures to Japan.

Owing to its unique location, much of Korea's history is a story of foreign incursions and the resulting struggles to maintain a precarious existence. From the world perspective, Korea was for long dimly perceived in the shadow of the towering China and then in the twentieth century as a colonial outpost of Japan that belatedly joined the ranks of the imperialistic powers. Lying at a crossroad in Northeast Asia, Korea, frequently known as "the land of the morning calm," belies its turbulent history: it has long been a frail, small kingdom that has been the trampling ground for the untamed nomadic hordes from the north and cultural upstarts from the south. Koreans put this historical fact in ironic proverbs, "a shrimp gets its back broken in a row of whales." Every Korean knows what this means. Nonetheless, depredations by invaders simply reinforced the will of Koreans to survive. Their resilience and stoicism found manifestation in their passive, mystical reverence for nature as suggested in a metaphor of water, which is the strongest of all elements because it gradually wears away even the hardest stone.

As they endured repeated foreign incursions, Koreans developed a sense of fatalism. They believed that life was transient and ephemeral, not worth being experienced with much gusto. The fatalistic view of life was fueled by Buddhism, which had touched the soft spot of their minds. Koreans take hardship for granted as a way of life. "Even if heaven falls, there is a way out." Food shortage used to be endemic in this resource-poor country, but the people fed on saying, "A cobweb does not stretch itself inside the mouth of a living man." In this way, Koreans have not lost a robust, satiric and sometimes uncouth sense of humor. They did not merely endure hardships but produced artistic, scientific and literary achievements distinct from the people of its neighboring countries.

The fatalistic view of life was tempered with a vision of something in their minds to be hopeful about. The combination of despair and hope consoled Koreans as they felt forlorn in living in the inhospitable world. Fatalism did not overwork itself to evoke pessimism. Immersed in the mystical doctrine of Buddhism or in the classic philosophy of Confucianism, they asserted that man should not be ashamed of coarse food, humble clothing, and modest dwellings. Rather man should be ashamed of not being cultivated in perceiving beauty. One verse has it: "Living on coarse rice and water, with a bent arm for a pillow, mirth may yet be mine. Ill-gotten wealth and honors are like floating clouds."

Foreign incursions brought forth an early advent of a centralized monarchical kingdom in the fourth century, which remained, without radical alteration, through much of history. It had clearly delineated boundaries, resulting in a remarkable accord between political, cultural and language identities. In this historical context, ethnic homogeneity was celebrated as a rare blessing hardly to be found elsewhere. Ethnic homogeneity, though, entailed a dear price they had to pay. Throughout much of its history, Korea shut itself from the outside world. Few contacts with outsiders resulted in a simplistic view of the world. Ethnic solidarity was sought at the cost of changes that might have lain golden eggs, as they basked in a blissful ignorance of the world.

The dimly perceived Korea, as known in the world, concealed the crucial role it has played, for centuries, as a catalyst for the mix of continental and maritime cultures, and in the formation of Japanese ancient culture. While most of its erstwhile neighbors receded into obscurity, Korea survived them and today retains a unique link bridging back to earlier tormentors that have long since receded into oblivion. Its past tribulations left a commonly heard metaphor, "a candle light before the wind." The major threat to their identity was the tidal surge of Chinese culture. Among the states surrounding China, Korea and Vietnam stand out for their persistent struggles to preserve their unique cultures.

Her adjacency to China says much about the Koreans' tendency to simplify the world and pour disdain on other dominant powers. Korea dismissed other ideas as not worthy of learning except those from China. This parochial view of the world, with a touch of xenophobic sentiments, explains the diplomatic inertia and naivety as Korea became the vortex for great power rivalries in the nineteenth and twentieth century. Koreans were slow to discern or appreciate dangers that befell it, resulting from its long-maintained blissful isolation.

Reactions to Western imperialism in the nineteenth century were different across the countries of Asia. China and Japan bowed to Western threats, but Korea, the weakest, resolved to maintain its blissful isolation, claiming itself to retain the splendor of Confucian idealism. This led to rash confrontations with the Western powers as Korea raised its torch high as the sole citadel of lofty Asian values, blaming China and Japan for cowardice before the Western threat. However, Korea's ignorance of the outside world, together with a long-simmering distrust of foreigners, came at a cost, dooming the intrepid puppy not to be afraid of the tiger.

After the Pacific War was over, Koreans emerged from Japanese domination with such a profound sense of worthlessness that they seemed to have lost any notion of who they were, where they came and where they should go. Korea once eluded the world notice with its people feeling worthless and powerless to have their identity known. No sooner had Korea begun to toddle than it became the first child to be traumatized by territorial division and the fratricidal civil war. The long-lasting division of

Korea continues to befuddle the world, resulting in a blurred, and sometimes mistaken, identity of Koreans. The irony is that the stronger ethnic and cultural bonds of Koreans were severed by a foreign-imposed ideology they had never heard of.

For a people who have gone through a long process of homogenization, the continuing presence of two Koreas may well be viewed as transient, stirring optimism that the division will be cast aside in a historical tide. Reference to the historical tide gives rise to romanticism sometimes taking the upper hand of a realistic indifference. The flip side of this optimism is that the passage of time creates ever widening gulfs, not only in their way of life but in value consciousness. Given this fact, as time passes, the more difficult it becomes to patch the differences in institutions, way of life and psychic makeup. The two halves of Korea have drifted so far from one another that perhaps they are beyond any point of reconciliation. Ironically, then, Korea, despite its professed ethnic homogeneity, sees its people split asunder, with no prospect in sight for reconciliation and reunification.

Consequently, Koreans inhabit the most dangerous region of the world. Dark clouds of tension and anxiety hover over the peninsula like a ticking time bomb. The economic growth of South Korea amidst such an uneasy tension is a story worth telling others. Its economic spurt can be likened to a wild flower sprouting through a cracked concrete. And yet, as they stood on the threshold of a new and vibrant era, Koreans made uncompromising efforts to fashion their traditional values into a force of dynamism. Hence, the economic development of South Korea is not haphazard but the dramatization of people's potential as the deepest recess of their aspirations met with a historical denouement.

Many Koreans bemoan Korea's geo-political location as the cause of hardships, but they have turned these into advantages characteristic of being a peninsula, fashioning them into an effective development tool. Value conflict continues to afflict Koreans, but it provides a new ground for the possibility of integrating old and new into a mutually reinforcing relationship. The exposure of Neo-Confucianism to a new frame of reference engendered a secular and utilitarian version of the philosophy. A majority of foreigners who imagined Korea as a traumatized child now marvel at the wonders brought by economic and social development. Despite all the changes, Korea still retains many of its traditions, though their influence has considerably abated. Visitors from abroad now wonder at the strange harmony of old and new. Not far beneath the surface lie value conflicts that are sorely in need of being refashioned into a new tapestry. Korea is a mess of contradictions – between the north and the south, between old and new, between homogeneity and diversity, between collective consciousness and divisive feuds, and between material improvement and social ills. The time is ripe to unravel the entangled skein of values and examine them in terms of their compatibility with modernity with an aim to create a road map that will guide us along the way to the future.

Chapter

One

—

Who Are Koreans?

—

Culture can shape and be shaped by a people's sense of themselves as a national or ethnic identity.

National Identity

||||||||||||||||||||||||||||||||||||||||||||||||||||||||||||||||||||

Culture, Social Behavior, Value and Institutions

The purpose of this study is to characterize Koreans in terms of their differences from those of other cultural or political communities. The premise is that each ethnic or political group has its unique traits that evolved from interactions of genetic-based social behaviors with cultural structures and institutions. Nicholas Wade attributes differences in civilizations to different institutions (2014,58-9) and states that "social institutions are a blend of genetics and culture. His notion of culture as a component of social institution contrasts with a prevailing belief that culture has greater importance as a shaper of collective traits. Culture is the opposite of nature, that is, what humans made and constructed in its struggle against a brute and untamed nature. Paul Horton defines culture as "everything which is socially learned and shared by the members of a society"(1964,59). David Landes singles out culture as a decisive factor: "culture makes all the differences."Therefore, social institutions, as organized by system of social relationships, may be viewed as the manifestation of culture, designed to meet the needs of society.

Given that social behavior has a genetic base, one limitation of this study is that it does not deal with genetics. Its exclusion by no means belittles the role of genetics in explaining the behavioral patterns dependent on the variations in culture and institution. Genetics are part of hard science and it is beyond the scope of this study.[1] The hypothesis is that each individual has his or her own identity shaped by living among the people of a common ethnic or cultural frame within boundaries that remain constant. Humans are social beings, marking them from genetically close animal species. Culture is neither a matter of choice nor something deliberately fashioned; it emerges and evolves in a manner that is beyond single person's control or logic. Members of a political or a cultural community hone their endowed characteristics against culture or institutions. Human wisdom and imagination work to make each person within a group identical in the ways they think and act,

What made Chinese minorities in Southeast Asia economically more successful than "native" people? The answer is that, in dealing with the sense of the core values and attitudes, culture comes to the fore. Culture evolves from social behaviors through interactions with the environmental features of the region in which people live. Culture is an alloy of socially and genetically influenced behaviors. Social behavior adapts to the challenges of surviving and prospering in a given place. In explaining the advance of Europeans over East Asians, both genetic and cultural influences account for differences.

Self-Centered Microcosm

Huntington defines "identity" as an individual's or a group's sense of self, evolved from self-consciousness that 'I' or 'we' possess distinct qualities as an entity. The sense of self differentiates 'me' from 'you' and 'us' from 'them' (2004;20). Although confined by ancestry, gender and ethnicity, people are relatively free to define their identities as they wish. Each of us builds our own microcosm, and our ego becomes the center of its world. The implication is that identities are imagined; they are what we think we are and what we want to be. Whatever it means, self-image is not necessarily congruous with one's true identity, unless the true identity is the reconciliation of self-image with perceived image. The perception gap between subjective and objective images suggests the need to develop a comparative perspective, and this can best be done by placing oneself in a different cultural context. Self-image changes as one comes of age, and maturity is the measure of objective perception of self. By analogy, understanding other countries provides clues into the other side of one's own country.

Any quest for the identity of Koreans may be thwarted by the fact that the world is increasingly becoming a global village. Hence, increased interaction among the countries inevitably shapes a common face of the world that can overshadow local peculiarities. Increased contacts between countries blur distinctions between values that are particular and universal, and the definition of identity may falter at the complexity of historical, cultural and value factors. A shared history builds up common memories of the past and set these to interplay with responses, active or passive, to the environment. The perception of historical events gives a unique substance to Korean characters. The interplay of culture with social behaviors underlies the historical path of Koreans. In this, "the history of a particular time is not a haphazard incident, separate from what had preceded it, but is part of an ongoing drama in which a people act as protagonists on the stage of history" (Hong Sah-myung, 2011,7). A new line of argument has it that the uniqueness of an historical event precludes the possibility of it being repeated. Therefore, the identity of Koreans is a product of a particular time frame, not a universal identity that has existed throughout history. The two streams run in parallel; one is particular to time, while the other flows like a river throughout its history.

Thinking about the relationship between culture and value on one hand and the historical experiences of a political community on the other, one asks "which of these is the cause or the effect?" This may be a classic 'chicken and egg' question, but there is no denying that the quest for the identity of Koreans accords importance to the nakedly true nature of a value system that underpins their social behaviors and institutions. But such a quest falters when we recognize that the value system of each state or ethnic group is a confusing tangle of different cultural and ideological strands. The maze of confusion defeats any attempt to single out a dominant value, let alone debate on which value is intrinsic or extrinsic. "Every culture is similarly made up of shreds and tatters from other cultures. These cultural elements are in a continual process of interactions; new syntheses and combinations are constantly produced" (Peter Farb 1968,28029).

The value system of Korea is a grand amalgam that evolved through a millennia-long process of mingling with alien cultures. Each emerging value over time becomes a distinctive layer which in turn is fossilized into oblivion or adulterated as a new layer is laid over it. It is through this process that values have become a conglomerate. An attempt to define the identity of Koreans may prove to be futile, because it is naïve to lump values together as a single group and claim categorically that they think and behave like this or like that. Intellectually challenging as it is, it makes only limited sense to talk about a national character. The small size of the Korean peninsula, with distinct borders and cultural uniformity, however, inspires an attempt to distinguish Koreans from others.

Identical Beings

Koreans are ultimately bound by an amazingly identical culture that has one-to-one correspondence with a political community. Although Koreans are not necessarily of common descent, they achieved national unity earlier than others under a strong and centralized monarchy. Their vaunted homogeneity derives from the millennia-old history of an integrated political community which dissolved all ethnic and cultural distinctions. The result is that Koreans' behaviors tend to follow a certain identifiable pattern that is distinct from others. Every Korean bows deferentially when he or she meets an old relative on the street. Such an act of greeting may be regarded as ritualistic, having little to do with volition. But failure to do it is the cause of displeasure in a seniority-conscious culture.

The quest for the identity of Koreans beckons a journey into the past to get at the roots of the Koreans' beliefs, that is, a blend of Shamanism, Buddhism and Confucianism. Koreans' class consciousness is the result of having attuned to a hierarchically arranged social structure. Hierarchical consciousness collides with confederate nations such as the United States and Canada whose citizens relished an egalitarian dream and pioneering spirit. Inhabiting a virgin land, these people broke free from the institutional inhibitions of the past and made a new start. Korea is not free from the weight of the past, and an inherited authority and status consciousness still remain fertile. "Even in the United Kingdom, everyone seems to know what class they are in and they just stick to it" (Hugh Mackay1993,152), despite the wide-spread idea that everyone can be prosperous, defying the same, rigid class distinctions. As egalitarianism was imposed upon traditional values, a question arises: is Korea a hierarchical society or an egalitarian society?

Koreans were once known as a compliant and restrained people. They used to accept the given status and played their role accordingly, doing things they considered good for family or country. The sense of individuality was lost in their commitments to their clans and small groups. The passage of time, though, wrought changes in the way Koreans behave themselves. In today's Korea, we see quite a few Koreans putting on airs, just because they live in a big house or drive luxurious cars. They do so to a greater extent than those of countries where the majority of people belong to middle class. This may be due to an innate longing to be better than others, an urge deeply rooted in hierarchical view of the world. How one is perceived is closely related to one's status in a group- conscious society.

The xenophobic trait of Koreans shaped by historical trauma is manifest in parochial racism. So far as individual interactions with others take place, man defines oneself in relation to others by specific reference to similarities and differences. The identity of Koreans is ethnic, historical, cultural and value-oriented, and such factors are not relevant to Americans. The identity of Americans based on White

Anglo-Saxon-Protestants came under attack, as new immigrants created a greater racial diversity. Unlike Korea with common memories of the past, Americans identify themselves by "their commitments to the political principles of liberty, equality, individualism, democracy, the rule of law, and private property" (Samuel Huntington 2004, 46). This creedal component of identity allows them to claim that Americans have a civic national identity in contrast with the ethnic and ethno-cultural identities of other countries. Japan, to justify colonial rule, claimed that Koreans constitute "divergence from one ethnic root," but Koreans insisted on ethnic origins in Siberia, arguing that there was slim chance for ethnic fusion. Geographical proximity was not a guarantee for a good neighborhood. In the nineteenth century, Japan's ascent to a new power sharpened Korean sensitivity to what allowed it to surpass Korea in industrialization and modernization. Koreans had traditionally disdained Japanese as backward. What a strange twist of fate it was that a suddenly stronger Japan preyed on its cultural precursor! Korean identity was shaped in the evolving context of its relationships with its neighboring countries. Many Koreans choose to be worse off absolutely but better off than Japan rather than better off absolutely but not as well off as that rival.

Koreans do not necessarily share a common ancestry, but the fact that they have enjoyed a unitary political and cultural community over more than a millennium explains how ethnic and cultural disparities were dissolved. Ethnic homogeneity fed off with cultural homogeneity to shape an ethno-centric perspective of the world and this created a gap between the subjective and objective view of history. Koreans talk with a sense of pride about the epic warfare of Koguryo, one of the earliest three kingdoms, against China.[2] But an objective light describes Korea as an anointed sufferer of foreign beatings. On the flip side, Koreans detect a streak of triumphant pride in the way they have endured the historical tragedy. The rash confrontation of 19th century Korea with France and America was another swelling pride: Koreans were triumphantly maintaining the citadel of lofty Asian value, when China and Japan fell on their knees before the foreign threats. Nevertheless, in the view of others, the confrontation with the impregnable powers cannot be considered in other ways than the manifestation of temerity that comes from the invincible ignorance of the outside world. Whatever its motive might be, the military showdown is taken for a reckless venture that China and Japan would have avoided at all costs.

Time brought significant changes in how Koreans are perceived by others. "Although not all Korean hearts beat to the rhythm of Confucian virtue, Korean society has been built on repressive norms in the absence of alternative ideologies. The Confucian interpretation of moral virtues is stoic and ascetic. Defying what appears to be a repressive society, today's Koreans impress observers from outside as more individualistic, more freewheeling and more outspoken than Chinese and Japanese. They fervently push themselves, exhibiting an inconceivable Olympian ambition, convinced that hard work will bring success. There is a touch of risk-taking or reckless dash. Such an impetuous proclivity of working habits finds its manifestation in everyday business activities today.

Koreans traditionally lacked a sense of tolerance for other ethnic groups and cultures, since they had few opportunities to interact with foreigners. There are signs of Korea moving toward a semblance of pluralistic society. In a movement to redefine the identity of a nation state, the cultural maturity of its citizens deserves a new emphasis. An apt analogy is that the nation is like an "adolescent," whose behaviors are subject to mind swings. "At one moment, adolescents long to be allowed to be dependent on their parents; at the next, they wage a furious battle for independence" (Hugh Mackay 1993, 202). Analogically, Korea may resemble an immature person – or an immature society – in that its confidence is quickly eroded by a negative experience; its small successes are held as justification for swaggering arrogance. Koreans may have little tolerance for words other than praises. Whatever the future may be, Korea should behave with maturity, drawing its particular strength from the depth and maturity of its cultural heritage. Its brand image will be enhanced by the global perception of its cultural heritage and on-going dynamism. The days when values underpinned the pre-determined codes of conduct have passed, and Koreans are entering an age of redefinition in which the future is fraught with uncertainties.

Ecological Influence

||||||||||||||||||||||||||||||||||||||||||||||||||||||||||||||||

Topographical and Geographical Factors

Ecological environment has so profound influence on the characterization of a people's identity. First of all, topographical factors help to describe traditional communities. Small scale peasant farming within the confines of villages, separated from other villages by mountains, helped Koreans maintain close blood relationships. Social bonds rarely extended beyond genealogy. The average Korean still subscribe to relatively closed social grouping and strong personal connections based on blood relations or daily contact. As a result, the collective-conscious Koreans are unusually strong in home-bound yearning, created by their strong sense of blood ties or by emotional attachment to the birth place of their ancestors. This is observed in their hectic rush, enduring the pain of breaking through traffic jams, to home towns on festive occasions. Still today, for the families who left their beloved ones in the north, family union remains a fantasy, and having no place to go on festive occasions brings them a visceral pain. They envy those who have hometowns to go on festive occasions. Koreans living in urban areas tend to organize molecular groups of hometown pals as a solace for their loneliness or sorrow. On a larger scale, incessant invasions by strong continental powers have reinforced the ethnic solidarity that is manifested in a blissful isolation of outsiders and a strong sense of nationalism.

Situated in the temperate climate zone, Koreans avoid continental weather and tropical heat. The traits of Koreans, by and large, have little to do with climate, revealing a contrast with the English melancholy ascribed to cloudy and wet weather. Gray, overcast skies make for gloomy landscapes, and the people in such climates tend towards indifference in their engagement with others. Koreans, by nature, are jovial, sociable, and optimistic when they are confined within their villages. Their abiding obsession with agriculture made Koreans compliant and submissive to the mercy of nature. In the past, Koreans stuck in their land lacked the courage to travel to see the worlds of strangers. As they succumbed to foreign aggressors, they suffered the ebb and flow of fortune. Korea is a unique case where its people failed to take peninsular advantages for trade and oceanic advance. The Roman Empire, Ottoman Turkey and Spain owed their ascendancy in wealth and power to the peninsular advantages.

Geography deserves attention for its role in characterizing Koreans different from their neighbors. The Chinese, by virtue of inhabiting a vast land, are imbued with continental characteristics that are not easily disturbed by trifles. They are relatively taciturn and seemingly impassionate, sometimes hard to read their minds by facial expressions. Koreans, in contrast, are easily swayed by emotions, and their facial expressions offer the straightforward reflection of their inner feelings. Today's Koreans are more outspoken and volatile than inhibitive Japanese. Alan Freeman portrays Korean temper as hot and spicy as their foods are. "A Korean will fight back loudly if he feels to have been violated" (1975,118). Despite the frequent emotional outbursts, it takes a good while for foreign residents to realize that Koreans have good senses of courtesy and a warm heart. Japanese kindness and orderly behavior engage the attention of foreigners, but the way they act in unison bewilders foreigners unfamiliar with the rift between the inner and outer beings: facial friendliness accompanies a ritualized behavior that does not necessarily reflect the inner minds. Japanese national character may have something to do with the insularity of the land which limited their contacts with continental powers. "The Japanese will more likely accept the slight and wrong, and seek vengeance later" (Freeman,115). A slur on one's pride or dignity led to vengeance resulting in death. Japanese attacks on British diplomats after it was forced to sign a trade treaty in 1855 was the manifestation of their collective vengeance on a slur on national pride. Many foreigners were victimized by a stab in the back.

Koreans, by and large, are more individualistic and freewheeling in behavior than their neighbors. To some foreign residents, Koreans are far more approachable than other Asians, contradicting the common notion that Koreans are clannish and inhibitive against strangers. Unlike other Asians that had been colonized by the West for centuries, Korea's bitter experience with Japan's colonial rule lasted for thirty-six years, imbuing Koreans with hatred and hostility. Physically, Koreans are bigger and more robust than Japanese. The Mongol heritage is more clearly stamped in their faces and bodies than the Japanese, who are a blending of many Asian racial groups. Koreans are compared to the Irish of Asia, though there are a lot more to characterize them apart. But they seem to share in more or less the same feelings – outgoing, ebullient, easy to sing, laugh and cry. Suddenly they turn into dark and brooding emotions.

The characterization of Koreans as emotional is inherently untenable, since it varies with its unfolding milieu. In earlier days, Koreans were known for stoicism and restraint from emotional swing. Advances in technology force people to move faster, and few things seem to be stable in today's world. The hectic pace of life is not only a challenge to norms which had been unswayable by the whims of the moment but constantly calls for improvised reactions. Korean youth has little sense of the tranquility in which human relationships have for long been nurtured and sustained. Modern society dispenses with safety valves that restrain emotional outbursts. Chinese today, are as open, if not more, to emotional outbursts as Koreans are. Chinese changed their characters with open access to the outside world. Being amidst Chinese tourists, one feels his ears attacked by loudspeakers. The rift between the outer and inner being finds its expression in the Japanese refusal to face the truth for which they owe apologies to their afflicted neighbors. When it comes to the shady side of their history, notably events subject to international censure, the inner being is at odds with the outer being. The shame of the past arouses violent tempers that are likely to blur the image of friendly, inhibited and prudent Japanese. It is worth noting, in this vein, the Germans' sense of history, reflected in their unflinching admission to the dark aspects of their recent history. Granted that the past is not a mere collection of our memories but justifies our beliefs in the present and future, it takes a lot of courage to have an objective perspective of one's misled past.

Owing to the gloomy weather, it is widely held that there are more misanthropists among the English than any other race, but this trait is, in a way, akin to indifference or apathy to the world of others. The English reluctance to be involved with others made England the first nation to worship individuality and privacy. The privacy of indifference, though, is not of a kind that shuts out the world but one that enables them to indulge in the comfort and solitude of a haven free of interventions. The popular image of the English home as a "castle" means that outsiders, to say nothing of foreigners, are seldom admitted in. English privacy may be regarded as "clannish" or "self defensive," an aversion to outside interferences, when it is viewed through the prism of Koreans' collective value.

Communitarian Spirit

Korean clannishness is distinct from the notion of privacy. Behind it, down at the village level, lies a communitarian spirit that allows no fences between houses and encourage the free flow of empathy among fellow inhabitants. A village is a clannish group and this proclivity, though, brings forth the exclusion of one village from another. Within a village or group, there can be no secret: all ears are finely tuned to gossip and rumors spread instantly. A Korean proverb has it "Birds hear words spoken during the day and rats hear those spoken at night." A Korean farmer has a phenomenal capacity to know how many spoons and chopsticks his neighbor has. All members of a village form the "we" into which "I" and "you" are merged. A Korean house open to others is the opposite of the English privacy, the latter, depending on the situation, carrying a connotation of snobbery.

The spontaneous will of Koreans to share all fortunes, good or bad, with their neighbors is salient in rural communities, and it brings home the importance of getting together to solve problems. "Get together" is a popular term meaning a collaborative attempt to find panacea for all social evils. Syngman Rhee, the first President of the Republic of Korea, used to say "to get together offers a way to survive; a heap of sands, slipping through the fingers, means death." Unity is the catchphrase of all schools where children learn to get together, but Koreans are not more spontaneous to get together than other races. There is a psychic urge to resist becoming identical persons. Another aspect of the willingness to share things within the village is the spontaneous participation in community affairs. A problem is that Koreans used to local life persistently refuse to stake out a broader community. A neighborhood was traditionally rooted within a parochial group or rural community. As villagers crossed the borders of their village, they became disdainful, jealous and envious to other villagers. Geographical proximity did not bring a good neighborhood between Korea and Japan. This was once the case between Germany and France.

In the village, rumors rapidly spread across the village because of the residents' instinctive impulse to share things, good or bad, but spreading rumors are not always intended to slander others. Everyone is offended by calumny or slurs on one's pride and honor, and Koreans have not learned to stay cool about the other doing this. It is ironic, though, that South Koreans are extremely patient with the North and its regular threats of unleashing Armageddon, with its rhetoric bombardment replete with scathing and vulgar invectives that exceeds any civilized norm. Perhaps, it comes as no surprise, given that they put up with a daily dose of hair-raising traffic and obnoxious drivers cursing at slow drivers. This is the price they pay for living in a diverse society that embraces the bizarre and unfamiliar. Still, Koreans stick to a narrow range of behaviors.

In the past, the village was a taproot to which all residents were attached and from which they could not stray far. Marriages and funerals were not family but community affairs that involved all villagers. The appreciation of "privacy" is recent for Koreans who become aware of it as a fundamental individual right of liberal democracy. To this day, the insensitivity of Koreans to one's privacy surprises foreigners. "Are you married?" "How old are you?" "What do you for living?" Koreans take these questions as a matter of daily life. But these questions lead outsiders to wonder why the Koreans have so much personal interest in other's business. Answering "mind your business" is a taboo in socializing with Koreans, except where congeniality is so strong as to make jokes exchanged among equals acceptable.

To Koreans immersed in a collective life, privacy matters little. Koreans spend much time fussing about what and how others do, let alone what matters to them. Their propensity to mind others, though limited to a small circle, should not necessarily be viewed in a negative light, for it is, in a large measure, an expression of their sympathetic concern for others. Their questions, intrusive as they may be, are useful in calibrating the relationships between people and establishing the reliability of the person to be associated with. They are the first step toward making a new net-work of human relations. Koreans' tendency to mind others is different from compassion in its true sense, since the former lacks concern for privacy.

South Korea was the first among the developing countries to revive the rural communitarian spirit in the name of the New Community Movement (Saemaul Undong)[3]. Launched in the 1970s, the movement dramatized the potential of rural populations to productive force for local development. The movement tried to channel the strong communitarian tendencies of Koreans into a dynamic force. At one time, the movement was an uplifting model for developing countries to emulate, but it was drowned out by the ringing rhetoric of industrialization and urbanization. The shrinkage of the rural population was coupled to the emergence of middle class urbanites. The latter was increasingly assertive of their privacy, a fundamental right of liberal democracy. Compliance and submissiveness to nature are no longer representative of Korean values. The middle class, enlarged to embrace a majority of population, claim to represent new Korean values. With the revolutionary change of information technology, the privacy of an individual, due to its vulnerability to violation, has become the most sensitive aspect of society.

Nature Worship

Koreans are endowed with unassuming naturalness. This is well expressed in old country houses in villages. The low straw-thatched roof, hardly discernible from its natural surrounding at a glance, makes a perfect match with the hilly landscapes. The integrated environment embraces trees, mounds, river and what not, all visible from the country house. Landscape surrounding a country house is its courtyard. There is no artificiality in the garden of nature. In contrast, Japanese gardens are bounded within a residence and have a contrived ambience. They reduce the world into a miniature that a viewer takes in at once: Lee O'ryung, a well-known literary critic, describes this as "diminutive propensity," noting "how they developed a phenomenal capacity to build a castle within a needle eye." Koreans, in comparison, may appear clumsy, but they take comfort in the knowledge that no other people have fingers strong enough to pick up a grain with slippery metal chopsticks. With the stronger fingers, Koreans can make something Japanese cannot.

There is a touch of serenity in a Korean house being nestled against the embracing arms of the surrounding mountains. Half seen through shrubs or hidden by hills, the country house does not shout its presence, but hides itself behind the hills like a blushing bride. From the road, those used to the monotonous landscape of flat land, marvel at the panoramic expanse of landscapes, with a village playing hide and seek as if frolicking strangers. The distant mountains come close and quickly recede into a fuzzy perspective. Koreans' attachment to nature may translate into passivity, submissiveness, and reluctance to move around to see the world of strangers. As people are unwilling to cross the village' threshold, the communitarian spirit appear closer to tribalism, distant from Alexander Tocqueville's concept of the American communitarian spirit that encourages spontaneous sociability. Koreans lack civic consciousness, that is, an intermediate consciousness which builds larger circles of trust.

Geomancy adds to the image of one's hometown: it finds auspicious places where wind meets flowing water for a grave, promising good fortune for the succeeding generations of the family. Harking back to my childhood in a small town, I remember a sacred place on the top of the nearby mountain, reserved by geomancy as 'no man's land.' Local legend had it that anyone who buried one of his kin would make his family rich and prosperous, but it came with a price to be paid by other families. The wife of a local judge in my hometown mysteriously died one night for no reason. Geomancy divination indicated that somebody had buried a corpse in that "no man's land." Excavations found a dead body buried. The man who had buried it, with hands tied behind his back, was dragged through the streets so that the town people could see. It conveyed a stern warning against others tempted to risk such a disgrace. The mortality of the hometown, according to geomancy, lies in where ancestors' graves are located; they form a mooring point keeping people from drifting too far from their ancestral roots.

Urbanization

In recent decades, the center of life has moved from rural communities to urban conurbations. This drastically altered the life style of Koreans. The communitarian spirit lost out, because urban life preferred the expedient and utilitarian aspects of living to the flow of human kindness. Until the Korean War, a quarter of the population was urban, but this percentage has tripled. As urban sprawl has hastened its pace, endless stretches of high rise apartments have encroached deeply into the soul of the rural community. Many, if not the majority, of rice paddies, have given way to new buildings or have been converted into long stretches of vinyl houses. The resulting dreary scene is a fallout of development, which should not be trifled for its detrimental effect on the environment. Such a phenomenon is not limited to urban areas. Even the countryside is occupied by the high rise apartments, becoming unsightly vistas that not only destroy the grandeur of nature but create an emotional wasteland. .

Contemporary Koreans will incur the wrath of their descendants by defacing nature to a point that may be beyond possible recovery. The timelessness of nature will never exonerate the contemporary generation from responsibility for what they leave descendants. Urban development brings squalid tenements in the shadows and egregious gaps between the few rich and the many poor. An elongated column between the two extremes is vulnerable to social ills. Many urbanites are sick of the density of urban life and long to settle in a rural suburbia. Nonetheless, many who return to their home towns find their pastoral life boring and frustrating for the lack of inter-personal contacts and cultural amenities. The countryside is today sparsely populated, and is no longer what it used to be. Fewer old people remain there to greet returnees. Those who long to slip away from the roar of traffic and the blight of industrialization are unaware of what solitude and reclusive life are like. Rural life is atomized, self-sufficient, and untouched by external pressures. Rural life befits those disciplined by individualism and seeking the pleasure of doing something that has been dreamed of hitherto. Many, if not the majority, of Koreans are better fit to the world of human bonds. Outside the boundary, they are "fish out of water."

Korean urbanites, despite their callousness and indifference to their neighbors, are accustomed to human contacts within small groups or fraternities. They hardly survive pastoral life that lacks such human contacts. The rosy image of reclusive life is incompatible with the reality of collective life. Many aged Koreans die of boredom, if not of sickness, when they are left out of human contacts. A majority of Koreans, regardless of age, opt to live in places which offers expedience, bereft of the aesthetic appreciation of rural life. Korean urbanites rarely feel an urge to return to nature - strong enough to overshadow the pain of living without much of human contacts.

Emotion Outweighs Reason

Urbanization is supposed to neutralize the emotional display of Koreans, but they often show temperamental character or emotion-charged behaviors. By and large, foreigners say "Koreans are easy to cry, laugh, and sing."Emotional displays of Koreans, however, occur within a parochial circle of intimates in tandem with communitarian passion. Such a free swinging emotional pendulum may in large part be a reaction to historical trauma or an ethical straight jacket that restrains behaviors to a standard norm. The thicker the layer of restraint, the more violent the emotional outburst. The prevailing ethical dictum notwithstanding, Koreans are given to emotional outbursts. Just as not all English are ladies and gentlemen, not all Koreans march to the drumbeat of Confucian stoicism.

A Korean airline was shot down by a Soviet rocket in 1983. All passengers aboard went down to the depth of the seas. One victim was an American representative aboard; his wife attended the funeral. Her quiet mourning, exhibited in a silent flow of tears, contrasted with the thunderous wailing of the Korean families. The irony is that Koreans were taught to restrain their emotions. An unendurable pain, of course, leaves little room for the bereaved to be conscious of their behaviors and look to emulate the quiet, dignified mourning of others. Some Westerners attribute their behavior to Christian emphasis on calmness and stoicism, but these virtues are also honored in Korea. What accounts for the difference? It may have more to do with the degree of class distinction, urbanization and civic consciousness. There is a difference in the way a ritual service is performed between civilized elites and untamed masses in Korea.

Koreans consider themselves as an anointed sufferer of foreign beatings. The Koreans' sense of historical trauma is expressed in chauvinistic nationalism which reached its apogee in the nineteenth century, when a surging tide of Western imperialism lapped on the shore of the Korean kingdom. The sense of ethnic superiority, coming from a long sustained isolation and supposedly invincible ignorance of outsiders, permeated Korean imaginations of the world, accompanied by hateful disdains for all other races as barbarians hardly different from the beasts.[4] Ahn Chang-ho, a foremost patriot better known by his nom de plume as Tosan, distinguished a peninsula character from Japanese insular character and Chinese continental character. He deplored Koreans' tendencies toward parochialism, depravity, laziness, and dependence and pleaded for character reform as the primary task to be carried out if Koreans are to become the citizen of an independent nation.[5] It took courage to be critical of his own people when chauvinistic nationalism pervaded the Koreans' imagination of the outsiders.

"Thorn trees bear thorns, and vines bear grapes. Even if people get rid of evil
social institutions, they would reappear, if they have not reformed their moral character.
Consider how democracy has taken different form in Mexico and the United States.
No matter how good the seed is, your work would be in vain, if the soil is poor."
(Ahn Chang-ho 1996,258)

The point of his argument is that the institution of a nation state is the product of social behaviors that could be refined by education and self-cultivation. In this connection, Ahn Chang-ho guarded against rash nationalism without people properly prepared to deal with the complex situation. Nationalism burst forth in a rash and intrepid confrontations with Western powers in the nineteenth century. Presumably, rashness and intrepidity are due to Koreans ignorant of their own weakness and the might of Western predators. Uniquely, such an exclusive streak against outsiders, when applied to a group, turns into a stubborn group egotism. The ignorance of the outside world made Korea pay dearly for having lost the opportunity to establish relationships with powerful countries, when the country was in a desperate need to get out of its stagnancy. To such stubborn Koreans, a born tendency to compromise means the inability to make up their minds and the lack of resolute stand.

Politics sets great store by one's capacity to compromise with opponents in democracy, but the compromise-prone politician is decried for the lack of will and cause. Making concessions to meet an adversary halfway would be to recognize one's weakness or lose in a power game. "Stick it out" until the other is exhausted is the best way to get a job done. Negotiations between political factions are dictated by face-saving and mannerism and there is little room for debates on substances. This strategy worked well for North Korea as it exploits the nuclear issue: the North's negotiators refuse to compromise his goal, no matter how long it takes. He adroitly exhausts his counterpart and thereby acquire the maximum gains. Group egoism works in politics in South Korea. A built-in tendency to compromise with adversaries is stigmatized as a perpetual turncoat which runs down generation after generation. Group egoism may find its genesis in the ethnic homogeneity prone to artificial fragmentation into numerous cells, especially when people compete for power. The Koreans' claim to solidarity, therefore, belies the tendency to factionalism.

Religious Pluralism

Primitive Religions

Religion deserves separate treatment as a powerful shaper of an ethnic identity. Korea shows a peaceful cohabitation of different religions, apparently strange to many foreigners who are used to one dominant religion within a political community. That an ethnic group displays strong commitment to one religion has been a norm, although in a few cases an ethnic group is split asunder by religious affiliation. Likewise, based on their claim to ethnic and cultural homogeneity, Koreans are supposed to have one religion. Far from this assumption, Korea exhibits "religious pluralism." And the absence of a dominant religion, however should not be taken to mean that Koreans lack religious piety or passion.

Religion is, according to Geoffry Parrinder (1971,69), the "recognition of superhuman controlling power, and especially of a personal god. A study of religious thoughts reveals human longing for value in life, a belief that life is not accidental and meaningless but has a teleological end. The search for its meaning leads to faith in a power greater than the human, and finally to a belief in a universal superhuman with intentions and will to maintain the highest values for human life. Given this definition, Confucianism and shamanism do not qualify as a religion, for both are oriented toward the contemporary life. Buddhism and Confucianism both were of foreign origin but failed to reach down to the masses where shamanism constitutes a folk belief positioned in a deep recess of Korean consciousness. Faith in multiple deities leaves little room for a dominant religion to take the ground.

Musok, the Korean equivalent of shamanism, is a cultural variation of Siberian shamanism, characteristic of Korean setting. It shares its root with animism, arguing that the spirit departs from the body on death and in some cases, stay within the souls of offspring or may float around, causing troubles for the living. The world of the spirits is thought to bring all the flow and ebbs of fortune to this contemporary world. Luck or bad luck depends on how a person appeases and maintains harmony with the spirits. Musok shares with Confucianism the idea that all fortunes, good or bad, are attributed to the spirits of the deceased. In Korea, ancestor worship is often believed to have originated in Confucianism; rather it is descended from Musok demanding that ancestors must be cared for, comforted and revered, as if they were alive.

Musok has neither moral value nor a teleological end."An ecstatic state is considered the religious experience par excellence, and the shaman is the great master of ecstasy"(Parrinder 1971,42). The shaman controls the spirits in the sense that she is able to communicate with the dead, demons and spirits without becoming their instrument. Claiming herself to be a mediator between the two worlds, she is capable of calling on spiritual hands to heal illness. For pre-modern people, shamanism, though lacking apocalyptical predictions, answers a human longing for help of the supernatural being, largely for material or secular reward.

The basic tenet of Asian beliefs is that nature is not created and will continue to exist into the infinite future through myriads of repetitions and cycles. Hinduism and Buddhism share this belief, as opposed to the Christian notion of an anthropomorphic God, the creator and the causer for all dead things to come into life. The Buddhism that reigns in China, Korea and Japan is primarily Mahayana, the Greater Vehicle. "Characteristic of Mahayana is the notion that the world of immaterial phenomena, nirvana, and extinction, are different manifestations of the Absolute" (Frits Vos 1995,95). "The strong point of Buddhism is that truth is not to be given by a god but an experience that exists in the purity of heart "(Lee Won Sul 1990;69). Experience is emphasized over knowledge; awakening is a conduit to salvation.

Native Korean belief, as elsewhere in Asia, regards life and death as a repeating cycle with no distinction between the two: the two are bound together through harmony and accord. The concept of a continuum underlies ancestor worship rites which foreshadows the return of the deceased to the earthly world. Ancestor worship rites invite the deceased to partake of the foods displayed on the altar, and descendants demonstrate unfailing commitment to filial obligations. There is no disjuncture that separates life from death for eternity, so far as life and death are regarded as interchangeable. Niravana is an ecstatic state that transcends the repeating cycle of life, that is, a sea of pains.

The concept of Han is expressed in the mythology of Tan'gun, the legendary ethnic progenitor of Koreans, the last person of a divine trinity, whose father was a son of Heaven. His father descended on the earthly world to save all humans. His arrival on the earth and subsequent return to heaven speaks of the integration of earth and heaven into a greater Han. Humans are the mediators between earth and heaven. Historically, Han has been a quintessential component in the naming of kingdoms: Samhan's (Three Confederated Leagues), through the late nineteenth century Dae Hanjekuk (Greater Han Empire) and today's Dae Han Minguk (Republic of Korea) stand for a united state, larger than its earlier shadow and continuous with the past. The notion of continuum is a revealing contrast with Christianity where the dichotomy between life and death, immanent in the transcendent deity, is evident.

Christians perceive corporal life as discontinuous, giving way to immortal life. Eternal life presupposes the immortality of the soul. The promise of an eternal life degenerates into the negative practice of degrading contemporary life into something meaningless, just as Buddhism regards the current life as a sea of pains or a passage to niravana. In reality, fatalism accompanies transcendentalism, as if a real life was preserved for the other world.

Shamanism is not different from Confucianism in its orientation toward the contemporary world, inspiring people to realize their secular desires. The secular orientation of both is no longer compatible with a sedate and static pre-modern society; both reflect the dynamics of modern and industrial society. Polytheism offers no ground for religious dogmatism to take its place."Koreans know of neither the crusades nor homicides in the name of martyrdom. Neither has their history seen the Reformation or the god-centered world." (Kim Seok-ju 2001, 142). So far as religious passion is concerned, Koreans can be described as passive middle roaders between religious fundamentalists and atheist extremists. Many Koreans owe their religious faith to non-religious reasons– moral guide, secular desires, refuge from mental distress, and prayers to assuage the ills of society –rather than their involvement with universal super-natural beings.

Buddhism

When Buddhism arrived in fourth century Korea through northern China then under the Tibetans, it appealed to the ruling class and became an agent for the spiritual unification of people, leading the way to the birth of enlarged monarchical kingdoms. Started as a highly disciplined philosophical religion, it seeks personal salvation through the renunciation of worldly desires. But its transcendental appeal was dulled by its integration with Taoism and shamanism. Buddhist definition of worldly desires as evil is consonant with Taoist penchant for a hermit-like life secluded from the secular world. Taoism teaches that the ultimate goal of a healthy eternal life can be achieved by discipline, by the control of breath, sex and food, and by distance from the secular world.

Niravana is not merely the awakened status of consciousness, but goes beyond the awareness of ego to reach a transcendental level, unaware of distinction between subject and object. "The true character of Buddha is hidden in the depth of human mind, not to be given by a sacred deity but to be found within the self"(Shim Jae Ryong 1981;381). The concept of the Buddhist "inner mind" is someway comparable to "St. Augustine's an unfathomable world of images, presences of our past and countless plains, caverns and caves. ...God, therefore, was not an objective reality but a spiritual presence in the complex depths of the self" (Karen Armstrong 1993,121). Augustine was the first to admit "sub-consciousness and shared divinity in the innermost of one's mind with Buddhism. Zen Buddhism teaches us to "empty our minds and wander the landscape without any more of it than to observe it" (Alain de Botton 2012, 156). It mocks our ego-dominant ambitions as the devil to be hunted out of every lair. The Buddhist virtues are egoless, purity, endurance and tranquility, comparable to Christian virtues of atonement, prudence, fortitude, piousness and hope. All the chief civilizations developed along parallel lines, when there were no commercial or intellectual contacts. Universally among China, Korea and Japan, the Buddhist's emphasis on patience and restraint is expressed in the way in which tea is served. Tea is brewed deliberately and slowly in a way that requires a lot of patience on the part of those to be served. The nature-scented taste carries their attention from secular desires to purity in the mind.

With its abstruse philosophy, Buddhism is diverse enough to embrace different religions, ranging from belief in the other world to contemporary orientation. "With the infusion of shamanism, Buddhism is quite often blamed for lacking a metaphysical orientation or theological hypothesis"(Shim Jae Ryong 1981,383). It views life as fantasy or as being empty of meaning. There is nothing that is immutable and every creature, once born into the world, is sure to perish. "What you are today is the result of what you were in the pre-birth world and what you do today determines what you will be in the other world. The past flows into the present which, in turn, flows into the future" (Shim 1981;386)."

"The Buddhist concept of 'no mind' identical to the Taoist 'nothing' is a persuasive call for return to the state of mind empty of preoccupations and earthly desires. This empty mind is the source of awakening and creativity" (Shim 1981, 386). Worldly life, sensual pleasures and material affluence are ephemeral, not worthwhile to be cared for. The Buddhist concept of soul is ambiguous, and reincarnation is the Eastern version of immortality. "Their concept of reincarnation is the passing of a flame from one candle to another. No self gets transferred in the deal, because there's no self to transfer" (Thomas Cathcart & Daniel Klein 2010,98)

Nature, according to the Eastern belief, is something to be awed, revered, and mystified as untouchable by humans. It believes in "one greater whole of man and nature and a continuum between the two" (Lee Won Sul 1990, 52). In the contrast, Illuminist thought seeks what humans can accomplish by exploiting nature, drawing on reason as a key to open up new vistas for human fulfillment. The latter stands for a state of mind freed from social and institutional inhibitions and authority which are looked upon as encroaching upon the realm of human freedom and creativity. The dichotomy between man and nature breeds the view of nature as objectified to be refashioned to meet human needs.

Buddhism and Confucianism have evolved through conflict and cooperation with each other, providing a vessel through which the past survived into the present. Some argue that there is no fundamental difference in principle between the two, referring to how Confucian 'humaneness' is consonant with Buddhist "benevolence.' Confucian humaneness is reflected in the reciprocity of virtue in establishing human bonds, while Buddhist benevolence stands for the fusion of 'I' and 'you.'"The transcendental element of Buddhism explains its lack of practical program as opposed to the Confucian orientation of functional approach which addresses the needs of human society" (Haboush JaHyun 1998,30)

Despite its fatalistic view of the world, Buddhism has some positive elements, such as charity, egalitarianism, stoicism and perseverance that helped forlorn Koreans to survive. The pervasiveness of these concepts has been eroded by the parochialism of Confucian reciprocal human bonds. Vladmir Tikhonov exalts Buddhism in the fusion of subject and object as a positive element which finds its manifestation in a relationship that blurs the line between 'I' and 'you.' Buddhist idealism is the complete banishment of the 'ego.' In reality, any relationship based on the fusion of two or more persons is not commonly found. Human nature does not allow a person to be a good neighbor to all; if he/she is good to one, he/she is bound to be indifferent to others. Yi Kwang-su, a prominent early twentieth century novelist, illustrates how certain strengths of a people can become shortcomings. Generosity and benevolence, for example, can hinder the inculcation of patriotism and nationalism against imperialism and colonialism. Most prominent among women's virtues was chastity which required their fanatic commitment to one family, even after they were widowed. Even nowadays, we see many of them forego personal fulfillment which would be made possible by choosing an alternative path of life.

In pre-modern society, Korean women made a personal sacrifice for the sake of family. For women troubled with contemporary life, "the egalitarian appeal of Buddhism and its promise of spiritual liberation had been a persuasive call to leave worldly troubles and enter the monkhood" (Martina Deuchler 1983,2). The loss of their husbands left widows to be troubled by the difficulty of living alone in their remaining life and placed them under pressures to remarry as a means of survival, though remarriage was thought to besmirch a woman's virtue. "Throughout the Koryo and Chosôn dynasties, many widows chose to enter the monkhood and ennobled themselves by life-long commitment to one husband and one family lineage" (Deuchler. 3).

Confucianism

Confucianism provides an elaborate ethical code accompanied by exacting standards f propriety that approached the force of law. Each society has an innate desire to idealize itself, and sets of ideals are integrated into ideology. The notion of "Greater Learning" (daehak) presents a paradigm of an enlightened man that everybody should aspire to reach. In Europe, Christianity has long been the idealistic guide to the life of people, defining the relationship between God and individuals. "In the world bereft of such a spiritual prop, "this world-oriented" Confucianism emerged to fill this spiritual gap. Confucianism centers on the ideal of the state and society, tirelessly reminding individuals of their moral obligations to realize the goal." (Dawson Christopher 1966,35). This task starts with self-improvement, suggesting an implacable link between an individual and society. What matters within Confucianism is a set of defined human relations that turns a society into an organism in which all members are related to each other. Interconnectedness brings the metaphor of Confucian society to a spider's web.

Rivalries in ancient China exhausted the imagination of its rulers with how to overcome the challenges of ethnic diversity in the unmanageably large territory. Confucianism began with a realistic approach to integrating diverse groups into a single state. This proved itself to be more workable in Korea that was free from the troubles of diversity. Public condemnation of Confucianism as a dead and rigid belief system led modern development theorists to point to its positive contributions to recent economic development in some of the Asian and Southeast Asian countries. Their success reflects in large part the Confucian work ethic and people conscious of "discipline and order" (Kim Jae-eun 1991,67)."

"Confucius, in contrast to Western thought, refused to speculate about Heaven altogether, though he accepted it as the abode of the venerable ancestors "(Thomas Cathcart & Daniel Klein 2010, 132) In the absence of religious belief, Koreans immortalized themselves through memories imprinted in the heart of their offspring and those with whom they had been in daily contact. Confucianism lacks the Christian concept of soul that is believed to survive physical death, promising another life of self-consciousness. In contrast with the passive acceptance of a given fate, Confucian values were the functional equivalent of capitalism. They stirred children to competition in learning and kept the educated perpetually motivated toward self improvement. Defying the placid and compliant image of the Koreans in the past, those steeped in Confucianism are perpetually dissatisfied with and refuse to stay at a given place. Confucianism captures the imagination of a few who try to present an idealized pattern of life. Confucianism encourages Korean children to live up to the parental summon to 'come up big.' Parents forever push their children to avoid the fate of tadpoles stuck in a well to run into the world of opportunity. Nonetheless, the Confucian moral paradigm is so demanding in an increasingly complicate society that it loses its relevance to daily life.

Of late, shamanistic culture, which had been dismissed for its naturalistic, crude, emotion-ridden values in the shadow of lofty Confucianism began "the counter-hegemonic assertion of itself as the popular culture" (Gregory Henderson 1983,135), Shamanism is present in the patterns of behaviors that actually shape the unconscious aspect of day to day life for the majority of Koreans. Sudden and often inexplicable illness brings a call for a shaman to evoke divine power to cure them. "The secularization of Koreans' spiritual life activated the functions of shamanism and shape the life and mind of the contemporary Koreans (Kim Jae-eun 1991,36). The fetish for an invisible deity in modern society recedes into the background. However, shaman rituals continue to be widely practiced, notably among petty capitalists whose fate rests on "the adventurous, aggressive, risk-taking, high-roller element"(Laurel Kendal 1996,518). Shamanism minimizes the role of humans in creating their own destinies with heavier dependence on invisible deities. Simultaneously, the secularization of faith, by virtue of its rebellious character against the established order, has provided a new dynamism for social change, and this is part of why shamanism is getting the better of self-restraining Confucianism.

Shamanism is no longer the belief of the oppressed or marginalized people, as it used to be, but has become a popular consciousness for the masses. Shaman rituals, once concerned with evoking healing powers for life-threatening illness, are now shifting to auspicious prognostications. It is often said that the counter-hegemonic assertion of shamanism brought volatile vigor, robustness, adventurism and materialistic display. These are risk-taking capitalistic elements but do not necessarily equate with Max Weber's Protestant ethic that advanced rationalistic capitalism to the drumbeat of individualism. It would not be fair, however, to hold shamanism responsible for the trend of high-risk capitalism. "Shamanic practices are not seen as fueling a particularly Korean "spirit" of high-risk capitalism"(Kendall 1996;522).Korea, once known for its aura of sedateness and impassive dignity, has witnessed an array of mind-boggling events in the path to today's society. Being abrasive or crude is a character trait which, together with the tendency to cling to immediate and self-centered problem-solving, indicates the lack of ethical consciousness inherent in shamanism.

Roman Catholics and Protestantism

Christianity, despite its late arrival, is often considered to represent the religion of Koreans, presumably due to the sheer percentage of Christians as well as the speed with which it grew. The rise of Christianity is the result of having survived large scale bloody purges of Catholic converts. The main reason for such rapid growth has been its messianic appeal that satisfies human craving for salvation after death, notably among the downtrodden. Roman Catholicism found its adherents among the intellectuals victimized by factional strife and the oppressed populace. But the arrival of Roman Catholicism in the seventeenth century brought it to a headlong clash with Neo-Confucianism which was essentially atheist theory. The ecumenical belief in a heavenly deity (haneunim) undermined the Confucian notion of the paternalistic ruler confined within a kingdom. Confucianism which valued "rule by righteousness" and an abstract projection of spiritual beings to an ambiguous heaven was unable to compromise with the anthropomorphic fatherly God.

It was not just the tenets of Christianity - such as the ecumenical view of "father"- that enraged the ruling elites. Korean Catholic converts performed rituals with prayers, but not ancestral worship with tablets. All-embracing government condemned some of the Catholics to death for not properly practicing ancestral observances. Congregations which were ever increasing in number were a serious threat to the state authority. Catholics were persecuted when the state authority was seriously threatened by the Western powers. The frequent appearance of foreign vessels in Korean waters was assumed to have connections with the Catholics which were assumed to have grown up to rival the monarchical authority.

Protestantism made an easier landing by following the path beaten by Roman Catholic. Its concerns with medical and educational service won the favor of the court. Korean nationalists were nurtured in Christian schools, many of whom staged heroic fights against the Japanese colonizers. Christianity was a new religion which nurtured dynamic values, known to provide a major impetus for modernization. Its most prominent influence, among others, is the universal idea of love and equality. Christian values, symbolic of modernization, was gradually planting the seeds of social change. "The notion of equality and a universal community of brethren was distinct from the predominant Confucian ideas which lay stress upon hierarchy and authority"(Lee Won Sol 1990; 106). Christianity was super-imposed on the secular orientation of shamanism to meet human desires. The accumulated effect of pious acts, many Koreans believe, invoke God's compassion to pay heed to their daily needs. Truly, shamanism's secular-orientation permeates Christian prayers: a priest calls this "a shamanistic frosting on the Christian cake."

Despite the appalling aggrandizement of the Christian establishment, it falls short of being a link from the past. "Until the end of the Japanese occupation, a greater number of Koreans were superficially touched by Christian ideas: their attitudes were basically shaped by the long Confucian tradition"(MacDonald Donald Stone 1990,43). Having seen Christianity come from advanced Western countries, many, including even prominent figures, became Christians believing that Christianity was the spiritual underpinning of the advanced countries. Still, if we consider the time span from the Chosôn Dynasty (1392 – 1910) which sounded the death bell for Buddhism, Confucianism and shamanism held a monopoly on Koreans' spiritual life and continues to influence Korea's present and the future.

The cohabitation of different religions may trace its genesis to a long-held polytheism of Koreans. This partly explains why Koreans bear no hostility to alternative religions, although they harbor exclusive attitudes. Koreans knew no religious dogmatism of the sort that gave full vent to the cruelties of the Crusades of medieval Europe. They know nothing of religious cleavages that are found elsewhere and deeply-rooted hatreds that refuse to heal. Political hostility can be patched up while religious hostility defies to compromise. Hostility between Christianity and Islam refuses to dissipate; the former lives up to a sense of today's greatness and the latter to a sense of pride in the past. Koreans have never had religious bigotry or fanaticism.

Koreans unambiguously manifest their religious commitment when they are Catholics or Christians, but they rarely manifest their affiliation with Confucianism, Buddhism and shamanism. Many Koreans unconsciously practice ancestor rites, though they are Catholics or Christians. These Asian beliefs have permeated the deep recess of their mind to a degree that they feel it normal to practice rites. By and large, all Koreans, regardless of their religious affiliation, are as much Confucians, Buddhists, and shamanists. These beliefs constitute the undercurrent of Koreans' consciousness, and a proper answer to religious pluralism may be found in the coexistence of different beliefs in their consciousness.

Geo-political Characterization

National character is shaped in the evolving context of its relationship with adjoining countries.

Korea borders on China, fifty times as large, Manchuria and Mongolia once strong enough to subdue China, and cradled across the sea by Japan that rose to a power that rivaled the Western imperialistic powers. Its adjacency to stronger neighbors produced a metaphorical expression, "a shrimp caught in a row of whales," implicating the precarious existence of an underdog state which had to withstand all the blows of its stronger neighbors. In comparison with other countries, the geo-political factors of Korea left stronger marks on the characters of the people. Koreans, due to their traumatic experience with their neighbors, shaped a xenophobic character and shied away from the vortex of power struggles between the continental powers, but drifted into it in one way or another against their will.

The self-perceived image of Koreans is the anointed sufferers of foreign beatings; they take the sufferings for granted as coming from their fated confrontation with stronger neighbors. Every accomplishment the nation makes, therefore, has reference to trauma associated with its unique geo-political location. On the flipside of this fatalistic perception, Koreans take a triumphant pride in the way they have borne the historical tragedy. "Economic miracle on the Han" has become a trope on every Korean's lips, meaning it to be comparable to the Rhine miracle of West Germany from the wreckages of the war. Whether we can draw an exact parallel between the two remains to be answered since different political backgrounds and policies were involved in supporting economic activities. Trauma metaphor inclines Koreans to build their self image different from the perceived image.

Chinese culture was like an ocean tide that could drown those of the surrounding states. All the alien rulers of China lost their identity in a sea of Chinese culture, but Korea, together with Vietnam, stands out for having preserved its cultural uniqueness. The medieval history of Korea was pockmarked with invasions by Mongols, Manchurians, and Japanese, but some of these tormentors, as we see these days, were reduced into the shadows of their former selves or dissipated into oblivion. Korea, the weakest of all, survived its tormentors and remains a single reminder of the past when these defunct monarchies reigned.

The Korean peninsula protrudes from the Asian land mass like a dagger pointed at Japan. All too often, this strategic land bridge was too tempting for its neighboring powers to seize. The relatively earlier advent of Korean monarchies is much attributed to Korea's ethnic and cultural homogeneity, and its traumatic experience with foes goaded Koreans to be coalesced into a tightly closed, centralized monarch. Beginning with the twelfth century, the Manchurian hordes haunted Korea through frequent incursions before they launched massive military expeditions against Song China. A century later, Mongols became not only the rulers of China but a trans-continental power history had never seen, and Koryô⁶ was involved in the Mongols' attempt to conquer Japan and drifted into collateral damage, teetering on the brink of extinction. Later, at the end of the sixteenth century, a triumphant Japanese feudal lord in the grip of megalomaniac ambition challenged M'ing China, involving Korea in a seven-year war, the most devastating in the loss of human lives. Subsequently, Korea suffered blows of the Manchurian hordes to which the king of Korea (Chosôn) was forced into a humiliating surrender in full view of the enemy camp. The Manchu invasions of Korea were again preludes to the premeditated expedition against China where they erected Q'ing to reign in China for 250 years. As new waves of imperialism lapped onto the shores of the Hermit Kingdom, Korea became a tinderbox for armed clashes between contesting powers. Every shift of East Asian hegemonic power turned Korea into a battlefield.

China shares the longest border with Russia and its appeasement policy was concluded with the 1860's Beijing Treaty which consigned its far-flung Maritime Siberia to the Russian Empire. Russian expansionism posed a threat. Vladivostok means "Conquer the East" and this gives the glimpse of how the Russian Empire turned its glare from the war-torn Europe to sedate East Asia, envying Korea and Manchuria endowed with rich reserves of mineral resources and strategic access to an ice-free sea. Japan was the first to take the Russian thrust as serious enough to endanger its survival since its northern islands remained vulnerable to it and saw the Korean peninsula as the bulwark to shelter it from Russian expansion. Having lived in an island, Japan was keenly sensitive to foreign incursions, more so than Korea where foreign incursions were taken for granted.

The imperial ambition of Japan was initially roused by its expansionary policy and Korea was the first to come into the purview of its continental expansion with a view to splitting it from the Chinese sphere of influence and creating a power vacuum that would favor its control of Korea. To Koreans fearful of the emerging Japan, China was an effective counter-weight, but it was no longer a big brother to depend on. The Sino-Japan War in 1894 was a turning point for Korea to part with China; without a power to depend on, Korea became a prey drifting into Japan's hands. Desperate to stave off the rising Japan, Korea placed hope on the United States, the partner of its trade treaty, as a counter-veiling power but met the latter's apathy. Korea was sidelined as the United States was in favor of Japan as an effective counter-weight to the Russian thrust.

The alternative was the Russian Empire which insinuated itself into the Korean court by claiming itself to the protector of the drifting monarch. But soon it stumbled into another armed clash with Japan. Had Russia won the war, Korea should have been a prey to Russia. The foreign powers were protagonists on the Korean stage, determining its fate. By winning the two successive wars with China and Russia, Japan gained an imperialistic foothold in Korea and found no obstacle in having a noose around the victim's neck. China remained a passive spectator to the Russian thrust southward after it was defeated by Japan in 1894. Needless to say, Korean leaders were lost for direction in the mess of confusions between the contesting powers, unable to deter its drift into the worst scenario of the unfolding historical drama. As such, the geo-political location of Korea left Korea ill-prepared for tidal waves of imperialism.

Fate again turned away from a liberated Korea, defeating its dream to rebuild the tattered country. The division of Korea was an offshoot of the ideological confrontation, known as the Cold War in the bipolarized world. To cite an example of Germany, it was Japan that should have been divided as the price the defeated had to pay. Ironically, Japan was spared territorial division and the occupation of the victorious troops because Korea was located to bear the Russian assault on behalf of its colonial master, followed by the American occupation of South Korea in quid pro quo. Is the territorial division simply a corollary of its geo-political location? Or was it made by Koreans themselves? To what extent are the super powers responsible for the division?

In the cold-blooded power dynamics of the world, Korea understands itself as impotent to become the master of its own fate; it has to depend on a stronger power for survival. The Cold War confrontation increased the dependency of South Korea on the United States. The relationship between the two has sweetened and soured over time. It can be said, though, that a friendly relationship remains steadfast throughout the disturbed period since the liberation. The Korea-U.S Defense Treaty speaks for the determination of the two countries to stand firm against common enemies. The confrontation between two Koreas is a microcosm of a global conflict. South Korea bore the important brunt of the war against communism but its exclusion from the signatories to the present state of ceasefire provided the North with a pretext to discredit the South as a partner to talk with. North Korea persistently insists on direct talks with the United States and South Korea is stymied in its initiative attempt to break through the stalemate. To further complicate the matter, the shaky balance of power between the two halves involves two adjoining and two distant powers in a tug of the rope. Each is so obsessed with its share of influence that any attempt to change the status quo involves risks; no one sticks its neck out for a change that will serve the goal of Koreans at the hazard of its interest. This stark reality allows no tolerance for anything but to perpetuate the division in the name of a balance of power.

Across the East Sea lies Japan now reigning as the third economic power in the world. Japan is retrospective of its triumphant victory over the invincible China and Russian Empire and an armed clash with the United States. China, once referred to as "a sleeping dinosaur," has become the second largest economic power, bent on restoring its erstwhile dominance in East Asia. Extrapolating from its stunning economic growth, China is expected to surpass the gross national product of the United States in 2025. Its exports total $183 billion mark in 2013, surging past that of Japan. Russia, having slipped back from the world power, is trying to restore its lost clout in East Asia. North-east Asia is the most dynamic region of the world.

In the power game between the United States and China, Korea is a dangling carrot, having to walk on a tight rope between the two: warming its relation with one will glaciate it with the other. Korea's partnership with China is of crucial importance in view of the latter's capacity to tame the bellicose North Korea. But an alliance with the United States is vital in confronting North Korea and other potential foes. The world is now watching how South Korea is trying to get out of the shadow of the two dominant powers. By weighing prudently on the shifting alignment, South Korea is expected to play a vital role in maintaining the regional equilibrium of power. South Korea is no longer a dwarf sitting on a giant's shoulder.

China's rise to a world power is in a way a psychic compensation for the scars on its pride, inflicted by its defeat in the Opium War (1839-42) and the Sino-Japan War (1894). There is an imperialistic bent in its nostalgic turn to Pax Cinica, flexing its muscle and asserting its strength abroad. China bewilders its neighbors with uneasy conjectures about the unfolding rivalry with the United States. Rivalry between China and the United States is in a way a contest between a memory of past greatness and a sense of present greatness, split apart across the gulf of irreconcilable interests. In earlier days, China's colossus in relation to its neighboring states and its seeming apathy to trifles built its image as a country of big heart and magnanimity. Rather, today's China is likened to an adolescent quite disturbed and unbalanced, for a time, by the rapid growth. It is often given to an emotional impulse to take a stick against strident voices in its neighborhood. One of the adjoining states sowed the wind and is now reaping the whirlwind. A discordant voice cannot be considered in other way than a daring challenge to its sacrosanct interests. China's reaction is a frenzy of uncontrollable fury and nationalistic bluster that features an enormous pot boiling with an instantaneous chorus of unanimous voices, demeaning of a big power supposed to be a conscientious sentinel of tolerance and self restraint. China with its neurotic tendencies foreshadows a bumpy road for South Korea to become its continuous strategic partner within the framework of alliance with the United States. China with an overweening ego cannot measure up to the lofty vision of world order that accompanies its power. Maturity is obtained when the mind catches up with the body. Petty nationalism obscures a greater cause to be served by a great power.

The emerging dynamics of the power game will incline Russia to line up with China against the American hegemony in East Asia. To hang on to its hegemony in this region, the United States considers Japan an effective counter-weight to the expansionist continental powers. Therefore, Japan's self-defense rearmament is tacitly endorsed by the United States to the chagrin of Korea. The United States is attached to a tripartite alliance with South Korea and Japan against the possible alliance of China and Russia. But there is a catch caused by Japan's emotional swing into the rightist nationalism that certainly irritates China and Korea. Japan's denial of its shady history and an imagined nostalgic turn to its imperialistic past haunts its neighbors fearful of its imperialistic specter. The United States is concerned that Korea and Japan may be estranged to an extent that hobbles the tripartite alliance. Japan, awash with nationalistic whims at the advent of a right-wing regime, served as a catalyst for Korea to be allied with China.

Centuries of existence in China's shadow accustomed Korea to quest, conscious or unconscious, for a power to depend on. Some of South Koreans are suspicious of the timelessness of the Korea-U. S alliance in light of the international power dynamics that is loath to a perennial ally. Modern China emerges to fill the Koreans' psychic gap to be caused by its imagined estrangement from its ally, the United States. All international relationships follow a cycle of birth, growth, youth, adulthood and senility. Koreans are challenged again to explore a way to survive in the most dynamic region of the world. An intriguing question is "Can Koreans break the historical myth of dependence on a 'big country' for survival?"

South Korea has its share of full-blown tension by inhabiting the most dangerous region. North Korea has developed a nuclear power to tilt the balance of military power in its favor and threatens to turn Seoul into a sea of fire in a few seconds. North Korea justifies its possession of nuclear power as a means for self defense, but the worldwide panic of nuclear proliferation goes deeper than the logics of self defense. Despite the nuclear Armageddon, South Koreans remain, to the surprise of foreign residents, undisturbed. The nuclear weapon, many reckon, is targeted at somewhere else, because North

Korea should be well aware of the unimaginably disastrous repercussions of its survival strategy that will surely boomerang upon itself. South Koreans are laudably patient with the rhetoric bombardment of all scurrilous invectives, all exceeding the bound of a civic-conscious nation.

South Korea has enough of fantasies about negotiation with North Korea but finds itself deluded by the north's enigmatic policy alternating between the illusion of dialogue in a reasonable garment and the acts of most profound perfidy. A psychological gap adds to doctrinal differences in explaining the difficulty of reconciliation with North Korea. The longer it takes, the more difficult it is to patch up the gap. For the North Korean ruler who has his character forged in the heat of revolution, isolated from the outside world, diplomatic approach to 'one Korea' is akin to a surrender leading to a slow death. This bleakest outlook for a diplomatic solution gives rise to an uneasy speculation that a miscalculation of its adversary may cause the North to gamble disastrously on his chances of winning a war. To make it worse, the nuclear power is in the hands of a man whose character is a smothered volcano. Above all, North Korea surprises the world by its 70 years of dynastic existence, defying all the prognosis of immediate downfall based on all logical arguments.

The Paradox of Globalization

Globalization has a profound impact on value structure, although its effect varies depending on the development stage of each nation state. As scientific advances shortened distances and obscured borders between nation states, persons and goods are free to move from one place to another. No nation state is any more an island onto itself. Whether we like it or not, globalization has become a fait accompli, an implacable process we cannot avoid in moving toward one world. It is important, therefore, to see the cognitive location of Korea in the world of globalization.

In the first place, globalization brought bountiful sunshine to melt the frozen lands and this was the cause for the downfall of the Soviet Union and Eastern European countries that Winston Churchill blocked as "behind an iron curtain." Globalization broke through what seemed to be impenetrable barriers to those in the shadow of an ideological dogma. Likewise, globalization brings us the hope of casting sunshine on the dark half of the Korean peninsula, creating a momentum toward the reunification of the two halves.

The so-called "global village" is an imagined society where all peoples live in peace beyond the strictures of particular cultures and values. The 20th century was greeted by ultra-nationalism that drove the world powers into fanatic behaviors. Then, nation states, each pursuing a policy for its own benefits, created tension and hostility between them and led to disastrous wars. Nations regarded one another, simply because it did not share the same ideology and institution, as an arch rival or a born enemy to be extirpated. On the ideal side, globalization is expected to put an end to such follies and create one global market that constrains excessive competition and allay tensions between nation states.

The globalization of technology and economy creates a common face of the world by means of standard cultures and values. Increased contacts between states cause universal values to marginalize particular ones. The result is that all peoples of the world, if this pace of change continues, will eventually be identical beings. On the other side, particular values assert themselves in defiance against the tide of universal values and remain diehard on their way out. The rapid pace of modernization, routinely defined as the acceptance of Western mores and technologies, generated a nostalgic turn to the past and tradition. Nationalism is a reactive quest for national identity defined in terms of traditional culture and value. The Soviet Union was a scramble made up of broken eggs. When each egg was broken, the Union was violently shaken with the resistance of the affected people. Even while the broken states remained part of the Union, cultural nationalism bubbled beneath the seemingly sedate surface. The downfall of the Soviet Union can be regarded as the triumphant return of cultural nationalism in each member state.

Globalization is often viewed through the prism of power dynamics of the world. As the United States is the most ardent proponent of globalization, others tend to be skeptical, viewing globalization as a way for the United States to refashion the world in its own image, continuously maintaining its hegemonic supremacy in the world. On a close look, the United States is rather losing its global influence in tandem with globalization. Globalization is violently defiant against one dominant power and its overarching influence.

Globalization declares ethnic nationalism as anathematic to societal advance. But Koreans regard a single ethnic patch as the touchstone of a state's legitimacy. Going one step further, the progressive view of history give legitimacy to North Korea, simply because it is based on the self-declared ethnic purity. The Korean concept of nationalism is ethnic-centered and its xenophobic tone cries out for seclusion from the outside world and condemns dependence on a foreign power whatsoever as the loss of sovereignty. This argument in the same breath condemns South Korea for having depended on pro-colonial elements and surrender to the neo-colonialism of America. A strong tone of ethnic purity is characteristic of a highly collective or regimented society and such a society is vulnerable to despotic and dogmatic rule. Nazism and Fascism were dressed in ethnic purity in tandem with an exalted state. North Korea is a case in point where ethnic purity is a counter-weight to capitalistic evils which they consider destructive of the social fabric of collective nature.

A society built on ethnic purity is more repressive of individual freedom, whereas one built around a shared experience and institutional or doctrinal commonality is tolerant of individual behaviors. Politics based on a single dogma is dehumanizing and coercive. Loyalty of Koreans to the nation derives from their ethnic consciousness but it is not necessarily as strong as American patriotism grounded in shared values or institutional and doctrinal causes. Koreans, with emphasis on ethnic purity, pay lip service to patriotism, but they are more emotionally nationalistic. Emotional nationalism unfairly disguises their duties with dogma rather than volition.

Economic globalization in particular has worked wonders and still keeps modern society in a high plateau of prosperity. It encourages free movement of persons and goods across borders and provides less developed states with easier access to the latest scientific and management know-how. The expectation of mutual benefits, however, is based on the premise that all nation states are on the same or similar stages of development. But wide gaps in national wealth and development stages likely leads globalization to anomie and discontentment in poorer, vulnerable countries. As demonstrated on several occasions, globalization creates economic tailspins in succession, since a problem stemming from a particular country can rapidly spread like an infectious disease to another. If one dominant country sneezes, all the vulnerable countries catch colds.

For all its achievements, globalization has a limited effect on political globalization. China has been cautious about the spill-over effects of globalization and opts to follow "economic globalization" against the background of political socialism. Its obsession with socialism is the result of not only anxiety about capitalistic evils and egoistic excesses but its refusal, under the weight of past grandeur, to emulate the Western concept of liberal democracy. The cohabitation of market economy and political socialism has so far proved effective but doubts are raised about the long-term cohabitation of the diametrically opposed systems. Solving capitalist problems by socialist means may prove to be workable in a myopic sight. But a longer perspective brings home the possibility that the rigidity of political socialism has the seeds of undoing social stability.[7]

Socialism serves better a state imperative to provide organizational antidote for the instabilities and uncertainties of modern society through the state's control of the masses. Socialism, due to its institutional rigidity, fares better where obedience and unanimity are taken for granted. But globalization inflames divisive feuds that challenge the rigid system in place. North Korea boasts of its system being an effective counterweight to a gaping chasm between the rich and the poor. Nonetheless, this problem has become as much serious in the casteless society as in capitalism, despite its avowed goal to protect the masses under the shield of equality. As its people are exposed to global trends, China will be torn over whether it should embrace Western liberalism or remain socialistic against capitalist evils; whether to remain in the shadow of Western civilization or to lead the countries within its cultural orbit through its own system. As one of the major cradles of civilization, China takes pride in doing a daunting work, that is, to test an impossible coexistence of two antithetical systems.

Globalization laid old values open to the scrutiny of reason, an objective light in today's world. From the global perspective, Confucianism can be blamed for its dogmatic ideology and for its questionable relevance to the modern world. However, there is a secular, down-to-earth side of Confucian ethics in coping with the challenges of a more vibrant society. We can observe how China and Vietnam made a soft landing in market economy, while their fellow communist countries in Eastern Europe came crashing to the ground. What explains the smooth transition of China and Vietnam from their erstwhile communist system? Any explanation finds the Confucian work ethic at work, a fundamental aspect of which is the subordination of an individual to the greater good of the state or society, willingness to restrain private interests to work for public goals.

Globalization places the rule of law in the foreground, replacing moral codes as a guide to individual behaviors. The law-consciousness develops in tandem with reason; where reason calls the tune, fairness and impartiality gain currency. Koreans who take to social order and harmony tend to discredit or flout the law. They rather see a strict conformity to the law as distasteful, since it dims personal feeling and compassion for others. Humaneness and compassion are workable in parochial circles of intimates but work against an expandable radius of trust that accompanies modern society. The limited radius of trust accounts for the lack of an intermediate values that extends to larger circles of association. Appeal for the mind, though, has its own shady side. When it encounters a charismatic leader, it is likely to inflame the passions of the disaffected masses into a misguided rally in support of a benighted form of politics, such that is based on racist and nationalistic megalomania. By the same token, a collective consciousness, wedded to an authoritarian leadership, creates willingness to bend, if not flout, the rule of law, when it runs afoul of his political dictum.

By and large, the global trend of the drive toward liberal democracy encourages the migration of cheap labors from periphery regions to the center and this continues to "weaken the claims of residency, cultural identity and citizenship" (Seyla Benhobib 2002, 182). There is a genuine risk, though, that the worldwide movement will create individuals less conscious of national identity and industries lacking moral responsibility. In this "global.com civilization," persons shrink into e-mail addresses in space, while tied to a worldwide network of human relations, with little sense of political and cultural identity. On a positive side, globalization inspires spontaneous commitment to a worldwide discourse of human rights and a collaborative attempt across borders to address problems of common concern, like environmental pollution and HIV/AIDs.

Globalization drowns a country's identity in support of a cosmopolitan cause in which ethnic nationalism and petty regionalism are shadowed out. The ineluctable consequence of globalization – with its need for cross-cultural communication –is that many languages spoken by smaller populations will be sidelined by a predominant lingua franca, and thereby the unique cultural perspectives of those languages will be lost. It stirs an uneasy conjecture that one's mother tongue, if not replaced by a lingua franca, may diminish in importance until it remains, at best, a secondary language. The loss of a mother tongue never allows us to claim a sense of self identity. Can we conceive a nation state without its unique language? No nation has even been great without its own sense of manifest identity. At this point, Samuel Huntington's prophesy is worthy of attention: "The classic conflict of the post-cold-war is about ethnicity, culture and faith. It is also a struggle between identities that brook no coexistence."

Another parallel of globalization is secularization bluntly reflected in social apathy to the spiritual or loftier goals of society in tandem with the materialistic orientation of life. Modern life is characterized by secularization and dehumanization feeding off one another. The crackling of the genetic code unraveled some of the mysteries of the human species and cast a positive light on the artificiality of creatures. But the result is its degrading effect on human dignity and value. Impersonality and objectivity have become the new watermark of rational conducts. Likewise, religion is challenged as it is forced to struggle with the voices of rational dictum. Religious orthodoxy is drowned by the pressure of secular issues, namely; divorce, abortion, homo sexuality, drug, and the counter culture. Nevertheless, Christianity carves out an intransigent stance harking back to the primordial values at the dawn of civilization. As an exalted state gave way to civic society, theocracy to democracy, and religious bigotry to religious tolerance, Christianity may have to redefine the social inhibitions of the primordial community and its messianic belief in biblical timelessness. Looking ahead, the world sees Islam enlarge its territory and silently prod Christianity to address an insoluble question of whether it should embrace Islam as an authentic alternative to salvation or relegate it to a threat by infidels. Secularization erodes the ground of religious fundamentalism and dogmatism, whether it is Christianity or Islam. Envisioning a peaceful coexistence of different religions allays dogmatic certainty and breeds the toleration of other religions, no matter what they are.

Last, but not least, globalization follows the tide of civilization like water running from higher and a lower place. One of the mistaken notions about civilization is that it mothers all cultures, institutions, mores and faith that endure the blow of time. The technological edge that Western societies maintain over the non-Western world is attributed to the civilization that claims its descent from the Greco-Roman civilization. Greek civilization glittered in the fifth century B.C.E, confined within the city of Athens. Given the consistency of the civilization, why did the civilization of early medieval Europe, marked by a chaotic presence of feudal states, differ from that of the fifteenth century, replete with intellectual spurts, oceanic advances and scientific discoveries? Norman F. Cantor is critical of deterministic civilization. "His answer was based on the premise that civilization is an organism which passes through a life cycle and then perish. Every civilization experiences a birth, youth, adulthood, senility, and death, as if all living things follow a cycle of seasonal change" (1963,504). The causes for the change of civilization are human freedom and will. Each stage of development writes about its own history distinct from those that predated and follow it. Globalization in the end is an attempt to challenge the deterministic civilization.

---

1. For genetic inheritance as a shaper of national character, see Nicholas Wade's "A Troublesome Inheritance" (The Penguin Press 2014), Chapter I and II

2. Koguryô was the strongest of the three kingdoms founded in the 1st century BCE and fell down in 668. It expanded its territory and crossed the Yiao river of Western Manchuria and offended Emperor Yan'ti of the Sui Dynasty. China launched a counter-attack on a large scale but was beaten back by Koguryô. His son Wen'ti launched a revenge attack employing 300,000 troops but they couldn't break through. One third of the forces bypassed and struck Pyeongyang but found the city empty of people. They were lured to a river valley and suffered a decisive defeat. The Sui Dynasty was replaced by the T'ang dynasty. Taichung, claiming himself as the Emperor of the World, invaded Koguryô but could not achieve his goal. The three wars,

starting in 598, continued 50 years. Koguryô's victory takes a special chapter in the history of Korea. But this is a small detail in the epic story of an anointed sufferer of foreign invasion.

3. The new community movement (Saemaeul Undong) was an offshoot of rapid industrialization in the 60s and 70s. Rural communities were stagnant with hardly any access to the fruit of development. The premise behind the movement was that the rural areas had people imbued with communitarian spirit that was deemed a potential resource to be tapped. This movement was to draw on the potential contribution of the communitarian spirit of the rural people and bring a new spurt of energy for local development. Self help burst forth in a rash of cottage industries which occupied the rural population with something productive to do. The Saemaul Movement is being emulated by many developing societies.

4. Choe Ik Hyun was one of the renowned Confucian literati at the turn of the century and was a stubborn opponent to the state's "open-door" policy. His passionate love of the country was expressed in a touch of chauvinism, disdainful of the Japanese and Westerners who were considered not different from beasts. He considered Korean values as the righteous way and reject alien thoughts as villainous. He labeled all foreigners as scoundrels to be guarded against. He was lauded as the conscience of the nation, his probity and integrity. He rallied peasants into armed forces fighting against imperialism when the Chosôn dynasty was teetering toward its downfall.

5. Ahn Chang-ho's plea for Character Reform shares the vein with Yi Kwang-su's Minjok Gaejo-ron (Reform of National Character). Ahn was a mentor to Yi who served as his biographer. Yi joined Heung Sadan founded by Ahn and both worked as fellow travelers on the bumpy road to national independence

6. "Koryô" has a phonetic similarity to Korea, but the former refers to a medieval kingdom (935-1392) that followed Unified Silla and preceded the Chosôn Dynasty. The kingdom was known to the world through the mediation of the trans-continental Mongol Empire whose eastern border was Koryô. This kingdom was subjugated under the Mongol Empire and participated in the two campaigns against Japan. By a strange coincidence, the two invasions met strong typhoons and left the two states teetering on the verge of a collateral damage. Koryô restored its independence in1350 while China was written off the world map for another 100 years under the Mongols.

7. One may be tempted to identify the political socialism of China with that of Scandinavian countries. A major difference lies in that Scandinavian countries have an assortment of democratic accoutrements, that is, representative systems, free competition among political parties for power, popular elections, and so forth. Chinese politics is dominated by one party, the communist party which serves as a policy deliberative body. There is neither popular election nor a representative body that serves a parliamentary function. Chinese have never experienced voting and election. The notion of representative system has never made its home in their consciousness.

Chapter

Two

The Historical Identity of Koreans

Ethnicity is not a unique substance but part of the consciousness of members belonging to a group. Ethnic consciousness is strengthened by a centralized ruling power and its confrontations with heterogeneous neighbors.
— *Kwon Tae-joon*

The Myth of Ethnic Homogeneity

A common notion of Korea, as perceived worldwide, is that Korea is a cultural offshoot of an overarching Chinese civilization, but Koreans chafe when a foreigner asks whether Koreans have their mother tongue. This is, in large measure, due to the fact that the true identity of Korea is dimmed in the shadow of a titanic neighbor. The complexity of undertaking the quest for Koreans' identity beckons a journey into the past, since history and culture, particularly in the case of homogenized Koreans, can be expected to provide useful insights. The particular nature of a historical event rules out the possibility of it being repeated in the constantly shifting frame of reference. Others argue that historical events are not a haphazard, separate from preceding events, but an ongoing drama of its people acting as protagonists on the stage of history. The quest for Koreans' identity also makes it imperative to compare with other peoples. Reference to other countries in terms of differences and similarities, is a repeated refrain that continues throughout the chapters that follow.

The primary evidence of cultural divergence between China and Korea, notes Hahn Young-woo, is the bronze cultures around the tenth century BCE, when the two were in the same stage of bronze age but not identical. "It was in the fifth century BCE that the Chinese began surpassing Koreans by using iron implements one century earlier" (Hahn Young-woo 1997, 43). Northeast Asian culture, generally known to the West as dominated by Chinese culture, is in fact made up of the cultures of many ethnic groups, each having its own uniqueness. These constituent cultures are grouped according to the names of countries: China, Mongolia, Korea, Japan, Manchu and part of Russia (Maritime Siberia).

The identity of Koreans was shaped in the evolving context of its relationship with China and other neighboring states. China regarded itself as the center of the world, reducing all states surrounding it into satellites that inhabited its periphery. When Mateo Ricci, the first Jesuit priest to serve in China in the late sixteenth century, showed the world map saying "China is not the center but a part of the world," we can imagine how it struck Chinese intellectuals. Hierarchy characterized the inter-country relationship of East Asia, in which China was regarded as the master and others as vassals. Chinese territorial definition was vague and the emerging gray areas leaves ample room for Chinese to assert their jurisdiction encroaching upon its surrounding states. China enjoys a vantage ground in claiming jurisdiction over its neighbors.

Chinese culture had the effect of drowning those of its surrounding states. Mongolian, Manchurian and Tibetan rulers of China had their distinct identities melted away within the Chinese cultural furnace. Some of these continental powers, as we see today, diminished into the shadow of former selves or disappeared into extinction. The unbroken continuance of Korean ethnic and cultural identities amidst the frequent rise and fall of its stronger neighbors is rather exceptional. Medieval Korea was pockmarked with incursions by Manchurians and Mongols in succession. The Chosôn dynasty withstood the blows of Japanese and Manchurians in a matter of 40 years between the two invasions. The philosopher Santanya expressed one of the profound truths when he remarked that those who ignore the past are condemned to repeat it (Norman F. Candor, 1963,547). Korea fits well with this generalization. Never has Korea been well prepared for the foreign incursions, though they were pained by memories of the past. While it was a trampling ground, though, Korea has been spared foreign rule by China taking foreign beatings and being placed under foreign rules. The marauders found China more enticing to possess by the size of the land with vast irrigable lands. Daunted by its stronger neighbors, Korea created a self image of "an underdog." But this description is not free of a tendency to blow up trauma in describing its achievement as if it were the hallmark of Koreans. But there are many others whose tragedies dwarf Koreans' to insignificance.

The History of an Ethnic Nation

Uniquely, the Korean national identity is defined in terms of political, cultural and ethnic accord. In contrast, Europe has rarely seen such an accord due to lingering feudalistic remains of culture-dominant sovereign states and the ever-shifting boundaries following frequent wars. While Western societies shared in history, culture and religion under the dome of Greek-Roman legacies, there is no common historical legacy in East Asia, such as the bond that brought Europeans into one political and religious emporium. Neither is there a religious vein that cuts across different political and cultural communities to facilitate the cross-fertilization of different cultures. The term, "Europe," refers to a cultural identity, whereas "Asia" is a geographical term, embracing different cultures.

Certainly, the professed ethnic/cultural homogeneity speaks for the absence of natural causes for cleavage. Koreans view historical movement as a progress toward homogenization and the earlier advent of monarchism in Korea is attributed to a rare accord between ethnic and cultural identities. But no nation has a claim to absolute racial or ethnic homogeneity, and this casts doubt on the Koreans' professed claim to a common descent that traces its lineage to Tan'gun[1] who began his legendary reign in 2333 BCE. The ethnic consciousness of Koreans is an imagined one, and such a notion cannot be conceived in a broader supranational identity of Europe.

Kim Jeong-bae traces the inhabitants of the Korean peninsula "as early as the later Paleolithic age. From the patterns of the pottery used, he surmised that the Ye-Maek tribes merged with the Paleolithic Asians who had settled earlier, while drifting southward, to become the progenitors of Koreans. Pae Hyung-il defends the theory of Siberian origin, linking Koreans to Tungus. Another theory has it that the earliest settlers migrated from Southern China, when the Korean peninsula was joined to this region before the sea level rose. The amalgamation of Ye-Maek with the Paleolithic Asians was followed by their integration with the southern inhabitants. After the downfall of the Chin Dynasty in China in 221 BCE, warring states followed, causing massive influx of Chinese refugees, and their eastward migration continued through the ensuing Yen and Han dynasties. The Han's occupation of the northwestern part of the peninsula must have facilitated the amalgamation of Ye-Maek with Chinese.

The professed ethnic homogeneity glossed over the historical fact that the ancient kingdoms of Korea, namely, Kogurŏ and Balhae² known as border states, were multi-ethnic states, composed of Ye-Maek, Malgals (Mohe in Chinese), Khitans, and Mongolians. Li Ki-moon, an authority on old Korean language, disclosed that the three kingdoms – Koguryo, Paekche and Silla – did not share one language. From the perspective of them belonging to the Altaic family, it is fair to say that their languages were within the distance that marked Swedes apart from Danes or Norwegians, and its structural difference characterizes the Korean language apart from the Chinese.

The homogeneity of Koreans, then, is based not so much on common descent as the fact that they have gone through a longer process of amalgamation than others. This argument is endorsed by the fact that history traces its earliest unitary state to 668A.D., when the three kingdoms were incorporated into a unitary monarchy. Encounter of a cultural identity with a political community is the pre-requisite for the amalgamation of languages. Koreans' belief in ethnic homogeneity is an imagined one shaped in the context of historical continuity and has profoundly influenced Koreans' national consciousness. "Ethnicity is not a unique substance but part of the consciousness of members belonging to an ethnic group in the formative stage of the state. Ethnic consciousness is strengthened by a centralized ruling authority and its confrontations with heterogeneous neighbors" (translated from Kwon Tae-joon 2006,240). There is little doubt that Koreans surpass other groups in ethnic and social solidarity in the absence of such causes of division that plagued its neighboring China.

Confined within a relatively stable territory, dynastic change served as a screening mesh to winnow out heterogeneous elements, as we see in the demise of Balhae, through Unified Silla (676- 935) and in the succeeding Koryŏ Dynasty (935-1392). Historical movement is the incorporation of heterogeneous groups into a larger group that is consistent with a society made up of like components and like-minded people. What matters in explaining ethnic homogeneity, therefore, is how long the people of different origins have formed one political community. Law, administration and jurisdictional boundaries have served to erase all ethnic and cultural distinctions and facilitated the formation of one nation state. When ethnic or cultural disparities were not dissolved, these factors served as connecting tissues. The integrative function of the state was given a greater importance in the ancient states of Korea. Emphasis on homogeneity reflects a gemeinschaft concept of a state - stressing a common ethnic descent rooted in kinship and emotional ties. But the concept of gemeinschaft contradicts the modern concept of nation state that goes beyond the ethnic and cultural confines to embrace various groups under one law and administration. The starting point of an ethnic integration is when minjok – an identifiable mass population – meets with a political community and Korea traces this encounter to Unified Silla (668-935) "The state was an effective guide to the proceeding of ethnic integration"(Gasett,1932; 180).

Balhae, the border state, came after the Silla dynasty had achieved political unification but fell down earlier than the latter. Unified Silla played a pot that melted all ethnic and cultural distinctions into one group. The succeeding Koryŏ kept its door wide open to integrate Balhae migrants into the mainstream population. Since then Koreans have enjoyed a cultural, language and political accord for a longer period than any other people.

Geo-political environment rendered Koreans keenly sensitive to a single ethnic patch. Occupying a peninsula surrounded by seas on its three sides, Korea had an opening in the north replete with rugged mountains and meandering rivers forming natural borders. Inhabiting the peripheral region of the Asian land mass, Koreans had few contacts with the outside world: isolation and forlornness helped a lot to galvanize peoples of different ethnic origins within the boundary to become identical beings. The underdog country activated the integrative function of the state within a self-contained territory. Phobia of the continental powers in its neighborhood was another to drive home the necessity of living together among compatriots in blissful isolation from its neighbors. The ethnic bond held the country together in its fierce confrontations with the invaders. As such, the inclemency of the surrounding milieu, coupled with the repeated blows of its neighbors, were the major shaper of Koreans' ethnic homogeneity.

Nationalism and Ideology

Nationalism in Korea is an outgrowth of Koreans' ethnic consciousness. This argument associates the idea of the state with a gens or volk, a people of common descent with shared culture, beliefs, language and history. Such an assertion has ethno-centralism toned with cultural chauvinism, largely due to the lack of contacts with outsiders. By virtue of its estrangement from the outside world and the resulting social solidarity, Korean society in the past was a self-imposed island, a haven for a dogmatic ideology to take roots.

The rapid pace of modernization, defined as the acceptance of Western technology and mores, spawned a reactive yearning for the past in this ethnical conscious country. Such a move is comparable to a centrifuge whirling within each society, often countered by a retrospective quest for the past and particular cultures. Supposedly on their way out, racial, religious and cultural distinctions reassert themselves. The collapse of the Soviet Union was followed by burgeoning nationalism in its member countries and the search for their identities rooted in their particular cultures and values.

Throughout much of its history, Korea remained secluded more tightly than Togukawa Japan. Ensconced within a protective wall of one dogmatic ideology, Koreans withstood foreign incursions. Hatred and distrust of foreigners, together with the resulting ignorance of the outside world, nurtured self-complacency about their cultural legacy, causing delay in opening the door to outsiders. Even after China and Japan bowed to the pressure of Western powers in the early 1800s, Korea remained a self-alleged stalwart citadel of lofty Asian values. Its intrepid showdowns with France and the United States respectively earned it "a puppy not to be afraid of a tiger." Temerity came from the utter ignorance of its foes and Korea's unflinching confrontation with the imperialistic powers awed both China and Japan as to what would befall this little and proud kingdom. While its neighboring countries were in the grip of "white phobia," Korea remained self-complacent and impervious to new challenges looming over the horizon.

Koreans' sense of nationalism is brought into a clear focus in comparison with the Europeans who persisted in maintaining stronger ethnic, cultural and religious identities more than political unity, and this fact owed much to the long-lasting remains of smaller princely states. "Even today, the modern nationalism of Western societies is a nineteenth- or twentieth-century phenomenon. This fact espouses the claim that while political ethnicity is of recent vintage, cultural ethnicity is much more ancient" (Patrick J. Geary 2002;33). "A shared cultural tradition is the precursor to the formation of a unitary nation state, as observed in Europe. A unique means of communication is the major promoter of community consciousness on the ground of shared history and culture" (Kwon Tae-joon 2006; 243).

The difficulty of achieving an ethnic nation state in Europe is also explained by long-simmering religious schisms. Further, efforts to achieve a unified nation state in the West were stymied by different languages spoken within one political community: this deepened the class schism between noble men and the commoners. In the former, a trans-national consciousness was formed through inter-dynastic marriages, lacking allegiance to their own monarchies, while the latter's view of the world was confined within the bound of a political community. Following the Napoleon era, ethnic nationalism was aroused among the Italians and Germans that had remained divided into many princely states. Their desire to bring all of their ethnic people into one nation state was stimulated by England and France in which nationalism served as a powerful driving force for imperial ambition and territorial aggrandizement.

The ethnic consciousness of Koreans was reinforced by frequent foreign invasions. The absence of external other is likely to undermine unity and breed divisions within a society (Samuel Huntington 2004,18). Among these, two invasions – one by the Mongol hordes in the thirteenth and another by Japanese in the sixteenth century – were most devastating in the sense that they made a deep dent in its social fabric and psychic make-up of Koreans. The Japanese invasion broke through the impenetrable barrier of a dogmatic ideology, leaving cracks in social fabric through which alien cultures could penetrate into its heartland, spearheaded by Roman Catholicism.

As the wheel of the Western imperialism was turning fast toward East Asia, ethnic consciousness reached its peak in the form of exclusive nationalism when Taewon'gun (1864-75) reigned on behalf of his immature son.[3] His seclusion policy reached a new height as displayed in its intrepid confrontation with the French armada and the burning of an American commercial ship in 1866. The temerity of Koreans was quite a contrast to the white phobia Chinese and Japanese held against the Western imperialists. Koreans were intolerable of any foreign intruder for fear that their sacred soil would be defiled by lowly barbarian cultures. The xenophobic backlash renewed the quest for Confucian idealism, refreshed by memories of the golden Chosôn dynasty that materialized under the reign of Sejong the Great four centuries before. The new era made it inevitable to develop industry and modernize military forces in preparation for its fated bout with the Western powers. The Western threat goaded the monarch into a reactive nostalgia for the luster of Confucianism. The historical progressivism of Korea suffered setbacks due to their ignorance of the new world.

Uniquely, Korea clung to its self image longer, even if it proved wrong. This speaks for the unfathomable depth of Koreans' ethno-centered nationalism. With a relatively easy access to the changing profile of the outside world, albeit fragmentary and partial, Koreans' belief in their self-proclaimed cultural superiority was shattered. Here, self image clashed with perceived image. Koreans have, as we see today, outgrown the bound of exclusive nationalism. Nationalism has changed its clothes from reactive and violent anti-colonial resistance to a swelling pride in more recent accomplishments.

A succession of events, caused by the Western encroachments, cast a dark shadow over the fate of the underdog state. The ideological quest for the true Korean identity in this context developed into a massive peasants' movement to repel corrupt officials and Western elements in the nineteenth century. Koreans' consciousness of their country in peril was kindled into a new height of defiance, calling for "getting together against the imminent barbarian incursions." Coming into the 20th century, the xenophobic orientation of nationalism was sublimated to embrace the concept of Koreans as constituting a nation state that approximates minjok" (Henry Eam 1999; 278). Nationalism in its true sense came from the meeting of minjok, volk, with a nation state.

Ironically, Japan whose centralized power was late in taking shape due to the lingering feudalistic legacy displayed the power of a unitary nation, goaded by popular awareness of national crisis before imminent imperialistic incursions. The defeat of China by Great Britain in the Opium War (1839-42) and the danger of its vulnerability to another invasion was the single most powerful motive for Japan's drive for modernization. The Koreans' failure to galvanize themselves into timely responses to an emerging national crisis was partly explained by the xenophobic-bent ethnic consciousness. For those who suffered from the Japanese colonial rule, ethnic consciousness gave full vent to a violent expression of anger and frustration fueling anti-colonial struggles. For those anxious to see an enriched country, ethnic consciousness goaded Koreans to rally around the professed development goals and fostering a willingness to make personal sacrifices to a greater good of the state.

After the Russian Revolution, some Korean intellectuals under the colonial rule could not be immune to the novelty of communism as the champion for the oppressed and as a guide to people trying to get out of the ruins of capitalism and industrialism. Communism bred a divisive feud in the Korean nationalist front, and Liberation from the colonial yoke further intensified ideological confrontations within it. The ideological rift of the Korean nationalist front led to a fratricidal civil war and territorial division. Caught up in a vortex of colossal events that followed liberation, the three-year old child was hardly given a breathing spell to totter on its own feet. As Koreans experienced a deep trauma in its nascent period of nation building, anti-communism became the mantra of South Korea, and its process of democratization was hindered and deformed within the frame of the ideological confrontation. The ideological occupation, created by an imagined "north phobia," gave birth to a succession of authoritarian regimes that threw their full weight to the state-driven economic development to catch up with the forerunners within the shortest period of time.

In fact, modern economic development theorists attributed South Korea's phenomenal economic growth to ethnic and cultural homogeneity. This creates a capacity for unhampered and effective communication and the standardization of the expression and comprehension of ideas, particularly those related to the state goals. It is easy to inculcate national values in citizens in a common language through the educational system, the mass media and state-sponsored organizations. The result was that the people were highly motivated to achieve a professed goal in modernization. Cultural homogeneity and class consciousness provided the ground for the rational authorization of bureaucratic leadership to dramatize Koreans' potential contribution to the country's ascendancy to a new economic power. The hierarchical order of the social structure wedded on rational authorization unleashed a new thrust of energy.

Among those locked in a self-perpetuating poverty in the shadow of rapid development, the encounter of ethnic consciousness with the successive authoritarian rules gave rise to anti-government struggles that were waged in the name of mass nationalism. Uniquely, anti-government struggles thrived on the authoritarian regimes which wielded iron fists to suppress them. The anti-authoritarian struggles earned the participating activists the name of democratic crusaders. "Like a scab on a wound, nationalism is often the ideology of the downtrodden" (Gerd Behrens, The Time, March 21, 1994). Some of the downtrodden were politicized into radical activities, and declined to recognize any regime in existence in the divided Korea. They called for the immediate reunification of the country, obsessed with ethnic nationalism but ambiguous about the ideological identity of what a unified polity should entail.

Due to a strong ethnic consciousness, average Korean is unable to distinguish between ethnic group and a state. There come new challenges as Korea is moving toward an ethnically and culturally diverse society. "Today, the previous boundaries of Korean society have been blurred due to international cross migration. The number of ethnic Koreans, who have left the Korean peninsula behind has exceeded eight million, while the population of foreigners who reside in Korea has recently exceeded two million mark" (Han Geon-soo, 2008; 13). Increasing numbers of migrant workers from abroad are obtaining Korean citizenship by marriage.

Ethnic consciousness in a parochial sense bred disdain for foreigners. Koreans who have regarded their culture as superior condemn foreigners poor at Korean language and lacking Confucian orientation. Koreans tend to become racists when they encounter strangers. It, therefore, takes a radical turnabout of their consciousness to embrace foreign workers as their fellow citizens. "As Korea proceeds toward a multi-ethnic society, it must go beyond merely recognizing cultural differences and strive to foster a mature cultural environment that appreciates and embraces cultural diversity" (Hahn Geon-soo, 13). National identity based on cultural homogeneity and chauvinism is outmoded today. Ethnic homogeneity has lost its ground to the historical dictum that Koreans should keep pace with the demands of the changing times as they embark on a path toward ethnic and cultural diversity.

Dynastic Continuity

Contrary to the frequent dynastic turnover in China, Korean history features dynastic continuity with a few turnovers, and the exceptionally long life span of each dynasty. Dynasty is a political entity ruled by a line of rulers from one family, with its power structure highly centralized to rule a large territory. In Korea, monarchical authority has been maintained, with a few exceptions, by the hereditary succession of power through the patriarchal lineage. There has been a singular line of succession of dynasties that never discontinued despite frequent foreign invasions. The Chosôn Dynasty (1392- 1910) followed strictly the male line of the ruling family whose authority stood above challenge by earthlings. Korea and China shared in aristocratic-centered monarchy founded on the thin layer of middle class and the impoverished masses, distinct from the monarchies of 15th century Europe whose ruler was seated on the enlarged middle class.

Reference to other countries brings into focus the characteristics of Korean dynasties. China with its vast land and ethnic and cultural diversity alternated over history between a unitary country and warring states. The dynastic continuity of China was frequently broken by the incursions of Northern nomadic hordes or the chaotic presence of small sovereign states. These petty states were ceaselessly locked in wars to gain hegemonic supremacy. The smallness of territory like Korea was a barren land for the rise of petty states, and the absence of feudal states put the Korean monarchy on a vantage ground to maintain dynastic continuity.

The Western dynasties are characterized by frequent resort to female line or succession by in-laws that was made possible through inter-dynastic marriages. The Holy Roman Empire elected emperors, with no hereditary succession guaranteed until 1440 when Hapsburg Austria appeared to monopolize the throne. Inter-dynastic marriage invited dukes of Orange and Hanover to claim the English throne. European monarchies have seen not only kings but queens put on the throne, not only home-bred ones but aliens from abroad, and this accounts for the frequent turnover of dynasties. "The Empire was made up of sovereign prince states, and the royal title was transferred from one to another princely state to preclude the development of any dynastic interest in the German crown" (Norman F. Cantor 1963, 303).

The five dynastic changes of Korea stands in stark contrast to the twenty-five dynastic changes in China. Silla was an one millennium dynasty and others existed longer than five hundred years. The life span of Chinese dynasties averaged 200 – 250 years with Tang China lasting 300 years. The average life span of the Western monarchs was 200 – 250 years and the longest one is seen in the Holy Roman Empire, an alliance of sovereign states under the loosely knit network. With regard to dynastic longevity, two questions arise; "what is the cause for the dynastic longevity and whether it is a blessing or burden?"

Korea traces the advent of a centralized monarchism to the fourth century. Political centralization in ancient Korea came with the introduction of Buddhism and Confucianism, the former giving the spiritual underpinning and the latter guiding familial and social relations. We can imagine a single body of people with a religious devotion and all loyal to the ruler. These two, interacting in a mutually complementary way, froze social life and institutional structures and the result was institutional and social stagnancy. In a comparative perspective, Korea offers a remarkable example of external strength and internal weakness. The former was expressed in social cohesiveness that enabled Korea to withstand foreign beatings and the latter is manifested in frequent factional division.

Confucianism is a dogmatic doctrine designed to order family relations and govern the state in a way that ensures the harmony of different elements and social classes. The earlier advent of monarchies in China and Korea is explained by the emphasized integrative function of the Confucian statecraft contrived to transform heterogeneous groups into an integrated one. The Confucian concept of the ruler has a metaphor to heaven that stands above challenges by earthlings, while subjects were referred to as earth. As the heaven and earth metaphor suggests, inequality is ensconced in Confucianism and its manifestation in family and social hierarchy is held to ensure the orderly functioning of the state and society. The Silla Dynasty owed its millennium existence to the rigidity of social hierarchy, expressed in the so-called "bone-rank" system,[4] consistently defying petitions for change. The downside of institutional rigidity is the lack of change and the resulting stagnation.

A hierarchical inter-state relationship with China was another that enabled the Korean dynasties to endure longer. China with its vast territory and people might have become a Roman conqueror, but moral obligations of the titular master for a peaceful order of the region kept it from predatory dreams; all feuds and conflicts were sublimated into a brotherly bond that appeared to be harmonious and peaceful on the surface. Unified China was too stymied by its internal problems, largely associated with rebellious local lords to prey on its neighboring states. Coming into the Chosôn Dynasty, the hierarchical inter-state system became more elaborate and subtle with M'ing China (1368-1644); its brotherly concern led China to dispatch 50,000 troops to help Koreans fight the overwhelming Japanese invaders in 1592.[5] There is another view of this matter, asserting that China's help sprang from its self defense: the downfall of the Chosôn dynasty would expose China vulnerable to Japan's attack. At any rate, the hierarchical order of East Asia was a counterweight to any state tempted to a rebellious act or bent on predatory incursion into another.

Distinct from the European continent beset by struggles between rival states, accompanied by ever-shifting distinction between foe and ally, Asian countries have maintained a static order within political borders contiguous with ethnic borders for a longer period. Medieval Europe saw no nation assuming the titular domination of China over others. European states, equal in power, vied for dominance and was perpetually locked in wars. There has been the equilibrium of power through alliance and de-alliance of states. States around a master state in Asia could enjoy a longer period of stable order. The Asian concept of inter-state hierarchy is not seen in Europe. One that approximates a vertical inter-state relationship is that of medieval Netherlands and German Empire, but there were as many to differentiate it from Korea in its relationship with its gigantic neighbor. The Netherlands was an underdog surrounded by its strong neighbors– such as France, England and Spain, and German

Empire. On the surface, the monarchy of Korea and Netherlands seem to share a common fate in this respect, but there are a lot more that characterizes the two apart.[6] The Netherlands was far from an integrated state, since it was made up of independent and autonomous cities. Located around the Baltic Ocean, some of the cities opted to stay separate from a confederate state to defend their trade interests. They were richer than others, though they were within one national boundary.

Korea's dynastic longevity has more to do with the Confucian notion of monarchical absolutism and the supremacy of moral politics. The king was elevated to heaven which defies challenge by earthlings. Although the dominance of military officials in the Koryô Dynasty reduced the kings into figureheads for more than a century, there was no interruption in the lineage succession of the royal clan throughout its five century history. Under the over-arching influence of the Yuan (Mongolian) Empire, Koryô kings were reduced into surrogates for the Yuan Emperor but the lineage continuity of the royal clan was not broken. The dynastic continuity is something unique of Korea. Comparing with China where Song dynasty was written off the world map by Mongolians for one hundred years, Koryô retained its dynastic continuity, though in a submissive status to the Mongolian Empire. Chinese historiography regards the Mongolian Empire as a Chinese dynasty, since the Mongolian rulers lost their ethnic and cultural identity in a sea of superior Chinese culture. Such an expansive interpretation of history is typical of Chinese scholars by taking advantage of the diverse ethnic and cultural make-up.

The royal lineage of the Chosôn Dynasty (1392-1910) was never interrupted, though two kings were dethroned by rebellious factions because of immoral acts. Assuming that monarchical ineptness and interregnum were more often the causes for dynastic turnovers in the West, Korean politics saw immorality as the decisive factor for ending the reign of the ruler in question, while ineptness, idleness, and shaky leadership were atoned. When an immoral ruler earns the wrath of heaven, the enraged heaven justifies the uprising of ruling elites to terminate his reign but not to terminate the reign of the ruling family.

The rebellious factions justified their actions by following what was known as the heavenly dictum but had never occupied the throne, thus discontinuing the lineage succession of the royal family. The ruling class consigned the throne to a blood kin within the royal family. Given the monarchical absolutism, the Western monarchs from the fifteenth century should have relished dynastic longevity. However, the absolute monarch in this period was built on an enlarged bourgeois or burgher class who were individualistic, enriched, civilized, and rebellious. The Reformation and subsequent intellectual spurts were the hotbed for individualism to gain currency, destructive of dynastic absolutism. The French Revolution was the culmination of civic rebellions against the established order; individualistic and civic consciousness grew as state authority declined. In the Western monarchism, aristocratic class atrophied on the rising tide of the middle class.

Power structure of the ruler and aristocratic class, mediated through a system of checks and balance, sometimes made the ruler relatively weak, contrary to the Confucian concept of monarchical absolutism. A strong monarchy finds its expression in Confucianism but, in reality, it was rarely found in Korean history. Moral supremacy was built into the institutional design to prevent the abuse of power or irregularities. Here, the ruler enjoyed an absolute status but was shaky in power. The longevity of each dynasty was ensured when the ruling class was content with the power-given privileges. But moral dictum discouraged them to covet the throne. The Confucian concept of absolute monarchism worked its way into prolonging the reign of each dynasty, but there was a price to be paid.

Viewing the dynastic longevity as a blessing is based on the capability of maintaining a stable and harmonious society. Koreans take pride in having maintained "an island of tranquility in a stormy sea.""Five dynastic changes without an interregnum" was made a high point of the Koreans' manifesto[7] declared by nationalists against the two superpowers intent to place a liberated Korea under the trusteeship of four great powers. In contrast to the Western progressivism based on armed clashes and cross-fertilization of cultures across borders, Koreans regard cultural flourishing as a product resulting from a long lasting stability. Likewise, Japanese take pride in "the unbroken continuity of the imperial lineage for 10,000 years" (Beasely W.G, 1993; 36). China, Korea and Japan all look retrospectively and admiringly at their historical continuity.

The frequent turnover of the European monarchies is rather regarded as the cause for progress. Kant referred to nature's method of developing the hidden capacities of life: "Struggle is the indispensable accompaniment of progress. If men were entirely social, man would stagnate; a certain alloy of individualism and competition is required to make the human species survive and grow" (Will Durant, 1961, 214). With Confucian emphasis on qualities of social kind, men might have led an Arcadian shepherd life in complete harmony, contentment and mutual love. But in that case all their talents would have forever remained hidden in their germs.

The memory of the once-great Roman Empire lived as a vital tradition in the hearts of Europeans. The historical continuity of Europe finds its expression in the resurrection of the defunct Roman Empire by Charlemagne, Otto the Great, Napoleon and Hitler. The Roman era is marked by the shared history of all Europeans, transcending ethnic, cultural and language differences. The dynastic turnover of European history brought the opportunities to renew ideology and institutions. In contrast, a dynastic continuity, though commended for a long-lasting static order, marked the absence of colossal upheavals such as the Reformation and French Revolution. Revolutionary changes should have put Korea into a violent shake to get rid of its stagnant past. Korea paid dearly for its dynastic longevity.

From 1800, Korea began to show fatal flaws of the monarchical kingdoms whose sustenance was made possible by sticking to hereditary succession through male lineage. Heir to the throne was a minor, inept, or nonentities in succession; they could have been disqualified, had it not been for blood connections. The new kings had never known their immediate predecessors not only due to distance between the blood relatives but because of untimely death, and the supremacy of blood siblings denigrated the leadership of the ruler. The anomaly of power succession repeated itself in Q'ing China after it was defeated in the Opium War. The imbecile rulers in the two states provided an opportunity for an in-law family to reign, foreshadowing the untimely demise of the kingdom.

The rigidity of the systems immobilized the monarch to derive actions from the time-brought pleas for changes. Transition to modern state, therefore, was more traumatic, as it was punctuated by the colonial rule, ideological confrontation, territorial division, the Korean War, the stressful post-war rehabilitation, and the untimely demise of the first and following Republics. A series of mishaps in its recent history rather shook the country out of the past and provided a new spurt of energy for survival.

Two Koreas

〳〳〳〳〳〳〳〳〳〳〳〳〳〳〳〳〳〳〳〳〳〳〳〳〳〳〳〳〳〳〳〳

Korea finds its historical identity in the present division of the people and land. Two Koreas still sounds awkward for Koreans to hear, although it is taken for granted by others. To Koreans, distinction between the nation and race is minimal since the term minjok (ethnic people) often connotes both. The ethnic consciousness of Koreans is extraordinary but they were the first victim of the Cold War, divided by an ideology they had never heard of. The divisions of Germany, Vietnam and Korea followed World War II, but they came from different political backgrounds. The division of Korea outlives a divided Germany and Vietnam. And yet Korea remains an island of ideological confrontation in a sea of de-ideological landscape. The juxtaposition of two antithetical ideologies offers no inkling of the two halves likely to become one. What characterizes Korea from other divided countries? Does it have anything to do with the collective trait of Koreans? Koreans find their identity in a tangle of events that belied their claim to ethnic homogeneity.

Ideological Confrontation

As the Pacific War was drawing to its close with the U.S victory becoming certain, the Soviet Union broke a three-year silence by declaring war against Japan whose fate had been sealed. It came on the day when the second atomic bomb struck Nagasaki on August 9, 1945, six days before Japan surrendered. This disaster galvanized Imperial Japan into an urgent cabinet meeting which subsequently made decision to surrender unconditionally. After a week-long participation in the Pacific War, Soviet troops marched into Korea. Little resistance of Japanese forces quickened their pace of advance into the Korean peninsula, threatening to sweep the entire territory into its sphere of influence, while the advancing contingent of the U.S forces were stuck in Okinawa. The rapidly unfolding situation in Korea gave urgency for the United States' action to thwart the Soviet's southward thrust, and the result was the declaration of the 38th parallel. This demarcation line was hastily improvised to contain the Soviet's southward expansion. Consequently, the northern half fell into the communist hands in the first week of Japan's surrender, while the U.S troops were aboard a ship sailing to Korea. South Korea was left drifting into chaos without leadership.

What caused the Soviet to enter the campaign that was sure to terminate soon? Adjacent to Korea, the Soviet was so much concerned about the fate of its neighbor: it could not simply stand all spoils going to the single winner of the war, its potential rival. What else could it be than to claim part of the peninsula, if not the land in its entirety, as a price for their one-week engagement in the campaign? Even a single day combat, the Soviet leader thought, would entitle them to part of Korea. The Russian interest in Korea was historical, whereas Americans for the most part not only remained apathetic but were uninformed about Korea. At the Yalta Summit Meeting, F. D. Roosevelt and Winston Churchill offered a bait; "in return for his promise to fight Japan, Stalin was promised the southern half of Sakhalin Island that Japan had won in the war against Russian Empire in 1904" (Samuel E. Morison, 1942, 412). The occupation of Korea by the two hostile foreign troops was a foregone conclusion that the country could not avoid division. The Cold War was a confrontation between the two super powers; each is deterred from attacking another by fear of the other capable of destroying the world. Some argue that the two Koreas were the surrogates for the big powers.

The occupation of Korea by foreign troops was discussed at the Potsdam Conference, the last of a series of the summit meetings that had preceded, with focus on disarming Japanese forces and restoring order in Korea. The occupation of a defeated country by victor has been the rule, but Korea was merely a colonial outpost of Japan, not a defeated country. The U.S troops arrived in South Korea following a three-week hiatus empty of political leadership. The post-liberation chaos of South Korea favored a communists' bid for power. Communists were well trained to thrive in a troubled water, and the communist faction had no rival in terms of its coherence, discipline and commitment to its goal.

To restore order from the post-war chaos, the Korean centralists authored the Committee for the Preparation of National Reconstruction (CPNR) with a view to orchestrating the rightist, centralist and leftist strands of nationalists into a coalition. The problem was that the leftists within it were never made to become bedfellows with others. In the south, right-left confrontations were a matter of daily grind. On the contrary, North Korea seemed to be uncannily silent under the Soviet-backed communist regime, but behind the scene, dissident elements were hunted down and ruthlessly persecuted. They were born enemies of class struggle, condemned for their inherited wealth and education to ruthless destruction. From the liberation to the Korean War (five years), two million North Koreans defected to the south to avoid social intolerance.

The communist faction in South Korea was gaining ground even under the nose of the U.S Military Command which maintained an air of studied indifference to the outcries of Korean political factions. The U.S Military Command was relatively tolerable of the communist party in contrast with North Korea's intolerability of the enemies of the people. The U.S naivety in dealing with leftists exasperated rightist nationalists. Syngman Rhee and Kim Ku who represented a broad spectrum of rightists and centralists were hypercritical of the U.S Military Command's inability to deal with a wide-spread anarchy; American troops were rather spectators to the unfolding situation, far from its support that the rightists craved in their struggle against the leftists.

The American occupation of South Korea came about as an incident of the surrender of Japan.

While the Soviet was consistent with its premeditated plan, the United States, without a long-term vision of its policy implications for the future, drifted into Korean affairs halfheartedly and found itself trapped into a tangle of problems against its will. In the absence of a long-term policy frame, the United States improvised policies in reaction to the Soviet's initiative."Bruce Cummings has it right labeling the United States as "a well-intentioned bumbler."

Division of the Country

At the initial stage of American commitment to Korea, the United States committed a grand failure by planning to place a liberated Korea under the trusteeship of four great powers. It immediately found an ardent supporter in the Soviets, though both had different dreams. The United States regarded trusteeship as a counter-weight to the sovietization of Korea, and the Soviet considered it would serve its interest in a long-term goal of expanding communism. This plan met the intransigent opposition of all Koreans, irrespective of ideological affiliations.[8] A unitary Korea without sovereignty is the resurrection of the body without a soul. Have Jews ever conceived Israel without Jerusalem? Despite the violent opposition of all Koreans, the proponents pushed the idea to have it confirmed at the three foreign ministers' meeting in December 1945. An outgrowth of the trusteeship agreement was the Joint U.S-Soviet Commission, the Korean equivalent of the German's Four Power Control Council.

The trusteeship plan of the United Sates met strong oppositions at home. Notably, Averill Harriman and George F. Kennan, both having served as American ambassadors to the Soviet, warned that trusteeship would rather more likely to be stepping stones to the Soviet ambition. The United States backed down from the plan, whereas the Soviet clung to it. Korean leftists, in conformity to the Soviet' pro-trusteeship stance, turned around from anti- to pro-trusteeship. This American blunder panicked South Korea into another round of blood bath between pros and cons of the trusteeship. Many of prominent political leaders, leftists and rightists, were assassinated by young ideological fanatics during this military occupation.

Korean nationalist activists forced out of the country under Japan's colonial rule were not immune to the seductive voice of communism in the host countries. The nationalist activists felt forlorn in combating Japanese forces in China and Siberia and the notion of "a common foe" was a persuasive call for their alliance with the revolutionary troops of the host countries. Some intellectuals were infatuated with the pseudoscientific vision of communism sure to become an alternative to capitalism that brought the collective ruins of the world. The repatriation of the ideologically aligned nationalists to liberated Korea dramatized ideological feuds into the foreground, drowning out a nationalistic outcry for "one people making one nation." In the north, the collective sentiment of anti-Japan was instrumental in fostering ethnic nationalism under the communist banner. But South Korea was seething with the coexistence of ideologically different extremists.

The chaotic presence of different ideological identities in the south defeated an attempt to form a unified nationalist front and a single voice. The nationalist front stumbled into the stone wall of ideological dictum: both the rightists and leftists stood pat to have their ideological visions reflected in a nation to be born. Middle roaders were sidetracked in the explosive Korean mentality of "all or nothing." The opportunity for Koreans to rebuild their tattered country was ill-timed to encounter the ideological confrontation in the bipolarized world. Given that the nationalist front split into ideological bifurcation, it can be said that the fate of a divided nation had been sealed even before Korea was reborn into the world.

A logical question is "whether Koreans, their political leadership in particular, were responsible for the division of the country or whether it was the result of the two confrontational super powers?" A progressive scholar argues that the "primary responsibility rests on the shoulders of the United States" (Bruce Cumings1994, 325).[9] His reference to the United States as the major culprit in the hierarchy of causation by authoring the 38th parallel oversimplified a tangle of factors that spanned a longer period. Doubtlessly, hegemonic rivalry between the two powers was started when they were fighting in partnership against the Axis power. Drawing the 38th parallel in a larger perspective was not an issue to be responsible for the division of Korea. It was part of an on-going drama that had started much earlier.

Franklin Roosevelt exhorted Stalin to participate in the Pacific campaign in a rush for the earliest possible conclusion of the war with Japan. It was in the Teheran's Summit Conference that Roosevelt and Churchill were convinced of Stalin's ambition for the peninsula as a price for its engagement with the Pacific campaign. In the ensuing Potsdam Conference, Harry Truman, fresh from ascendancy to the presidency, was suspicious of the Soviet scheme and wanted to 'go it alone,' triumphant on the successfully tested atomic bomb. But it was too late to thwart the Soviet ambition. It simply remains uncertain when the Soviets would engage in the Pacific War. With regard to what motivated the Soviet to declare war against Japan, nothing is more erroneous than a naïve conjecture that the Soviet's belated entrance into the Pacific War had little to do with its hegemonic motive for world domination. The futility of this prognostication proved true in consideration of the Greek and Turkey's civil wars in March 1949 disclosing the Soviet ambition for global expansion. Korea was the first ground for communism to measure its feasibility on an institutional base.

The imperialistic ambition of the Soviet Union goes far into the past when the Russian Empire was brought into an armed clash with Japan in 1905.[10] Given the imperial ambitions built into the two powers, discourse on what caused Korea to be divided crossed the threshold of "who authored the 38th parallel" The issue should be considered within the context of a great global struggle. The Russian policy toward East Asia had consistently been expansionary from the time of the Russian Empire. The Pacific War presented an ideal opportunity for the Soviet to be a free rider on the tide of the American winning streak and inflame its imperialistic ambition.

With the conclusion of the Pacific War, the Korean peninsula, due to its geographical proximity to the Maritime Siberia, was the first to receive the Soviet blow on behalf of its colonial master. Citing the German case, it was Japan that should have been occupied and divided but Japan was spared punishment by Korea taking the beating on its behalf. The northern half immediately fell under communism according to its pre-set scenario of communization and still remains an enigmatic island of revolutionary fervor. Under the Soviet occupation of the northern half, Stalinism had a practical appeal, for it filled a vacuum created by the withdrawal of the colonial model. Marxist-Leninist theory was fading out before Stalinism which offered an organized, complete, systematic blueprint for economic development and modernization. Omnipotent leader and rigid surveillance systems do not allow any rival. Bloody purges were a popular means for weeding out political foes. Mystery and secret surround their doings, personality traits and even families. Collectivization of agriculture did not allow even a modicum of freedom to be creative and productive. Such a regimented society was by no means envisioned by Lenin and Trotsky.

In the post-liberation period, the southern half continued to suffer from murderous confrontations between the leftists and rightists until the North launched a massive surprise invasion in 1950. So obsessive with a way that could have spared Korea the division, Bruce Cumings puts fingers on the United States, critical of "its support for a rightist political group which had a lame grip on the south and next to nothing on the north" (1994,312). The flipside of his argument is that the United States should have supported the leftist, if it had supported the goal of avoiding division. Expecting the United States to support the leftist faction in the south is tantamount to expecting the Soviet to support the rightists in the north which had been totally eliminated by that time.

The communist faction was growing stronger in the south, as they were identified with true nationalists acclaimed for their heroic anti-colonial acts. It was able to exploit the enthusiasm of some segments of intellectuals. Nationalism resounds its strong emotional appeal for "one people for one nation," but the ideological dictum drowned out the nationalist pleas. The rightists and centralists were as much nationalists as the leftists were in terms of their heroic struggles against the colonial power. So far as nationalism was concerned, both were friends, but they became foes when it came to ideology.

The communists were obviously growing stronger in their network in the south: no political faction in the south rivaled the communist faction in terms of their discipline, fanatic commitment to goals, and act in unison. The notion of social overhauling against the existing order made a great appeal to the underclass, notably the tenants and workers, for they expected a new world where they could dominate their masters. There was a silent majority, though, blind to ideological colors, and a few radicals made a loud voice to drown the voices of the majority. A Korean saying has it that "one tadpole is enough to muddy a pond." A strong and cohesive leftist group was powerful enough to break through the ideologically blind majority. Within the CPNR, the communist faction lived a parasitic life and in the end seized the centralist leadership. The irony was that the communists reduced the mother organ to an outpost for the purpose of communizing South Korea. To communism, coexistence with those who did not share in the same ideology was anathema. During the three-week hiatus following liberation, their action was so meteoric that it stole thunder from other factions. One day prior to the U.S troops landing South Korea, the CPNC declared the People's Republic, flying the communist flag, claiming it as the sole party ready to rule the south. The U.S Military Command's decline to accept their draft of cabinet members sent them to the streets to wage massive demonstrations and abetted walkouts and sabotages.

The U.S Military Command resolved to stay above affiliation with any political party and this explained why the People's Republic failed to win the recognition of the U.S Military Command. Even the Provisionary Korean Government, the largest group of nationalists in exile, failed to win its recognition, despite its claim to the legitimate succession of the forcibly dissolved Korean government. The declared ideological neutrality of the U.S Military Command soured its relationship with the rightists who expected the U.S backing in their struggle against communism. Syngman Rhee among others was hyper-critical of the U.S Military Command for the naivety of its political vision.

The Asian landmass was most vulnerable to the expansion of communism at this particular time. Communism, starting with Russia, spread with amazing rapidity into Eurasia and Siberia. All independent states were broken into a Soviet scramble. Another titanic country – China – was undergoing a civil war with Mao Tse-tung's leftist army winning victory against Chang kai-shek's nationalist forces. North Korea had been communized, and South Korea was drifting into rightist-leftist confrontation, with a metaphorical reference to "a flickering flame before the communist gale."

The Birth of Two Regimes

In July 1946 in the middle of the trusteeship chaos, Syngman Rhee made clear his intention to set up a separate government in the southern half. Rhee's remarks on a separate south panicked the nation into chaos and goaded the creation of a rightist-leftist coalition led by moderate centralists. Noteworthy was the spurt of a coalition that envisioned a government that excluded two extremists, Kim Il-sung and Syngman Rhee. But this coalition did not last long, since the left-tilted centralists bolted out in protest against the coalition playing into American hands.

Rhee was a legendary nationalist, but his idea of two Koreas laid him open to denouncement as a traitor, and his life was endangered when nationalistic fanatics were rampant. His stand for a separate south was fast and firm, based on a fait accompli - that one nation was most assured of salvation by communism. Rhee's intransigent stance soured his relationship with Kim Ku, another prominent figure who had chaired the Korea Provisional Government in exile. These two figures had been travel fellows along a long, bumpy road to national independence. The grueling anti-colonial struggle had woven the lives of these patriots together into a relationship of mutual dependence and respect, that could have withstood the test of time. Kim Ku, desperate to avoid division, went to see Kim Il-sung despite Rhee's warning against a trap and his reputation was marred by the cold-shoulder treatment by a man of his youngest son's age. Kim Ku discovered that Kim Il-sung had crossed a river of no return. Two months after he returned empty-handed, Kim Ku was assassinated by a rightist fanatic. At this tragedy, the wailing of people built up to a painful crescendo at the loss of a man of so towering a figure.

The idea of Rhee's separate government was not a matter of 'right' or 'wrong' but a matter of value choice between two alternatives, that is, between civil society and a rigidly regimented, coercive society, the validity of which was to be determined in the hindsight of history. Rhee was as much anti-communist as he was an anti-Japan nationalist, but the situation dictated him to choose either nationalism or ideology. Opting to stand for ideology, he had to discard his nationalist stand. Rhee and his adherents were waging an upstream battle against the tide of communism resounding an egalitarian plea for the suffering majority of population. "Rhee was initially in favor of the communist ideal of equality but frustrated by the egregious gap between the ideal and reality" (Rhee In-ho:108). Soviet troops repatriated after six months of occupation from North Korea, convinced that communism took a firm ground. But the U.S. troops were unintentionally implicated in a more complicated situation and stayed against their will for three years in South Korea. The internal situation of South Korea was uncertain and the withdrawal of American troops was expected to worsen the situation.

In May 1947 the U.S-Soviet Joint Commission, an administrative apparatus contrived to seek a mutually agreeable path to a united Korea, opened the second meeting but failed to be productive in a way of producing an agreement on a single issue. The United States favored the participation of all Korean political groups in the meeting, whereas the Soviet insisted on excluding the groups in the south which opposed trusteeship. From its beginning, it became dysfunctional, because of an unbridgeable gulf between the two powers. In March 1948, the United States, aware of the futility of the apparatus, transferred Korean issue to the United Nation which subsequently adopted a resolution for free election that was to be conducted across Korea, but it met the Soviet opposition. The reason for the Soviet's boycott was that free election would favor South Korea because its population was twice as big as North Koreans. Election was conducted in the south in May 1948, hoping that another will be held in the north, should a situation allow.

The Republic of Korea was formally inaugurated on August 15, 1948, the third anniversary of liberation, followed, in two months, by the inauguration of Democratic People's Republic of Korea to rule the north. The Constitution of the Republic of Korea declares its territory as the Korean peninsula and its subordinate islands. This declared North Korea as an extra-nuptial child to be eliminated. The Republic of Korea claimed itself to the legitimate one by obtaining sanctions from of 30 U.N member countries. The 38th parallel, improvised to contain Soviet expansion, became a border separating millions of families. The Republic of Korea made a difficult start, harassed by communist assaults and frequent walkouts and sabotages. The communist riots were more violent in the south-western province and Cheju Island. One regiment of the South Korean constabulary forces refused to board a ship to suppress the riot in Cheju and turned their guns to the police stations. They seized the southern ports, Yŏsu and Sunchôn, for two weeks and retreated into the nearby mountain to wage guerrilla wars. South Korea naval ships met no obstacle to go to the north. The presence of powerful communist insurgents in the south led Kim Il-sung to miscalculate its power to destroy the south.

The Korean War

The Korean War was a grim and inevitable episode in the grinding globalization of the Cold War. Viewed through the confrontation frame, the south and the north were surrogates for the big power game. Each side deployed their constabulary forces along the 38th parallel. With regard to the origin of the war, debate is heated over "who triggered the guns first?" Leftists put fingers on South Korea as the starter of the war. Some of them argue that South Korea offered at least a pretext that provoked the North to attack. Military clashes had taken place along the dividing line and the South was held responsible for the root cause for the disastrous war to follow. According to this argument, the Korean War did not begin on 25 June 1950. The origin of the war, they argue, should be traced back to find connections with what had transpired before the Korean War broke out on June 25, 1950

With regard to the origin of the Korean War, a common sense is based on South Korea's unpreparedness that is backed up by the loss of Seoul in three days after the war broke out and the loss of its territory in two months, excluding Taegu-Pusan perimeter 50 miles in diameter. South Korea was saved by the collective defense of the United Nations. But the leftists denied the logical reasoning of the events and their position was endorsed by Bruce Cumings' controversial "The Origin of KoreanWar"[1]. Koreans were drawn into a new phase of a daunting debate with the progressive view of history. According to his research, South Korea had its own share of responsibility for the war. The 38th parallel had seen scatter-shot skirmishes, and many of them, he attributed, to the south's preemptive maneuvers. In the hostile confrontation seen in a series of attacks and counter-attacks, however, none of these skirmishes carried ominous overtones of an impending war on such a scale that daunted the imagination of the world.

Cumings in Korea's Place In the Sun (1997) pointed to Syngman Rhee's bluster about "march north." According to his research, "Rhee had long sought to touch off a fratricidal civil war. He incessantly provoked clashes at the front line: in preparing a northern expedition, he had gone so far as to collude with their sworn enemy, Japanese militarism. The south opened the fighting on Onjin with an eye to seizing Haeju" (1997, 264). Nevertheless, in the daily confrontations of hostility, it is doubtful whether his bluster was taken as serious enough to provoke the hard-beaten North that made little of the military power of South Korea.

Having devoted much of the volume to "who started the war," Cumings deliberately sidetracked the question into a marginal concern. In reference to the American Civil War he observed. "Who started the Korean War? is the wrong question. Americans do not care anymore that the South fired first on Fort Sumter; they do still care about slavery and secession. No one wants to know who started the Vietnam War" (1997, 264). It should be noticed, however, that the American Civil War gave way to a unified state on a higher plateau of its historical vicissitude. Vietnam was unified and entered a stage of prosperity. Certainly, Koreans do care about "who started the war?" because the war-inflicted scars remain raw to be rubbed by the on-going ideological war. But Koreans relish a dream that there will be a time when a drama of high stake fades into an episode to be laughed away.

The situation at home and abroad was so ripe for beating the South in the years that preceded the Korean War. Repeated leftists' assaults on the police stations and public facilities were exhausting South Korea's capability of defending itself. Frequent walkouts destroyed the nascent industrial structure. The U.S forces had left, exposing South Korea to attack when South Korean regime was formally inaugurated. In1949, the United States declared the Acheson defense line. "The defense perimeter which run from the Aleutians to Japan and goes to the Ryukyu Islands"(Dean Acheson 1969.466). This left South Korea and Formosa vulnerable to attack. Further, the repatriation of the war veterans, who had fought for Mao Tse-tung in the Chinese civil war, to North Korea, was an added spur, whetting North Korea's ambition for the dominance of the peninsula. Park Hon-yong, the most celebrated communist, abetted Kim Il-sung to gamble disastrously on the winning chance of the war for the liberation of the south. In later years, Park was purged on charges of traitor. After the death of Stalin, Soviet Premiere Khrushichev's memoir disclosed that the Korean war was the direct corollary of the collusion of Stalin and Kim Il-sung. Despite the disclosure of the clandestine event, a talk about the South's pre-emptive attack refuses to dissipate.

The eerie silence of the morning of June 25, 1950 was broken by the roaring tanks crossing the 38th parallel on the hitherto largest scale. Sunday morning found one third of the South constabulary forces relaxing at home or out of the camps. North Korean troops, well trained and superior in number and weaponry, streamed south almost undeterred. South Korea had no single tank when 200 Russian-made tanks rolled over the 38th parallel. The United Nations Security Council issued a statement urging North Korean troops to withdraw to the 38th parallel. Defying the statement, they continued to carry the day and were ecstatic with great fanfares that a few days were numbered until Koreans celebrate a united country. As the war continued, the United Nations appealed for its member countries to send combat troops to rescue South Korea. The United States was the first to respond to the call, followed by the United Kingdom, Canada, Australia, New Zealand, and all European countries, including even a small country like Luxemburg, except for the former Axis powers, all numbered 30 nations. Non-Western combat participants were South Africa, Ethiopia, Turkey, Thailand, Philippines and Columbia.

The United States dispatched the largest number of combatants, followed by the United Kingdom. These foreign contingents were fighting under the United Nation flag. The war met a turning point as the U.N forces landed at Inchon on September15 and recaptured the capital on September 28. The landing operation at Inchon was considered improbable due to the big tidal differences. Even General MacArthur made a pessimistic assessment of the landing in favor of a 5,000-to-1 risk. Undaunted by the overwhelming opposition of the chief of staff and advisors, he saw a guarantee of an essential element of success in a deceptive surprise landing."I can almost hear the ticking of the second hand of destiny. We shall land at Inchon and I shall crush them"(Acheson,580).

Energized by the successful campaign, the U.N forces broke through the stalemated defense line surrounding Taegu and fought their way to the north across the 38th parallel. They had scarcely come close to the northern border when Chinese troops intervened in overwhelming numbers. Outnumbered by Chinese troops and suffering from the merciless cold, the U.N forces made a strategic retreat to the south, accompanied by two million North Korean refugees streaming to the south. General MacArthur tried to see it through to a complete victory by expanding the war but this military strategy met the political decision of the U.S Government to localize far from the border with Manchuria. Pushed back by China's human ant tactics, Seoul was lost to the communist troops and was recaptured. The forces on both sides had a brutal seesaw of attack and counter-attack, forming a new combat zone later to be known as the Demilitarized Zone (DMA). This was the line where the hostile forces were deployed along when the ceasefire was announced on July 27, 1953.

The intensive combat came to a halt, but it left the country divided. Korea is still in the state of uneasy ceasefire, but economic euphoria dulled South Koreans' sensitivity to the precarious status of ceasefire, while North Koreans had to endure a life of extreme austerity, jittery over an imagined war. The signatories of the ceasefire were the United States on behalf of the U.N. member participants, North Korea, and China. It should be noted that South Korea was not a signatory of the ceasefire, though South Korean troops took the brunt of defense against communism and suffered the heaviest casualties. Syngman Rhee vehemently opposed the cease fire, arguing that it would not only leave the country perpetually divided and make waste the blood that youngsters let out to soak this land. He insisted on marching to the north with South Koreans forces alone. Owing to Rhee's intransigent opposition to the ceasefire, South Korea was excluded from the signatories of the ceasefire. Rhee later acquired the U.S guarantee for defense of the south in the name of the U.S-Korea Defense Treaty in return for his belated recognition of the ceasefire.

Rhee was known among American politicians as a curmudgeon who would not yield to American pressure. Rather, Rhee did more to displease America in the post-liberation period. There was another shocking event that panicked the world. The northern prisoners of war under captivity on a southern island were murdering their fellow prisoners simply because the latter did not want to go back to the North. The former engaged in murderous extirpation of their fellow prisoners condemning them as traitors. Murder was an order of the day, and it was carried out in most inhuman way. Rhee was extremely concerned that anti-communist prisoners will be diminished into a few to survive this ordeal, if the situation is allowed to take its course. Again, Rhee took a bold action to save their lives as many as possible, even violating the international law. A childish unruliness took possession of him. He ordered the Korean military police to disarm the American military guards and flung the gate wide open. His rash action stunned Eisenhower into a state of near traumatic shock, and Winston Churchill was so frightened to scar his face with a razor blade. It brought a spate of protests from the leaders of the war-participating countries. Rhee's boldness to flout the law represented the typical nature of Confucian scholar, cussed and obstinate. He was not a person who could be threatened to take his words back.

When the ceasefire was imminent, neutral countries under the U.N aegis conducted interviews about the intentions of the North Korean prisoners of war. The anti-communist prisoners were given a choice of country where they wished to reside between South Korea or a neutral country. However, Rhee's rash action entailed a price to be paid when the war was brought to an end. North Korea retaliated by refusing the release of sixty thousand southern soldiers under its captivity in the falsified pretext that they did not want to return home. The hapless South Korean soldiers in the north languish in mines, pining for their homes and families. The Korean War is remembered among the foreign war veterans as a "forgotten war." There was neither winner nor loser of the war. More than two hundred thousand South Korean soldiers and fifty-four thousand American soldiers were killed in the battlefield. The deaths of communist troops were three times as many. Looking at the exorbitant human sacrifices, let alone physical and psychological damages, both parties paid too dearly for the ceasefire. The American veterans never had much of a welcome home. Many of the war-veterans who survived inhumane treatments under captivity try to forget the past but are still haunted by nightmares.

Forbidding Gaps

Ideological, institutional and psychic make-ups underlie a daunting gulf between the two halves. The notion of "people are the master of the state's fate" is blurred in North Korea where the state is exalted over people. One class society reveals a born enemy to be destroyed and extirpated. Communism thrives on the presence of enemies; without enemies, it can never summon people into fanatic revolutionary fervor.

In the first place, the leadership features a revealing contrast between the two. Kim Il-sung, having assumed a virtual assumption of divinity, evoked a chorus of acclaims from his people for having elevated a little, resource-poor country to the self-styled, sole rival for the world power. He commanded an absolute following as the lode star who guided the country along a bumpy road to the self-claimed world power. Communism, though, refreshes our memories that the iconoclastic revolution took a painful human sacrifice. In the communist world, there is room for one master – a jealous and implacable master whose price of friendship is complete submission. Like his mentors, Stalin and Mao Tse-tung, Kim Il-sung allowed no rival for himself. Other Korean communists of towering stature – such as Kim Won-bong and Park Hon-young par excellence– were prey to the absolutism of one ruler. Mao's cultural revolution was no more than an attempt to reshape the country and renew the loyalty of people to him by ridding himself of all political foes who tried to kick him upstairs to an honorary title. Leadership in communism is premised on the utter absence of a rival or an opponent. Even in the monarchical absolutism of pre-modern Korea, the ruler was challenged by ruling elites. The ruler was haunted by an endless flow of critical memorials from scholars and lower officials and their sit-in demonstrations before the palace.

Kim Il-sung was a self-styled guerrilla leader when he was ten years old, and Syngman Rhee of South Korea was a legendary anti-Japan nationalist and a radical anti-communist. Kim was 33 years old when he rode on the Soviet coattails to premiere, and Rhee was 75 years old when he was elected the first president of the Republic of Korea. The former received a patchy education up to secondary school, and his biography sanctified him to the pantheon of heroes before he reached adulthood. Rhee was the first Chair of the Korea Provisional Government in exile while he was actively engaged in diplomatic maneuvers abroad for the restoration of independence before Kim Il-sung was born into the world. Rhee was well grounded in Confucian classics and modern political philosophy by studying at George Washington and Princeton University, working toward a doctoral degree. The Kim's family has ruled down to a third generation while South Korea has seen turnovers of the regime. Even today, Kim's biography is thoroughly worked over to mystify him and his family, and people are buried under layers of fable extolling him as a divinity. The Kim's family impresses the world as the avatar of an absolute monarchism, harking back to the most benighted politics of the world. Rhee was a charismatic leader who gathered many young patriots around him.

Concocting an inspirational mythology around the nation's founding father is by no means a North Korea's monopoly in the communist countries. But the personality cult of North Korea is carried to previously unknown heights, intolerable of heresy to this concocted truth. South Koreans are divided into pros and cons with regards to Rhee's doings. Rhee's ambition for power through the stressful times scarred his reputation he had built as midwife for the birth of the Republic of Korea. Rhee's authoritarian rule reflects his solipsism – that he fits the bill in a country tossed on the stormy seas of unforeseen events. Deung Xiaoping paid an absolute respect to Mao Tse-tung as the founding father of a unitary, communist China despite his intolerable flouting of human dignity in later years, including a harsh punishment meted to himself. Red guard riots alone brought the death of four millions during the cultural revolution.

Communism draws inspiration from Karl Max's prophesy of history –"historical development is purposeful and will come to an end with the achievement of a communist utopia." The utopia, noted Marx, stands at the end of the historical process. Structural contradictions between capitalists and workers invite a class struggle to weed out those blessed with greater wealth and cultural capital and build a proletarian society where all citizens enjoy absolute equality. One of the greatest fallacies of capitalism, Marx noted, consists in its inherent tendency toward a cycle of devastating depression. But every system contains within it the seeds of its own undoing and is in the process of change. Even liberal democracy finds its reason for viewing it in a state of change. Communism has a fanatic belief in the ideological consummation –an absolute belief that communism alone brings history to its consummation. Viewed from liberal democracy, Marx's dialectical view of history is flawed by seeing historical process through a dogmatic and materialistic prism. In communism, nothing bulks larger than materialistic ends, with no attention given to moral values, human dignity and the appeal of the inner being, let alone immortal soul. Marx explains historical positivism through the relationship of 'dairyman and milk.'[12]

Poverty is in the person as well as in the purse: to do away with poverty demands the restoration of a human being's self-respect and dignity as well as meeting his or her material needs. The quality of life lies in the total human being, not just economic man, but economic, political, and for that matter, cultural and spiritual man. The concept of a new utopia came from an intransigent pessimism about poor workers in the capitalistic system. Therefore, all attacks against capitalism had an incendiary and agitating element."In the end, the knell sounds for the forcible overthrow of all existing conditions. Let the ruling classes tremble." Class struggle lay bare enemies of the people and revolutionary passion is fueled by having an enemy to be pleasurably crushed. Absolute equality that communism declares as its virtue not only runs afoul of the law of nature but goes against the grain of Koreans endowed with ambition to move up along the social ladder.

In the countries which profess absolute equality, an elite group within the society made of one class was created like a frosting on the cake of the masses. Like absolute power, absolute equality corrupts from within. Equality in possession is gained at the cost of individual freedom. A utopia founded on absolute equality may be feasible if all human differences in ability, aptitude and skill are ignored completely. Equality built on a coercive force breeds habit, as observed in the East Germans who found it difficult to break with the tyrannical and protective hand of the government even after reunified. Zbigniew Brzezinski noted the ills of dependence on the state: "Impregnated with torpor, boredom and stagnation, habit and inertia perpetuates themselves in a vicious cycle" (1989,258). For the world traumatized by liberalism and capitalistic exploitation in the name of industrialization, communism made its appeal as a new guidepost to life. Communism condemns imperialism as an evil product of capitalist development intent on self-interest and the exploitation of workers. For intellectuals disillusioned by the colossal war, communism established itself as a viable alternative to the flawed capitalistic imperialism. Their argument that a few rich is blamed for living off the sweat and tear of the poor made a strong appeal among the downtrodden people in that particular time frame.

The grand failure of communism lies in its scoff at historical progressivism by perceiving it as an alternative to the institutions evolved from the existing stockpile of experience and culture. Communism finds its role not as supplementary to the existing system, but as an alternative. Many Korean intellectuals under colonial rule could not resist the temptations of the novel theory. The downtrodden imagined a society where they could replace their masters and dominate them. The problem is that those who were once passionately attached to communism had no way out of it unless it is paid with one's own life. "The new ideology is a kind of infection like smallpox. Either men get it and are permanently scarred, or they escape it because of some effective inoculation and are untouched" (Galbraith J 1971, 57).

Communism, many argued, had a potential match with Korean traditional values. Going down to the village level, there is an element of communism with its constituents willing to share the last bowl of rice even in times of crisis. The clannish proclivity of Koreans or small group dynamics give rise to a silent pressure to reject a few becoming richer or excellent over the pack. Those blessed with intellectual superiority or material wealth are not the object of envy but to be ridiculed or denounced for the lack of compassion for others. In terms of a tendency to share things and fanatic commitment to group goals, Koreans are said to be more receptive to communist tenets in principle than others.

Attuned to a hierarchical society, however, Koreans strongly long to be distinct from others; there is an intensive desire to land in a privileged fold as a means of distinction not only in materialistic satisfaction but in social status and dignity. Man is inherently endowed with desire for recognition of his worth or, probably, more than what he is. Koreans are so much individualistic as far as they long to be identified as something special. Market economies based on free competition and creativity are repellent to those who argue for equality for all. The Confucian defense of inequality is that everyone is not born with equal talent or creativity. An ideal society is built on social harmony which is achievable by orchestrating different roles and classes depending on individual competencies and hierarchies. "Excessive equality makes for cultural uniformity and monotonous life" (Galbraith 1971, 65). The capitalistic stand for hierarchy reflects a greater concern for incentives that reward hard and creative workers.

In traditional wisdom, authoritarianism is regarded as the product of Confucianism. Some argue that totalitarianism is a short step from authoritarianism. The resulting tendency is to block the South and North into a totalitarian package. The way North Korea is ruled is an anomaly, far-fetched from authoritarian rule. State exaltation and personality cult create an atmosphere repellent to any type of rule that smacks of a paternalistic authoritarianism. Heavy use of kinship metaphors ("the dear fatherly leader), however, is the manifestation of a Confucian notion of the absolute power holder imbued with fatherly care for people. The metaphor of the king to father justifies the extension of filial piety to the ruler. Communism strengthens a bond of absolute loyalty and obedience, from which one has a difficult escape once trapped in it. The notion of a fatherly figure in its true sense is solicitous of the welfare of people, fundamentally different from a society that forces the people to be silent, obedient and unanimous.

The exaltation of people in the south reduced the state into an instrument to serve its citizens. Even under authoritarian rule, South Koreans enjoyed a modicum of freedom and were tempted to challenge the ruling authority and institutions. North Korea is heavily dependent on social engineering characteristic of a regimented society. "Society is simplified into a gigantic machine to be manipulated to achieve the state goals" (Zbigniew Brezenski 1989,7). And the people are mere cogs of the machine. Whenever famine or natural disaster befalls, the people are the first victims forced to undertake a grueling march. The representative democracy of South Korea is considered an antidote to the "personality cult" or "state exaltation" inherent in the revolutionary doctrine. A few elites surrounded by men of uncritical adulation insulates the ruler from the reality.

The ruler's assumption of divinity in North Korea absurdly exceeds the cult of personality Stalin and Mao enjoyed. It is the manifestation of an idolatrous passion grown out of neo-Marxism's institutional uniqueness, a carefully contrived version of the statecraft to preserve a tightly sealed society. Its political system holds together society in isolation from the world, and this is the way in which North Korea survives its fellow communist countries. As soon as fresh air is let in, such a society crumbles to ashes like an Egyptian mammy brought out of its encasement. Typical of an isolated society, North Korea has no choice but to resort to radical nationalism as its only political salvation. Its mad pursuit of mythical nationalism breeds extreme antagonism to other countries.

Political indoctrination is carried to a pathological extreme, even creeping into home and schools. Total submission to the ruler is cloaked in a deceptive appeal to be selfless. Absolute loyalty to Kim and his family was the touchstone of political purity. The end of the day's work is followed by hours of lessons, focusing on the tale of Kim's heroism and the superiority of communism, and the populace is hardly given a spell to drown the cares of a long hard day. News is strictly censored, and radio churns out nothing but propaganda. Disinformation is fed to make rhetoric triumph over reason. The whole nation is sliding into double speak, and words become divorced from reality and people's real thoughts. Solicitation of self criticism is a trap to uncover those who dare oppose the ruler. People are under the watchful eyes of unknown informants all around with standing exposure to the terror of the secret police. The party's all-round intrusion into people's lives is the process known as "thought reform." Dissidence festers but cannot find an outlet for eruption. Everything personal is political: in fact, nothing is regarded as "personal" or private. Prying into personal details is a way of ensuring a thorough soul-cleansing. The people are worn down with the frenetic pace of forced-draft industrialization, the rigor of ideological indoctrination and the excesses of a pervasive personality cult. Even at this moment, they are trudging a weary way.

Ideological fanaticism caused ethnic nationalism to bulk larger as the measure of the legitimacy of the state. North Korea declared South Korea as an illegitimate child for its being dependent on and remaining in thrall to a foreign power, while it is proud of its nationalistic purity. Given nationalistic purity as a reference for legitimacy, North Korea is not faultless, for it depended on the Sovietized Koreans in laying the corner stone for the construction of the communized society. Its claim to self independence is discredited by its emulation of Stalinism and economic dependence on the Soviet and China. North Korea was placed under the communist banner of alien origin and embarked on an unprecedented social reform modeled on the ideological version of the Soviet Union. Kim Il-sung was submissive to Stalin in the hierarchy of communist leadership. Syngman Rhee, even before he became the President, was hardened by widespread anarchy and carved out his independent stance to the displeasure of the United States. North Korea and the Soviet enjoyed a complete match of policies, whereas South Korea and the U.S Military Command squeaked through disharmonious chorus in the post-liberation period.

No sensible South Korean would favor a utopia where the hold of a dogmatic ideology is gripping enough to reduce its citizens to adult children incapable of making rational decisions. The political castration of society demands nothing but the subservience and political unanimity of its members. An individual is no longer the master of his own fate; one has his fate determined by the state. The politics of regimentation is better explained by the manipulation of the masses, exactly the way mass game is performed. The mass game is calibrated to the gage of the ruler, not to the masses who participate in it. Instant and reflexive acts in absolute unison to an orchestrating command are crucial. The power of actions in unison is formidable in such a regimented society. This simply means that a state machine produces identical beings pliable enough to act at the ruler's fingers: it offers a tasteless uniformity of life pattern, stripped of diverse tastes and ways of life.

Outlook for Unification

Now that more than three quarters of a century have elapsed since the division, Korea should have created a new climate that would bring its two halves into a collaborative search for a viable path to a unified Korea. And yet, such a cooperative mood is far from being built. Different institutions and goals create insurmountable barriers for their search for an agreeable path to reunification. Each came up with its own strategy. The north-proposed confederation of the two systems is dismissed by the south as a disguised plot to communize the south. "One government and two systems" obstructs an effort to moderate the ideological and institutional gaps that are poles apart. Such a system cannot find its parallel in human experiments with institutional improvement. The confederate system of the United States is built on the principle of state autonomy based on local particularities and ideological and institutional commonalities.

The south-proposed "one people for one economic community," a loosely knit web that resembles the British "common wealth model, "was rejected by the north as perpetuating the division of Korea. The north argues for an immediate unification, while the south for a step-by-step approach starting with economic and cultural programs to reduce gaps, to be followed by political reunification. The two parallels in no way offer an inkling of meeting half way because of mutual distrust built into the psyches of the people on both sides. From a realistic viewpoint, the enriched south considers it inevitable to play with time to avoid catastrophic damages coming from a hasty unification. In dealing with an impetuous state, the only way open to a better future is to steadily reduce its abject poverty.

From a pragmatic viewpoint, a confederated Korea stands a slim chance to become a reality unless efforts are made to reconcile the present diametrically opposed systems in a way that produces a common frame of governance. Both should make such concessions that are virtually improbable for each party to accept. The south-proposed commonwealth approach is justified on the grounds that the egregious gap of living standards and doctrinal differences should be tackled in the first place as the condition for creating a control tower binding on both. The downside of this approach is that the passage of time is not a sufficient guarantee for change in the north.

"In 1989, East Germany's per capita national income was one-third of that of West Germany. North Korea's per capita national income remains at five percent of South Korea's. This gap stirs a nagging disquiet, particularly among conservative circles about the disastrous consequences of an immediate unification. Further, the population of West Germany bearing the huge unification costs numbered four times that of East Germany. South Korean population is only twice as big as North Korea's" (Korea Focus Winter 2009; 101). The South's proposal is flawed in its naïve expectation that time will play its role in the utter absence of a governing mechanism binding on both. The one-way flow of aid, unrequited by North Korea in the form of a policy turnaround, is not likely to ensure that an appreciable change takes place to guide North Korea in a desirable direction. The paradox is that the longer it takes, the more elusive it becomes to achieve a united Korea.

The issue of reunification crossed borders. The continued balance of power in the form of a ceasefire involves two neighboring and two distant countries. So long as no foreign power wants to toy with an idea that will change its status quo, a divided Korea is deemed an effective means for maintaining the peace of North-east Asia. The involvement of the concerned foreign powers has pushed the issue of reunification beyond the reach of the two Koreas. South Korea has thrashed out devices to break through this stalemate, and the sunshine policy initiated by Kim Dae-jung proved to be effective in a myopic view. Obviously, it represents a monumental undertaking in that it tried to create an opening in the tightly sealed kingdom, through which sunshine could penetrate. Some critics were skeptical of the sunshine policy in view of its one way support unlikely to be reciprocated by change on the part of the receiver. Nonetheless, it was a bold undertaking to get the secluded North out of its encasement, see the tidal wave of changes in the world, hopefully to lead the north to join in a search for the institutions that bring mutual benefits.

Kim Dae-jung's historical visit to North Korea on 15 June 2000 was expected to open the floodgate for the reunions of dispersed families. All at once, the disillusionment of the four millions of North Korean refugees in the south were rekindled into drowsy hopes to see their families. As the north was half-hearted to open the door wide, a faint light of their hope further flickered into darkness. The North Korea leader is gripped by a paranoid fear that continued reunion with South Korean families will help to demystify the enigmatic society. When the increased contacts bring sunshine to dispel the morning fog, North Koreans will rub their eyes in wonder to see how miserable their life is in comparison with countries outside. Living without reference to others breeds ignorance and stagnation.

The major obstacle to reunification lies in the rigidity of North Korea's politics in response to new demands. The state machine tries to obscure the true image of itself to the world as well as to its own people. Under the proclaimed Jucheism,[13] Kim's family refined a national solipsism into a virtual assumption of divinity, exceeding Stalin's and Mao's cults of personality. The term Jucheism literally means self identity, economic self reliance and political autonomy. This concept in the highly centralized power structure leaves ample room for distortion. From the voluminous exegeses by Kim Il-sung, this concept narrows down to "the masters of revolution and construction are the masses of the people and they are also the motive force of revolution and construction. In other words, one is the master of one's own destiny and has the power to shape it oneself" (Koh Byung Chul, 1974,84). How does master of one's destiny match with pressure for obedience and silence? Under the authoritarian regime, South Korea asserted self reliance, meaning it to epitomize "Koreanized democracy" when Park Chung Hee attempted to prolong his reign.

"The dilemma of North Korea is that the aperture of a long dark tunnel is ever avoiding human catch as a shadow does. Isolation builds the paradoxical cohabitation of economic development and political stability. Economic development requires the country to open the door to the outside world, since it cannot 'go it alone' in total absence of capital, technology and infrastructure that must come from outside. The problem is that the open door shed light on the outside world and generates human craving for liberalism. Then, people discredit the state and in the end sound a death knell for the secluded north. Given the dictum of choosing either one or the other, North Korea stands for political stability, throwing millions of its people on the verge of starvation.

North Korea is the reminder, in many respects, of the nineteenth century hermit kingdom in that it avoided contacts with foreign countries, teetering on the verge of extinction. All programs beamed over airwaves are completely jammed. In the case of Germany, the demarcation line was porous enough to allow the dispersed families to meet. East German youngsters developed "Western fantasy" through their inhibited contacts with T.V programs. The Korean demarcation line is tightly sealed off to allow no single ant to break through. In the deliberately created darkness, the North cranks the state propaganda machine to lure the people to the workers' paradise. The isolation of North Korea is illustrated by comparison with East Germany. Since the barbed wires were set up, "each year saw a million of East Germans visit their relatives in West Germany and 6-7 millions of West Germans crossing the border to East Germany. Those who broke through the barrier and sought residence in West Germany numbered 4.5 millions in comparison with 25,000 North Koreans defectors to the south. (Choson Daily Press editorial dated Sep.12, 2015). Reunification of Germany is not a miracle coming out of the blue but the result of each part understanding the other. Reunification is made possible by making a miracle, not by expecting it to come.

Frequent turnover of the ruling party in South Korea is indicative of human experiments with new devices to improve the conditions for human life. The political castration of North Korean society reduces the people into subservient masses and social unanimity. By all accounts, North Korea refuses to be a true identity of Korea. Stumbling blocks to reunification are not only doctrinal differences but a forbidding psychic gap resulting from the North's bungled emulation of communism. The politics of regimentation had deeply ripped into individual initiative and creativity. The psychic passivity, resulting from so gripping the hold of ideology, has eroded the common bonds of Koreans. North Korea is distinct from the Eastern European countries because of its historical and institutional uniqueness. Neither will a unified Korea be the unified Germany. Reunification requires that each partner understand the other and vice versa. Nevertheless, the North refuses to clarify its true identity and this makes it impossible to create a cooperative mood that leads to a well-intended dialogue for reunification.

The nuclear issue adds a new dimension to discourse on reunification. North Korea argues that nuclear power is a self-defense mechanism against the standing threat of America. It means its intent to match its military power against the United States, that is, as a means for having direct dialogue with the United States on an equal basis. But an uneasy conjecture goes beyond the simple logics of self-defense; its proliferation effect is a worldwide panic. The dismal weapon is in the hands of an unruly despot prone to dangerously calculate on a gamble.

Reactions to the nuclear issue show contrasts between the near-hysteria with which North Korea is viewed in Washington and near indifference with which South Koreans greet this news. After decades of living through the North Korean threat, many South Koreans seem to view North Korea more like a crazy aunt than a direct military threat. They either dismiss its threat or assume the United States will deal with them in the end. South Korea stands in favor of reunification through a peaceful means and North Korea pays lip service to peaceful reunification. But this possibility is delusional unless it is premised on the wills of both parties to reach an agreement, free from foreign powers' interference.

Supposing the present stalemate continues, the alternative is the German model, that is, to incorporate the north into the south. Reunification under the aegis of the south surely bumps into China's refusal to share the border with a country that is allied with the United States. China needs North Korea as lips to protect its teeth from the cold: China is inherently pitted against American hegemony in this region. While communism lost its favor with the world, North Korea alone manages to squeak through the world's beatings, by altering its course to survive. Despite all logical prognostications of sages in favor of its imminent demise, North Korea survives its fellow communist countries, although it stirs conjectures about how long it will last. North Korea is an anomaly, by intents and purposes, to which the universal rules of law do not apply. The eternity of such an anomalous society is questioned, if it does not make a crash landing on the ground. In the meantime, the people's shrill cry of pain will be heard louder.

Can Time Heal?

During the period between liberation and the Korean War, two million North Koreans defected to the south, and another two million accompanied the retreating U.N forces during their renewed bout with Chinese troops. In the south, four million refugees and their dependents account for a quarter of the South Korean population. The migration of population has been a one way flow from the north to the south. A few of the first generation refugees are still alive, still having not forsaken the dream of reunion with beloved ones, but a majority of them passed away, carrying their dream into graves. Even today, the demarcation line is eerily silent, often to be broken by loudspeaker's cackling. The demilitarized zone (DMZ) is the sole man-made 'no man's land.' North Korea keeps its people in the dark about what is happening outside of their domain. Then, a titanic propaganda machine cranks in to create the most perfidious imagery of itself. The endless stoking of the fires of ideological ardor wearies the populace.

On July 1983, KBS launched a hitherto largest campaign to bring the reunion of dispersed families. The KBS building was pasted all around with leaflets that provided clues into how they were dispersed. The plaza was packed with some hundred thousand people holding high their pickets. There were quite a few who were happily reunited to exhaust their pent-up wells of tears. A lot more, on the other, were frustrated and went back. The scene of reunion was something more than ecstatic. The shared sense of high emotion turned into a sea of tears. The TV producers, announcers, cameramen and reporters cried when watching the people reunited. The human mind was made of the sort of stuff, like musical instruments. If one makes a sound, all others join to sing, laugh and cry. They are crying, I am crying, and everybody is crying. They had been separated during their desperate southward flight just a few steps ahead of the marching communist soldiers. There were two little sisters whose mother was bombed to death. Their cries over the dead mother exhausted tears. An elder had gone for a bottle of water. When she returned, she found her little sister, five years old, had moved out with the rest of refugees. By reviving their dimmed memories of the moment, they were brought into reunion when they became adults. Each and every case of separation and reunion is itself a theme of the profoundest human drama. Even the slightest physical marks and faintest clues remembered played crucial roles in identifying their blood siblings. Every refugee has a story worth a book. Some of their hometowns are visible from the demarcation line, where their wives are worn down with hopes for reunion. Humans are created to enjoy the residence of their choice anywhere under heaven. But the North Korean refugees are denied the right to settle in their home towns.

There are thousands upon thousands of families yet to be reunited. These people never forget their duty to perform sacrificial rite for ancestors on the top of the mountains nearest their home towns. When they defected to the South, they were seventeen or eighteen years old. They promised to return home within ten days. But no one expected these ten days away to become seventy year separation, possibly leading to eternal separation. Imagine the pains of their siblings in the North making a grueling march against an imagined enemy. The sad stories of separated families are indelibly imprinted into their consciousness. Time is no longer the remedy for the collective pains of Koreans.

Their yearnings for reunion with their siblings and hometowns may well be considered in tandem with the institutional uniqueness of North Korea that explains the difficulty of fulfilling their hopes. There is an explicit disjunction between the dominant elites and the dominated masses. The former is a family corporation aided by a few party elders who were guerrilla fellow fighters for Kim Il-sung and their progeny. The apparent stability masks instability at the center and this makes it inevitable to ensure a dynastic succession of power within the family lineage. "The Achilles' heel of the system, whether the ancient regime or the North Korea of today, is that it does not have great leaders or philosopher kings, but human beings of a certain subjectivity" (Bruce Cummings 1997, 433). There is no sense of the virtues society seeks to realize. There are twenty-two million human beings who go about their daily lives without the sense of being the masters of their own fates. Despite overwhelming predictions on the imminent demise of the kingdom when Kim Il-sung died, the core of party politics remains cohesive and strong. These elders are comparable to the "dead loyalists" of the Chosôn dynasty who sworn allegiance to the immature king, Dan'jong, enthroned on the untimely death of his father Mun'jong. Anti-colonial nationalism is the spiritual rock on which North Korea sustains itself through the post-Cold War world. We cannot but wonder how long it will last in this most dynamic region.

Modernization

Miraculously, the war-ravaged Korea rose to a new economic power. War-inflicted damages gave way to the spurt of renewed efforts to get the country out of its long-sustained stagnancy. From the 1960s, South Korea embarked on a grandiose program, never attempted before in scale, oriented toward the industrialization and modernization of the country. Ostensibly, modernization was defined as the acceptance of Western technology and mores. This means that advanced societies present an inspiring model for the non-western countries to emulate. We can think of two wheels of modernization, economic growth and industrialization on one hand and political development in favor of liberal democracy on the other. Industrialization per se is not only to borrow updated technologies from the advanced countries. Koreans' traditional values, in company with new technology, galvanized the working masses into a dynamic spurt of energy. The development of the South Korean economy is one of the great stories worth telling others as it owed much to the rare combination of the factors, external and internal. Modernization involves much more than meeting our eyes. Integration of old values with new ones plays a more fundamental role.

The economic success was illustrated by breathtaking contrasts: a per capita GND of $87 in 1962 versus $5,5000 in 1990 and $10,000 in 1995. Development theorists singled out South Korea as a beneficiary of the post-war bonanza which brought all conditions needed for the countries just broken loose from their colonial masters. The withdrawal of the colonial powers, stripped of all economic advantages, created a vacuum in the new developing countries for socialism to fill. Socialism, by virtue of its revolutionary departure from the existing order, was accepted as a universal validity. Revolutionary reform may bring forth an analogical allusion to communism: "revolution and communism are by no means synonymous with each other, although it is undeniably true that communists are working for and eager to lead a revolutionary thrust" (Robert L. Heilbroner 1971, 79).

Despite the overwhelming trend of a socialistic approach among developing countries, South Korea stood alone in applying capitalist solution to problems. South Korea, once referred to as a traumatized child born in the post-liberation maelstrom, outpaced its forerunners. "When South Korea pushed its per capita GNP to $968 in the mid 1960s, Malaysia, Argentina, Thailand and Brazil registered $2,950, $3,459, $1,037 and $2,045 respectively. By 1990, South Korea earned $5,000 in comparison with Thailand ($2,879), Argentina ($4,030) and Malaysia ($4,727)" (Eckert Carter 1990, 388)

Seoul under the Japan's colonial rule was no less than an overgrown village of straw-roofed houses and landscapes dotted with cottages in the countryside. The state-driven development on the ruins of colonial exploitation was truncated by the Korean War. As we see nowadays, Seoul became the most bustling city with towering skyscrapers that the sky limits their height. The south's economic growth was acclaimed as bordering on "the miracle on the Han River," likened to the miracle of the Rhine. The term "miracle", however, fails to do justice to the story: still the process of development is simplified as a windfall extraneous to its cultural and historical legacy. The traditional values of Koreans turned into a dynamic force when they met national tribulation.

The modern history of Europe has seen individuals divorced from the state, authority, tradition, norms and even family. Individualism fueled a move towards free pursuit of personal interest. And this was supposed to provide a rational base for a market economy. Development theorists argue that market economy thrives on the mix of individual initiatives and competition in response to the diminishing state power. In contrast, South Korea shows a typical case of how state-driven development has been used. Softened authoritarianism, subordination of the private sector to state goals, and bureaucratic interventions represent traditional values. The rational dictate of the market paled before the urgency of achieving specific development and industrialization goals within a short span of time. Single-minded pursuit of state goals and the way they were achieved were detrimental to the free market principle.

Economic development took off the ground through a series of five year programs under the military regime. The policy of export promotion was implemented, giving exporters in the selected industries special licenses, tax favors, and financial privileges. The U.S aid was an added spur to the development of exporting industries. South Korean goods enjoyed a privileged access to the U.S market on its take-off stage. Along with the export-led development, import substitution was promoted, beginning with the development of the textile industry built on its colonial base.

Development is the function of social, political and cultural factors. The strategic importance of Korea as the outpost for containing communist expansion kept the United States committed to material and technical support. The influx of American capital into South Korea was accompanied by a corresponding flow of technology and technical expertise. Timing is an elusive factor for development, since its impact on economic growth can be rather fortuitous. Timing, by definition, is a new conjoining of conditions for events to occur simultaneously and combine to give economic growth a new spurt.

As the economy was taking off the ground, South Korea benefited from its friendly bond with the United States and Japan. One good example of the fortune was South Korea's economic opportunity in Vietnam, which came precisely at a time when the country was in dire need of new sources of foreign earning. Another was the construction boom in the Middle East which came just as the Vietnam War wound down, after the Korean companies had gained experience and credential in Vietnam. South Korea's industrial development was not attributed to technological advance alone. The human resources of South Korea are as much responsible for the development. First of all, South Korea was endowed with a well-trained and informed working class capable of rapid assimilation and adaptation to new technology and economic expertise in their early stage of development. High education levels helped workers raise the quality of their work and kept their products highly cost competitive. Another contributor is cultural homogeneity. A nation state is best held when it commands a thick frame of shared value and a strong commitment of the people to shared responsibility. The standard language and value made it easier to bring consensus on the virtue and development goals that society seeks to achieve. The absence of ethnic and religious cleavages made it possible for workers to expand their loyalties to corporations, the state and society. A disciplined leadership dramatized the dormant vertical and collective consciousness of Koreans into a functional equivalent of Max Weber's Protestant work ethic. Creativity, viewed from the collective morality, follows from flashes of insights coming from the sustained exchanges of ideas between co-workers.

Status or class consciousness in a hierarchical establishment engenders a strong upward stream that sucks up men of competency to a privileged fold in a sea of mediocrity. The stereotype image of Koreans as compliant, submissive, and decorous has long since gone. The dynamics of modern society awakened the dormant characters of Koreans to a hard working, deep drinking, high risk-taking, free swinging, aggressiveness, ambitiousness and 'devil takes the hind most.' (Gregory Henderson 1983, 254). The pragmatic version of Confucianism renders Korean workers perpetually discontent with the given status. Collective consciousness is impatient with the search of personal interests. Self-effacing and individual subordination is sublimated into self-sacrificing spirit characteristic of Korean workers. Extra-familial loyalty inspires individuals to serve group or state goals at the cost of their personal interests. The rough edge of the Korean persona was honed and sharpened to display its luster and Koreans have become workaholics.

The world media is paying attention to how South Korea coped with the economic illness and how it grew, outpacing other countries. Its economic success is validated by quantitative analysis conducted by IMD (International Management Development). The index of nation's competitiveness places South Korea among the top ten. South Korea's per capita income posted close to $31,800, surpassing Italy's and following right on the heel of Japan's ($34,400), the third economic power. Sitting behind these stellar achievements are Samsung Electronics, LG Electronics, POSCO, and Hyundai-Kia whose products are strutting the world market. South Korea ranks at the top in the production of new-fangled semi conductor chips, TV screens, cell phones, automobiles and ship-building. In other areas of products, Korean enterprises rub shoulders with topnotch ones in the world. South Korea maintains a technological edge over modern China in manufacturing technologies but this competitive edge is a matter of time in this most dynamic region of the world. North Korea's per capita GDP is perhaps five percent of South Korea's. Koreans, no matter where they are located, are a people of one culture and language. Given the millennia-long sharing of commonalities, this egregious income gap between the two halves can be explained by nothing other than the system, institutions or infrastructure in place. The regimentation of society into a state inhabited by depoliticized masses and social unanimity leaves no room for an individual to be independent and creative.

As we see in other countries, there is a dark side of rapid development. A forward look captures the future looming over the horizon with a host of problems, some stemming from the hasty growth and others nurtured in the hotbed of state-led development. The state-led development resulted in the loss of opportunities for businesses to thrive on market dynamism. Business concerns, particularly those selected to spearhead export-led industries, were a fish out of water when they were dismantled of the government's support. The lack of experience with market dynamism cost them an ability to survive when they felt the pinch of shrinking state support and oil shock. With Korea's economic boom turning into a rout from 1997, Asian values were vulnerable to recriminations in the aftermath of boastful claims of superior 'Asian values.' Blame was heaped on 'the Asian way,' the wastes' created by the incestuous relationship between the government and corporations. The economic rout invited the IMF bailout program, a vociferous voice for return to the dictum of the market based on openness, transparency, equality, rationality and emotion-neutral policy. It advocated neo-liberalism which stressed the minimal role of the state and the maximum role of the market. Protectionism and mercantilism could not survive in the world of ruthless competition. A law was enacted to justify the layoff of workers for business reasons, but its encounter with the paternalistic emotion of Koreans made it a rough going, spawning pugnacious problems.

The initial reliance on foreign capital allowed South Korean business to develop into exceptionally high debt-equity ratio and made the country the largest foreign debtor. Such a high debt-equity ratio reflects much of intrepidity and risk-taking adventurism of robust Koreans. Petty entrepreneurs failed to calculate prudently when starting business. The main social problem of South Korea is the issue of economic justice in the distribution of wealth. As the economic boom benefited one sizeable segment of population, with absolute poverty perceptibly reduced, the entrepreneurs reaped a disproportionate share of the new national wealth.

South Korea became a fast-aging society, as the percentage of aged population is becoming larger. The average life expectancy of South Koreans is 80 years in comparison with 47 when the Korean War broke out in 1950. Despite tangible improvements in conditions for living, South Korea hit a record-breaking suicide of the aged people: the old poor accounts for 45.5 % of those aged 65 years or above, compared to the OECD's averaging at 13.0 % (Choson TV, Aug.26,2014). Social welfare and ecological concerns were brushed aside in the rush for economic growth and have become topical issues in political debates these days. The government pays dearly for its belated response to the social needs. Economically, Korea is making its weight felt throughout the world. It is the United States' seventh trading partner, a key supplier of materials and labor in the Middle East, and a significant economic actor in Africa, Latin America, and elsewhere in Asia. Modern Korean-built ships roam the seas under the flags of many nations. Some of the large conglomerates, headquartered in Seoul, are making their influence felt far afield, sometimes having an effect of the foreign policy decisions of other nations. Today nations from the third world are pleased to accept Korean advice on patterns for development. This miracle is not a myth but a clearly existing reality that had resulted from a functioning market mechanism, pragmatic macro economics policies encouraging domestic savings and investment, and the governmental abilities to initiate and monitor performances to success.

The splendid façade of the economic edifice is defaced by new problems accompanying its development. The bleakest aspects of industrialization, a malaise of spirit and the nightmare of environmental collapse are looming over the horizon. Social welfare, grappling with the gap between a few wealth and masses in poverty, is once again sensitizing a segment of Koreans to the lure of socialism, giving an added impetus to the on-going ideological confrontation. An increasing percentage of aged people, coupled with a low-birth rate, offers no promise of another economic leap forward.

Historiographical Warfare

The historiographical warfare in Korea is a unique phenomenon which hardly finds its parallel anywhere else. The warfare occurs on two levels. One traces its cause to different interpretations of Korea's modern history marked by its struggles against colonialism and imperialism. An ideological stance is an important factor that helps to shape a historical perspective. Ideological confrontation sharpens contrast between progressives and conservatives, leaving little room for narrowing perception gap. Another follows from Korea's historical experiences with its neighboring countries, particularly in relation to China and Japan. Each country projects its own interpretation of history on others. It inevitably entails a perception gap much likely to create a tension-ridden inter-country relationship. Unlike the Western countries which can be blocked into one historical emporium, the countries in the East have little to share. The on-going historiographical war between Korea and Japan stands out: it is an emotional war that has been shaped in a victim-victimizer relationship.

Legitimacy of the State

The presence of two Koreas provides the ground for an endless debate on "which side truly represents a legitimate state." Each side seeks its legitimacy in its declared continuum from the past. North Korea claims itself as the orthodox that has descended from the Joseon Dynasty and this claim negates the last monarch, Daehan Jekuk,[14] that preceded its downfall. Physically, both South and North Koreas lost their connections by a hiatus of 36 year alien rule to the last monarch. The bridge that connects the pre-colonial monarch to the present is the Korea Provisional Government in exile.[15] North Korea asserts itself as a legitimate child born of the Korea Provisional Government in exile. But Kim Il-sung had never associated himself with the Provisional Government. Why does North Korea skip Daehan Jekuk to establish a connection with the Korea Provisional Government? The answer is found in Daehan Minkuk (the Republic of Korea) asserting itself as the true successor to Daehan Jekuk, as implicated by Daehan, a common prefix. Daehan (a greater nation) was a quintessential component of naming a new state, meaning an enlarged state continuous from the past. Daehan Jekuk was the extension of the Chosôn Dynasty as it was under the same monarch, but with titular upgrading to put it on par with China and Japan that had departed from monarchical legacy.

Progressive scholars argue that the Korea Provisional Government in exile marks the inauguration of a new nation state and this argument accordingly degrades the birth of the Republic of Korea to that of a government. The dichotomy between the state and the government sounds strange to laymen, for one was unconsciously equated with the other. To be precise, the Provisional Government in exile came closer to a unified nationalist front organized by patriotic-minded expatriates ten years after the downfall of Daehan Jekuk, with the purpose of restoring national independence. "It fell short of a new nation state, since it had neither land nor sovereignty, which, combined with people, could have provided the conditions for a nation state" (Cho Kap-je 204,258). It did not obtain sanction from any of the nation states. Neither did it obtain formal recognition from China, the host country that helped it to sustain its precarious existence through the dark days of its struggle. Further, the extreme leftists, led by Kim Won-bong, bolted out of the Provisional Government, leaving it to face the danger of falling apart at the seams. But the mainstream of the provisional government members, embracing moderate leftists, centralists and rightists, remained to patch the cracks and played their role in the birth of the Republic of Korea. In light of the Korea Provisional Government assorted with the democratic trappings, it was a hotbed for democratic sprouts to be transplanted into the democratic bed of the Republic of Korea.

The Constitution of the Republic of Korea declares its continuity from the legal and institutional foundations of the Provisional Government in exile. The progressive view of the Korea Provisional Government as the inauguration of a nation state cannot be considered other than an attempt to obscure the legitimacy of the Republic of Korea as a new nation state.

Nationalism in the post-liberation Korea, amid its bout with colonial vestiges, was equated with anti-colonial credential. In a country which suffered the evils of colonialism, nothing was harsher than being stigmatized as a pro-colonial element. North Korea bashed South Korea for its collusion with pro-colonial elements, notorious for having hunted down and tortured Korean patriots, in creating the leadership of the post-liberation government in the south and in their imminent confrontation with their ideological foes. Nationalism identified with an anti-colonial credential was the holy grail that measured the legitimacy of the government. South Korea has been bashed for its failure to dispel the colonial sediments.

A similar instance is found in East Germany's accusation of West Germany whose legitimacy was suspected by its failure to dispel the Nazi's vestiges (Mark Kurlansky,1988; 14-45). Nationalism had so strong an appeal to Vietnamese pitted against the new colonial master that North Vietnam declared its regime as the genuine manifestation of the Vietnamese Nationalist Front standing above ideological frays. In terms of anti-foreign credential, both South and North have no claim to legitimacy. Ko Eun, a progressive poet, enunciated "the true identity of Korea rests with the political entity which meets the popular aspirations for welfare and decent life"(Chang Jak kwa Bipyong, 1993,41-45). According to his view, both nationalistic and ideological criteria reflect the needs of a particular time, and the true identity of Koreans is non-ideological and non-nationalistic.

Textbook Debate

A new round of the ideological war revives in an on-going debate on the high school textbooks of modern Korean history. In light of Koreans having shared in history over millennia, one may presume that it leaves little room for different interpretations of history, particularly when it relates to colonial and imperialistic legacies. The modern history of Korea, as taught in high schools, is blamed by the conservatives for a left-oriented interpretation of history under the influence of students' antagonism against the military regimes and anti-American sentiment. They say that the afterglow of leftist orientation is still burning bright, dominating the intellectual circles of these particular age cohorts. Progressives burst into a counter attack condemning the criticism as a plot to invoke a colonial and autocratic specter of the past. Now that three generations have passed since the colonial power receded, argument over the shady past raises skepticism about its relevance. Many Koreans ask why they should be the captives of angry sentiment over the past.

In the presence of bipolarized historical views, bashing of the adversary is often blown out of the fact. Progressives covers a wide spectrum of different brands and defies a categorical image of pro-North Korea stance, as held by conservatives. Likewise, the progressives accuse the conservatives' attack as regression into a dark history, trying to resurrect pro-colonialism and autocratic rule. In actuality, the market of textbooks is dominated by the left-oriented textbooks that are suspicious of the legitimacy of the Republic of Korea (South Korea). If this mutual castigation is tinged with a political motive, it surely constitutes a black hole of ideology into which all political activities are sucked to the virtual exclusion of other political agendas.

Scholars of Korean history, due to their manifested focus on Koreans' struggles against colonialism and imperialism, are strong in the sense of ethnic nationalism. Viewed through this prism, the Republic of Korea (South Korean regime) is not free of its own share of dark history by dependence on and subjectivity to a foreign power throughout the period of national foundation and its bout with communism. The recent phenomenal growth of South Korea is discredited as the result of collusion between a few powerful enterprises and the government, exclusively dependent on foreign aids. The dark side of the economic development is that it fattened a few, leaving the masses exploited. A heavier dependence on a foreign power is condemned as an act of depreciating Koreans' energy to stand on their own feet. Given this argument, the 1997's economic downturn of South Korea was a matter of rejoice for those who beat the drum against "a castle built on the sand beach." They were heartened to see their prognostications verified by the reality. North Korea, according to the progressive view, casts a positive light on its tenacious struggle to break free from foreign powers. For all plausible pretensions on both sides, it is clear that an anti-foreign mantra alone cannot be the measure of the legitimacy of a state.

Progressives regard the conservatives' critique as a plot to revive the pro-colonialism and dictatorship of the earlier rulers. But it is rather the progressives that lock themselves as much in the past by evoking memories of the past to be equated with the reality at present. Obsession with the past leaves little room for political flexibility. A new era has long since condemned colonialism and dictatorship to death. Nowadays, no sensible ruler wants to go back to the benighted form of pre-modern politics. The best strategy for Koreans to beat their adversaries is to broach the scandalous doings of their ancestors, that is, a subjective cooperation with colonialism. Inter-generational responsibility remains strong with Koreans and becomes a convenient means to vitiate the honor of a family. Judgment of one's past behavior in the present framework has its own limit. A distortion begets another distortion, perpetually locking Koreans in a vicious cycle of feud and confrontation.

As debate goes on to a new height of intensity, passion and sentiment prevails over reason. As words are inflated, they are divorced from the reality, and people are intoxicated with their own words empty of meanings. The cause of ideological debate is rooted in dichotomy between volk (ethnic people) and the state and debate is heated over which one comes first. Conservative circles put the state over volk with greater concern for the future of the state, whereas progressives stand for the reverse, stressing volk as eternal. Progressives unfailingly subscribe to ethnic nationalism that hold foreign powers responsible for all kinds of misfortunes that beset Korea.

Every single fact has the two sides that are antithetical to each other. Syngman Rhee was a towering figure in his anti-colonial struggle and in his role in the birth of the Republic of Korea. But his image as the founder of a democratic society is significantly obscured by being a dictator who mocked the rule of law he had legislated. He is bashed for collusion with pro-colonial elements in his fight against communism and having spearheaded a course of events leading to the division of Korea. He was denounced by the nationalists as a traitor by standing for a separate government and the division of the country. A fact tinged with an ideological color is categorically denied by both as muddying the true identity of Koreans. Ambitious Korean youths in the colonial period volunteered to be the loyal subjects of Japan, but these people were outnumbered by those who were forcibly drafted into the military service. After Korea restored its sovereignty, these people resolved to serve the country to which they owed allegiance. The question is whether the record of having served the colonial master should perpetually disqualify them for serving their country that had been placed in peril.

One may argue that the current textbook system that gives publishing companies free access to the market can be improved by upgrading criteria, since it encourages competition toward a higher quality of the textbooks. The shortcomings of the present system may be remedied by a consummate organization of authority standing above scuffles. But the situation has been too much muddied to allow this common sense to work itself. A publishing company, writers and teachers are allied into a cartel to work in the interest of the textbooks they worked for. The problem is that schools are not given choice of the textbooks they want to use. Given this, the on-going bout with the government's plan to standardize the textbooks cannot be considered in other way than an attempt to protect their vested interests under the disguised shield of free right to choose. The progressives' argument for a free market, nevertheless, contradicts their current engagement in an aggressive sale campaign that seriously limits the right of schools to make an informed decision. They pay lip service to the diversity of opinions but are not aware of their acts with a possible result of hobbling diversity itself.

The dichotomy between pros and cons is ever present in modern society. The motive for a standard textbook, if given the benefit of doubt, may follow from an earnest concern for a fair treatment of contents, not biased in either direction. The sudden turnaround of the government to the standard textbook, moreover, reflects its resolute action to end the debate on what is correct or false once and for all. A resolute action to end debate may be at odds with the nature of the task that should be approached in a flexible manner that reflects the needs of time.

The Paradox of Neighborhood

Geographical proximity does not breed a good neighborhood. The perceived image of Japanese by Koreans is categorically negative due to the earlier piracy of Japanese, a devastating war triggered by a megalomaniac ruler, and the colonial rule. But Koreans take pride in having been a cultural precursor to ancient Japanese. Japanese, on the other hand, regarded Koreans as half-awaken to be enlightened by them. In relation to China, Korea has been awed by the giant, and accepted its identity as a partner to the Sino-centered world. Korea's hierarchical relationship with China, however, was far from being a smooth sailing that was assumed to be typical of a brotherly bond. Koreans have a mixture of feelings alternating between envy or admiration and jealousy or distrust. China still lives off its pride in its past splendor and burns its ambition to restore its erstwhile hegemony. The on-going historiographical wars between Korea and its two neighbors follow, in large part, from the fact that Asian countries have never shared in one cultural and historical legacy in contrast to the Western societies. 'Europe' conjures in our minds an unambiguous, cohesive cultural identity against the amorphous diversity of Asian cultures. Unlike European countries that trace their cultural genesis to Greco-Roman civilization, Asia has no common legacy that binds all countries into a greater cultural and religious community. The lack of common legacy leads each country to assert its own ethnic, cultural and historical identity that refuse to be reconciled.

Although Western societies are separated by language, culture and institutions, there is one vein that cuts across these differences. Historical and cultural bonds left little ground for disputes on historical issues, though armed clashes transpired with greater frequency when national interests were at cross purposes. In the Eastern hemisphere, history has never seen any state rise to the Roman Empire that brought different political communities under its imperial dome. China, though larger than the sum of its surrounding states, has never conquered East Asia. Each state has evolved along ethnic and cultural boundaries. For the lack of a common legacy, Korea is inevitably drawn into historiographical wars with its two neighboring countries. The problem followed from both trying to impose their prisms of interpretations that are quite different from each other. Korea's perception of Japan in terms of a victim and victimizer relationship rejects any Japan's argument to justify its doings. Nevertheless, beating the drums of colonial atrocities will drown out thoughtful voices that could have given solution to the inter-country disputes.

China's nostalgia for the grandeur of the past finds its manifestation in its breathtaking rise to a new military and economic power. To Koreans, China's enhanced status is the reminder of the imperialistic specter of its former self. China, owing to its blurred borders, tend to expand its view of history encroaching upon the historical identities of its neighbors. Korea fears that the Korea-China relation may again turn into the traditional hierarchy. Granting that China has a strong leverage to restrain North Korea from rash behaviors, it is inevitable for South Korea to be a friendly partner, if not in a hierarchical relationship. Being a friendly partner means that the two should share in purpose. When it comes to the reunification of Korea, however, the two countries have different dreams, though they share a strategic approach to peace in this region. The Korea-China honeymoon has its own limits, because China will never become a fellow traveler of South Korea in a daunting journey to a unified Korea. The irony is that China regards North Korea as its courtyard or a buffer zone against American hegemony.

Distortions of History

Korea is separated from Japan by a strait, but these two have never enjoyed a friendly relationship. A narrow strait that separates the two countries was wide enough to discourage any one from crossing. It was in 1876 that the two countries were brought into a formal contact in the name of the Korea-Japan

Trade Treaty. Given the geographical proximity, the belated opening of a formal diplomatic relationship is extraordinarily out of the norm. Japan has the dark side of its modern history, ridden with injustices and atrocities done to Koreans. How to face the wrongdoings committed by their ancestors exhausts the imagination of contemporary Japanese rulers. How to apologize for the victimized countries is another issue of the rulers whose views vary with its reigning regime. Korean perception of Japan is fixed in the past, whereas Japanese perception of Korea is whimsical and illusive, depending on the regime in power. It should be noted, however, that conscience weighs heavily on a significant segment of Japanese individuals; they feel shameful of injustices and atrocities done to the neighboring people.

Koreans fear that imparting historical facts, as Japanese perceive through their own prism, to their younger generations can reinforce their collective propensity to overlook their ancestors' wrong doings, if it does not result in a perpetual oblivion. Historical distortions are found in the Japanese middle school textbook published by the right-wing's Japanese Society for History Textbook Reform in 1997 which rebelled against apologetic remarks made by every Japanese ruling regime. All aggressive acts of Japan are clothed in words that justify self-defense of Asia from Western imperialism. The victimized countries, on the other hand, view them as an overt invasion encroaching upon their sovereignties. The dichotomy in view owes much to the two countries locked in a victimizer-victim relationship.

When it comes to the shady aspects of its history, Japan tones down the wording of textbooks or delete the relevant materials partially or entirely. The wording of historical material plays an important role in changing the content of history itself. The result is that it dulls the sensitivity of Japanese youngsters to "right" or "wrong." In a broader perspective, this helps to revive the ethnic superiority of Japanese to other races. The deliberate distortion of history by Japan, of course, inflames the fury of Koreans and others. This illustrates an example where history is reduced into a tool to buttress a state's policy in relation to its neighbors. With regard to Japan's forced annexation of Korea, Japanese use 'advance' (jinchul) as opposed to aggression (chimnyak).

Japanese distortion of its history is not confined to its modern history. Debate is heated over the so-called Imna. Japanese historians argue that the southern part of the Korean peninsula had been under Japanese occupation, and it was timed with the Korean peninsula divided into three kingdoms. Japan's twentieth century advance into Korea was justified by the restoration of its lost territory. This region, history testifies, was a battleground between Paekche and Silla, the mightier monarchical kingdoms of Korea which locked their horns for territorial expansion. Given that Paekche was aligned with Japan against Silla, this area could be presumed to have housed the allied forces of Paekche and Japan, serving as a site for a joint military command against Silla.

A fabrication of history is found in respect to the tomb of a Kogurysô king. A band of Japanese soldiers on a reconnaissance mission during their 1931campaign against Manchuria discovered a stone monument in Jinlin Prefecture, which proved to be the tomb of Kwang'geto, the Great of Koguryô who reigned from 391 to 412. This great stone monument was built by his son Changsu in 414 to honor the military exploits his father achieved. The stone-carved epitaph was in full text of Chinese characters about how Koguryô was founded and reached its apex of territorial expansion. No one expected that the fortuitous encounter of Japanese soldiers with the stone monument would be an opportunity for Japan to steal history from Korea. Part of the epitaph reads "Imna was conquered." Some of the epitaph characters were worn down, leaving room for Japan to distort the text in favor of Japan's historical claim to the southern part of the peninsula. According to the text, the allied Paekche and Japan forces invaded Kaya Confederation, adjacent to Silla. King Namul of Silla asked for help from Koguryo. Kwang'geto himself led 50,000 strong and sacked the Imna commanding post.

The occupation of Imna receives greater attention in connection with its colonial policy to blur the ethnic distinction of Koreans from Japanese. Japan's colonial rule over Korea, according to their own interpretation, dates back as early as the first century B.C when the southern part of Korea was under the reign of Samhan, the three tribal confederations. These were powerful enough to awe any feudal state of Japan. The island of Japan, divided into feudal states, was suspected of its capacity to send their troops across the strait and conquer much larger and powerful confederations of Koreans. In the third century, four hundred years after Japan's claim to Imna, there were thirty ruling domains in Japan against Korea made up of three confederations (Kim Young-woon, 2000,71). The Kaya Confederation consisted of six walled towns, and Imna was one of them. In light of this fact, Imna might well be viewed as the location of a Japanese office in this walled town sate, in a status comparable to the Netherlands' residential office in Nagasaki of Edo Japan.

The relationship between Paekche and Yamato received new light as historical dig into classical materials was intensified. Any slight suggestion that the imperial clan of Japan might have Korean ancestors continues to be regarded as heresy in Japan. Nevertheless, the relationship of Paekche and Yamato was made indisputable by the Emperor's confession in January 2002. "A defeated royal clan of Paekche left blood to run in my vein." In his statement, he must have referred to Homuda, a Paekche prince and the founding father of Yamato Kingdom. Kanaku Niekasa, descended from the last king of Paekche, was mother of Emperor Kanmoo who settled the capital on Kyoto (781-806) (Kim Yong-woon, 2002,83). Noteworthy is the text of an epistle that appears in the chronicles of China Liu Song Dynasty dated 478. "The text identifies its sender as the Wae King, Mu, the crown prince of King Kaero of Paekche. The archeological and historical evidence excavated from his tomb led to the conclusion that the King Mu of Wae Japan became King Muryong of Paekche" (Kim Yong-deok, 2003). Hong Won-tak's investigation identified Homuda, the founder of Yamato court, as son of King Kye of Paekche (2003, 35). The Kojiki and Nihon Shogi, known to be the most monumental records of the ancient history of Japan, identify Homuda as the 15th reign and obscures the period that preceded him in mythological accounts.

The bloody connection of Paekche with Yamao is evidenced by the latter's attempt at military campaign to deliver Paekche on the verge of extinction (Hong Won-tak, 2003, 35).Yamato Japan hastily organized and dispatched a military contingent, made up of 26,000, after Paekche fell down. But the loss of 10,000 at a decisive battle of the lower basin of the Kumkang River, leading to the heart of Paekche, brought the military expedition to a virtual halt. "Given the total population of Japan estimated at 5,000,000, this military strength reflected a desperate effort of Yamato to rescue the falling kingdom" (Kim Young-woon 2000, 83). From that time on, the Yamato court entered a long-sustained seclusion while the ruling lineage of the Yamato was indigenized. Why did the Yamato court so suddenly reverse its attitude by trying to erase its earlier connections with Paekche? The aborted military expedition in support of Paekche left the Yamato court open to a possible retaliatory attack by T'ang and Silla allied forces after they had triumphantly pacified Korea. The succeeding king, Denmu (673-686), needed to distance himself and sought to create a new identity of the Yamato court and ordered that a new history of Japan be written. The Kojiki and Nihon Shoki were published in 712 and 720 respectively.

Geographical proximity is no guarantee of a good neighborhood. Some scholars in Japan recognize Korea's role in transmitting bronze culture, Neo-Confucianism and pottery-making skill, but "the dominant view of Japanese regarding Korea was rather pejorative" (Hur Namlin 1998, 10). Such negative perception of Korea was evident in the Tokugawa period and became acrimonious in the Meiji period. National Learning scholars in particular, full of narratives asserting the heavenly origin of the Emperor, went so far as to claim that the ancestral lineage of the Three Han states in Korea's southern part was started from Busano Mikoto. This theory developed into a "theory of the same ancestor of Japanese and Koreans" which was adopted to justify Japan's rule over Korea. The annexation of Korea and Japan in 1910 was justified in the name of "enlightenment"– that "a civilized Japan needed to occupy a culturally lagging Korea" (Hatado Takashi, 1983,33-37).

The dichotomized view of history is also observed in their view of Korean diplomatic correspondents who were regularly dispatched to Japan since the Japanese massive invasion into Chosôn in 1592. Korea's claim was that they were commissioned to enlighten the uncivilized Japanese to see the light of the humane and moral world. In contrast, Japan regarded them as a tribute mission to pay respect to Japan, characteristic of the vertical relationship between the states. "The diplomacy of maintaining a friendly relationship was overwhelmed by a deeply dichotomized frame of reference" (Huh Nanlin 1998,11).

Territorial Dispute

The same principle applies to the disputed ownership of Tok-do islands (Takeshima in Japanese). These inhabitable rocky islands might have been relegated into a minor issue, but their location on a midpoint between Korea and Japan – to be exact, it is little closer to Korea –gives it so profound a strategic significance, allowing no party to make concessions. Korea refers to the forced signing of the Protectorate Treaty with Japan by which Japan had control over Korean territory and the Annexation Treaty in 1910 incorporating Korea, including Tok-do, into Japan. Liberation from the Japanese colonial yoke justified Korea's claim to these islands. As the Pacific War was winding down in August 1943, Franklin Roosevelt, Winston Churchill and Chang Kai-shek met in Cairo and declared the Cairo resolution to the effect that Japan shall be dismantled of all territories it illegally and forcibly obtained prior to and during the war. But Japan asserted that Tok-do were a different matter, not subject to the Cairo resolution, because it had legally obtained the islands from Korea. A crucial question is whether any sovereign state is willing to give away part of its territory, if it was not done by force and threat?

It was in the fifteenth century that the Chosôn dynasty recognized the presence of the islands which now include Ullung-do and Tok-do islands. Tok-to is 120 miles away from Ullung-do, while it is about 210 miles from Okinoshima of Japan. Coming into the eighteenth century, foreign vessels began to appear, and a French vessel discovered the islands in 1849 and called it Liancourt Rocks. Ullnung island was thick with forestry, and Japanese began to reside there for lumbering. As the Chosôn Dynasty moved Koreans to settle down from 1883, all Japanese residents departed. Ullnung Island has been an indisputable part of Korean territory since then. Korea takes a firm stand, asserting that Tok-do cannot be treated separately from Ullnung-do as they had been blocked to be called Woosan-kuk from the time of the Silla Dynasty.

In asserting that Tok-do is an integral part of its territory, Japan refers in its documents to a fishery license issued by the Tokugawa administration to Yonago residents in 1618. In 1897, the Chosôn dynasty declared Daehan Jukuk (Greater Han Empire) and issued Decree 41 claiming these islands as lying within Korean territorial water. One of the most important Korean maps, the Ch'ongku-do drawn by Kim Chong-ho in 1834, also has it that the geographical location of the islands was within Korean territory (Kim Won-sik 1965,pp.48-9). "Chosen Engan Suiroshi" of the Japan Navy Department drawn in 1923 (cited from Hahn Ki-ri, 1965, p.47) and "Kangoku suiroshi" in 1908 drawn by Iori Genbun of Japan clearly marked Tok-do as a Korean territory (Sin Sok-ho, 1977,p.47). After the Republic of Korea was born, President Syngman Rhee sealed its ownership by assigning coast guards to defend the territory. In this connection, how to name the sea that separates Korea from Japan remains a sensational issue. This naming on the map had a direct bearing on the ownership of Tok-to islands. Koreans have called it the "East Sea." Since the outbreak of this territorial dispute, Japan calls it "the Sea of Japan" and embarked on an intensive campaign to draw the world's attention to the logic of their argument. The United States took an action to suspend the use of the Sea of Japan.[16]

Comfort Women

Another internationally sensitized issue is the so-called "comfort women." The right-winged Japanese regime under Prime Minster Abe denies coercive recruitment and inhuman treatment of Korean women during the Pacific War. Leaders of Japanese administrations, starting with Yasushio Nakasone, made apologetic remarks on Japanese aggressive war and inhuman treatment of comfort women. Most conspicuous were the apologies of former Prime Minister Moshiro Hosokawa in 1993 and Dominich Murayama in 1995. Dominich Murayama in particular was hyper critical of Abe's regime for its attempt to obscure the issue in alliance with the rightist wing. Beset by domestic and external criticism, Kichi Miyazawa issued a statement in the name of Chief Cabinet Secretary Kano, assuming official responsibility for comfort women. The statement admitted that the Japanese military was involved directly or indirectly in the establishment and maintenance of brothels for soldiers. Abe in his demand for the retraction of Kano's statement in May 1997, observed "there was no evidence of coercion in recruitment."He further tried to obscure "coercion" by saying "there is no fixed definition of coercion."His ambiguous statement suggests an attempt to obscure coercion by substituting the fabricated "volition of Korean women" to trade their souls for livelihood. A majority of the comfort women, he said, came from the impoverished families.

Abe's statement cannot but be viewed as a deliberate attempt to degrade the decency and dignity of women in general, if not intended for Korean women. Is there any woman in the world who volunteers to subject herself to sexual enslavement? Every sensible Korean who experienced the colonial rule witnessed "women hunt" that hastened Korean parents to get their daughters married even at earlier ages to avoid the coercive recruitment. There are millions of Japanese who appeal to their honesty and consciences to recognize their wrong doings. They air critical voices warning against the diplomatic isolation of Japan resulting from the right wing's denial of truth. The rightist movement in general is considered an outgrowth of the nationalistic sentiment of the masses to protect their country from the Western predators. In Japan, it is more than the love and defense of their country; it is an emotional outgrowth of a collective reluctance to face the truth.

In 2007, the comfort women controversy received global attention, as it became a human right issue in the U.S-Japan relationship, when the rightist members of the Japan-Ruling Liberal Party tried to discredit Kano's statement. Some of U.S congressmen moved for a new resolution concerning the wartime human rights abuse of these unfortunate women. The continuing move to revise the Kano's statement generated concern within the U.S Government. The comfort women which had been limited to the dimension of historical perception took a new turn to a question of human right and war crimes which the American public and international communities could no longer condone. House 212, initiated by the Foreign Affairs Committee of the U.S House, passed the whole House in mid July, 2007. The resolution called for the Japanese government to admit responsibility and provides an official apology over the comfort women.

On the part of Korea, some Koreans admiringly look at the civic consciousness of modern Japanese and their incredible capacity to get things done in unison in times of crisis. The self restraint of Japanese and their high sense of order enabled them to overcome earthquake and Tsunami disasters. A majority of Koreans, however, view Japan as a country which refuses to be enlightened. Such a negative view is grounded in the past, following from the piracy of Japanese which plundered the coast villages of Korea from ancient time and the bitter taste of colonial experience. The categorical image of the Japanese discourages Koreans' effort to understand the true picture of Japan. Japanese remarkably lack the courage to unflinchingly face the truth in contrast to Germans who no longer incur the wrath of the victimized countries for their war-time atrocities.

Expansive View of Chinese History

The on-going historiographical war with China was rather a recent occurrence. China broke its millennia-old silence by declaring a historical jurisdiction over Koguryô, one of the earliest three kingdoms of Korea. Koguryô was a border state which occupied the northern half of the Korean peninsula and the middle plain of Manchuria. Its territory was inhabited by Ye-Mak tribes, Manchus and Mongolians. Koreans trace their ancestral root in Ye-Mak tribes, the ruling class of the kingdom. Denial of Koguryô as an ancient kingdom of Koreans would most likely lead to the negation of Paekche that occupied the middle part of the peninsular, since both originated in a tribal confederation called "Fuyu." The founders of the two kingdoms were of one confederated tribal league.

China, made up of 55 ethnic groups, enjoys a vantage ground in claiming an expansive jurisdiction over its neighboring states. Since ancient times, China has viewed all other states as subordinated to the middle kingdom, and Korea was apparently placed in the shadow of the Sino-centered world perspective. China's claim to the ownership of Koguryô, in large measure, follows from the fact that all surrounding states were in a tribute relationship with China. In reality, China enjoyed a titular master over its surrounding states, and what seemed to be a vertical relationship was rather ritualistic and ceremonial. Local gifts were exchanged and investiture was contrived to confirm China's approval on the new kings of its surrounding states. The fallacy of the Chinese argument is the failure to distinguish between subordination and ownership. Rather, the tribute relationship was defined as moral obligations that were reciprocally honored in order to smooth inter-country relationship.

China regarded itself as the middle kingdom surrounded by satellite sates. Therefore, its borders extended beyond the pale of its administrative authority. Chinese have a vague notion of borders, and their expansive view of history evolved from its territory being unmanageably large. Uniquely, the Chinese historical claim is based on the present occupation of the territory of the old kingdom. Koguryô is a historical identity that cannot be projected into the present. Historical identity is not congruent with its present territory. The territory-centered view of history is in contrast with the historic view of the Balkans. This region embraces a tangle of ethnic or religious groups, and a political identity that exists today is based on "a right to govern its historical territory, defined in terms of early medieval settlements, regardless of who own it" (Patrick J. Geary, 11). Historical identity overwhelms the present occupation of a land. Their ethnic and religious make-up is complicated by the occupation of the Balkans by the Roman Empire, Hapsburg Austria and Ottoman Turkey. Their claim for a territorial jurisdiction is based on their earlier settlements that date back to the medieval ages. This contradicts the Chinese claim that projects the present occupation of a territory into the past, thereby encroaching upon the historical jurisdiction of an extinct state. The inhabitants of the Balkans left their distinct ethnic, political and religious traces that endure to the present, and settlers in a region renewed the process of ethno genesis. China's present occupation of the territory has no ground for asserting jurisdiction over the history of the state that has long since been extinct.

The historical identity of a state is determined by the people who inhabited a region in a particular time. Man, among others, is the maker of history and, given this fact, Chinese claim based on its present territorial occupation leaves much to be refuted about. China's present occupation of three-fourth of the old kingdom's territory, according to their argument, entitles them to a jurisdictional claim over the history of a defunct kingdom. Koguryô is a historical identity that remained outside the territory old China claimed. Historical territory cannot necessarily be identical with contemporary territory. Chinese claims to its historical jurisdiction over the old kingdom means that they can move a historical fact along a time span and fit it into a particular time frame which favors their historical assertion. This means the advantage of flexibly interpreting its history based on the presence of ethnic groups within its present territory.

Chinese view the shaper of history as not people but the territory which they have occupied since the downfall of Ming China in 1664. If the present territorial claim is the determinant of the past, how do they explain the history of Koguryô after its capital moved in 426 to Pyongyang from a town in the basin of the Yallu River. According to Chinese interpretation, the history of Kogruyô should be divided into two parts, one covers the first part from its foundation and the later period that stretches from the transfer of the capital to its downfall. This begs a question of whether a dynasty which had been ruled by one family clan changes its identity depending on where its capital is located.

The Chinese argument is flawed by ignoring time-brought changes. The power, size and land of a state change over time. The territory of Koguryô had been inhabited by ethnic tribes called Manchurians who erected Q'ing China in 1644.[17] Since then, the Northeastern region has been sanctified as the birth place of the founder of the new dynasty. Before the People's Republic of China was born in 1949, Han Chinese had never directly controlled the northeastern region. All of Chinese chronicles set the region aside to be inhabited by Eastern barbarians (dong Ie Minjok). If the historical identity of a state is not locked in a particular time, Italians could have reclaimed Roman dominance over all of Europe by conversely projecting the past to the present. A historical fact is not allowed to traverse a time span to lay its claim to the present.

It remains clear that Koguryô engaged in a series of military confrontations with the Sui and T'ang dynasties that Chinese had proudly declared as the largest unitary states following the long-lasting warring states. The T'ang dynasty in particular was the world power that awed its surrounding states into submission. Given China's claim to historical jurisdiction over Koguryô how should it explain the wars of Sui and T'ang with Koguryô. In the presence of a giant country, small states should have showed timidity rather than risk frays, unless forced by a compelling situation. Koguryô was a border state destined to serve as a breakwater against a tide of Chinese invasions into the peninsula. China considered the wars with Koguryô as one of a series of skirmishes accompanying the expansion of its territory. But these wars, each employing a huge military strength up to 300,000 at most, exceeded the normal bound of a skirmish. The three wars Koguryô engaged in confrontation with China were not of such a scale that suggested a skirmish. So, what would have happened, had it not been for Koguryô? China left its borders to be blurred by time by leaving the ground for other ethnic tribes to settle in; these people lived beyond the pale of China's monarchical authority.

North Korea's dependence on China symbolizes the resurrection of the traditional hierarchy between the states. China has tacitly regarded North Korea as its buffer zone against its rival, the United States. Projecting China's expansive view of history into a distant future, who would deny the possibility that China will claim North Korea as its courtyard? North Korea may see it better to remain its courtyard rather than to confront the risk of incorporation into the south. From this viewpoint, the reunification of the two halves into the unitary state may not be achievable.

---

1.   Tan'gun is a mythological figure, known as the Korean ethnic progenitor, who was believed to reign the oldest country of Korea, Old Chosôn, from 2333 B.C. Reference to Tan'gun appeared in "Tales of Three Kingdoms" authored by a Buddhist monk during the medieval Koryô. Although Tan'gun was a legendary figure, he has been a rally cry for Koreans to rise up against foreign invaders. Koreans draw inspiration and courage from the belief that his spirit is with them in their dauntless struggle for existence. Koreans consciousness of their progenitor stirred awake nationalism based on ethnic homogeneity.

2.   Koguryô and Balhae were border states that inhabited Southern Manchuria and the Northern part of the Korean peninsula. Due to their adjacency to China, the people were made up of Khitans, Jurchens, Mongols and Yemak. Coming into the Unified Silla and Koryô, they were homogenized under one political and administrative system. The process of homogenization was started in 668 when the kingdoms were incorporated into one large political entity. Dynastic change serves as a screening mesh that winnowed out heterogeneous elements.

3.   Taewon'gun was the regent for his immature King Kojong enthroned in 1864. He was notorious for extreme isolation policy against imperialist incursions. Hatred for foreigners was built into his mind and this inflamed his stand for chauvinistic nationalism. Under his reign, Korea was known as a hermit kingdom, which left no states willing to approach. He was an Confucian idealist, with his belief that Confucianism offered the way to survival when its neighbors opened the doors and tried to accept foreign mores and technology. He refused to compromise with corruption but his radical turnaround of the policy provided symptomatic relief of social ills. During his reign, Korea had rash confrontation with French and American fleets.

4.   The bone refers to the status of family. Even today, Koreans talk about a family of high bone or low bone, depending on what their ancestors were in a hierarchical society. The Silla kingdom was marked by rigid adherence to the bone ranking which applied to the royal family and populace. The royal family was divided into sacred bone and true bone. The former requires a king to marry a spouse of another sacred family, Park. Failure to marry the designated family disqualified any royal member for the ruler. True bone refers to a royal member who married a spouse from other families than the Park. This family began to rule the kingdom after it pacified the peninsula. The populace was divided into six bone rankings. Any one born into a particular class had no escape from it generation after generation. The rigid classification of social status was instrumental in ensuring dynastic continuity but at the cost of the opportunities for change.

5.   M'ing China's military intervention in Chosôn campaign against Japan was said to have followed from the

brotherly bond where an elder voluntarily takes the responsibility of protecting the younger. In an analytical view, the military intervention was no so much to help Koreans fight against the enemy as its own self protection. Chosôn served as a buffer zone for China which loathed a direct confrontation with Japan. This is exactly what North Korea is to China in the latter's effort to constrain American power in the Pacific region. This very fact is explained by the fact that Chinese troops entered immediately into negotiation with Japanese military leaders for ceasefire during the 1592 invasion. They were more often on-lookers in the armed confrontation between the Korean militia and Japanese forces. It was not Chinese forces but Korean militia which bore the brunt of combats.

6.   The medieval Netherlands was not a centralized kingdom of the sort we are familiar with, each province approximating an independent political unit with provincial sovereignty. Several feudal states, due to flourishing trade, developed to an extent that dismisses the necessity of joining a confederate system. Economically they had outgrown, able to dispense with a federal protection. The Netherlands is a case in point where one ethnic group was divided into two religious groups. See "A Short History of the Netherlands by P.J.A.N. Rietbergen

7.   U.S.A colluded with Soviet Russia to place a liberated Korea under the trusteeship of foreign overseers and Koreans, irrespective of ideological stands, vehemently opposed and declared a manifesto that verified its ability to preside over the history of five dynastic changes through its millennia-old history. The five dynastic changes that correspond to the 25 dynastic changes of China speaks for the ability of Koreans to rule the country for themselves, and the manifesto decried the trusteeship plan as a scheme to prolong the colonial state of Korea. The trusteeship plan was initiated by the United States and accepted by the Soviet Union. The former had an idea of the trusteeship as a defensive mechanism against the perceived scheme of the latter to sovietize Korea. The U.S dropped the trusteeship in dread that it would be a stepping step to sovietization.

8.   The United States came across the idea of trusteeship after it realized the Soviet scheme to sovietize Korea, taking advantage of the continuing turmoil in South Korea. Placing Korea under the trusteeship of great powers, the proponent surmised, will have the effect of blocking the Soviet scheme. Prominent American diplomats – Averill Harriman and George F. Kennan – vehemently opposed to the plan, citing it as a stepping stone to sovietization. The United States backed down from the trusteeship plan and was therefore called a "well-intentioned bumbler."

9.   A tangle of interplays between the United States and Soviet Union does not allow for clarity in holing the former responsible for the division of Korea. There was neither major culprit nor minor culprit. Fixing the turnaround of the situation on the day when the 38th parallel was drawn, the United States could be blamed for the division. But the assessment of the situation cannot be fixed on a particular event. Attention goes to what provoked the United States to draw the line and what motivated the Soviet to belatedly participate in the campaign. Rivalry between the two powers goes back to the time when they were fighting in partnership

against the Axis.

10.   The Russo-Japan War was the armed clash of the two imperialistic powers. Japan, having defeated China, was tightening its grip around the neck of Korea. Korea sought a counter-weight to Japan in the United States, convinced that it would come to rescue according to 1883's Treaty, but met its apathy. It turned to Russian Empire. Since then, Korea increasingly leaned toward Russia. The growing Russian influence exasperated Japan. The two contestants entered a negotiation to draw a line that would indicate the sphere of influence. Japan offered Manchuria to be consigned to Russia, while it has Korea under its own influence. But Russia came up with a counter-proposal which claimed the northern part of Korea above the 39th parallel, rich in mineral resources. The deadlocked negotiation was the detonator for the Russo-Japan War

11.   The author has access to classified materials about the American policies that have bearing on the Korean issues related to the division of Korea. He is picky on the autocratic character of Syngman Rhee insinuating that Korea had an unfortunate encounter with such a character responsible for the tragedy of modern Korean history. The advantage of his work lies in the documentation of historical facts based on concrete evidence. But the way of treating facts seems a bit hued to the progressive perspective of history. He is not free from his own biased value on which to perceive things. The illustration of historical facts even to trivial minutes did more to obfuscate the clarity of the events that led to the division of Korea. His progressive view had a wide following among the progressive elements of Korea, particularly those radical activists defiant against the military regimes in the 1980s.

12.   Materialistic orientation is explained by the worker-employer relationship which was fondly referred to cows-dairymen relationship; "the dairyman feeds his cows more than the maintenance ration since they give him more milk." The materialistic orientation of life lies in "more bread make men work harder. The material orientation of life reflects the oversimplification of diverse social needs. A society which knows only things they feel, see, touch, hear or smell is far from a mature nation that brings physiological tempo in tune with spiritual life.

13.   Juche Sasang literally translates into "self-reliant thought, an outgrowth of Kim Il-sung's desperate device to outlast, shocked by the downfall of his fellow communist countries. North Korea divorced itself from the orthodox communism and adopted its own system, anomalous by any standard of communism. It is Kim's own creation to steer his country free from interventions from outside and hereditary succession of the throne has never seen its parallel in communist societies. In short, Juche thought is an improvised thought to create a dynastic politics, reminiscent of the monarchical kingdom, in the face of the crumbling front of communist societies. The thought marks the paradox of equating absolute subservience – to do as the party expect you to do – and absolute freedom as the master of revolution.

14.   Daehan Jekuk, Grater Han Empire, was declared by King Kojong who was emboldened by Russian backing to put the country on par with China and Japan. It was the time that Japan's victory over China provided

chances to tighten its grip on Korea. Korea sought a counter-veiling force in Russia against the dominant Japan. Korea was not an empire in its own right, but staying as a kingdom might have reduced her into her former self overshadowed between the two towering neighbors. This was the first recognition of the self as an independent nation state equal in status with its neighbors, providing the ground for her assertiveness of interests.

15. Ethnic nationalism attaches great importance to KPG in exile as heir to the defunct kingdom while struggling against the colonial Japan. KPG represents the allied front of all ideological threads, all united under the nationalist front against the colonial power, but it fell short of the unified nationalist front, since the communist nationalists parted company with KPG. The leftists lost a claim to direct descent from the unified front. A hiatus between KPG and the Republic of Korea was filled by a majority of the KPG members involved in the founding of the Republic.

16. The disputed ownership of Tok-do was drawn on a collection of materials by Hosaga Uji, a Japanese-turned Korean scholar who has devoted his studies to the relationship between Korea and Japan. His materials are known to be most reliable. This narrative is summed up from these materials.

17. Jurchens inhabited the eastern part of Manuchuria pitted against Khitans in the western part. Both were the citizens of Koguryô and the succeeding Balhae. After the downfall of Balhae, they were dispersed into nomadic tribes. Once they were reassembled into a unitary monarchy, it became a mighty continental power which tormented Korea. The Chin dynasty sent its forces invading the Chosôn dynasty and extracted a humiliating surrender in 1637. This invasion is marked as the most humiliating surrender in Korean history. They overrode Ming China in 1644 and continued to rule China until 1910. Q'ing China is considered one of twenty five dynasties of China, although it was under Manchu rulers. As they were incorporated into China, their ethnic and cultural distinctions were blurred. The foreign rulers were much more changed by China than they changed the latter..

Chapter

Three

Intellectual Foundation

*We owe boundless gratitude to our parents for the gift of birth and
rearing us. We are born with a duty to care for them in old ages as we
do for our children.*
— *Shiao Ching (Hyo Kyung in Korean)*

Native Thoughts and Confucianism

Indigenous thought of Koreans, as reflected in mythology surrounding the foundation of the first proto-state, sanctifies heaven because early Koreans believed that they had originated in heaven. Its metaphor to heavenly mandates was deduced from the order of the universe, the way in which the universe works. Korean mythology tells how the heavenly prince, Hwanwoong, coveted human society as a place to live in and descended on a northeastern mountain to build the City of Heaven. Ruling over it, he contrived to build an ideal society, the Korean version of utopia, that would be worthy of emulation, for it would bring benefits to all who lived in it. Society in which humans live mirrors heaven, the invariable and sustained order of the cosmos. Embedded within this is a universal continuum in which man is inseparable from nature. All components of the universe are brought into a greater whole, and this causes mankind to exist. The unity of heaven and earth gave mankind a towering stature commensurate with their role as the sole mediator between heaven and earth. Koreans took the totem of bear, erasing distinction between mankind and animals by placing them on one continuum.

The cult of bear indicates the indomitable and inscrutable forces of nature that elude historical validity. Mythology, then, is merely a willful belief in the unbelievable. It is trans-historical in the sense that it is ever present. The idea of a heavenly being coming to earth in the West gives a god with anthropomorphic form as well as creative force. But the heavenly being conceptualized by Koreans enters this world as a remote potentate who rules all things. There is fatalism by enjoining humans to follow Heaven-ordained path. An emphasis on the impersonal and merciless nature of a creator god resonates with the Newtonian "the ruler of the universe" idea most detached from the world of humans. There is no distinction between the spiritual and the natural or between the created and the accidental occurring. The universe is a product of interactions between two opposite forces, Yin and Yang, and the way these two opposites encounter each other is considered to produce a creative force without intention or will. Nature has no teleological end.

The notion of one continuum describes a female bear which became a human by winning a race of endurance against a tiger. Marriage of the heavenly prince to a bear-turned woman gave birth to Tan'gun, the alleged ethnic progenitor of Koreans. Tracing family origins to a sacred animal (or bird) was common in the misty ages of early Koreans, based on a notion of transmutation and reincarnation. This was not limited to Koreans alone; other ethnic groups give historical significance to the animal totems of founding mythologies. Can any reasonable person conceive of a twin suckling a wolf? The ambiguous mystification of family origin that resulted from the other species reflects an attempt to elevate the family over ordinary people, ennobling some to rule by conjuring up extraordinary qualities that set them apart from the pack.

Human-centered thought shares the sacrosanct nature of mankind with the Confucian notion of ennobled mankind. Confucianism has an enlightening effect on man. The gift of one's birth is celebrated and glorified, but resigning oneself to natural growth is not the way to become human. Moral precepts are contrived to characterize man as different from animals. "Great Learning (daehak) postulates that self-cultivation is the very beginning of the way to become a person who will culminate in an impeccable character (Dae In)" (Keum Jang-dae 2006; 29). Nature worship is identified with the cult of humanity in the sense that it gives man a proper dignity to cultivate the self toward the highest version of existence.

Earlier Koreans were ambiguous about distinction between "I" and "you." A strict separation between the two still sounds somewhat awkward or impersonal to contemporary Koreans, since it implies egoism against collective consciousness. In routine conversations, Koreans feel more comfortable with the word "we" than "I". When it comes to referring to the country or people, it is customary for Koreans to say "our people" or "our country." Distinction between "I" and "you" is obscured when it comes to defining interpersonal relationships. "The concept of 'going Dutch" is hard for Koreans to accept, since it draws a line between oneself and the other. "Pay for my own" in a positive light may convey the message of autonomy or independence, but it certainly drives one to become a lonely being, ostracized from friends. Confucianism condemns "self-ego" as evil and celebrates what is good for all"
(Keum Jang-dae, 22)

Unlike Buddhism which transcends the contemporary world, Confucianism has a secular concern for human ethic and accords importance to man as the fabric of society. Nevertheless, both have asceticism in common. Buddhism enjoins earthlings to renounce their secular desires, whereas Confucianism is repressive of individual behavior spurred on by emotional or intuitive impulses. Individual behavior is disciplined through rituals and make man conscious of propriety. Society is defined as spider's web, a network of human relations where individuals are related to one another. The hierarchical arrangement of the social structure and institutions is meant to provide social order. The king stands on the top of the social hierarchy. His heavenly anointment as the ruler raises him to absolutism above the challenges of earthlings. What the ruler is to his subjects parallels what a father is to his children, so the ruler should treat his people as if they were his own siblings. A righteousness associated with heavenly dictum is the guidepost for the ruler's statecraft directed towards the realization of social justice. Moral supremacy enjoins the ruler to self -cultivation toward self-perfection: correcting himself is to straighten matters in the right way, enabling him to perform "virtuous rule."

Confucianism is a collection of the teachings of ancient sages, including Confucius, Mencius, and many others. It is an ascetic morality, postulating the codes of conduct intended to create a grand harmony. Coming into the Song Dynasty, Zhu Xi reinterpreted Confucianism to give it a cosmological backing by relating ethical and social norms to the cosmological principle" (Hahn Woo-keun 1970;194). Man's existence continues not as an individual; man can exist only within the 'between people' framework. And this 'between people' framework raises the visibility of anthropocentrism within Confucianism, thereby striking a cord with ancient Greek philosophy. Aristotle held man to be a political animal and defined "live" as being among men (interhomines esse) and death as ceasing to be among men (interhomines esse desincere). The human finds its raison d'etre in influencing and being influenced by others (Hannah Arendt

1958;7-8). Man, then, is a social animal whose existence is inevitably reliant on inter-dependence.

The Confucian notion of inter-dependence is expressed as the binary-relative relationship such as king and subject, father and son, wife and husband and the like (Kim Jae-un 1991;58). These form the basis of all social relations to follow. The Koreans' view of the world reflects a kind of dichotomized or binary cognitive structure that is conceived in the very abstract over-arching conception of two antipodal forces, Yin and Yang. The Korean perception of nature rejects a heavenly being equated with the creator of universe. Confucianism believes in Heavenly Being that presides over the order of the cosmos, distinct from the concept of an anthropomorphic God. Taekeuk, the equivalent of Hindu rita substitutes for the creative force of God.

Taekeuk begets the binary forces and interactions between the two forces give rise to natural phenomena. "This world view is perceived through the prism of dual elements interacting to create and change the world in a constant dialectical interplay" (Kang Shin-pyo 1983;123-129). Again, "the cosmic force generates natural phenomena, and the five binary relations, perceived to be in harmony with the cosmic order, are the warp and weft that weave social fabric"(Song Young-bae 1994;18). The law of nature is equated with an orderly society based on inequality. Nature abhors equality and inequality is the norm of human life, contradicting Plato's advocacy of equality as the attribute of nature. The ancient belief of Koreans is an anthropocentric interpretation of nature.

The sacrosanct nature of the family gives utmost importance to harmonious relationships among its members in favor of the family's interests. It often makes a family clan a redoubtable power bloc, strong enough to overshadow the ruler. The family is the centerpiece of all human relations, and familial bond extends to a clan, a community, a province and, ultimately, to society. In the time of primitive society, therefore, Koreans had no sense of "I" separate from others. Neither was there the sense of private ownership. Morally defined relationships, when properly observed, bound individuals to a network of relations. "Korean society is network-oriented, and this network is extremely important for Koreans because it is through building and maintaining ties that they order their world and pursue their goals. It is also an important means to build trust" (Lew Seokchoon 2000;126). Imagine a world where we lose touch with each other. Would it not be comforting to restore a stronger sense of community in our lives through greater personal contact with family, friends, and neighbors?

The family in particular was believed to have a high degree of solidarity. This was necessary to ensure hereditary succession into an infinite future. Conversely, the neglect of proper relationships among family members is bound to invite moral decline and with it, the eventual collapse of society. The Confucian belief in the immortality of society evolved from a cycle of status quo that needed to be maintained by resisting change. The Confucian definition of society as an extended family underscores the belief in an unhindered extension of familial relations to a more complicated organization such as society. Idealistically, the moral virtues should facilitate the extension of familial solidarity to social cohesion, establishing a touch stone on which the moral righteousness of mankind's behaviors can be measured. This conceptualization by no means recognizes natural discontinuity between family and larger entities such as state, and consequently it contrasts the Greek notion of distinction between a natural association - the first cycle of life - and political community - the second cycle of life. This notion emphasizes the dichotomy between what is one's own and what is communal. The exaltation of the former over the latter is an open invitation to corruption.

The Confucian notion of "immortality" is predicated on the human capacity to leave its name through immortal things he creates. This concept of immortality bears some semblance to "the Greek's immortality that grew out of their experience of an immortal nature and immortal gods which together surrounded the individual lives of mortal men" (Hanna Arendt 1998, 18). Human life is viewed in the light of a repeating cycle, contrary to the notion of a straight progressivism.

To attain social eminence through one's achievement, according to Korean traditional thought, is the way to leave nonperishable traces that can be perpetually remembered by one's descendants. As a Korean proverb has it, "man leaves his name imprinted on time as a tiger leaves its skin to clothe mankind." Man realizes immortality through his association with nonperishable objects. In the foundation period of the Chosôn Dynasty, Neo-Confucianism fueled the reformative zeal of the ruling elites. As this dissipated into inertia as it struggled to cope with new challenges, the institutional fixation based on Confucian ideals became a drag on progressive changes. The decline of Confucian influence opened a path to a new approach, with a greater concern with effectiveness and egalitarianism, that addressed the problems spawned in the routine round of daily life. New voices were heard, arguing for a realistic approach demanding an end to the formalistic and speculative nature of Neo-Confucianism. The new school of learning blamed neo-Confucianism for inhabiting a tower of speculation, which was apathetic to the pragmatic aspects of lives. It kicked off a process of adapting Neo-Confucianism to fit the indigenous setting of Korea.

Spider's Web: The Five Binary Relationships

The matrix of the five binary relationships, which grew out of the philosophical account of the interactions of the two opposite forces of Yin and Yang, underpins the quintessential quality of human relationships. The moral virtues identified with the five binaries are connecting threads that make the dual forces mutually complementary and tie them together into an abiding existence. These five fundamental relationships underlie the moral values of society that aim at perpetuating the binary bonds, once the two have been paired. The family is thought to be the very foundation of all social relationships. The binary bonds, contrived to ensure harmonious order in agrarian society, have left their traces which find manifestation in their pervasive influence on modern Korea.

Ruler and Subjects

According to Confucian tenet, the king is ordained by heaven to rule on its behalf, and his rule over the state is a response that realizes the heavenly mandates. What the ruler is to their subjects is what the father is to children. The heaven-bestowed authority demands that the ruler be a moral paragon for other people to emulate. Monarchical authority is maintained through loyalty paid by subjects to the ruler. Loyalty is a voluntary action of subjects distinguished from uncritical obedience or adulation. This paired bond binds the ruler and his subjects into a rock solid unity that can weather the test of time. Loyalty is much more than a mere obedience: the ruler is not only obeyed but is respected, honored and served. The loyalty of subjects is reciprocated by the ruler bent to govern his subjects justly and correctly. What we call "minbon" means that people matters most in the mind of the ruler and that in this response they honor their obligations to serve the ruler in good stead. The moral mandate of the ruler to benefit his subjects entails a set of behavioral norms that are identified for him to internalize toward self perfection.

The modern version of the ruler-subject relation is the relationship between a paymaster and employees. Employees are perpetually indebted to their paymaster for the opportunity to work and this recognition is expressed in an abiding sense of loyalty that promises one's life-long commitment to one's master. The traditional concept of loyalty to an 'employer' or 'master' involves more than just a contract-based working relationship, since it entails an emotional aspect of the relationship. The concept of life-long employment is something characteristic of an intimate relation between an employer and the employees, in which emotional concerns can obscure the rule of law. Ideally, employer or master is a fatherly figure who should have paternalistic concern for his employees. Workers find security not so much in a contract as in a personal relationship with the boss. A worker's life-long commitment to one master presupposes the ability to resist what may be lucrative temptations, and the durability of the relationship cannot be explained by a relationship sealed by a contract alone. Any relationship that results from working together is sure to entail a more humane, emotional and personal aspect that survives a working relationship stipulated and controlled by law. The two dimensions of a relationship - public (or working) and private (or emotional) - feed off each other to make for more solid bonds. It is for this reason that distinction between the private and public domains in Korean corporations is very often obscured, if not consciously overlooked.

Emphasizing the public (or working) aspect of a relationship within an organization is often frowned upon as an impersonal act or an indication of a relationship deprived of a warm heart or sympathetic understanding. This accounts for the prevalence of emotion over rationality, objectivity and legal constraints. A member of a corporation who adheres to the rule of law in every triviality may thus be ridiculed and marginalized as an outcast. A vertical relation between a senior and junior is based on reciprocity: one's loyalty to a senior is reciprocated by the latter's favor and tolerance. Such moral reciprocity diminishes the importance of the rule of law in conducting public affairs. Often, emotion dominates the rule of law and many will find it more convenient to abide by moral obligations.

The ambiguity between private and public domains is reflected in a tendency to personalize the leadership of an organization. An enduring personal relation depends on displays of unfailing loyalty, even at the cost of self-interest, to the boss. Politicians are fraternized around a factional leader and their loyalties are for the person in charge rather than to a political belief or creed. A leader of political party, particularly when he was the founder of a party, is likely to abuse his authority as if he owned the party. Such a privatization of leadership is characteristic of a hierarchical structure where the focus of loyalty is often a person. In Korean politics, a party represents neither a class nor a creed: it is a faction organized around a leader. Loyalty to a person is the major determinant for one's political fate, and one's success in career depends to a large measure on the demonstration of a selfless loyalty to the leader.

The life-long loyalty of party members dims the leader's consciousness of public commitment and this encourages wanton judgment about his status as a public figure. The leadership of every Korean president was marred by personal concern that takes precedence over public interest. He is safely protected by a human barrage made of a few intimates or confidants, and the result is seclusion from the masses of the people. Authoritarianism and charisma are the outgrowths of the tendency to privatize leadership. Loyalty in a privatized vertical relationship structure establishes the view that seniors are moral paragons with such characters that inspire others to emulate. What the boss says is accepted as an undeniable truth to those lower down the ladder of hierarchy. In return for loyalty, a leader owes his subjects a paternalistic concern that is manifest, for example, in his promise of life-long employment that is rooted in a continuing personal relationship. Such a paternalistic care explains the characteristic reluctance of Korean employers to sack their employees though they have the legal right to do so. If someone is sacked, he regards it as unjustifiable in light of his whole-hearted devotion to a corporation and is more defiant and explodes with uncontrollable fury. When a company has to fire someone, it is done in a subtle way – by relegating the employee into a less important post or posting him to a local branch office –so as to minimize his anger.

The society that values human relationship will rarely see a subordinate spill the beans about a superior in public, much less to file a lawsuit claiming malfeasance or misconduct, which might have tarnished the boss' image. In other words, juniors are tolerant of their boss' wrong doings and of their transgression of social justice to such an extent that puzzles their Western working partners. The sense of loyalty douses any impulse to be candid and honest for fear of a negative impact on the credentials of their superiors. When it comes to serving as a witness in legal suits which involves superiors, the witness credibility can be doubted, as his mind is dictated by what is thought to be good for his superior, even scorning the rule of law.

The Korean version of loyalty is brought into a clear focus in comparison with the Japanese version of loyalty as expressed in the conduct codes of Samurai, warriors in profession, which might well be considered the equivalent of the knights of medieval European fiefdoms. In feudalistic Japan where wars frequently transpired between fiefdoms, the loyalty of Samurai(warriors) to their master was selfless. Their readiness to renounce their life for the master, however, led to treason when their martial arts expertise in battles was laid idle or where they were insulted or had their reputation slurred. Loyalty that knows nothing but self sacrifice becomes treacherous under the very circumstances that justified it.

The Korean version of supreme concern for filial obligations is lost in "the layered loyalty of Japanese that goes up to the Emperor as the supreme being so sacred and inviolable as to command absolute loyalty of all, including the feudal lords and shogun's" (Beasley W.G 1994;26). Loyalty to the Emperor is the supreme virtue coming from an ecstatic contemplation of a fantasized Good Father untainted by secular contacts. Nothing comes up to challenge the divine status.[1]

Husband and Wife

The traditional relationship between husband and wife features sexual distinction that permeates space, role, status, education and many others. Even the way house was built reflects spatial distinction, say, between an inner quarter and outer one, and female members were stuck within the former, minimizing their contacts with outsiders. A Korean admonition bans boys and girls over seven years of age from sitting next to each other. The cosmological view of nature does not differentiate gender. The notion therefore views marriage as the merging of two personalities into one body and one mind. In reality, different personalities rarely form a perfect match that requires or allow the complete subsuming of different personalities into one. No marriage is free of feuds, dissent or tensions. Neo-Confucianism established "a hierarchical order between husband and wife to ensure the proper functioning of human order and conceptualized spatial division that assigned women to inner and men to outer domain of works"(Martina Deuchler 1983;5).

Division of gender roles was based on the belief that a binary relationship maintained at a certain distance invites decorum so that one views another with deference. Confucianism itself draws on the cosmological principle of one continuum in prescribing its normative values, and its attempt to keep husband and wife at a distance seems to be at odds with this cosmological view. The moral concept of spatial division involves an institutional device to maintain distance, in which the division of gender role goes hand in hand with gender hierarchy.

The early notion was that "distinction between public and private realms is the root cause of women's subordination to men" (Rosaldo Michelle Zimbalist 1974;42), and this still commands a wide following.[2] The division of gender role is an institutionalized social construct designed to compensate for intimacy that erases differences between husband and wife. It underscores the concept of propriety in the sense that it formalizes and ritualizes the relationship between husband and wife. Less stress is laid on manifest affection in the Confucian concept of husband-wife relationship than propriety that seemingly defies emotional expressions. The formal and ritualized relationship is impersonal, and no affection is shown at the surface. The idea behind this is that propriety brings their hearts closer to each other and thus perpetuates this binary relationship. The moral injunction is that the closer the relationship, the greater the need to be decent and discreet in act.

Koreans carry strong sediments of their past, characterizing Korean women as distinct from their counterparts in the West because of their greater awareness of role division by gender inherent in the traditional family which is the citadel of the Confucian values. This awareness is more evident in high-class people, but it is fading out in intensity with the atomization of family life in modern Korea. Likewise, the Chinese writer Lin Yu-tang (1895-1976), despite the fact that he was much westernized in his thinking, lauded the beauty of women, especially when she was at domestic work.

Nowadays, there are myriad professional Korean women. They enjoy the same treatment as male counterparts within corporations, although they still suffer discriminatory treatments in some aspects of life. They remain well aware of their roles vis-a-vis what they expect their husband to do at home. When it comes to making important decisions, a professional woman will step aside, allowing her husband to call the shots, although her opinions may be solicited in the process of decision making. Role distinction, initially intended to ensure peace and harmony at home, has resulted in what seems to be a perpetual dichotomy into male and female domains of work, each called 'sanctum" in the sense that the dividing line was hardly crossed. Korean women are culturally disposed against encroaching upon man's sanctum, and injunction such as to "never cross the border" reinforced the manhood characteristic of a patriarchal culture.

Role distinctions reflect the Confucian notion of natural inequality. "The hierarchical order between the sexes is cosmologically sanctioned and is imperative for the proper functioning of the human order (Martina Deuchler 1983,54). Although each side asserts its domain of work, the wife is brought under the husband within the family—and, as such, she is often likely to be abused. Inequality is justified if it serves harmony and peace within the home. Two leaders in a family were considered the cause for endless altercations, and Korea abounds with aphorisms against loud-voiced and dominant women as an ill omen of family doomed to collapse. Role distinctions shaped in the context of long-practiced, prejudiced self-fulfillment expectations are frozen into absolute beliefs in what each gender can or cannot do. This misleads our expectations of what each gender is capable of doing in their innate or developed capacities. Women's activities, in particular, were for centuries circumscribed by the bias of performance expectations. A few decades ago, a women soldier on the battle field was inconceivable.

An emphasis on manhood characterizes Korean culture. Masculinity is fostered through women's expectation of what men ought to do or to be like, and is epitomized by taciturnity, equanimity, and tolerance. Masculinity enjoins men to distance themselves from domestic trivialities or titillating details. A fastidious man is frowned upon and ridiculed by women as a small fry. Men of whimsical temperament have nowhere to go in traditional and contemporary Korean society. A hen-pecked husband is not expected to reach this ideal manhood, for a decent Korean man is not supposed to be attentive and accommodating to wife's demands. A man who boasts of his wife's merit is taunted or ridiculed as a dimwit. Likewise, role expectations give men expectations of what women should be like. Confucianism untiringly depicts womanly characters and womanly ways as the ideal norms for behavior. A woman was supposed to follow a prescribed path to become a virtuous woman ideally vested with an assortment of affection, warm heart, unadorned and clean appearance, discreet and prudent manners, less talk, and chastity. Going astray from this beaten path condemns a woman to social chastisement. Considered in a broader context, role distinctions are intended to idealize women as an exemplary of unblemished character distinguished from man wallowing in secular affairs and subject to moral contamination.

The Korean woman in a traditional family was an angel, depicted as the heart of the family, comparable to English women fantasized in Victorian novels, secluded from the sordid world. Masculinity in a traditional Korean family is manifested in the figure of the sunbi, a Confucian scholar who did not covet a prestigious post, though vested with competency. Rather, his taste for study and erudition made him revered as a behavioral model. Devotion to study distanced him from the sordid realities of earning money, since to be otherwise would sully the purity of his mind. He was proud that he was unable to read a balance sheet. In his family, a wife had to labor like a horse to earn livelihood to keep her children and family. But, incompetent husbands rarely appreciated the self-sacrificing devotion of women.

The role domain marked for wives is justified on the ground that it protects them from possible abuse by her authoritarian husband, thus minimizing the deleterious effects of male dominance within the family. It also explains how a powerless daughter-in-law becomes a formidable mother-in-law, a guardian of the family clan. Such a role was dramatized into novels which portrayed them as a dignified grandmother, a woman of immense insight, ability and devotion, able to preserve the family through the sea of storms that it faced. In such a family, a husband who squandered his youth with wandering lust is a pale figure before the lofty tower of his wife. The woman's role in maintaining a cultural ideal and ensuring a familial stability at the height of social disintegration cannot be glossed over.

Rapid social transformation has made changes in role distinctions tangible. The family has been squeezed into a smallest possible unit, and this effaces the need for role distinctions within the family. Role distinctions fade so that role switching or role sharing has become familiar, particularly among young couples. The pace of change in role perception dazzles our minds, so much that it widens the inter-generational gap. Many newlywed couples consider role switching to be unavoidable or implacable within a nuclear family, particularly when both husband and wife are employed. Husbands consider helping their wives in domestic chores as a matter of daily life, although not necessarily desirable. The problem is that role change is a cause for altercation, often involving in-laws within a tightly-knit familial structure. Although a couple lives at a distance from their respective parents, the tight mother-son bond keeps the mother revolving around and poking her nose into every nook of domestic life that takes place, no matter how far they are distanced from each other. No mother is happy with her son cleaning dishes in the presence of his wife, even though it is justified by the latter's occupation with something else. So far as role distinctions are concerned, the generational gap appears to be becoming more serious than the gender gap. There is no guarantee that a young woman will not over time turn into a nosy mother-in-law, although she favored role sharing when she was young.

The son with a strong sense of filial obligations and his attitude toward his wife in particular shape an elderly woman of whimsical character. For the husband, his wife is only tangential to 'the circle of kin, for his parents remain a central concern. A man of strong moral character with a high sense of filial obligation accepts his mother's decision for him to divorce his wife for a simple reason that she was infertile. Many couples bound by affection have to tearfully part in the face of an intransigent mother.

Although divorced, they may continue to meet surreptitiously far from the mother's watchful eyes. The husband's love for his wife, no matter how passionate it is, is obscured with age by the beck and call of an intolerable mother.

An American veteran who spent years of miserable life as a prisoner of war uttered words of excitement when reunited with his wife and children. "How delighted I am to see my beloved ones, my wife and children." But a Korean returnee in a similar situation would express the bulk of his feelings toward his parents, repressing his feelings for his wife, wary of the watchful eyes of his jealous mother. Apparently, filial obligations to parents leaves a wife as little more than a stranger, at least ostensibly in the public vista. Even if a marriage is happy, a wife is rarely placed in the circle of intimates. A man may elevate his relations to his wife to the level of his feelings towards parents, but it is not so openly made in public speeches, notably in the presence of his mother. A Confucian credo of silent reserve still works to constrain emotional display toward his beloved one in contrast to more articulate Western social behaviors. Members of a family think it irksome to express love, respect and other high emotions to one another.

The process of democratization and industrialization has brought about a dramatic turnaround in Koreans perceptions of the husband and wife relationship. A noticeable change attendant to the trend towards nuclear families is a shift from hierarchical to conjugal ties. Korean women who were of university age in the 1980s, the era of protest against the authoritarian regimes, were highly conscious of equality and freedom, challenging the patriarchal culture of family. Many Korean women were thereby emboldened to challenge the established order and assert their self identity. They refused to become another asexual and self-sacrificing women like their mothers. Their participation in social and economic life elevated their status, and some reaped success, as the authority of husbands was obscured as a bread winner. They are no longer objects to be possessed, dominated and conquered by their husbands, with the exception of a few at the base of the social ladder. There is a lot that formerly would have been considered masculine in the way young wives talk and behave. The women's movement is booming with open discourses on female identity, feminine waywardness and sexual subjectivity that would have been driven to furtiveness. The generation gap ultimately explains difference in the women' perceptions of their self-identity in Korea, while race does in the United States.

Parents-children

Filial duty is the most fundamental moral obligation of offspring to parents. This duty takes precedence over others since it extends to other relations. The extension of filial duty to the ruler leads to loyalty, and a broader interpretation of filial duty heightens concern for propriety or manners in relation to seniors in age and position. When filial duty extends to relations between peers and equals, it becomes identified with fidelity and righteousness. What precisely is meant by filial duty varies depending on the nature of the human relations involved. The primordial form of filial duty is found in the relationship between parents and offspring. Hence, the preface of Xia Jing (Hyokyung – filial piety - in Korean) reads, "We owe to our parents boundless gratitude for the gift of birth and nurturing. We are born with a duty to provide for our parents' comfort and attend to their needs with utmost attention."

Every country has a normative value that celebrates, albeit in a varying degree, filial duties to parents. What characterizes the Korean notion of filial duty is that it celebrates the self–sacrifice of offspring for the well-being of parents. Those who had done exemplary duties involving self-sacrifice receive social acclaim as a monument that glorifies the hereditary line of the family. In search for a spouse for marriage, it is customary to favor somebody identified with such a glorified family. This means that anybody born from a widow who was remarried is frowned upon. Divorce may have been viewed as a matter of daily life in many industrialized countries, but divorce in Korea exposes children to be cold-shouldered, if not being scoffed at by their peers. Children are traumatized by the divorce or separation of their parents.

Self-sacrifice is clearly shown in the well-known folk tale of Shimcheong. Shimcheong was a lass growing up in a coastal village, whose mother died while giving birth to her. Her blind father carried the baby on his back crying out for milk. Village women, moved by compassion, breastfed the baby. As she grew up, she took care, with great devotion, of her blind father. The village ritually sacrificed a virgin to the water god as a ritual to ensure the safety of fishermen, and Shimcheong offered herself as a propitiatory sacrifice, in return for a reward that would provide for her father's living. The water god, moved by her filial piety, sent her back to the land. This story ends up with the reunion of father and daughter. When the father met his daughter who was thought to have died, the impossible pleasure shocked him to open his eyes. Her father miraculously restored his sight thanks to his daughter's filial duty. The tale teaches that self-sacrifice for one's parents will surely lead to blessings.

The parent-child relationship is part of an ordained continuum, and patriarchal family inheritance denotes the timelessness of the father-son relationship. The Confucian classic had it thus: "We receive our bones from our father and flesh from our mother. The flesh gives birth, growth, temporal needs and emotional satisfaction, but the flesh rots away, while the bones endure. The bones are the structure, that is, a continuum of the father-son relation, stretching back to time immemorial and stretching into the infinite future". The father-son relationship is like a flowing stream. "Your parents flow into you and you flow into your children." There is a mystical strength in this flow from parents to sons which makes life more meaningful and blissful.

A man's single and most important duty in life, according to the old tenets, is to father children, while a woman's duty is to bear them. Parents work like a slave to provide for their children, ensure their proper upbringing and do whatever is required to make them succeed in life. They in return enjoy total loyalty from their adult children in return. Until recently, children from needy underclass families outperformed those from well-to-do families in school. These were filial children who were most profoundly motivated by compassion for the sufferings and the pitiful state of their parents. Their own success, they thought, would atone for the past, wiping away all the ancestral pains. Every biography of an achiever is punctuated by a deep sense of indebtedness to their parents as the major source of courage and inspiration.

Filial duty goes beyond the life-time of one's parents. After a parents dies, filial duty takes the form of ancestor worship, accompanied by dutiful performances of sacrifice rites. So far as filial duty is concerned, there is no distinction between the living and dead parents, and the posterity pledge to continue the performance of filial duty and ritual service. The continuity of filial duty beyond life time breeds a sense of inter-generational responsibility.

Elder-Younger siblings

Reverence characterizes the relationship between the elder and younger brothers (or sisters), and this is regarded as a way to maintain orderly relations between siblings sharing the same blood. Propriety formalizes this relationship, binding brothers to a vertical bond that endures. The eldest brother is the symbol of authority, as heir to the family leadership. He is austere in manner and dignified in bearing, awing younger ones into paying respect and addressing him with honorifics. Conversations between brothers are carried in a way that differentiates status based on seniority. There seems to be much formality permeating brotherly relationships, particularly when the age gap is wide. The seemingly rigid and stern attitude of elders dismays foreigners who often feel there is impersonality and the lack of affection between brothers. But, for all the impersonality on the surface, elder brothers lavishly pour love on his younger siblings. Impersonality is the surface but affection is hidden beneath the surface.

In the old days, reticence and restraint were emphasized to deter the eruption of emotions. The vertical relationship gives elders a greater sense of responsibility for younger siblings, acting on behalf of the father. The absence of a father requires a greater self sacrifice of elders for the wellbeing of younger siblings. An immature elder fathers younger siblings while parentless children stick together, refusing to be adopted into non-relative families. What troubles the orphaned children is the fear that they may be dispersed when adopted into families with whom they have no formal relationship. The notion of family integrity is firmly embedded in the minds of these children.

Reverence goes beyond blood relations to render Koreans manner-conscious in the company of seniors in a social network. Reverence to elders is supposed to extend to senior relatives and superiors in school, organizations and society at large. In an extended social network, Koreans are keenly interested in the age or position of any person they associate with, and their first questions on meeting somebody revolve around age, status, and position. This baffles foreigners who feel them as intrusive into their personal matters. It seems to them that Koreans are poking their noses into private realms with no sense of embarrassment. A slip of the tongue becomes a frequent cause for altercations between seniors and juniors. In school, a single year age gap manifested in a higher grade is enough for an elder to require proper conduct from a younger. A junior failing to show proper manners to a senior– associated, in large measure, with the failure to use proper honorifics - incurs the wrath of the latter, occasionally leading to physical punishment, all of which is justified by the school's unwritten law.

Korean children are well disciplined, but they deserve this word when it is confined to hierarchical relations. Manners are proportionate to one's perception of the status or position of a person one is addressing or interacting with within an organization of a close circle of intimates. A Korean conscious of required propriety to his senior within an organization may go wild in relation to seniors in age outside the group of familiar faces. Koreans are blamed for the lack of manners when they behave outside the circle of intimates, where their behavior is considered imprudent and rude, and their words truculent. The hierarchical structure of relationship breeds durable brotherly bonds, but it also creates a somewhat parochial character which accounts for a low threshold of tolerance when interacting with outsiders.

Friend-Friend

Fidelity guides relationships between friends. Once friendship has been cultivated, it is desired that the friendship should be built on a rock of fidelity to endure. The Korean concept of friendship puts emphasis on consistency and timelessness and is, for this reason, referred to as a tree deeply rooted underground not to be swayed by the wind. The cultivation of friendship itself is a carefully selective process, and the Korean concept of friendship has depth and roots which keep it from being swayed by the vagaries of situation.

In contrast, the American concept of friendship is considered to be more like seeds scattered in the wind. They move from one place to another, giving no time for them to take roots and bear fruits. Koreans look upon such a concept of friendship as superficial and fleeting. Friendship in Korea is deep, but it is parochial in the sense that it is limited to a certain circle of people. Beyond the circle of association, Koreans tend to be impersonal and remiss. Friendship in the American sense is considered shallow but mobile and pervasive: Westerners treat strangers with a degree of intimacy. To Koreans, breaking up friendships gives a visceral pain or emotional explosions, as if they were bound by a romantic tie. Koreans' timeless and parochial concept of friendship is at odds with the American ephemeral and pervasive concept. As observed elsewhere, friendship is pervasive and expandable across national or ethnic borders, and so the moral demand that inter-personal relations be based on fidelity will finds resonance in the minds of Americans. But, the Korean sense of friendship tends to dwell within a circle of intimates or peers and rarely expand over this bound. Friendship is multiplied by being shared in fortunes and misfortunes, and such an experience is made possible in a closed circle. The human circles of daily association deter the expansion of friendship to larger groups in Korea.

Parochial networks of association creates an impenetrable crust that thwarts outsiders trying to develop an intimate relationship. Such group solidarity gives rise to informal groups within an organization; Koreans work within a narrow circle of classmates, hometown pals or those who shared the same religious creed. The proliferation of these informal groups occasionally distracts one's sense of group loyalty when one is torn between the requirements inherent in maintaining several groups. There remains a greater tendency for Koreans to form molecular groups and this imposes difficulty in expanding the circle of association into larger organizations. Parochialism breeds a depth of relationship but hinders the expansion of the relationship.

The Moral Characters of an Awakened Man

The Confucian view of social order as harmony with the lex naturalis created another set of moral characteristics, the so-called "four beginnings" of cultivating ideal moral characters, namely; humaneness, righteousness, propriety, and wisdom. A human is a moral being and what results from the four beginnings represents the ideal characters that man aspires to cultivate. "Compassion for a wretched soul leads one to warm his heart to help. A man shameful of his misconduct strives to correct his behavior. A high regard for others makes one deferential and conscious of manners. An ability to discern "wrong" from "right" requires wisdom, and man ought to be prudent about his behaviors" (Song Young-bae 1994;221). Frequently, "reliability" is added to the list, making it into the so-called "five constants" that refer to an ideal state of mind. These characters, although occasionally spurred on by motives based on emotion, become emotional neutral. While the five human relations denote connective threads binding individuals in personal and social relationships, the constants stand for the characters of a morally cultivated man. The five relations and five constants are value-laden; they represent a set of behavioral or attitudinal norms that guide the cultivation of the human mind. While the five relations stipulate fundamental codes of conduct for social relations, the five constants point to the direction one should take toward perfection of the self.

The five moral characters belong to "Li," meaning the principled, original or undisturbed nature of mind, representing the inner nature of all things. Mencius said "Man's nature is purely good by birth."The nature of mind is disturbed and blurred by the Seven Feelings, desire, hate, love, fear, grief, anger and joy. These feelings are called "Gi", the initial response to a given situation or stimulus. "Li" tells the way to go, and "Gi" gives the force of going along the way. Li and Gi are complementary to the point of being virtually monistic. Equilibrium between the two leads to harmony, the universal path. "The condition before the seven feelings are aroused is called equilibrium; after they are aroused and each attains proper measure, it is called harmony. Equilibrium is the great foundation of the universe: harmony is its universal path" (Michael Carlton 1994, xxvii).

The first character to cultivate is In (Chinese Chen, Japanese Chin) which translates as humaneness or warmth of the heart. Who would leave a forlorn wretch to be taken by somebody else? Compassion is the beginning of warming one's heart to help others, and such a sympathetic trait characterizes humans as different from animals. Nonetheless, what is meant by the term goes beyond the bound of humaneness. "Confucius defines In as an willingness to constrain one's desire and act with warm concern for the good of others" (translated from Song Young Bae 1994;47). The essence of "acting with warm concern" is deference to others and, viewed in a broad context, this is coterminous with propriety. This notion finds its manifestation in the Analects of Confucius: "Treat every man as a big guest to your house. When ruling the state, treat people as you do your ancestors. Don't force others to do things you don't wish for yourself" (translated from Song Young -bae;57).

Confucius saw the warmth of human mind as an innate trait of man and Mencius developed this concept into "heaven-given goodness"(Lee Won Sul 1990;97), hidden under secular desires, opposed to Christianity's original sin, imperfection, and infantile dependence. In is something incomplete, that accompanies man from birth to death. Confucianism strikes the same chord as does the Illuminist philosopher's cult of reason, with confidence in man's ability to reach perfection. Christianity, on the other hand, perpetuates childhood throughout life, arguing that perfection is achieved only by dependence on God.

In, comparable to Ralph Emerson's puritan divinity of the human mind, is muddied and obscured by secular desires and ambitions. Buddhism echoes the Confucian character through "benevolence' but this definition broadens the warmth of heart beyond man to all creatures. Buddhism sees the cultivation of this virtue as leading to personal salvation, transcending a cycle of re-birth giving rise to all sufferings of man in this world. Confucianism sees In as goodness to be reciprocated, leading, ideally, to the wellbeing of man in society and to social stability. Where do social evils come from, if In is embedded in the human mind? Here, the role of education assumes greater importance, for social evils come from ignorance. Education was regarded as something like honing a stone until it radiates its luster.

The internalization of In is only possible in tandem with Eui (Chinese Ii, Japanese Gi) or "righteousness." If one does not have a feeling of shame and dislike for evil, he is not human, according to Mencius. Eui denotes the sense of righteousness which keeps a man from shameful or malicious acts. Viewed in a broader context, righteousness is equated with social justice that guides statecraft in a right direction, but this concept has no escape from parochialism, when it is related to the five connective threads: an action performed for group solidarity or group interest is justified, even if it is at odds with a greater social good. The behavioral manifestations of Eui are honesty, accountability, self-control, and transparency, and readiness to fight for a righteous cause even if risking one's life. The political meaning of Eui, though, varies depending on the collective entity being served. The art of ruling a state is guided by the "heavenly way" - perceived as the righteous way equated with social justice. Heavenly way enjoins the ruler to ensure harmony between man and the cosmos while a ruler loses his credibility when he turns away from the cosmos. Heaven justifies the termination of his rule.

Virtue is associated with goodness; hence a so-called "virtuous rule" was an idealized form of statecraft guided by Eui." Virtuous rule means the art of ruling in conformity with heavenly mandates that meet the harmonious satisfaction of upper and lower peoples"(Tran. from Song Young-bae 1994;38). In a broader sense, Eui denotes righteousness or justice, but, when applied to a group, Eui means one's unfailing commitment to a group or faction which is not necessarily congruous with a greater social goodness. Inter-personal relations define Eui in terms of an enduring bond between men and a relation of an individual to a group that withstands the test of time. Honesty, truth and transparency are obscured by a greater concern for human bonds. A man of Eui is not supposed to break with a group to which he belongs. With the intervention of humaneness, Eui becomes laden with emotion, dulling one's sense of objectivity. At this point, Eui embraces a steady and fast commitment to human bonds and to organizations. Breaking a relationship between a senior and junior or between equals is regarded as a disgraceful transgression of Eui. Being turncoat remains a permanent blot in one's career, subject to public recrimination when a person seeks public appointment. In a parochial sense, Eui is equated with justice one considers worth fighting for, even to the degree of sacrificing one's life. Such a notion runs high within a highly cohesive group when it comes to competing with another group. Gangsters may lose themselves in fighting for the honor of their group in the name of Eui, and this indicates that Eui can be detrimental to the public goodness.

Ye (Chinese lie) is a set of behavioral or attitudinal patterns which are ritualized and formalized by deference for others. Deference for others enjoins one to exercise self-control or self-discipline, as manifested in civilized conducts and demeanor. Socialization plays a role as a form of social control, enabling man to live together peacefully in the world of others. Man needs the culture that nature brings for survival, and culture involves the renunciation of instinctual impulses, that is equated with self control. Deference for others presupposes that human character is good by birth, since it is bestowed by heaven at birth. The purity of humane character lose its luster in secular human interactions that expose social evils, and self-cultivation brings Ye into play when it is normally concealed behind the deep layers of consciousness. As such, the search for the innate good of human nature provides the starting point for developing Ye. The Confucian idea contradicts Freud's social control from a darker vision of instincts. Drawing heavily on the Darwinian metaphor of his day, Freud portrayed humankind "as only incompletely evolved, torn by a fundamental rift between bestial motives and civilized conduct and demeanor, between an animal nature and cultural aspirations. "

Confucianism regards Ye as "an idealistic social order"(Lee Won Sul 1992;97) and human observance of it characterizes mankind as distinct from animals. Going further, Confucian literati eulogize Ye as if it were the supreme goal of mankind, the highest self version man aspires to realize. Confucianism emphasizes that the more complicated the ritualistic patterns, the more civilized the society becomes. When a society has developed a culture of elaborate rituals, ritual knowledge constitutes significant cultural capital and can be used as a source of authority. Confucian emphasis on the ritual and formal aspect of propriety blurs the vision of reality or substance. Formality and face-saving take precedence over substance in political bickering, this engendering the metaphorical expression of "the tail wags the body."

Ji (Chinese Qi) or wisdom is another guide to human behavior. The disposition to approve and disapprove is the beginning of acquiring wisdom. "Learning" is to work the mind within itself, not necessarily drawing on the mirror-imaging role of the mind. The so-called "great awakening" stressed in Confucian cognition is different from Rene Descarte's experimental theory. Ji involves subjective meditation to discriminate between right and wrong. Education is an on-going process of becoming a person, moving toward the highest version of the self. Cultivation of character is referred to as the grinding of a gem stone to get at the shining surface of it. The traditional orientation of education toward self perfection contracts today's education of forcibly feeding knowledge.

The Confucian term of wisdom refers to erudition of a general nature, and does not relate to specific aspects: it lacks a sense of analytical or inductive reasoning. It was far removed from the absolute belief in reason, as enshrined in Illuminist thought, known to stress its role in sharpening human potential into unlimited ability. Whatever the pattern of learning, Confucianism makes much of the motive found in a person who has exemplary behavior, and this is particularly characteristic of a stratified society whose sages command an absolute following. However, the meditative concept of learning, by engrossing oneself in moral debates and character formation, darkens the scientific vision of knowledge, lacking Bacon's inductive theory and Rene Descarte's deductive theory in post-Renaissance Europe. Knowledge was identified with virtue. It was an abstraction of what came from acquiring a new thing while virtue means deed. One who possesses knowledge was supposed to behave with decency and goodness to others.

The last of the five contestants is Sin that is equated with fidelity that governs the binary relationship between friends. The reciprocity of fidelity is highly visible between friends within small groups but reduces as the circle of intimates enlarges. The resulting intimacy of two characters invariably emphasizes emotional aspects of the bond and makes it deep and parochial. Such a friendship fuses "I" and "you" into one, the friends clinging together and dependent on each other to a point that erases differences. Trust merges two characters into one so that all fortunes or misfortunes are shared. The degree of trust is possible only when one accepts the other in wholeness or as an alter-ego. Emotional fusion is what friendship is all about and there cannot be anything else. Once trust has been built into a person, it remains fast and steady, no matter whatever happens to blur his credibility later. The flipside of emotional dominance is the temptation to consider inter-personal relationships in terms of total goodness or total badness, a matter that contradicts the selective trust of man, based on cold calculations of personality traits that can be seen and judged. No man is good in every aspect of his being; he may be good in creative work but lack his credibility. The selective trust of a person is the measure of one's maturity, and modern society makes it imperative to be selective about what aspect of a person to trust. Diffusive trust brings an unendurable pain to those who suffered broken relations. It may lead one to commit suicide out of frustration especially when one's acceptance of the other in wholeness is not reciprocated by the other.

Despite its emphasis on shin as a desirable social norm, Francis Fukuyama classifies Korea as a non-trust society in contrast with the high trust society of Japan. His classification may be based on the Korean trend to form molecular groups that tend to exhibit group egotism. Koreans rarely expand the network of trust to more diffusive groups governed by the rule of law and rationality. This is exemplified by the general reluctance of Korean business concerns to open their doors to professionalized managers. No Korean want to face the risk of employing somebody whose trustiness has not been verified. The strong fraternity within molecular groups breeds exclusiveness against those from outside the groups.

The Japanese trust network has a different historical background. Before Japan became a nation state, each fiefdom functioned as the lowest unit of communal living unlike the family clans of Korea, where all were tied to familial fraternity. The feudal lord of Japan functioned as the patriarchal authority, caring for all communal members as if they were his own siblings. The lord-subject relation was bound by paternalistic care which was to be reciprocated by a life-long loyalty of people. The fraternity unit of Japan was much broader than the sphere of blood relatives and hometown pals characteristic of Korea. Therefore, trust has an appeal for larger groups or more diffusive circles of associations. A society built on pervasive fidelity is considered to be healthy and solid. From the Confucian viewpoint, the cultivation of humaneness, righteousness, propriety and wisdom conspire to contribute to the cultivation of fidelity. By virtue of the inter-relatedness between these elements a reliable man is supposed to have all of these virtues.

The five matrix view of the world, as we have discussed, expects human relations to apply to social relations. Man is part of nature, and the view of man as a continuum of nature collides with the Illuminist's advocacy of the dichotomy between man and nature and between subject and object. While the Korean view fostered a sense of fear before a mysterious nature, the Western view inspires an intrepid man to encroach upon and fashion nature into its own needs. Restraint and self debasement before a formidable nature are reflected in oriental artifacts. By analogy, attention is given to the low-squatting straw-thatched huts dotting the rural landscape. They were concealed behind hills, as if they were shying away from being seen. Oriental paintings leave part of the landscape mystified to inspire conjecture as to its meaning in comparison with the realistic depictions of Western paintings. Part of the painting remains hazy or blank, as if it chose to remain congruous with a mystified nature. Nature worship led to the analogy of the ruler to heaven: he was anointed to be the lode star guiding the path in the dark, and his act and decision whatsoever commanded an absolute following. The morally awakened few were entrusted to rule a perpetually depoliticized majority.

The Asian view of cosmic order stresses harmony with nature. The world abounds in symbols that reflect the cosmic order. The palace of the Q'ing emperor (China), for example, had 365 rooms, the number of days in a year. The colors of the armed forces carried a picture of the celestial world and the emperor's costumes were embroidered with the sun, moon, clouds and dragons. The nature-oriented outlook, Max Weber argues, created a patriarchal bureaucracy, and bureaucratization under a patriarchal authority tended to stifle individual creativity. It is within such a gigantic system of governance that a certain set of group norms emerged, subjugating its constituents to ritualized and formalized behavior. Once human ears and eyes have been attuned to the rhythms of ritualized behavior, their vision of the world is stuck within a parochial bond. Substance and reality are sidetracked amid greater concern for formality and face-saving, this making political compromises difficult.

The five human relations and five constants constitute a system of general ethics, from which the Sino-Korean concept of law is less sharply differentiated than would be the case if the Western concept of law applied. Ethics were the chief path to harmonious conduct and had, in effect, the force of law. The observance of ethical norms was dependent on autonomous will. "Rule by the force of law rarely put the subjects to shame for punishable behaviors. Rule by morality, however, makes a stronger appeal to their volition to follow the ruler"(translated from Song Young-bae 1994;38). If family and clan heads fulfilled their roles in accordance with ethical norms, a Rousseau's version of a state without law and government is expected to prevail. Only when ethical solution failed was the law required as an extension of the ruler's attempt to harmonize society.

All men in Korea tend to avoid resorting to law or reserve it as the last resort, since it is considered a slur on their reputations. "Those appearing in courts were regarded not as defenders of their rights but as quarrelsome, unruly, and in need of better education "(Gregory Henderson 1968;240). Chong To-jon, a famous early leader of Korean Confucianism, put the case well: "The sage proclaims law not to rule with force but in order to rule without it." Social discipline and abiding by law made the Chosôn dynasty distinct from modern Korea. Many Koreans are reluctant to have their behaviors judged by law rather than moral arbiters, and this attitude inhibited the development of legal system based on rational or institutionalized justice.

Encounter with Heretic Beliefs

The seventeenth century in Korea is considered the period of intellectual hybridity, growing from the Koreans' encounter with the Western thought. In those days, it was hardly conceivable that anything of value could be obtained from foreign countries other than China. Throughout the centuries of Korea's seclusion, annual pilgrimages to Beijing, the celestial capital and cultural center of Asia, evolved into an educational and cultural institution for Korean intellectuals. Any things other than those originating in China were dismissed as heresy.

Cheong Doo-won, an envoy dispatched to the Q'ing court, made the first contact with a Jesuit priest in Beijing in 1630 and brought with him Matteo Ricci's text, The True Meaning of the Lord of Heaven. Ho Gyun, a prominent literary and political figure of the time brought books about astronomy and science. Lee Seung Hoon who followed his father on a diplomatic mission was the first Korean to be baptized in Beijing. A Chinese priest Chu Wen'mo was smuggled into the heartland of the Chosôn dynasty on underground missionary work. The seventeenth century was referred to as the Korean version of the Rennaissance.[3]

Matteo Ricci set his feet in Beijing in 1583 after years of staying in Macao. He was the first European to awaken Chinese that China was not the center of the world but a part of it. The world map he showed punctured the millennia-old fantasy of China as the "middle kingdom" surrounded by backward satellite countries. Matteo Ricci not only taught Western thought and the world of Christianity but insinuated himself into the Chinese intellectual circles by learning the Chinese language and classics. He was the first to cross what had seemed a forbidden gulf between the two worlds.

The True Meaning of the Lord of Heaven explored how the world was created and presided over by God. The heavenly kingdom is where one settles down for eternity, and this contemporary world is a contrived passage to the heavenly kingdom. The messianic appeal touched a soft spot – man's craving for immortality. Matteo Ricci humanized God - as the final causer of life and the paramount ruler- and drew a distinction between substances and accident. All objects, he argued, are dead and are bereft of anima, and there must be the efficient causer for them to have life. God stays within and outside the realm of mankind as the causer of life and final arbiter of all human deeds.

The humanized God resembles the Chinese concept of "heaven" (Changti) who is supposed to rule the cosmos. Mateo Ricci thus argued an affinity with Confucianism. This conceptual affinity must have facilitated the Chinese understanding of an alien Western thought. An anthropomorphic God, however, contradicts the "taekeuk," the principal non-human force that is supposed to create the cosmos, according to Neo-Confucianism (trans. From Song Young-bae,2004;48). For Matteo Ricci, Neo-Confucianism could not be viewed as others than an atheism, since taekeuk was not a substance endowed with its creative force but an accidental cause through which substance comes into being. Christian theology argues that all objects in the universe are bereft of anima and incapable of making a reasonable judgment. Since they cannot move for themselves, there must be a causality, a being that in Christianity becomes the ultimate God, residing outside the realm of objects (Matteo Ricci 1-3;40). Although humans are born with goodness, this does not guarantee that humans do not make fallible judgment of their deeds. God is the final arbiter of human acts sure to be accompanied by a rewarding or punitive measure in the other world. Faith in rewards to come for virtuous deeds brings forth the supposition of the existence of God.

In contrast with the theological definition of fallible humans, the Illuminists stressed reason which was believed to consist in the depth of human consciousness; reason radiates its luster as it is constantly honed. Mencius argues that every human is born with "goodness" and stressed the importance of self-cultivation to access it. The Illuminists exalted a human-centered world over the God-centered world of medieval Europe. The Illuminist belief in reason conformed to the theory of natural selection – that human nature from its rude and primordial form is constantly improving itself towards perfection, because humans have a technical capability to lead an examined life with self awareness, memory, foresight and judgment. Darwin believed the human species to be a moral one – in fact, the only moral animal species capable of moving toward higher morality. Natural selection itself was thought of as a benign deity, constantly improving human species for the greater good.

Every object, according to Matteo Ricci, has a living end, that is, existence is teleological and cosmos moves towards its teleological end. Before every object came into being, there must have been the ultimate causer who presides over movements of any object to its teleological end. God-bestowed goodness does not necessarily guarantee that man is immune to evils. Matteo Ricci stressed the importance of a high moral standard as a means to polish the abrasive surface of the mind to get at God-bestowed goodness. Earlier, Thomas Aquinas maintained that humans were reasoning intellectuals capable of distinguishing between goodness and evils with an end view to realizing justice for a greater whole.

Matteo Ricci's residence in Beijing coincided with the religious wars that followed the Reformation in Europe. It seems that his religious belief was not affected by the Reformation that set individuals emancipated from the church, the Pope, the state authority and law. The Illuminist movement thrived in the soil of individualism, and its cult of reason brought dichotomy that separated man from nature. Nature becomes an object to be altered and refashioned to serve human needs. The period of intellectual awakening saw monumental scientific discoveries in Europe. The invention of a movable metal type printing in 1443 kicked off a series of scientific discoveries. Copernicus' "The Revolution of the Celestial System" was advanced by Galileo. His theory went across the border to bear fruit in discoveries by Newton and Einstein. Scientific discoveries obviously brought material wealth, but scientific development is blamed for functional inertia to bring a mutually complementary interplay and balance between wholeness and individual constituents and between nature and humans" (translated from Song Young-bae 2004;41).

Confucianism provides ethical codes of conduct and, in this context, its primary concern was with statecraft based on morality that is conducive to a world where all live in peace and harmony. Confucianism boils down to the idealization of individual behaviors in an attempt to realize the highest version of society. The ruler was constantly enjoined to keep his ears to the voices of the people. Moral supremacy is reflected in the system of checks and balances between the ruler and the ruling class in order to prevent the abuse of power by one against anther. The past, it believes, is the mirror to look at to derive desirable actions. In Song and Ming China, Neo-Confucianism prospered to provide the classical Confucian tenets with a metaphysical backing and every ethical code, it claims, is linked to the cosmic order.

The Book of Rites explains the inherent structure of the mind, in reference to the law of the cosmos, as the combination of *li* and *gi*[*]; nature casts its shadow over man's mind and this is consonant with St. Augustine's theology – that human mind reflects the shadow of God. Divinity resides within our soul, waiting to reveal itself to sages and prophets. Like divinity, *li* is an innate goodness, the universal and immortal principles, whereas *gi* is phenomenal and variant forces. *Li* is obscured and eclipsed by gi, that is, feelings subject to whimsical changes. Neo-Confucianism regards *li* as something to be restored by honing the abrasive surface of the mind hidden under *gi*. (trans. from Song Young-bae 2004, 59). Man has emotional and irrational tendencies, precluding the following of the dictates of reason. Neo-Confucianism prefigured many of the teachings of modern psychology.

Interactions between *li-gi* can be explained through Voltaire's "a cold clash between intellect and instinct" (Will Durant, 2004,187)."It is one of the rare coincidences that the juxtaposition of the antithetical forces was dominating the intellectual circle of Koreans when the sophisticated soul of the French divided up into Voltaire and Rousseau."The quest for reason leads one to move toward self-perfection. Whether one is to realize *li* for self-perfection, however, rests with his or her voluntary will, and it has nothing to do with rewarding or punitive anticipation" (Will Durant, 60). In this sense, Matteo Ricci's belief in God as the arbiter of human behaviors – to reward good doings and punish bad ones - encountered difficulty in persuading Chinese as well as Koreans. Christian morality is utility-oriented since good doers are expecting God's grace, a heavenly reward. This utilitarian morality clashed with Confucian morality whose motive is based on one's voluntary will. Confucian morality is the manifestation of humanness flowing from the well of one's consciousness; it denies the existence of an arbiter to guide human deeds" (trans. From Song Young-bae 2004, 63-77).

Neo-Confucianism is a metaphysical conjecture devoid of experimental evidence. The heavenly deity in Confucian terms is not a transcendental being residing outside the contemporary world, but a righteous way that resides within every individual. By contrast, Christianity's transcendental being is an absolute law giver and ruler who presides over the cosmic order. There is an intent and purpose in the existence of every object. Matteo Ricci denied Neo-Confucianism's five human relations and taekeuk created by the interplay between *Yin and Yang*; he declared that there was nothing that has been created by accident. The creative force, taekeuk, has no character or will capable of infusing an object with an intended goal. The existence of an object presupposes that there had been the causer before it came into being. Discussion on a series of causes leads to the final causer posited by the Aristotelian definition.

Challenges to Neo-Confucianism

Neo-Confucianism is not different from Confucianism in its emphasis on ethical codes of conduct and moral politics in accord with the heavenly way, but Neo-Confucianism links the workings of society to cosmic order. Neo-Confucianism is a metaphysical speculation that consider human affairs not separable from cosmological background. It refers the workings of the mind to cosmic principles and, therefore, is too highly abstract and speculative to undertake an effective approach to pragmatic problems which bear on daily life. Wedded on a state of a single ethnic patch, it became a dogmatic ideal. The Chosôn kingdom lived in a blissful isolation, entrenched within an impenetrable ideological shell.

Due to its obsession with speculative discussions, Neo-Confucianism created inertia in coping with new issues in a more complicated social structure. As its appeal diminished, grounds for the gestation of more utilitarian approaches were generated; hence, in the later years of the Chosôn Dynasty, Neo-Confucianism was the major cause for factional feuds, locking the intellectual society in a vicious cycle of division into hostile blocs. The internal schism of Confucian scholars dismantled Neo-Confucianism of its intellectual appeal and created an upsurge of interest in searching for the utilitarian value of Confucianism. Yoo Hyung-won was critical of the Confucian inability to distinguish between the ideal and the real and between body and tail (trsns. from Keum Jang-dae,2006; 200).

Although Catholicism was not compatible with the hierarchical society, reference to a new frame of reference revealed the fallacies of Neo-Confucianism and brought forth a new school of Confucianism known as Silhak (Pragmatic learning). Access, though on a limited scale, to the outside world brought a new perception of the country in the world. Intellectuals were awakened to the new world entirely different from the China-centered world they were familiar with. It was in such a global context that Silhak demanded an end to formalism and ritual trivialities and return to the true spirit of Confucianism. Silhak cried out for the ending of social stratification and the slavery system, land reform, equal taxation, the wellbeing of the people and a scientific approach to problems of daily life. Silhak was considered an attempt of Koreans to transcend the bound of China-dominant scholarship and develop an independent school of learning relevant to Korean culture. "And some of the intellectuals endeavored to convert the metaphysical cosmology into science-centered cosmology" (Keum,78)

The most prominent proponents of Silhak were Hong Dae-yong (1731-1783) and Cheong Yak-yong (1762-1836). Hong, critical of abstract speculation, called for a practice of morality that would address the affairs of daily life. Hong went on to define the China-centered scholarship as "empty" of pragmatism and referred to the limitless change of the cosmos that eluded the Confucian grasp. He denied the absoluteness of knowledge in favor of relativism. Earth was no longer the center of the celestial sphere but just one of innumerable planets in the cosmos. His understanding of the cosmos was unique in that it denied *li-gi* theory and demanded an end to the speculative nature of Neo-Confucianism. This new school of pragmatic learning mocked an anthropomorphic interpretation of the cosmos, and taught us to learn to submit ourselves to the law of the cosmos. Hong stressed inductive reasoning in studies and had little patience with the speculative metaphysics of orthodox Neo-Confucianism. Another aspect of Silhak is that man cannot be differentiated from nature, and these two make one continuum. Neo-Confucianism stresses the importance of self-cultivation to develop a desirable human character, and this interpretation views human character as superior to animals. Hong asserted that there was nothing superior in human to animals. In the China-centered world, he argues, discriminating other ethnic groups from cultured Chinese, thus calling them barbarians, is absurd. Viewed from a broader perspective, such discrimination fades into insignificance, since it simply asserts the superiority of one civilization to another.

Cheong Yak-yong divided substances into those with shape and those without shape, much as Matteo Ricci divided into visible and invisible objects. Reason in particular was an important attribute that characterized man as different from animals. His argument is consonant with Christianity by stressing the importance of "moral will" and insisting on reason as the starting point of self cultivation. Like Hong Dae-yong, Cheong denied the Li-Gi theory of Neo-Confucianism as groundless. He was also critical of Neo-Confucian "goodness" as something bestowed by nature on each individual. Instead, he noted that morality could be obtained when one shaped a moral character by the accumulated effect of free will, much as outlined by Mattteo Ricci's "The True Meaning of the Lord of Heaven." According to his theory, there was no moral virtue that preceded human experience; moral character was shaped by the experimental process and by the practice of free will, and not to be obtained by speculation.

Matteo Ricci defined God as shapeless and voiceless, and this can be compared to Cheong's definition of an invisible and voiceless being, absolutely required to fend off evils and guide our moral footsteps. Cheong Yak-yong was the first to teach that the measure of human value was not based on nature. His emphasis on the practice of free will as the starting point of moral cultivation represents a creative encounter between traditional Confucian and modern thought. By placing human deeds under the glare of Shang'di, an invisible deity, he encouraged individuals to attain self perfection. His stand was consonant with the Christian precept by subjecting individuals to a rewarding or punitive measure by an invisible deity. In relation to a rewarding or punitive measure, reference to hell and paradise was a repeated refrain throughout the "True Meaning of the Lord of Heaven." However, there was no word that referred to the other world in Cheong's writing.

Cheong maintained a touch of the Confucian notion of self realization in the form of character perfection. His theory should be regarded as a step forward by emphasizing the practice of ethics over Confucius and Mencius "heavenly way." Another Silhak scholar Li Ik was the first to admit Christian ethics as coterminous with Confucian ethics but considered Christian imagination of paradise and hell preposterous. He was in favor of a selective imbibing of Western learning. Lee Soo Kwang stood in favor of the Western learning of science, geography and belief, all worthy of scholarly scrutiny. By and large, Silhak denied the conjectural nature of Neo-Confucianism and inspired us to develop our reasoning ability to winnow out unacceptable and barren truth. Its emphasis on reason renders Silhak akin to the Illuminist philosophy that paralleled a new epoch of scientific discoveries in the Western hemisphere. Scarcely had Silhak taken roots, than the Choson Dynasty was swept into the vortex of world power struggles. The uneasy social milieu hardly provided the ground for the new learning to take its root.

The state's persecutions of Catholic converts strangled any new idea which might have produced golden eggs. How and to what extent this new learning actually contributed to the modern transformation of Korean society is open to question. The advent of Silhak is coincidental to the politically stabilized period under the reign of two kings, Youngjo and Chôngjo (1724-1800). This period is referred to as an "intellectual awakening" or "ideological hybrid" in the sense that dogmatic Confucianism was giving way to new thoughts that basked in a short spell of sunshine before Roman Catholicism was severely persecuted. The monarchical inertia from 1800 brought the dominance of in-law families, and there was no progress made in the way of ideological consolidation. Ideological diversity was the spawning ground for the progress of civilization. Amid the ensuing political melees, the Chosôn dynasty saw Q'ing China humiliated in its confrontation with England in the Opium War (1839-2). Koreans dismissed this new power as a barbarian predator to be guarded against. Q'ing China was erected by northern barbaric hordes, taking the place of Ming China from which Korean intellectuals could hardly tear themselves.

The increasing congregation of Catholics, the Royal Court figured, was assumed to have something to do with the frequent appearance of foreign vessels, and the state's persecution of Roman Catholics was intensified, followed by its rash confrontations with the French fleet in 1866 and American marines in 1871. The latter was an Americans' retaliatory attack on Koreans for having burned an

American vessel that had penetrated into Korean territory. The xenophobic sentiment of Koreans, largely stemming from centuries of foreign-imposed trauma, emboldened them to challenge the mighty foes. To reclusive Koreans, the entry of a strange vessel was considered an overt invasion into its sacred land. The arrival of Protestant missionaries in 1880s toned down Koreans' xenophobic sentiment, and the Royal Court allowed Catholic priests to move around freely. Protestant missionaries convinced Koreans that they were doing lordly works with a genuine concern for the wellbeing of Koreans.

Another ideological child born of Koreans' search for their indigenous value was Tonghak (Eastern Learning), in opposition to the Western Learning. Tonghak styled itself as the true belief with its roots embedded in the traditional religion, but it was nothing more than the improvisation of the existing beliefs and religions. Choe Ja-u, son of a defeated yangban clan[5], founded Tonghak based on the heavenly mandates he claimed to have received through his communion with the Heavenly Deity. Tonghak taught that "man and God were the same and that the spirit of God dwelled within the mind of man, thus everyone is "a heavenly being" born with a precious and ennobled life, irrespective of status. Man is immortal when he or she lives in harmony with the will of heaven (Hahn Woo-keun 1970,123). Tonghak drew on Taoism in its call for a hermit life far removed from the secular world. It is also Buddhist in that it renounces worldly desires. It bears affinity to shamanism by regarding the cause of illness as imbalance between yin and yang or between man and nature. It is as much Confucianism in honoring and glorifying moral virtues and making much of human relationship. Despite its claim to the indigenous identity of Koreans, it blended the existing beliefs. By blending the Confucian tenet with "one god" and egalitarianism, it gained a wide currency and was spreading fast among the downtrodden peasants and served as the tinderbox for the peasants' riots called Tonghak Rebellion.

The peasants' riots were spreading across the nation like a prairie fire beyond the monarchical authority to put them down, thus becoming an open invitation for China and Japan to dispatch their troops to Korea under the pretext of suppressing the peasant riots. The presence of two opposing armies in Korea was conducive to the "Sino-Japan War in 1894. The two countries were the protagonists taking the center stage of Korea to determine the fate of an enfeebled kingdom. Tonghak's dream to build a new social order free from foreign interventions and corrupt officials was dashed into pieces as the two powers locked their horns in a struggle for hegemonic supremacy. The peasant movement was driven underground where it remained a tinderbox to inflame anti-colonial sentiment against Japan. Tonghak had its ideology linked to the peasants' grievances, producing a formidable force of anti-colonialism. Tonghak revolution, had it ever succeeded, might have become a civil revolution comparable to the French Revolution.

Across the Border

The logics of discourse on the intellectual legacy of Koreans suggests the desirability of crossing the border and see how regional variation of values is related to the perception gap. Each region followed a certain paradigm dictated by natural and geo-political factors, creating its unique civilization. To begin with a gross characterization, people in the East are said to be fatalistic, though not categorical, by resigning themselves to the mandate of heaven imagined to preside over human affairs. Heaven is the epitome of fatalism which brooks no objection. Behind Koreans' reverence for heaven lies their acceptance of its authority as the law-giver and ruler of the universe. As heavenly way is defined as a just and righteous way one must follow, the society we live in is held to be the microcosm of the heavenly world. Koreans accept the fate of an underdog in rows with its stronger neighbors and considered themselves the anointed sufferers of foreign beatings. At the same time, they detect in this drama a streak of triumphant pride in the way they have borne the historical tragedy.

The West is identified with historical dynamism by transgressing its ordained path and challenging the wonders of nature. Contrary to the Eastern fatalism, Western culture has been influenced by a religious faith that gives every living object a teleological end. The contemporary world we live in is not merely a sea of pains; there is an intent and goal in the existence of every object and the world we live in is a contrived path to another world to come. A pessimistic view of the contemporary world evokes human longing for a new world to come with the promise of an immortal life. An anthropomorphic interpretation of nature personifies and dramatizes nature and cover it with a cloud of deities. Monotheism defines God as the final causer of life and creator, omnipresent and omnipotent, positing that there is nothing created by chance.

The fundamental base of Confucianism is anthropocentricism that gives humanity the supreme value. Its primary concern is how to maintain social harmony, and morality refers to all behaviors that subscribe to human relations and social solidarity. The maxim of Koreans in relation to daily life is "Saram dap'ge salara." Translated literally, it means "live like a true man." The word "true man" refers to what Freud calls "a consciously formed personality" as opposed to "the undifferentiated, amoral realm of primitive yearning." By positing an exemplary life, humans articulate the codes of conducts that enable one to live in harmony with others. There is an altruistic element in its constant call to seek happiness in others and perfection of the self. This constitutes the basic tenet of statecraft that the monarch had to follow. Idealistically, moral consciousness in Korea begins with "deference to others" and "self-cultivation."

The West owes its recent development to the cult of reason, assuming that reason opened the vista for what humans could accomplish in their innate capacity and that all social problems are capable of a rational solution. Reason is a god-given faculty that put man above plants and animals. "Man molded in God's image has an innate urge to reflect reason in his social behavior" (translated from Kim Hyun 2006, 206).

Reason, the innermost sense of righteousness, enables one to make a reasonable assessment of a given situation and an informed decision about ways to behave. The cult of reason, together with the myth of growth, blinds us to the limited capacity of the ecosystem. New technology created devices that enriched our life and offered the convenience of life but "we have not assumed moral responsibility for how they are used – to the ends to which new technology and systems are put" (Charles A. Reich 191, 172).

There are two modes of moral thinking that are fundamentally contradictory to each other. Collective consciousness appeals to the heart for behavioral guidance, whereas ego-centered consciousness looks to the head for a guide. A man of collective consciousness is emotional in principle and an ego-centered man shows a tendency toward emotional neutrality. Collective consciousness stands for what is good for a group or community and the ego-centered consciousness sanctions a rational pursuit of personal interest. A saint in one realm is a miscreant in another. The liberal democratic mode of politics is confrontational politics, considered "culturally inappropriate" to Koreans whose ears are tuned to the rhythm of communitarian ideals, harmony and consensus. "Deference to others," viewed from a self-centered perspective, sounds something out of the ordinary, if not considered a quirk. By the same token, a collectively conscious man is disgusted with an individualistic motive since it breaks loose the close network of human relationship and leads to a free-for-all chaos. Collective moral consciousness restrains an individual's free will to be rational and flexible in the pursuit of his own interest.

There are more sentimentalists among Koreans who equate emotional neutrality with impersonality, apathy, or even cold bloodedness. Anthropocentricism envisions a world of human networks that is workable when every individual is warm in the heart. Koreans weep over a society bereft of compassion and human feelings. The human face, they thought, forestalled forced lay-offs, even though it was justified by business downturn. A warm heart, of course, is a good way to guide one's moral behaviors, but it loses relevance to a mass and mobile society. Emotion, going to an excess, obscures one's sense of fairness and impartiality so important to public performance. "Yet if feelings are not to degenerate into indulgent, aggressive or unhealthy emotionalism, they need to be informed by critical intelligence" (Karen Armstrong 1993, 394). In reality, every reason-motivated behavior cannot be insulated from an emotional motive. Come whatever, a motive is, in one way or another, accessible to questionable personal experience, precarious inference or fallible reasoning. The conceptualization or perception of an object is open to an emotional impulse at least in its initial reaction to a stimulus. An emotion-driven motive is more likely to be distanced from its intended behavior.

From the time of the polis, Greek philosophy has drawn distinctions between private and public domains. Koreans' blindness to the distinction owes much to the Confucian emphasis on affective behaviors whose utility is questioned in the public domain. Humaneness[6] proves to be useful to enable individuals to live peacefully within a parochial circle of association. But this virtue loses its luster when applied to public life. The Christian notion of an all embracing brotherly love evaporates the moment it has public exposure. "Public" means something seen, heard and accessible to everybody, and emotion-neutrality becomes a measure of fair and impartial conduct. Average Koreans shy away from the public display of love; when it is displayed within a close circle of intimates, it is likely to become nepotism that favors particular individuals or groups. Confucian values, by its emphasis on affective behaviors, proved to be workable within a social circle of family or clan relations and others with deep, life-long bonds. Mass and mobile society premises an expandable radius of trust. The limited radius of trust explains the underdevelopment of an intermediate value that extends to larger social circles of trust.

We notes, with foreboding, the credibility gap of politicians in general and particularly in relation to the presidential leadership of today's Korea. This appears to have much to do with the Confucian stand for warm heart and affective behaviors and the resulting apathy, conscious or unconscious, to distinctions between the two domains of life. This tendency invariably haunts every president with so much damage done to his stature as his term is drawing to its close. The human mind is basically selfish and egoistic, bending to serve private interests rather than working for public interests. Private concerns are held in check while one is conscious of public service; where power grows to an excess, the balance between the two falters. The resulting lack of prudence and discretion in the exercise of power dims public mindedness, silently prodding the human mind to assert private interests. In such a hierarchy-conscious culture as Korea's, lacking in strong institutions or voluntary associations, elites and masses are sharply dichotomized, power converges on a few on the top, inclining the president to ensconce himself behind these confidants. Leadership in the shadow of human barrage becomes increasingly dogmatic and arbitrary, feeling little prick of conscience in disavowing public commitment. "Even the greatest forces of intimate life – the passions of the heart and the delights of the senses – leads to an uncertain, shadowy kind of existence unless and until they are transformed, de-privatized and de-individualized, as it were, into a shape to fit them for public appearance" (Hannah Arendt; 50).

Filial duty is an absolute imperative in Korea and Confucian societies, while this virtue is not held in so a high regard in the West, though it is celebrated in different ways. For Koreans there is no crime more heinous than the dereliction of filial duty, whereas it may be dismissed as a misdemeanor permissible somewhere else. Any Korean who neglects or disavows filial duties cannot avoid a moral cudgel by blood relatives or community members, though not subject to legal punishment. This does not mean that all Koreans are better bred to treat their parents than any others. The ideality of human life is distanced from reality. Likewise, the Korean monarch lost his authority or was dethroned when he was found morally flawed. But no Korean king was punished for unreasonable, inept or irrational conduct which might have terminated the dynastic continuity of the Western countries. In the moral-conscious kingdom, Koreans laudably showed an abiding patience with an imbecile and inert ruler.

Speculative thinking was the hallmark of Korean intellectuals, pertaining to a privileged few in old Korea. The thinking mode of a conjectural nature has something to do with the metaphysical character of Neo-Confucianism. In a situation devoid of empirical evidence, speculative thinking creates different interpretations of a doctrine, each sticking to its position. This explains that Korean officials were contentious doctrinaires squabbling over peripheral issues or rituals. Within a hierarchical and centralized power structure, grouping is artificial. The contentious argument still finds its parallel in the modern politics of Korea. Neo-Confucianism aims at building a spider's web society that boasts coherence[7] but the result can be far from what it tries to achieve. Identical beliefs and practices have inspired diametrically opposed courses of action (Karen Armstrong, 2015, 393). The irony is that Korean history, despite its claim to a legendary social cohesiveness, attests to the impossible coexistence of cohesiveness and division. Every moral issue in Korea comes unstuck into an impossible "right or wrong" dichotomy. In moral debate, Korean intellectuals slog it out, as if they were in "a win or lose" game.

While the Western hemisphere progressed in a dramatic departure from the past, the Eastern hemisphere stagnated for long. The sluggish development of the non-Western world may be explained by many factors but most crucial, the advantage of analytical and inductive reasoning is evident over speculative thinking in the race. Those conscious of human relations, in general, are strong in ability to synthesize and generalize while they are relatively weak in analytical ability. "The great century of creation" in the West - from 1760 to 1860- was the dazzling heights of intellectual and cultural grandeur, that was never experienced in the East. The Eastern hemisphere has seen a plethora of sages but never seen scientists like Copernicus, Galileo, Newton, Bacon and Einstein.[8] But the cult of reason tilted the balance of development in favor of material pursuit as reflected in the utilitarian or philistine orientation of the Western values. The myth of growth has reduced nature into a mere object to be fashioned to serve human needs.

Ruthless objectivity is replacing warm humanity as the touchstone of good conducts. Where impersonality calls the tune, man is increasingly alienated from his inner needs and loses, at last, his being. With the loss of the self, man means nothing else than role, occupation and machine. It leaves man to be dictated by the most impersonal of the substitutes. On the other hand, mass industrial society, by virtue of its fluid and complex nature, increasingly owes moral decisions to situational ethics. Each individual inevitably becomes the author for moral decision. It is neither possible nor desirable to develop an ethical principle that answers every moral question, transcending the whims and notions of the moment. In this connection, an ability to make moral decisions without reference to priori norms will be an essential quality.

The Eastern notion of humanity is not a lonely island to be submerged by the expanding domain of reason. "It is defiant against science that sees the natural world in explicit disjunction from humanity" (Wilfred C. Smith 1984,10). The altruistic touch of humanity is resonated with the Puritanical asceticism, that is, to suppress personal feelings and make personal sacrifice for the benefit of others. The question is "how we can develop a new consciousness that places humanistic values over the machine." The moment has come for us to recall a stern reminder by Aurelio Peccei, President of the Club of Rome. "None of us seems to be fully aware of the fateful role that willy-nilly we are all playing in shaping human life for a long time to come."

---

1. Japanese history has witnessed such an absolute loyalty galvanized into fanatic patriotism and a paradigmatic display of unitary power in confronting their foes. Loyalty in the Confucian concept, imbued

with the Shinto concept of the Emperor, turned into an errant form of patriotism. The supremacy of filial piety to parents in Korea has ruled out the possibility of clash between the two obligations observed in Japan. Ironically, absolute loyalty to feudal master often led to a betrayal against the Shogun when the two came into conflict, and the only way open to be loyal to both was to commit a suicide. Classical dramas (Kabuki) are full of stories of the heroes being torn apart between the two obligations to have a tragic ending of their lives. Disloyalty to a feudal master was quite often observed, when the warriors were laid idle during peacetime.

2. Note that Koreans make no distinction between private and public realms. Their view of the continuum implicates a naïve expectation that the two domains constitute a single continuum, and that moral virtues work in a positive way to promote public goodness. This concept overlooks the reality that Confucian values are relevant to the private domain and cease to be effective in the public realm. A blurred division between the two explains the lack of public sensitivity of Koreans. Greek philosophers asserted that the rise of the city-state, that is, the public realm, occurred at the expense of the private realm of family and household. A distinct line was drawn between the two.

3. This period corresponds to the reign of Youngjo and Chôngjo (1724 – 1800). The wise kings not only stabilized the country by terminating factional strife but created a liberal aura for scholars to imbibe new thought from the West. It was during this period that Roman Catholicism made inroad and spread among the downtrodden. Western thought grafted on Confucianism gave rise to a new thought, notably, the pragmatic school of learning. Had this period continued longer, Korea could have taken a different historical path. This period was a lull before the dynasty was swept into a stormy sea, followed by in-law family dominance.

4. Li-Gi theory represents the duality of the cosmic order made of two diametrically opposite forces, Yin and Yang. Since the world we live in is the miniature of the cosmos, it is managed by "principle," an absolute and immortal truth that is super-imposed by "emotional force" that changes every minute. The former is a reason-dominant character lying in the inner depth of the human mind while the latter stands for force or energy which moves objects around. The appropriate mix of principle and emotion makes our society properly function.

5. Yangban refers to the noble, landed class, which enjoyed high status. Unlike the hereditary succession of the status by birth in Europe and Japan, their attainment to yanban status was strictly based on their own merit. Those who passed the high civil service examination were entitled to be the ruling elites, and they were distinguished from the landed aristocrats. In time, the status was inherited by their descendants by birth through privileged appointment. The ruling elites were divided into factions, each so much avid for power. They made strong power blocs often to such an extent that allowed them to challenge the ruler.

6. The word "In" is interpreted to mean different things, depending on the situation. Its meaning is elastic

and there is no English counterpart to catch the term in a neat and clear definition.. Warmth of heart or humaneness comes closest but neither captures its true sense. A man who sees a beggar or a person in a miserable and pitiful situation is likely to be moved to help. If one fails to have a sympathetic concern, he is not a human. In is a virtuous behavior with warm concern for others. In represents the beginning of moral cultivation. It is regarded as one of the essential virtues that an enlightened man has This character has, in a way, an emotional tone, in contrast to the emotion-neutral "reason" of the Illuminist thought. Rather, In stays closer to the Buddhist notion of 'charity' which set one ready to benefit others at self sacrifice and be tolerable of one's sins. In a broad sense, it means a character that distinguish humans from other species.

7   Confucianism set forth five human relationships. Each shows a binary relationship including two partners with a moral virtue to serve as a kingpin. Once a relationship has been built up, it is hoped to be perpetual. Confucianism is primarily concerned with the durability of a relationship. The relationships between king – subject, wife – husband, parents – children, elder brother – younger brother, and a friend – friend are the very beginning of a more extensive and complicate social relationship. Therefore, the Confucian view of society is a spider's web society, in which everyone is one way or another related to another. This network is supposed to create a highly cohesive society

8.   Copernicus' "Revolution in the Celestial System" was consigned to Galileo, Newton and Einstein, each making his own contribution by way of accretion or denial. One discovery has been snowballed into a great invention as it traveled across cultural borders. It cut across different cultures, each adding a new dimension to the discovery. Scientific discovery in this sense is the result of cross-cultural fertilization. A new discovery would not have been made, had it not drawn on the existing stockpile of theories.

Chapter

Four

Characterization of Koreans

Man can be defined as the animal that can say "I" that can be aware of himself as a separate entity
— Erich From

The Value Consciousness of Koreans

Characterization of an ethnic or political group may be considered something of a reckless effort. No single group fit a distinct pattern of behaviors or attitudes. What follows is gross characterization of Koreans, although it is based on recurrent patterns. Still, the characterization of Koreans leaves a lot to be desired. We may say that Koreans are increasingly temperamental and volatile, but many would reject this characterization as a significant departure from the popular image of Koreans. The problem is that phenomenal description does not necessarily accord with that of the fundamental characters. Despite the fact that Koreans have experienced breathtaking changes, Korean familial and social structures remain essentially hierarchical and collective. It is fair to say that the modern society of Korea is still the seat of traditional values, though they have been in decline. Below what appears to be dynamic on the surface are values inherited from the past, resisting the tide of new values. The persistence of traditional values suggests the desirability of looking retrospectively at the past to examine how they have changed over time.

Until the nineteenth century, Korea had been completely shut off from the rest of the world, and the isolated kingdom provided a haven in which Confucianism tapped its root deeper in the minds of Koreans. There was no attempt to develop an alternative ideology. While Korea's neighbors were restless with the double imperatives of enriching the country and fending off imperialism, the intransigent opposition of Confucian literati to any opening of its borders locked Korea in isolation. This spoke for the unfathomable depth of ideological dogmatism. Access to the outside world, they thought, would muddy the sacred land inherited from their progenitors. Korea took legitimate pride in being the citadel of lofty Asian values.

Hierarchical and collective consciousness is the most fundamental values of Koreans. It has a profound impact on not only social and institutional structures but on the way Koreans think and behave. Hierarchy and collectivity constitute the themes that are constantly repeated through discourses about the characteristic behavioral patterns of Koreans. They survived the colonial rule, post-liberation chaos and the Korean War. In contemporary Korea, consanguineous solidarity maintains an ideal lineage unity. Lineage identity cannot be explained in separation from these quintessential elements of the Korean value system. .

Hierarchical consciousness

Hierarchy and the vertical order of relationships are the most fundamental elements that characterize Koreans apart from others. Hierarchical consciousness generates a strong vertical pressure to obscure one's horizontal perspectives. Seniority still marks each step up a hierarchical ladder. Confucianism encapsulates inequality as the law of nature, and this justifies the vertical arrangement of human relations and institutions. The so-called "five human relations" are based on the concepts of inequality and order. Neo-Confucianism defines the vertical order as the mirror image of the cosmic principle which provides an orderly change of season following certain moving trajectories of sun, moon and constellations of stars. The metaphor of the ruler and subjects to "heaven and earth relationship" reflects an attempt to follow a cosmic order, and "it is through this ordained vertical order that the universe maintains its orderliness and peace" (Lee Sang-eun 1976;240). The concept of inequality was elevated to the way of maintaining order and a viable society.

Not all humans are born with the same intelligence or competency; a few bright are qualified to rule others who are fit to be ruled. The vertical differentiation of role is built into the structure of Korean corporations and officialdom, accompanied by a set of ethical obligations. To be in a position to lead others, one is enjoined to internalize all virtues to reshape himself toward the highest version. The hierarchical structure of Confucian society justified the heightened status of the ruling elite as a social device to preserve an orderly society through generations. Class distinction was hereditary in a class-conscious society.

Virtuous rule is based on the spontaneous loyalty of subjects to the ruler, and this obligation is not something to be forced upon individuals. The ruler's right to command loyalty depends, at least, on his dutiful observance of Confucian ethic. By following the heavenly dictum, the ruler thought that he could keep himself up to the flow of popular opinions and search an effective way to meet the popular desires. While the ruler expected his subjects to pay loyalty, he acted as a fatherly figure with the paternalistic care of his people. The infusion of the heavenly dictum into human life bespoke the Confucian notion that human life itself mirrors the cosmic world. There is unity between human life and cosmic order.

Hierarchical order also applied to inter-state relationships. Korea's relationship with China was vertical, characterized by a self-debasing attitude, while the proud little kingdom sought to compensate its self-debasement with a snobbish attitude toward the others. Vertical order finds its manifestation in patriarchal family structures, and vertical relations bred a strong sense of social status and humans are perpetually endowed with a longing for upward social mobility. "It also helped to consolidate a stratified structure rooted in the vertical order of ruling elites (scholar officials) - farmers-craftsmen-merchants-low born" (Ahn Byung-man 2003;14).

In the cult of vertical order, inequality is equated with a harmonious social order. The social smallest unit is the family which embodies inequality in its structure which is expandable to state and society. The notion that society is a large family reflects the Confucian failure to understand a modern society that sees the pluralistic nature of human relations and the presence of conflicting factors. The hierarchical order justifies the enlightening role of the ruling elite endowed with a superior faculty. Koreans are used to authoritarian aura which foreigners find suffocating and stifling. It reduces an individual into a passive performer of orders from above. Nevertheless, an effective leadership that stems from rational authoritarianism is meant to stir individual members to their best ability and this trend is typical of an organically structured corporation.

The Collective Consciousness

The Collective Consciousness of Koreans begins from familial relations. The small territory, stable borders, and a universal value system helped to homogenize the culture and spawned the tendency of Koreans to group together against strangers. In the absence of natural causes of cleavages, Koreans tend to organize themselves into molecular factions, of which family and blood lineage are the strongest solidarity.[1] Under the centralized ruling system and homogeneous culture, grouping is artificial. Pierre Cohen Aknain, a resident French diplomat, captures the grouping propensity of Koreans.

"It seems that Korean individuals are subsumed into a collective entity. Personal sacrifice is glorified if it serves a greater good of a group. There is no altruistic concern for those outside a group. Personal shortcomings are buried behind a group as women conceal their faces under a thick paste of cosmetics and plastic surgery. When French friends meet after a long separation, they enjoy talk over wine. To Koreans, the reunion of friends involves much more than enjoying over sake. There is the emotional fusion of Korean friends—an emotional bond that bounds them without interstices. There seems to be no space for privacy. Koreans seek comfort and solace in retreat into a group" (translated from Chosôn Daily Press dated 4October 2003)

Average Koreans still subscribe to relatively closed social groupings and strong personal connections based on blood kin, hometown pals and close intimates. In the constantly disturbed ancient China, Confucius came up with the idea that harmonious bonds and peace within the family were the corner stone of a healthy and stable society. Paramount concern for familial harmony and peace is well reflected in moral obligations that stress filial piety to parents, respect for elders and fidelity between wife and husband. All of these virtues denote a call for commitment of individuals to a greater good of family and state at personal sacrifices.

Some are critical of Confucian emphasis on family, "viewing its plea for individual subordination to a greater goal of a group as an anachronistic practice resulting from the ignorance of humaneness and reciprocal equality enshrined in the five human relationships" (Lee Eul-ho 1975,35). In light of Confucianism cast in its role as a connective thread for a clan-centered society, Confucius himself must have seen loyalty in a more diffused context, extendable to nation and society at large. Whatever may be said of family supremacy, the fact remains clear that patriarchal authority is the base for the expansion of loyalty to monarchical authority. Attitudes toward monarchical authority or the state were determined in the context of parental discipline rather than institutions or voluntary organizations which might have served as bridges between the family and the throne. Confucius envisioned a world in which familial relations directly applied to one's relation with the monarchy.

Koreans' sensitivity to "relatedness" or "connectedness" became more acute because of the strong attachment to family serving as the pace setter for all social relations. This spawned the ethical norms of the family binding on all constituents. A disciplinary action taken against a spoiled man by a group of blood relatives illustrates a strong ethical concern of the family relative to the weaker sense of the law. A noticeable tendency was that family or community floggings substituted for the rule of law. Networks of kin, blood relatives, alumni and home town chums weaved the social fabric of the Chosôn dynasty, and this continues to do so in today's Korean society. Strong family fraternity engenders exclusiveness or antagonism against other groups, drawing a line between friends and foes. There is no ground to stand on for politicians trying to compromise or make concession. The problem is that such acts are considered serving others' interest. The intractable nature of Korean factionalism, as reincarnated in today's politics, is thought to result from the strong sense of the clannish group or "getting together" around molecular groups.

Hierarchical and collective consciousness are antithetical to egalitarianism and individualism enshrined in Western thought. Debate on Western thought brings Christianity into focus. Behind Christian history lies a host of different ideas, inter alia, the Illuminist philosophy that attempted to demystify the theological interpretation of God as creator of the universe. This intellectual movement made its share of contribution to emancipate individuals from the authority of the state, its law and its institutions. The Protestant work-ethic is more often singled out as the prime mover of Western development. In defense of Protestantism, Max Weber "portrays Confucianism as most traditional by including elements which hinder capitalistic development." Weber echoed Karl Marx, Talcoot Parsons and Karl Wittfogel, all appearing antithetical to Ikeman's theory which attributes the recent development of Confucian countries to familism, discipline and morality. Weber theorizes that Confucianism, by stressing harmony and cooperation, leaves no room for "rational warfare" characteristic of competition and conflict between interest groups. "China, for example, sought to remain a unified state, notwithstanding the normal causes of division, and has never experienced 'armed peace' which had beset but advanced Western Europe. The absence of armed peace, according to Weber, provided a barren land for capitalistic development based on the lending and borrowing of money. This argument cannot escape skepticism. Koreans have seen historical cases where harmony and peace became a leaven for changes in favor of progress.

The Confucian values that once dominated the ethical sense of Koreans diminished in the scope and depth of its application to modern Korean society. Nonetheless, some of them die hard, playing crucial role in shaping Koreans' outlooks on particular issues. Many Koreans are still caught in the emotion of hierarchy, authoritarianism, personal connectedness, and ritualism, albeit abated to some degree. The human-oriented conception of social relations and hierarchy are the persistent theme of this book that explains how they affect behavioral patterns of Koreans. Reference to the values of other countries is expected to develop a critical understanding of what is desired in Korean values.

The Cult of Family and Blood Ties

Of the five moral underpinnings of the human relationships, three subscribe to a hierarchical structure of the family with its emphatic tones of orderliness and cohesiveness. Such a structural pattern of family is meant to be extrapolated to greater collective entities such as community, state and society. The family sets the pace for all social interactions, and it is within the family that each individual finds meaningful life. Contrasting the Western view of an individual as an independent member with its own identity, Koreans consider family members to be fused into one entity. An individual loses his or her identity in a greater concern for the good of family. There is no personal goal that is at odds with that of family, since personal interest is shaped in terms of its integration with the latter. The glue that holds family members together is a fixation on blood line. A network of trust is formed within the family whose members shape a primary group that extends to blood kin, school chums, community, and the nation.

Contrary to the idealized expansion of the network of trust, a strong sense of family solidarity works as a gravitational force against the expanding networks of association. It is not easy for Koreans to extend trust beyond the family and the bound of close friends. The sphere of intimates is something like a trench where one feels secured with a sense of connectedness to others, and only the bold goes beyond it, venturing out into the world of uncertainty. Francis Fukuyama put Korea among non-trust societies for the lack of spontaneous sociability that otherwise keeps one ready to be associated with strangers. "Family, generally, defined as an extended rather than conjugal family system, features an extraordinary preoccupation with its solidarity and involves heavy dependence on kin networks for various types of support "(Denise Potrzeba Lett 1998;223). From a shamanistic view point, the family is an enclave in a sea of spirits, the unhappy dead and ancestors, all of whom are prone to get angry and wreck our life if not appeased through a proper sacrifice rite. This notion defines home as a fortress against our fear of assault and as our corresponding obsession with privacy, suggesting that everyone beyond the family is a potential bastard.

The family is a kind of trench where one finds the comfort of love, sacrifice and support to avoid loneliness and self-doubt. It is from here that Koreans face the world of strangers and uncertainty with a sense of fear and clenched fists for the unknown. Outside the sphere of kin, each Korean is a fish out of water. They are impersonal and remiss about outsiders and show a remarkable lack of decency and demeanor. Familial parochialism is an abiding drag on expanding the circle of association, and this can be termed a form of "tribalism." "History suggests that it is virtually an axiom of human nature that, when the tribal sense is in decline, the moral sense is similarly threatened" (Hugh Mackay, 1993; 273). Consanguinity remains strong among Koreans. In the eyes of anthropologists, Korea remains a primitive society, banning marriage between siblings of the same blood. There have been a number of legislative actions on the part of law makers to abolish this ban, but each has been aborted under desperate opposition from conservatives who accepted nothing other than Confucian morality. Blood tie is a sacred cow in Korea, and anybody who argues for the logics of marriage between distant kin is susceptible to public recrimination as a social obloquy. So far as the family is concerned, tradition and custom form an immensely strong counterweight to change. With the sacredness of blood and the abiding obsession with family integration, social aversion to divorce or remarriage still remains strong, although divorce more frequently transpired these days. This view underscores the social norm that eulogizes a saint woman who renounces all personal desires for the good of children and family after her bereavement.

In order to understand how remarriage is perceived, take the case of a mother who, after bereavement, raised her two daughters by herself while working as a civil servant. In time, she remarried another man, a father of two daughters. However, his family name was different from that of her children. On account of this, their daughters were taunted by peers at schools. "Why is your family name different from your father's?" Such a careless question could seriously damage the children as well as the family, casting a dark shadow over their happiness. "The matter troubled the mother; she was a victim of the structure of our current laws and system that still upholds the original family name as unchallengeable. Even lawmakers are torn between frequent demands for amendment and the strong voices of conservatives struggling for the sacredness of blood" (Kwak Bae Hee 2003;49). This incident speaks for all troubles that blended families, non-kin families or transient families suffer in Korea. Children whose mothers are remarried are depressed.

The strong sense of family defines business companies or social organizations as extended families. Business culture in Korea mirrors the patriarchal authority in families, and leadership rarely goes beyond the sphere of blood ties or school chums. Even multi-national conglomerates are run by family members and blood-relatives who occupy the top management positions. The leader is an austere fatherly figure, the center pillar of the company. Authoritarian leadership is reflected in a strong central leadership which is believed to create its own security. Koreans are not so much keen on seeking job security in contract or the rule of law. With loyalty directed to persons who run an organization, lifetime employment is ensured by displaying an unfailing loyalty through a continuing relationship with an individual on the top. Although the leaders have the authority to sack people on the spot, they rarely do so. Firing someone comes as the last resort, since the severing of human relation is considered inhumane. Though someone is fired, it happens in a subtle way lest he feel the impersonal act of the employer. The Korean business owner rarely makes trust leap to open the company's leadership to professional managers outside the sphere of kin.

The importance of human relations in a parochial network offers few grounds for decision-making to be based on rationality and transparency. Emotional bonds denote certain aversion to business-like contractual interaction which is largely reserved for outsiders. The more intimate the relationship, the less importance is attached to the rule of law or contract: resorting to legal solution or insisting on a contract is regarded as an insulting indication of mistrust. If contracts are broken, extra legal channels are evoked to resolve a dispute. It goes to the court only when all else has failed, but the fact that legal means intervened is often taken for the symptom of institutional insecurity by outsiders.

A family clan in Korea denotes a lineage under one progenitor. In China and Korea where family clans developed, the family name was given importance as a means of identifying with the progenitors. The given name consists of two characters: either the first or the second indicates the generation of the lineage. In Japan, surnames and genealogies were not important, particularly among commoners. In China, all carrying the same surname are considered belonging to one family clan. But the Korean surnames pose difficulty identifying with a family lineage, since all carrying the same family name are not considered belonging to one lineage. Family lineage is identified by a family name prefixed by the progenitor's birth place. The family name 'Kim' is most common. But, there are more Kim's than you can count. Each Kim may be as distant from another Kim as it is from Park, Choi, Cho and the other. An Andong Kim, for example, is not more closely related to Kyungju Kim than to Park, Choi, Yoon, etc. The family system which values blood tie inhibits marriage between those of the same family clan even when a common ancestor was ten or twenty generations distant. Such institutional inhibition has evolved from ancestor worship. Incest is banned in almost every society known on earth, no matter how primitive or advanced, simply because it is abhorrent to human instinct. From an economic viewpoint, marriage to a non-kin family in primitive societies was expected to bring an alliance of families, adding more laborers to hunting or farming.

Ancestor Worship and Rites

|||||||||||||||||||||||||||||||||||||||||||||||||||||||||||||||||||||||||||||||||||||||

In connection with the bloodline cult, ancestor worship deserves a separate space for explanation. While the Korean family is the basic network of social relations, it is parochial in scope but so deeply rooted in the consciousness of Koreans in a way that weathers all the blows of time. The honor of the family denotes something that cuts across the past, present and future. Posteriors fondly refer to a shining achievement made by their ancestor hundreds of years ago, and it passes down, as a proud family legacy, to the succeeding generations. Few Koreans fail to eulogize their ancestors and family legacy. The Korean concept of family line is characterized by "timelessness": once a family is formed, it is hoped to be immortal. Immediate family members are links in a chain that goes back to the time immemorial and stretches into the infinite future. Ancestors and posterity form a single unit for which Koreans have a sense of trans-generational responsibility. A strong sense of family ties and obligations may translate into what Westerners would consider outright nepotism. Ancestor worship and filial piety are the fundamental elements, which, for millennia, have supported society, nation, and family, as well as serving as a matrix for human relations.

In the absence of the Christian version of immortality, a question arises: how Koreans satisfy their longing for immortality. Confucianism defines immortality as the memories of the deceased that inhabit the minds of the livings he was intimate with. "One's existence finds its immortal place in continuing human relations. Every Korean finds great comfort in having blood siblings who keep ancestors in their living memories; one sees his own image in a son and grand son, and children are links that perpetuates 'me' into the infinite future" (Lew Seok-choon, 2013). Korea is a land free from the prevailing passion to "live for yourself: Koreans live for predecessor and for posterity. Korean youngsters, however, are fast losing the sense of historical continuity, unaware of each being a link in a succession of generations.

The vertical conception of a family makes it imperative to have the chronological records of the family from the progenitor down to contemporary generations. One finds his identity in the succession of generations, and every family holds, with pride, "jok'bo (pedigree), a lineage tree that records the illustrious names of ancestors and their deeds. Even a lowly man has a jok'bo, forged to show the hallowed ancestry, since a family without this is treated as one who must have come from a humble origin. Koreans who have shady aspects of family history are reluctant to face the truth, contrary to the Australians openly admitting their convict ancestors. Where ancestry is hallowed, sacrificial rites for ancestors are complicated, but they are something that cannot be done without, although its ritualistic complexity has been simplified considerably.

An annual sacrificial rite is performed up to the fourth generation from the living generation. This imposes heavy burdens on sons, notably the eldest son who bears responsibility to continue the family legacy. In the past, failure to conduct a ritual service or to do in conformity with the approved procedure justified state intervention, leading on some occasions to capital punishment for the transgressors. State's intervention speaks for the all-embracing role of the government, contrasting to the European separation of the secular from the spiritual domain. Early Korean Catholic converts fell victim to brutal persecutions simply because they infringed on the state demand to practice ancestral rites. In Japan, there is neither a cult of veneration for ancestors nor a tight clan of groups descended from a common ancestor. Instead of the pedigree, each Japanese family has a family insignia, the version of the coat of arms in Western countries, passed on to the succeeding generations. Their consciousness of ancestor's worship has been overshadowed by their obsession with commune as a common fate. Sacrificial rites for ancestors are overshadowed by their worship for deities and the Supreme Being.

Ritual service for ancestors in Korea keeps posteriors within the living memories of their ancestors, thus reminding them of filial obligations which go beyond one's life. There is no distinction in the way descendants honor their dead and living parents. A thought runs down a timeless line of family to refresh the memories of ancestors and develop a sense of closeness to and togetherness with them, as if one's encounter with them were a matter of yesterday, however remote they are in time. Likewise, what will happen to their remote descendants becomes their immediate concern.

The free-wheeling of a thought through a limitless time corridor gives immediacy to the past and the future. Chong Sun-mok singles out the diffuse and undifferentiated conception of time as the central feature of Korean culture. With respect to time conceptions, the present is seen as holding in it the past, and hence one's forefathers nest in one's body. Moreover, lodged in the present body is the 'future' that all my ancestors already in me plus myself transmit to our descendants. Embraced in such a time concept are the three phases of past, present, and future, and in the present are the three existences of ancestors, self and descendants. Son preference was fostered in the context of entrusting the son with perpetuating the family line and performing ancestral rites. Underlying this is the belief that blood flows through the male line, because a daughter becomes a member of her husband's family on marriage and is therefore in a position to take care of her in-law parents. Korean parents find the eternity of their life in the birth of their sons in succession, and filial piety keeps the wheels of family turning around intermittently. Familial solidarity is maintained by filial piety which ensures the continuum of father-son relations. One's identity is defined in terms of his position in a succession of generations and the sense of family continuity is one's supreme concern. In the timeless continuity of the family, "no son" leads to a disgraceful and painful discontinuance of the family line which has been sanctified by ancestors: having "no son," then, was thought to be the most dreadful sin ever committed by human beings. Those who have not given birth to son are constantly haunted by the specter of their ancestors and live in fear of the day when they meet their ancestors in the other world.

From the Confucian viewpoint, ancestor worship is an extension of loyalty to deceased progenitors: the focus of loyalty is not only the living but the dead. Whatever the object worshipped, ancestor worship finds its genesis in shamanism – a belief that the dead remain with their living offspring in the form of spirits that guard against evil forces. The spirits may remain malicious most of the time, unless they are appeased through ritualistic service. Koreans therefore attribute all good fortunes to ancestors in contrast to the Christian notion of God's blessing and grace. Complex ritual services are observed on the anniversary of an ancestor's death and on festive occasions like the Korean Thanksgiving Day (Chuseok) and the New Year Holiday (Seolnal). Foods that the ancestors liked are placed on the altar, as if they were alive. According to Shamanistic interpretation, the dead are viewed as living souls that partake of the feast.

Filial piety does not distinguish between the living and the dead. Descendants pledge their filial duty through ritual service. But the rite itself is so complex and redundant, let alone a drain on the pocket book, that it takes much self sacrifice and patience on the part of the first son responsible for it. The Koreans' adherence to their ritual aspect of ancestor worship is undergirded by Confucian teaching, "the more cultured the people are, the more complicate the rituals, for this characterizes human beings as different from animals." Many Koreans worry about the spirits of their ancestors who may go astray when there is no one to perform proper ancestor worship rituals.

Filial piety to parents is exalted over allegiance to the ruler, and this tendency is an outgrowth of the cult of family whose solidarity in a way undermines one's consciousness of allegiance to a greater entity such as state or society at large. The Japanese concept of filial obligation, on the other hand, shows relatively weak identifications with family and clan, since each used to subdue the self to the feudal commune and the Emperor. The absence of strong family consciousness helps to exalt allegiance to a more diffusive, non-familial fiefdom, where the constituents shared a single fate and collaboratively find ways to survive in confrontation with other fiefdoms intent to prey upon them. Emphasis on a fiefdom unity accorded crucial importance to the sacrificial loyalty of the warriors, Samurai, to a feudal master. The exaltation of loyalty to the Emperor is attributed to Shinto's deification of Him to a divine and invincible being beyond frays with secular rulers. The divine concept elevated the Emperor to a heavenly realm divorced from secular affairs. The Emperor is a symbolic figure whose authority is heightened without ruling the state. The Confucian concept of filial piety to parents was distorted to fit the Shinto's hierarchical demand. "Filial obligation to parents or a petty lord could be abrogated only when it came to conflict with one's obligation to the Emperor, but not certainly because one's parent was unworthy or when he was destroying one's happiness" (Ruth Benedict 1946;119).

Authoritarianism

IIIIIIIIIIIIIIIIIIIIIIIIIIIIIIIIIIIIIIIIIIIIIIIIIIIIIIIIIIIIIIII

The Outgrowth of Vertically Arranged Society

Authoritarianism is characteristic of the hierarchically arranged social structures. Notwithstanding its professed claim to a democratic society, Korean society is not free from residual elements of the traditional class structure. A discussion about authoritarianism brings patriarchal authority to the fore, but this hierarchical structure is not limited to the family alone. The vertical arrangement of relationships regards a society as a super-extended family, where proper human relations become normative. By extending the familial structure to the political realm, vertical relation allow for the dominance of an elite over the masses. Authoritarianism is the quintessential quality of the ruling elites in a centralized system or a strictly ordered tower of power, reinforced by the militaristic bureaucracy that dominated Korean politics for three decades.

Where society is vertically arranged, obedience of the younger (or lower) to the older (or higher) is imperative. It is in such a hierarchical structure that one's craving for higher status becomes so stronger that any political game ends up with bitter hatreds and hostilities that linger for generations. In the structure of power, status is the key to social relations and is therefore an object to be vigorously sought. Authority and status feeds off one another into a frenetic drive for social mobility. But the mad search for authority offers a fertile ground for formalism, ritualism and mannerism to become dominant ethical concerns. Bureaucracy in particular is replete with an aura of authoritarianism, and bureaucratic posts were most envied by those who wish to advance in career and strive for a successful life. There is a built-in avidity to dominate others in Koreans' preference for bureaucratic posts.

In the closing years of the Chosôn Dynasty, Homers Hulbert, an American Protestant missionary, noted "a passionate desire" among Korean people "to ascend a step on the social ladder, as they tried in every way to insinuate themselves into good society" (Denise Potrzeba Lett, 1998.38). Status consciousness creates a desire that is satisfied with distinction from the pack. Passing the so-called high civil service examination (Kwago) was the entry to higher status, and merit and seniority marked each step upward. Every candidate for the examination dreamed of the day when he would return triumphantly to his hometown clothed in an embroidered silk robe. The resulting creation of a few on the top echelon is at odds with the Confucian defense of harmony, since it engenders feuds and competition. Koreans frantically seek education, making unbearable personal sacrifices, for its own sake or as the entry to elite status. Nonetheless, we cannot overlook the positive side of status consciousness. "This desire to acquire status, coupled with new opportunities available to this effort, has been a driving force behind the development of South Korea's human resource in general, of its new middle class in particular, and ultimately of South Korea itself" (Denise P. Lett ,41).

Authoritarianism coupled with status consciousness engenders an impulse to aggrandize oneself beyond what one actually is. The dignified look of a boss is ubiquitous in the hierarchically structured setting, and it whips subordinates into submissiveness or compliance. It is quite common that a man in a powerful position assumes an arrogant demeanor. Although authoritarianism has been in decline, it persists relatively strongly among those at the top echelon. Authoritarian ambience of an organization exerts a brake on free-wheeling behaviors and unrestrained self-expression. Koreans take it for granted, but foreign visitors to Korean public agencies are sure to note petty officials bowing and cringing to their superiors. In a society or an organization where authoritarianism prevails, lay workers often feel it best to bite their tongues rather than to be assertive or speak out. There is a passive majority within a vertically structured organization, and this hardly encourages them to work in a spontaneous and creative manner. In the hierarchical order of bureaucracy, subordinates humble themselves before seniors and pay respect to him: seniors are exalted by uncritical adulation beyond what they really are. Petty officials attribute all achievements worthy of praise to their superiors, even though they may have been the initiators or authors of new ideas.

A New Father-Son Relationship

Authoritarian people have low tolerance for views different from theirs, and "no" answer is hard for them to accept. Those bold enough to say "no" is often viewed as presenting an open challenge or threat to authority, and must brace themselves for what will befall him in return. A problem is caused by improper manners of a junior to a senior, including an inadvertent slip of tongue or failure to differentiate hierarchy in their speech. This is seen in the way Korean students are treated by their seniors at school. Seniority rule punishes failure to perform proper conduct before seniors, an ordeal that comes in the form of physical punishment or mental stress. Indeed, a school itself is vertically structured and in a way resembles the military academy in that juniors are conscious of proper manners. The aura of a military establishment is ubiquitous due to the pervasive presence of strictness, austerity and formality. The positive side of authoritarianism is that it is easier to have consensus among members and enlist support and cooperation down the hierarchical ladders of a bureaucracy, when it comes to implementing a policy. Westerners exposed to such an authoritative climate may find it dull and, at worst, suffocating in the absence of controversial issues. Authoritarianism thrives on a climate that inhibits open debate and challenge: it sees virtues in unity, one path, one system and one race.

The patriarchal family leaves sediments of parental authoritarianism. Filial duty required of children served as an added impetus to foster parental authoritarianism. Within the patriarchal family, father and the first son enjoyed inordinate power. They carried an authoritative and dignified look which strike outsiders as impersonal and lacking in affection. Unlike their own fathers, today's Korean parents are increasingly permissive - even to an extent of spoiling children. The dictum "spare the rod and spoil the child" fall flat on the ears of devoting parents. Still, parental influence remains strong, albeit considerably abated, when it comes to important issues such as career choice, spouses, and others relating to their future. Filial duty brings the bond of parents and offspring closer and tighter, but we note clashes that result from the mindless attachment of parents to repressive intervention in their children's affairs. Authoritarianism carries paternalistic concern, accounting for the greater dependence of Korean children on their parents. But the general trend today is that children are becoming more self-assertive, liberal, self-initiative, and inclined to move away from the shadow of parents. Clashes of opinions are unavoidable, but the generational problems become more serious in the case of Korean expatriates abroad, particularly in Western societies, where self-initiated and independent children are increasingly rebellious to authoritative parents.

Authoritarianism and Personality Cult

An authoritarian ruler used to be a national hero praised for having united contradictory components of national life into a harmonious interplay. Sediments of the monarchical authority of traditional society continued, albeit considerably abated, into the post-liberation regime and the following regimes. These regimes were marked by a strong authoritarian streak to an extent of stifling the principles of liberal democracy. Authoritarian rule is not characteristic of South Korean regimes alone. Joseph Stalin, Mao Tse Tung and Kim Il-sung are the classical examples of the authoritarian ruler that followed from the dictum of managing collective societies. The fate of a coercive state rests with the function of the hero-despot. The military, economic, political and religious powers are pledged to one man through loyalty or submissiveness. But these hero despots distinguished themselves from other authoritarian rulers by identifying themselves with an extraordinary personality cult. An analogical leap leads us to assert that personality cult is a short jump from authoritarianism and that authority and the personality cult feed off each other into an absolute power that gives them claim to the pantheon of heroes.

Many gravitate toward the notion that the absolute power of North Korea's leader is rooted in the authoritarian soil of Korean Confucianism. However, Korea history has never witnessed an absolute power holder like Napoleon, Hitler, Stalin, not to mention Kim Il-sung, who is absurdly deviant from what is expected of the Confucian climate. The dominance of morality in Confucian societies moderates authoritarian brutalities by emphasizing self-restraint in the exercise of power, and this explains the monarchical weaklings against the powerful aristocratic class in the highly centralized system. Since the monarchical kingdom is based on authoritarian rule, it set much emphasis on moral dominance in politics - that the people matters most and caring for them is the supreme concern (minbon in Korean).[2]

Morality and authority were mutually complementary. Morality empowered an authoritarian leader to supervise, intervene, reward and punish all on assumed moral grounds. Moral demand follows one into higher rank. It was maximized at the center in the person of the ruler who exhibited moral charisma and faded as one descends the administrative hierarchy and moves beyond the pale of authority into the marginal orbit of ordinary citizens. Aspirants to higher ranks within bureaucracy are subject to severe scrutiny with regard to their moral transparency. Personality cult, many believe, is the child of authoritarian rule. But it is not compatible with authoritarian rulers. Rather it is an outgrowth of revolutionary zeal that entailed pleas for national unity against an imagined enemy and energized the downtrodden with hopes to be better off. Kim Il-sung borrowed the idea of personality cult from Stalin and Mao but outdid his precursors. As we witnessed after the death of Stalin and Mao, all legacies of personality cult disappeared into the shadow of irony. Nevertheless, Kim Il-sung, even after his death, continues to be blessed by mass fantasy that makes people believe he is still alive to take care of the beleaguered country. A rainbow seen over his statue brings thousands of spectators into kneeling, praying and sobbing in admiration. Obviously, there is a belief in the reincarnation of the dead into the contemporary world to save the people in need of help.

Rational Authoritarianism

In a hierarchical and orderly society, authority plays positive role in fostering shared values that lead to social integrity. Korean workers perform better when they are aware of the presence of a competent leader, not because they are dependent on him but because they draw inspiration from the expected efficacy of his leadership. Personal leadership yields its effect when it is based on rational authoritarianism. As authoritarian role is made visible, loyalty broke a new ground for its achievement. The object of loyalty can be a person, a collective entity, social justice or religious creed. Due to its high propensity to serve a person or a personal interest, loyalty is likely to deepen the chasm between factional leaders or to obscure distinction between the personal and public domains. When loyalty is directed to a group or an organizational goal, it unleashes a powerful collective force that contributes to national development. Authoritarian rule under a contingency situation served as a catalyst for dramatizing Koreans' potential into stunning accomplishments. The sense of loyalty to a collective goal stirred individual workers into pushing themselves to new limits, exerting their best efforts, directed toward a greater good, whether it be for a private firm or a public agency. Korean workers in the 1960's and 70's lost themselves in their whole-hearted devotion to a greater goal of the company - even to the point of neglecting their obligations to their families. It is a collective response to a compelling need for the nation to get out of its long-lasting stagnancy.

Trauma theory explains why South Koreans were so highly motivated to achieve: they were traumatized by ideological confrontation and still on tenterhooks about what will happen in its continuing fray with the north. They were pushing hard to hoist them high enough for the miserable northern brethren to see them climbing high along the development ladder. The unique sense of loyalty held by Koreans is the root cause of hard work and unfailing dedication to something other than personal concerns. It makes it easier to secure social consensus notably under a situation where the authoritarian rule encounters national tribulation.

Humans, once born into the world, form hierarchical networks of relationship where authority becomes something they live in company with. Authority is distinguished from authoritarianism: the former is given by a given post or power, whereas the latter comes from the encounter of a personality trait with an working environment. These two can be put on a single spectrum: access to authority can cause Koreans to bask in an authoritarian air, when one achieves a status of envy. By an analogical extension, dictatorship can be fostered by the people's fawning on or cringing to a figure of authority. Authoritarianism is antithetical to rationalism, and the decline of authoritarianism is considered to be a necessary and desirable phase of historical progress to give room for the working of rationality. However, "if authority had been eliminated along with authoritarianism, something far from the desirable would have resulted" (Kwak Bae Hee 2003;50).

Europe experienced trauma in the 18th century, as the Illuminists aggressively challenged the authority of family, churches and monarch under the banner of "rationalism." A blind pursuit of rationalism in politics inevitably threatened the foundation of a state itself by undermining people's sense of community. The incompatibility of authoritarianism with rationality is plausible since "a social community is not the product of a rational process; rather the community is the unintended product of the shared customs and traditions that various people have experienced over time" (Hahm Jae Bong 2000;35). Despite this contradiction, Koreans witnessed reason making a soft landing on authoritarianism. Authority is the central pillar that holds a family together: without authority, family crumbles with its members falling apart like sand.

A destructive force against the family was intrinsically built into Illuminist thought since it regarded family as an institution encroaching upon individual right and freedom. Given an implacable move toward the frequent breakdown of families, a question arises about whether it is possible to dispense with authority that pervades every aspect of social institution in modern society. "Is there any ideological tool that can substitute for authority?" Some argue that authoritarianism can be an easy way leading to dictatorship and totalitarianism. While this argument has an element of truth, European history abounds in the cases where a sudden breakdown of authority set loose a mighty force that panicked the country to anomie, and this proved to be the fertile ground for totalitarianism to raise its head.

Rationalism, once considered the panacea for all evils, failed to guide the steps of social progress.

The essence of leadership theories emphasizes that authoritarianism tempered with persuasive reasoning and people's voluntary action provides breakthroughs for the problems caused by the absence of authority. The psyche of Koreans, attuned to hierarchical structure of power, is more receptive to authoritarian rule. Authoritarianism will remain, though in a slow decline, as long as organizations are vertically arranged. An authoritarian figure is strong in solipsism. Syng-man Rhee was an authoritarian figure claiming himself as the man who fits the bill in the country that was undergoing stressful post-war rehabilitation. But he failed to reap what came out of the seeds he embedded. The weakness of authoritarian leadership is that the ruler is easily given in to fawning people.

Morality

IIIIIIIIIIIIIIIIIIIIIIIIIIIIII

Retrospective of the Past

Neo-Confucianism draws its ethical principles from the cosmic order and, therefore, its view of morality is static and retrospective. The Confucian analects are the reminders of the old sages: their demeanors are the mirror for posteriors to look at to seek moral guidance. It assumes that ethical norms defy changes as they are considered an abstract heavenly way, the final arbiter, to which all personal interests and aspirations subscribe. Such an outlook exalted morality over the rule of law and institutions. It deters the gestation of progressive thoughts since it risks discontinuity from the inherited ideas. "The essence of Confucian morality is the continuity of and consistency with the past" (Paul B.Horton and Chester L. Hunt 1964;565).

"A realistic approach to morality tends to regard human behaviors in terms of 'right or wrong' and 'good or bad': It sanctions certain actions and forbids others" (Kingly Davis1969;256). In the absence of clearly defined standard criteria, mores, folklores and customs are the important determinants of such an intuitive dichotomization. Morality in its true sense is differentiated from emotional or intuitive decisions by laying stress on an inner feeling drawing on one's consciousness in moral decisions. The moral norm is observed not simply because others around one observe it, but because one has an attitudinal disposition to subscribe to justice, honesty, purity, fairness, truth, etc. Underlying these conception is the assumption that there is a universal and necessary ethics, a priori principle that is absolute and certain as mathematics.

Moral decisions based on customs and habits are retrospective of the past. In contrast, the concept of morality changes with time, as exemplified in the Western Europe. Eastern morality, particularly the

Korean concept of morality, has not changed drastically. In the maelstrom swirling with old and new values, the traditional concept of morality seems to taper into a fuzzy gray, but it raises its voice in the domain of vertical and collective consciousness. The concept of morality readily reveals two contrasting views between Korea and the West. The old Korean concept of morality is based on the moral virtues identified with the connecting threads of the five binary relations and five constants, and morality is judged in terms of the degree of conformity to these pre-determined moral norms.

Chong Yak-yong, a prominent Confucian scholar in the eighteenth century, argued that moral life began with the duty to serve parents and ended with serving Heaven (Chung Yak-yong Chong Seo 2 chip 4 kwon). His view of morality spans a wide spectrum by sublimating familial obligation into the cult of Heaven. "Underpinning morality with its transcendent reference was a novel idea in his times" (Chung Jae-sik 2003;269). The final arbiter of morality is the abstract and over-arching idea of Heavenly Way which defies definition in substantial terms. The Heavenly Way implicates the law of the cosmos. For those living in a modern dynamic society, however, this argument cannot avoid a question; whether the pre-determined norms, often relegated to the static fossil of medieval ages, are still practiced with some degree of intensity? What happens in modern Korea clearly indicates a tendency to subscribe to old values in moral decisions. Social malaises which we experience today more often attributes their cause to the absence of such moral virtues that hearken back to the pre-modern age; any incident of juvenile crime stirring mass media invariably evokes a unanimous shout from across the social spectrum to "return to the old value".

Situational Ethics

In Western societies, moral judgment is made on the basis of individualism and freedom, stressing the individual's ability to make moral decisions by assessing a given situation. With much less dependence on the pre-determined norms, human behavior is guided by the logical and rational working of the mind, the voice of conscience, and religious pleas. Rationality thrives in the soil of individualism, and these two feed off each other to provide important guide posts to moral decisions. "Self interest is the clue to rational choice that plays a moral guide" (Scruton Roger 2002;60). Emanuel Kant echoed the same chord; "Our rational will is the very source of our moral duty and it comes from the inner self, not reliant on questionable sense experience or precarious inference" (Will Duran 1961, 209). Even reason is a fallible guide to morality. For Koreans whose moral behavior is guided by shared values, the Western assertion of self interest as the rational base for morality is not persuasive.

The liberal orientation of morality argues for the maximum scope of moral autonomy while interfering as little as possible with others' freedom. Those steeped in a collective form of living tend to see the egoistical aspect of individualism as destructive of the social fabric. Moral decision based on the ego is incompatible with a society that embraces the diverse needs of its constituents. That an individual has the sole authority for beliefs and action leaves little room for external intervention. Rather, individualism is subject to personal prejudice and bias, built-in dispositions of each person. From a religious viewpoint, if a man or woman wants to live a moral life, it needs an overseers that guides moral behaviors in the right direction. But many dismisses this conception as moral obscurantism.

The Korean concept of morality, in contrast, reflects a group norm; morality is what is good for the majority of the constituents within a group or society. A group norm presupposes that external standards or principles constitute the authority that dictates one's beliefs and actions. While the Korean concept of morality is fixed around pre-set norms, the Western view of morality is rational-dominant and situation-specific. The Western concept of morality emphasizes the capacity of an individual to make moral choices with a resulting variation in behavioral responses, contrary to the Asian standardized behavioral norms that commands a wide following, observed by all members of society. Such predetermined norms, forced on all, gives clues to a set of predictable behaviors through which Koreans respond to particular stimuli. Koreans, the people of an underdog state, are more conscious of national symbols than those from more powerful states. Every Korean feels his heart beat to the national anthem and stands to attention while singing. Such a passionate love of national symbols that Koreans take for granted looks quite strange to "any English intellectual who would feel more ashamed of standing to attention during 'God Save the King'" (Jeremy Paxman; 12)

Criteria for Moral Judgment

There once were moral principles in the West, that were the equivalent of Korean predetermined norms. In medieval Europe, the religiously faithful people sought ultimate sanction for morality from Christian ethics. "Ten commandments" and the New Testament were laws best applicable to all men. Christian moral virtues narrow down to atonement, piousness, rectitude, and prudence –and refusal to recognize them was meant to abdicate one from being personhood and to deny the possibility of real community living. The Christian world, however, underwent a process of secularization with the resulting separation of the state from religion. With the Illuminist philosophy, reacting to the God-centered world, the quest for innate human ability brought forth a tendency towards moral decisions based on individualism and freedom. Christian moral virtues, contrived to cross the bound of parochial networks, paralleled material wealth and scientific discovery, with the concomitant loss of any cause for ethical instructions. The Reformation emancipated individuals from customs, traditions, church, and even family, defeating the effort to embrace a common and clearly framed set of ideas on which to base value judgments. Moral actions have become diverse in modern society, hardly providing the basis for moral judgment. Morality has lost its lofty place and is reduced into a pragmatic business of living subject to situational whims. The existentialist's view of an individual as a unique life gave full vent to situational ethics, asserting that moral principles are determined by particular situations in which moral decisions are required. Such a view left little room for the standardization of human behaviors.

The Korean concept of morality emphasizes the humane character fit to maintain a harmonious relationship with people, and pre-determined norms are still the useful measure of moral behavior. The

Western view of morality, on the other hand, is concerned with "good or bad" and "correct or wrong" in a given situation, leading to inquisitive and analytical questions contrived to seek an absolute arbiter. It appears that such an analytical view of morality seems to lose relevance, since a moral issue, in the absence of external criteria, is a fuzzy gray rather than black and white. The result is an increased resort to the rule of law.

The traditional concept of morality in Korea gave sympathy to an underdog or a pitifully deprived person and anathema for ambition. Humaneness (In) is equated with compassion or warmth in the heart. According to Korean folklore, morality is a warm heart but devoid of action and ambition."Hungbu Chon (The Story of Hungbu) features a protagonist named Hungbu, an ideal man, emotionally moved by a little swallow with a broken leg, but he was inept. He is depicted as a moral paragon in contrast to his elder brother notorious for ambition bent to improve his lot" (Kim Jae-un 1991, 243). This story reflects the Korean tendency to give higher value to the affective aspect than duty, ambition and competency. His brother is aggressive, ambitious, and stingy. Thus, a good Korean is self-restrained and humble, warmly affectionate and patient to endure hardships. Implicit in this definition is the belief that the self-effacing element of moral character stores up heavenly reward. Such a vision of a moral paragon bred the cult of underdog or victim. There has been a strong tendency towards giving sympathy to an underdog candidate for an electoral office, irrespective of political credibility. Repeated failure to be elected places a candidate in a better position to appeal for votes from compassionate people.

In the Korean concept, morality invariably evokes concepts such as propriety, integrity and decency, and these were apparently the moral strength of Koreans of traditional society. The downside of these virtues was a lack of ambition either to achieve expansionist goals or to accumulate wealth. Koreans have rarely hatched dreams of military expeditions against foreign lands but, instead, have weathered foreigners' beatings. Koreans' distaste for abrasive ambition and assertiveness discouraged a Faustian pursuit of self interest and self aggrandizement. Ambition and assertiveness carried a negative connotation in Korea, and it made an ambitious man an outcast or at least someone to be marginalized in the collective society.

In reference to Korean moral consciousness, Kim Tae-gil defines three major constraints on human behavior. One is the force of a stronger person or authority and threat from an external force. Law constrains human behaviors by having a binding effect on all who might breach it. Second, how one's behavior is perceived by others is an important behavioral guide in collective society. There are the eyes and ears of others which exert influence on one's act and motive. Third, the voice of conscience is an internal call for action, and the behavioral manifestation of it is self control and a discreet and prudent act opposed to acting on emotional impulses. In a collective society, one's concern for the greater good of the group outshines the voice of conscience, and the resulting behaviors are self-effacing and group-centered, blurring what is good for society at large.

In the frequent display of bonhomie characteristic of Koreans, reason or logics comes a distant second to harmonious human relations. On the contrary, the Western culture regards the rule of law and order as an absolute arbiter of morality with less concern for norms or mores. Moral judgment based on human relations are relative in the absence of objective standard measures that are supposed to reside beyond the sphere of human relations. The absence of objective measures invites emotional intervention to calibrate the distance in human relations. Fairness and honesty are relative terms in a society where connectedness or relatedness prevails over reason. Koreans' penchant for relatedness leaves ample room for 'bending the rules' of law in order to serve a group interests, and one's commitment to honesty can become ambiguous when it competes with group commitment or loyalty. Koreans are often torn between honesty and loyalty, and occasionally find themselves in favor of group loyalty over honesty and justice. The heart is the moral guide of the Koreans, whereas Western morality is guided by the head. "The heart has its own logics that the head cannot understand."[3]

The emotional aspect of moral judgment is also attributed to a blurred distinction between private and public domains. Confucian norms, Cheong Jae-young notes, are "relevant to the private domain where the heart is the moral guide." They, however, lose their relevance to the public domain where moral decisions are based on impersonal assessment of reality, fairness, rationality and objectivity. Western societies have long since departed from Gemmeinschaft relationships replete with favoritism, nepotism, and regionalism; they developed public consciousness based on service and duty, no longer obsessive with particularistic likes or dislikes. Objectivity, rationality and honesty are restrained or obscured by emotional concerns when they apply to a parochial circle of association.

The Circle of Association

The clannish proclivity of Koreans invites criticism from foreigners for the lack of an intermediate values that can extend trust to larger, more diffused circles of association. The familial network of trust is regarded as a trench in which one feels comfortable and secured, but life, for Koreans as with others, is all about existing among others, bound to a network of relationships. Loyalty to the molecular group has proven to be an obstacle to expanding circles of association. Warmth in the heart deepens relations in the parochial circle that comes from the people who get together to embrace no other manifest goal than a group's solidarity or fraternity. For a people who are bound by fraternity based on the warmth of the heart, there is the pathetical lack of public consciousness. It is widely held that Koreans lack the communitarian spirit of the early American settlers that fascinated Alexis Tocqueville. Francis Fukuyama calls this intermediate value 'spontaneous sociability' which makes it easy for a parochial concern to leap to a larger one. He went on to classify the countries into 'high-trust' societies endowed with an intermediate value and a 'low-trust' ones known for the lack of it. As society grows in complexity, greater importance was given to an individual capable of freely alternating between parochial and larger groups. The family in Korea creates a greater gravitational force to make the expanding circle bounce back, countering the centrifugal force built into circles of association. A community demarcates a space where Koreans are too shy to say "high" to others. Moral virtues lose their luster in a world of strangers.

The basic concept of Korean morality derives from loyalty or a sentimental attachment to a group, more frequently a small one. Koreans tend to be too shy to move on to an enlarged realm. An individual tied to a parochial group is, however, not unwilling to renounce his or her interest in favor of the greater good of all. As demonstrated by Koreans on extraordinary occasions, parochial loyalty has a potential match with greater communitarian concerns. "What makes the facile expansion of one's circle in a world of strangers is the citizenship bound by duties to their fellow citizens" (Scruton Rogers 2002;60). While this concept has yet to develop, Koreans demonstrated greater concern for the state or for a more diffusive entity, since there is consensus in their perception of society as an extended family. This notion activated popular responses to the country's crisis. Obsession with a parochial circle provokes a sense of patriotic nationalism within the homogenized society. As ethnic and religious consciousness united all Jews to confront their hostile Arabs, the concept of an extended family activated Koreans' patriotism in times of crisis.

With many moral virtues confined within the private domain, social justice is a recent development associated with liberal democracy. The importance of justice glitters in the public domain. The Korean tendency towards small groups makes the measuring rod of justice elastic as if it freewheeled between the private and public domains. In the public domain, it is equated with moral righteousness which is supposed to guide statecraft. The public perception of justice under the authoritarian rule does not necessarily require the legitimacy to achieve a goal when it serves a greater cause. Koreans' loyalty, ethical or unethical, to a small group is frequently viewed as a righteous act, even if it has a potential clash with the greater good of society. The policy of authoritarian regimes to put democratic dictum in abeyance could not avoid public approbation, but was justified when it served the greater cause of rapid development.

Morality vs. Legality

The diverse interests of modern society give rise to myriads of behavioral motives. The fixation of morality as the motive for human acts is anachronistic, since it denies the presence of an array of alternative motives that grows in proportion to increasingly diverse society. Situational fluidity obscures the clarity of fairness or decency in human behavior. With the trend to reify abstract standards into specific attributes, it seems that there is no alternative but to base moral judgments on the voice of conscience and on a careful assessment of alternative motives and the social acceptance of its consequence. Whether a motive to act comes from within or without makes a significant difference in its moral value. An act initiated by one's internal call or volition is much more desirable than one done under pressure or threat. Although an act is justified with regard to its motive, its consequence may not prove to be acceptable in society. Reversely, an act done under pressure may prove to be socially acceptable, since social acceptance is another element which qualifies one's behavior as moral.

The Korean emphasis on moral motives reflects a greater concern for "acting by volition" before the rule of law intervenes. This casts into a question how morality relates to the rule of law. In the authoritarian climate, the rule of law is considered the fist of moral authority employed to shield the regime from its real or imagined enemies. The law is rarely, if ever, considered a moral or politically neutral force to be used by the populace to protect their interests from the intrusive state. To draw on Marsilio, "the essence of law lies in its imperative and coercive character. Law does not have an ethical content" (Norman F. Cantor 1963, 510). In the symbiotic relationship between morality and authoritarianism, the rule of law is at the behest of a moral authority, producing a tendency to avoid laws or bend them, if ensnared, to serve its moral purpose. Institutional legitimacy matters little if a charismatic ruler better serves the moral purpose.

The interpretation of law cannot escape the prism of culture. Remarkable differences in interpretation are explained not only by circles of association but, more importantly, by the sense of moral responsibility. A case in point is the judicial treatment of on-duty offenses or misdemeanors by American soldiers in Korea. In a legal case involving misdemeanors of lower officials on duty within an organization, the Korean legal system holds their senior officials responsible for renouncing their moral responsibility. Punitive measures including dismissal or suspension is expected to follow, though the senior officials are not directly involved in the misdemeanor. Often then, moral responsibility leads to harsh punishment that goes beyond the bound of rationality. As Korea has not escaped the elements of a patrimonial society, moral responsibility remains almost unabated.

A typical reminder of moral responsibility was the reactions of Koreans to the acquittal of two American soldiers responsible for the death of two Korean middle school girls. The offenders were brought to the U.S military trials on charge of killing Korean teenagers while they were operating an armored vehicle. The trial of the two offenders was placed under the glare of Koreans, since the issue was so much sensitized in the middle of the presidential campaign. The American legal treatment of this case sets great store on the intent of the offenders as the crucial factor that would affect the verdict. As a U.S Forces spokesman said, "we have acknowledged that it was our fault. It was our vehicle, it happened during our exercise. We have apologized and paid compensation to the families."

The apologies were too abstract or rhetorical for Koreans who perceived moral responsibility as requiring somebody's head to be chopped. Under moral dominant perspective, moral cudgel should have been no less stringent than legal cudgel. The U.S military decision to acquit the offenders – on grounds that they had no intention to kill the Korean school girls –may be justified on legal grounds but sparked massive candle-lit demonstrations nationwide. To the astonishment of Americans and Koreans alike, this legal dispute had spiraled into a crisis that threatened to mar the bloody ties of the two countries. Unfairness in the trial was regarded as an American over-arching dominance flouting the pleas of Koreans and a direct affront to the nation on a surging wave of nationalism and pride in the nation's flurry of stunning accomplishments, including the outstanding performance of the Korean soccer players in the FIFA World Cup Game. It not only magnified a fundamental rift in their interpretations of the legal case but aroused nationalism that complicated the matter with anti-imperialist sentiments.

Korean grief and anger have become a collective sentiment which would never be placated by the American president's apologies. Koreans perceive SOFA (Status of Overseas Forces Agreement) as contrived to protect and insure that the American forces in an overseas mission receive just judicial treatment, to ensure their impunity from local legal sanction. Nationalism over this issue involved passionate emotions that blurred the clarity of distinction between on-duty offenses and criminal acts against local citizens. A question is raised: could Korean public will tolerate their soldiers in overseas mission subject to local sanction against on-duty offenses? The moral obsessions of Koreans involve anti-foreign nationalism, especially when it relates to a giant country like the United States. This case demonstrated the triumph of moral sentiments over legal judgments; the moral cudgel is, at least, as much acrimonious as legal punishment.

We can imagine a domain of morality clearly distinct from that of law. The common notion is that where the moral continuum ends, the law continuum begins; morality refers to a more desirable means of averting unwanted consequences before the rule of law intervenes. Morally undesirable behavior is not necessarily subject to legal punishment; a son who neglects his filial obligations to his parent cannot be punished unless he commits a criminal act. Some moral norms have a binding force which may result in a more stringent punishment to befall a spoiled son than a legal cudgel. In defining morality, the voice of conscience is as of crucial importance as an act of internalizing all factors and making an informed decision which is justified in terms of its motive and social acceptance. The voice of conscience is expressed in the rational and logical working of the mind. It is the quintessential quality of democratic citizenship that "the exercise of my own rights requires as much respect to others' rights" (Kim Tae-gil;1981;243).

The old concept of morality accentuated "the virtue of obedience," and this enjoins the weaker to comply with the stronger. Moral education that stresses obedience will produce stronger men whose behaviors are hard to control in relation to the weaker one. As mentioned earlier, the eyes and ears of others, together with moral or social norms, are an important behavioral guide in the collective society. One's sensitivity to these external pressures may dull his sense of what is good for others and society at large. If a woman is sensitive to what her rich friends wear within a social group, she may go against her will to "keep up with the Jones" and finds herself somewhere beyond the reach of her financial means, if not bankrupt. The words like "envy" and "jealousy" are the products of living within a group whose norms mold all members into an identical pattern of life. One or few who raise others' eye brows by displaying their opulence in luxurious ornaments arouse envy or jealousy among those who cannot afford it.

Koreans within small groups are egalitarian, but they run wild once they are outside the group where they no longer see familiar faces. Autonomous morality is an antidote to enslaving the self to the external pressures. It is imperative that moral education be reoriented to develop a new consciousness of social justice, free from parochial interpretations, and voluntary will to observe. The concept of citizenship defined in terms of 'rights and duties' may produce an ideal society to which humans aspire. Citizenship is a constant call to duties based on spontaneous participation in other affairs than personal ones. Citizenship enjoins one to live up to 'my right means other's duties' and 'I prosper on the duties of others'(Scruton Rogers 2002;34). Duty is simply the other side of one's free choice of action. The linkage of one's rational choice to benefit others provide an ideal guide post to moral decisions. "Citizenship is enshrined in the individual sense of being part of a community. The concept of morality derives directly from our relationship with each other" (Hugh Mackay, 1993; 270)

Nationalism

|||||||||||||||||||||||||||||||||||||||||||||

The definition of nationalism varies depending on the history of a country. Dictionary definitions refer to "love of and pride in the country or "desire by an ethnic group to become an independent country." In democratic societies, "nationalism became a power for overturning the old order and cementing the new one " (George Novak 1971,118). England justified its imperial aggrandizement to bear Anglo-Saxon freedom and civilization on its dominions. France built its empire under the ensign of exporting the values of its cultural enlightenment to the natives. In those countries that had divided into princely or feudal states, nationalism turned into 'irredentism,' a movement to bring all ethnic groups into one nation state. These countries were late in joining the rank of imperialistic powers. "To this day, nationalism retains its progressive potential in backward countries, thus involving them in their democratic revolution" (Novak, 119).

Ethnic Nationalism

The relatively small size of its land, steady national borders and ethnic and cultural homogeneity characterize Koreans from others, and nationalism in non-European countries neatly fits this concept. Nationalism in the West was an ethnic pride in a train of accomplishments and became a driving force when it met with the national goal. It strengthened state' power and enlarged its territory encroaching over others.

Foreign residents in Korea complain that the single biggest obstacle to understanding Koreans is their exclusiveness, a matter that is often equated with ethnic nationalism. Their view of Korean nationalism identifies it with parochialism or exclusiveness that discourages them to integrate into the Korean circles of intimates. Koreans rarely nod in a friendly greeting to strangers. The exclusive aura of Korean nationalism has much to do with the historical trauma in relation to its neighboring and other countries. Nationalism befalls the homogenized people with a greater sense of ethnic unity reinforced by a millennia-old consistency of cultural, ethnic, language and political identities. Love for a country, its language, culture, symbols, and history is a natural instinct of people clustered around a racial or political group, and this patriotic sentiment pervades the traditional definitions of nationalism. It should be noted, however, that Korean nationalism, as it exists today, contains complex sentiments not confined to exclusiveness or xenophobia alone.

For a people who have shared cultural homogeneity, the gemeinschaft concept of nationalism is associated with the nation of gens or volk, a people of common descent with a unitary culture, a common religion, language and history. Nationalism in its relative term is a kind of collective sentiment of people against the stronger nations, aroused when their country is driven into a perilous state by the predatory incursions or overbearing attitudes of stronger powers. The exclusive nature of nationalism was occasionally sublimated into an intermittent political movement to resist a dominant foreign power when their country is teetering on the brink of extinction.

Nationalism and Ideology

During the colonial period, Korean ethnic nationalism fueled anti-Japan struggles for the restoration of national independence. After liberation from the colonial yoke, Koreans held the foreign powers responsible for a succession of tragic events that left their country in a miserable state. Nationalistic sentiment was aroused by the perception that foreign powers were shaping their country's destiny. Here, nationalism reacts to the mass perception that a stronger power is intent on subduing a weaker one. As the first country to be traumatized by the Cold War, nationalism lost its integrative force to bring all Koreans into a single political entity. Nationalist activists at home and abroad split over the ideological identity of the new state projected in their visions of a unified Korea. In the ideologically bifurcated world, however, ethnic nationalism retreated into the backstage.

While nationalism was considered the guiding star for nation-building, it was by no means possible for it to remain immune to ideological persuasion under the confrontational rivalry between the two powers. Nationalism without anti-communism in South Korea could not survive, while North Korea seethed with ethnic nationalism and a passionate zeal for revolution, thus shaping its political identity loaded with hostility against their brethren in the South. It condemned South Korea as the proclaimed surrogate of the United States. If the south is the surrogate for the United States, what the north was to the master whose ideology dictated it?

A typical example of ideological rift over nationalism occurred between the two most prominent nationalistic figures of Korea, Syngman Rhee, the First President of South Korea, and Kim Ku, Premier of the Korea Provisional Government during the colonial rule. Both were well known for their heroic struggles against the colonial master. Kim Ku asserted nationalism as the dictum for "one people for one nation state." He was bent to avoid the establishment of two governments, no matter what their ideological stands, and critical of Rhee's plan to establish a separate government for the south. Kim Ku was assassinated after his aborted meeting with Kim Il-sung in 1948 in a desperate effort to avoid "two Koreas and this knelt the death toll of nationalism as an integrative force to realize a unified nation. In contrast, Rhee perceived the futility of negotiation with the communized North, when communism dominated North Korea while leftists in the south were growing into a dominant faction taking advantage of widespread anarchy. The merciless reality was that a unified nation would surely lead to a communized Korea, leaving Rhee with no alternative but to save the southern half from surrendering to communism. His staunch nationalistic stand compromised with an anti-communism dictum, and his foresight into the contagious expansion of communism dramatically turned his back against a unified Korea. In a haste to defend the southern half, he organized constabulary forces whose leadership was filled by experienced soldiers, mostly those who had served Imperial Japan.

Ethnic nationalism fanned public sentiment condemning Rhee for an outright collusion with pro-Japan elements. On the part of Rhee, nothing was of greater urgency than to keep the southern half from turning red, though it involved risking his life for his collusion with the colonial elements. The irony of history was that the foe of yesterday became the friend of today in the south.[4] From the communists' viewpoint, nationalism is based on ethnic purity, and North Korea flaunted its claim to ethnic purity free of foreign contaminants. Ethnic nationalism provided an excuse for the North to be hyper critical of the south whose nationalistic purity was muddied by collaboration with its erstwhile foe and subjugation to a new colonial master (the United States).

Nationalism under the banner of communism had its own limits. It smacks of ethno-centralism and a xenophobic sentiment. The cult of nationalism was a large part of the reason why communism appealed so much among Koreans in post-liberation Korea, as if the communized nationalists had been the sole winner of the war for national independence. It should be noted, however, that parochial nationalism confines North Korea to an island in a sea of foes. No nation in the world stakes its claim to ethnic purity, and ethnic nationalism has long since been fossilized, as if caught in a time warp, although, exceptionally, occasional outburst of ethnic nationalism can be observed in underdeveloped countries against their former colonial masters.

The Radical Turn of Nationalism

In the 1980s and early 1990s, South Korea witnessed a mass movement spearheaded by radical students. This resulted in a radical shift of nationalism from anti-communism to neo-liberalism. Neo-liberalism was not free of ideological flavor by insisting on one Korea.[5] Neo-liberalism was so strong that it even challenged the authoritarian regimes in the south clothed in liberal democracy. Shouting voices for a better life for the deprived majority became louder as a result of so many problems which had been glossed over under the mantra of an all-out growth policy.

In North Korea, as in other communized countries, the notion of a proletariat utopia was allied to nationalism under the banner of anti-imperialism. North Korea regards its confrontation with the United States as a revolutionary front enjoining them to liberate South Korean brethren from the new colonial rule, American imperialism. The new nationalistic stand of North Korea was identified as Jucheism, the ruling philosophy of the North, allegedly contrived by Kim Il-sung and became the ruling philosophy of North Korea. Juche emphasizes "independence" as its core concept and defines the development of history as a process to liberate a suppressed people. A 1982 publication quoted Kim

Jong-il as "In human beings, independence is life itself and the history of mankind is the history of struggles to achieve the independence of the masses to protect themselves from the unfair authority of others." Liberation of the downtrodden people draws on Karl Max's dialectical progress of history.

In 1986 when Gorbachev's "glasnost" and perestroika" were the catchphrase of the Soviet policy, North Korea emphasized the primary importance of Jucheism, and upheld the official viewpoint of its own system that was inherently different from its fellow communist countries. It meant a return to an exclusive policy that insulated the country from the outside world. Confined within the ideological barrier, North Korea became a tightly sealed hermit monarchy. Nationalism inevitably assumed an ideological color, reducing itself into a defensive mechanism for political and institutional identity. Choi Chang-jip sees this phenomenon as "the nationalistic front crumbling before the rock of ideology." This does not mean that nationalism dissipated into obscurity with the ideological division of Korea; rather it remained dormant to be rekindled into struggles against the dictatorial regimes of South Korea which were blamed for being a surrogate for America, and a straight ideological jacket of the north did not allow anti-government struggles of any kind in the north.

Nationalism wept over the ethnic oneness split into two parts in contrast to the recent European history that saw ethnic dispersion brought into a nation state. In the presence of poverty-stricken masses, dormant nationalism erupted into mass nationalism that was antithetical to state nationalism. Mass nationalism does not recognize any existing regime in a divided Korea, and its effort to strip nationalism of ideological colors was, at some point of time, made coterminous with the North-proposed "Federation of Two Governments." Again, though, the North's approach to reunification is greeted with skepticism about the dubious co-existence of the two ideologically opposed systems. A confederation of states is workable when all member states have ideological and institutional commonality.

The Source of Surging Pride

Nationalism was at the outset a reactive, anti-foreign sentiment aroused by the realization of the country in peril before the predatory powers. Later it shifted to active nationalism by drawing inspiration from national pride in a string of accomplishments. A country which made a dramatic turn from its fate and stamps its feet for world recognition of its heightened status is highly sensitive to how it is treated by the mass media abroad. Any words short of praise by an outsider, not to mention taunt, are more often than not taken as outright affronts to its burgeoning national pride. Hell has no fury like a nation state scorned.

The American media's focus on poorly-lit sweat shops on the outskirt of Seoul in the years running up to the Seoul Summer Olympics in 1988 might be justified from the feisty media's intent to reveal the true reality of the host. On the other hand, it would have been more sensible to think that this media attention shattered the dream of a country endeavoring to show its achievements to the world in its hostile confrontation with its northern half. The Seoul Olympics symbolized the sweat of the

Koreans' brows, and the media criticism did much to stir nationalistic sentiment at home against the world power that had once been acclaimed as the war savior and as the major donor of support for the Koreans' effort to rebuild the nation out of ashes. This world power instilled in the minds of Koreans its image as a permanent ally, protector and helper, and Koreans developed a sense of emotional dependency and reliance on it.[6]

Korea's impressive achievements in modernization gave rise to a tidal surge of pride and confidence that gave full vent to active nationalism. Koreans were stirred to heroic efforts to enhance their role in partnership with America. The donor-receiver relationship kept Koreans in an emotional tie, immune to winds of changes. Had Koreans known the cold-blooded dynamics of the competitive world, they might have hardened to face new challenges with a degree of equanimity. There was, on the other hand, a significant segment of the population who wished to see the role of the United States eternalized as a merciful brother. Sustained dependence on a big brother would have reduced Korea into a perennial child. This underscored Koreans' penchant for an enduring relationship, but any act that contradicts this expectation is liable to invite a fitful outburst of rage in a country devoid of generosity. Modernization is, in a way, the acceptance of Western mores and technology. When damage was dealt to national pride, anti-Western sentiment was aroused, drawing inspiration from the ethno-centric consciousness. The low threshold of tolerance of Koreans at the take-off stage set loose emotional outrage verging on xenophobic sentiment.

Korean nationalism deserves attention in relation to the Confucian impact on Koreans. Confucian emphasis on blood ties speaks for a narrow band of experience of Koreans and parochial circles of association. The resulting exclusive and clannish trait of Koreans discourages many foreigners to break through what appears to be an impenetrable shell of kinship. Exclusivity works its way to create boundaries between individuals or factions, but they are not of a kind of ice that defies attempts to breakthrough. What is shared among Koreans would make a strong emotional appeal for group solidarity and social fraternity, but, once the ice has been broken, outsiders have an easy access to the core of a group and build an enduring relationship.

It is true that Koreans are clannish, but treating this as a categorical image of an ethnic group simplifies the complexity of Koreans' mentality spanning a wide spectrum. Some Koreans are more open-minded to foreigners than are the Japanese, though both show a tendency to look upon strangers with reserve or awe in the first encounter. It takes a good while to get acquainted with one another across the cultural border. Clannishness finds its manifestation in the enclaves of Korean expatriates abroad, isolated from the mainstream culture. Nationalistic consciousness explains the transnational homeland consciousness of Korean diasporas, expressed in their determination to preserve cultural and ethnic links with the home country. Exploring Korean-Americans, Nancy Abelmann notes that the American dream and a homeland consciousness complement each other. "In this way, national identification - not with the United States, but with South Korea - is seen as the key to such success" (Nancy Abelmann and John Lee 1996;13).

Nationalism represents a collective sentiment of people who share one cultural or political identity, while patriotism is individual love, a kind of a mindset to work for the country and the people. While the former has its meaning clearly etched against the backdrop of competition or confrontation with a foreign country - but not necessarily xenophobic or hostile to it - the latter is merely an emotional manifestation of a personality trait. Koreans are strongly nationalist but not all of them claim themselves to be patriots. Korea was in the 1980s criticized for its nationalistic, xenophobic and mercantilist economy branded as unfairness, dumping and closed market policy. Apparently, nationalistic sentiment permeated its economic policy. Protectionism is common in the world, albeit its intensity varies from country to country, and the fact that Korea was singled out for beating rather suggests an excessive nationalism at work. Opening the door to the domestic market led to fierce debates, as it brought intransigent opposition from Koreans, notably farmers, branding it as a collaborator with Western predatory economies.

For the United States that was the major market open to Korean manufactured goods on its take-off stage, its trade deficit with the developing countries were the major motive for giving full vent to strong voices for fair trade based on a reciprocal basis. Koreans regarded U.S-proposed fair trade as a new wave of protectionism. Had Koreans known that a cold head dominated a warm heart in impersonal power dynamics, they would not have been so shocked by the American protectionism. It takes common sense to realize that the United States actions were motivated by self-interest. The naivety of Koreans - belief in the warm heart of Americans – left them unprepared for the cold-blooded policy based on self interest. There is no grey area between the two extremes of protectionist and open economists. The cold heart of a merciful big brother inflamed the outburst of xenophobic nationalism. A Korean proverbial metaphor depicts a stingy man as "one trying to wrestle liver from a flea." Americans were blamed for being a stingy big power, after they had been acclaimed as bountiful donors

Globalization keeps a centrifuge whirring on and nationalism is driven into perspective. As global communication and commerce mold us all into identical souls, nationalism is at work in defiance, serving as a drag on the move toward larger circles of association. Supposedly on their way out, racial, ethnic, and religious differences are reasserting themselves, not only say in the Balkans but in every corner of the globe. Cultural homogenization still grips Koreans in an unambiguous identity. Amid the global trend, each nation strives to preserve its distinct identity. The more identical the people become, the greater an urge to be different. People long to be recognized as something special; they draw their identity from differences vis-a-vis others. If universalism is a cold, neon-lighted room, nationalism is a cozy corner filled with comfort and camaraderie. For many who defected south prior to and during the Korean War, ethnic nationalism is a fantasy. There is something of an irony that ethnic, cultural and political division befell the Koreans most conscious of ethnic homogeneity; the notion of one people belies the mutilation of the land. Ethnic consciousness is blurred in the rising pain of dislocation. Nationalism is nostalgia for the lost home, and this nostalgia often haunts the psyche and imagination of the displaced like a hungry ghost that refuses to be appeased.

Emotional Pendulum

The human face is the hallmark of every social or working relationship and shows much of what lies in a deep recess of consciousness. One Korean characteristic, as many observers have pointed out, is their strong emotional involvement, particularly among persons within the circle of intimates. "Not only do people tend to act emotionally, but they have certain aversion to business-like contractual interactions which are reserved for 'outsiders' without significant collectivistic connections" (Kim Jae-eun 1991;243). The insider and outsider dichotomy is attributed to a social value inclined to calibrate interstices between persons. Warmth of the heart pervades interactions between insiders, but such a virtue is lost in the public life. When it comes to extending association beyond the established circle, Koreans rarely have interactions with the same degree of affection, passion and personal involvement. Parochial and in-depth grouping keeps the circle from stretching into larger ones, contradicting the Confucian ideal of unhindered expansion from family to society.

According to the Confucian ideal, Korean heroes are loyal subjects, filial sons and respectful husbands, and to cultivate these virtues in combination takes much pain and patience. Restraint, soberness, and impassive dignity might have pleased old Korean sages, but these traits are rarely found among contemporary Koreans, particularly in their relations to outsiders. Moral values are supposed to fashion all Koreans into idealized stereotype, but, in reality, life in the hustle and bustle of the city rarely befit the idealized pattern. Often, Koreans' excited volatility is observed in contrast to Japanese inhibited behaviors. It seems that there is no safety valve to moderate emotional explosions among contemporary Koreans.

By and large, Koreans are perceived to be fractious and argumentative, as observed among contemporary Koreans, and this is more often observed among Korean politicians. They pounce on minor mistakes, and a minor slip of the tongue is very likely to start off a contentious argument. Having lived in a hierarchically stratified society, Koreans are used to being bullied by fathers, teachers, seniors, dictators, army officers, big brothers, and anyone else with greater authority. They are increasingly status conscious as they rise in rank or position within the hierarchy of an organization. Status consciousness renders Koreans less tolerable of 'no' answers or 'leveling with him' since these are very likely to be regarded as challenges or affronts to one's status. Koreans' behavior is portrayed as a pendulum swinging between the idealized patterns of Confucian sages and emotion-ridden acts.

People who have proved patient with repression are more inclined to find outlets to vent their pent-up emotions. The stronger the repression, the more violent the eruption of rage will be. Extreme self-restraint or control entails extreme emotional explosiveness in an increasingly permissive society. As social transformation drives Confucian asceticism into the background, Koreans conveniently attune their behavior to emotional imperatives and situational whims. During the Korean War and the stressful post-war period, Koreans lived a life of extreme austerity. They were so obsessive with a 'survival complex' fixated on immediate survival needs that they couldn't afford to heed the voices of soberness and manners. Now that the repressive norms have given way to 'id' impulses, instincts are expressed in their survival struggle, the frantic drive for materialistic wealth and higher status and political freedom. The static psyche of Koreans flies into a storm and just quickly subsides into placidity. Swinging between emotional extremity and restrained soberness suggests that the ideal behaviors are still at work as a counterweight to emotional explosion. Harmony is ensconced in the cosmological make-up, as reflected in the co-existence of heaven, earth, and man. Man finds his raison d'etre in the holistic totality of the three wherein his role in balancing with nature is emphasized. This notion views man as part of nature that contradicts the Western view of man as an independent entity that justifies man's role as a predator against nature. Harmony with nature inspires submissiveness to the rule of nature, as expressed in "the heavenly way" that mirrors itself in the norms of human relationship.

The volatile behavior of contemporary Koreans contradicts the concept of harmony reinforced by constantly inculcating "means" (jung yong in Korean), which literally denotes 'middle' or 'non-excessive.' Lin Yu-tang defines Jung Yong as "half and half" which enjoins man to maintain a middle position between behavioral extremities. It involves moderating and humbling oneself, cognizant of mankind's paltriness and vulnerability. There is no fixed principle to guide behavior, and this encourages the human ability to make informed decisions which befit a situational dictum. Jung Yong derives from a criticism of the strict tenets of Confucianism that emphasizes soberness, hard work and self restraint. In this sense, statecraft based on Jung Yong is an art of reacting to the prevailing situation, rather than necessarily being dictated by ethical principles. Freedom, power and wealth seem to be available in unlimited quantities. But excessive pursuit of them requires a price to be paid by another, and this argues for the necessity of self-restraint. Unrestrained ambition for wealth has its own limit, for it requires others to suffer harms. The flipside of Jung Yong is the leeway for the elusive nature of human behavior that allows no objective measurement of moral righteousness. So far as human beings are bound to emotional ties and affection, then, warmth of the heart and compassion prevail over reason and the rule of law.

Confucianism requires that all inter-personal and social relations be given a human face. Where humaneness has greater appeal, resorting to the rule of law is frowned upon as an impersonal and cold-minded way to get matters resolved. For emotion-ridden Koreans immersed in their vertically structured society, the rule of law is likely to carry negative connotations - as something imposed from above. Many Koreans believe that harmonious relationships based on humane concern provides antidotes to social problems and that the rule of law comes a distant second to harmony. 'Solving problems in a human way' takes precedence over resort to the rule of law. In a business that requires a kind of contract, many foreigners are dismayed to find that the Korean business counterparts come up with a few pages of contract, sure signs of no or little attention to and unpreparedness for possible legal problems. Koreans very often spend much of time defending their behaviors or thoughts, particularly when they are subject to censures by others. It has been noticed that contemporary Koreans slog matters out in heated debates, no matter how long it takes, until a winner is clearly etched against a loser. Such a debate in the end may go to court, however trifle the issue is. Emotion-ridden Koreans have little patience with losing a game or face, since they regard it as a fatal blow to their pride and honor. It is something of an irony that Koreans who used to avoid the rule of law more frequently go to the court for the defense of their righteousness. Courts are snowed under by pending law suits, mostly trivial enough to have been resolved by compromise at an early stage. .

Koreans easily cry and laugh, both occurring in a blink of the eyes. Koreans are full of compassion for the dead, even if the dead were a curse to society. These emotional swings have nothing to do with ethical principles. Koreans are free to vent pent-up feelings, and emotional explosions are more violent with the downtrodden or the poverty-stricken farmers when they rail against government policies. Some aspects of Korean's behaviors cannot be explained by ethical norms. Repressive politics in this mutilated country can partly be attributed to the emotional extremity of Koreans that obscures reason. In the next section, I will explains how moral benchmarks – such as honesty, fairness and truth - yield to emotional whims.

Euiri

In the cultural context where humaneness prevails, Koreans set great store by what they call euiri. This word literally means 'a righteous cause,' but this concept has its meaning distorted to denote moral commitment to group solidarity in a way that produces a greater concern for an enduring relationship built on the rock of fidelity. Should a group goal go against the grain of social sanction, euiri loses its meaning as justice or righteousness; it simply turns into a connecting thread that hold group members together. Some moral commitments are not justified in the rule of law.[7] An emphasis on euiri pervades every aspect of human relationships, and the transgression of it is condemned as the denial of justice, honesty, correctness, and truth. A turncoat or telltale is 'a man of no euiri, somebody to be guarded against, no matter how his act is justified. A man who turned his back against fellow members is not to be trusted. Euiri is in this context equated with loyalty or unfailing commitment to an enduring bond with his fellow workers. Euiri takes on an aura of trustworthiness or reliability, so far as it contributes to the solidarity of a collective entity. By the way it is used, this term suggests that an enduring relationship and fraternity are primary concerns, though it transgresses the rule of law.

Euiri is taken, on a higher plane, for what borders on social justice or righteousness, and here it becomes the final arbiter of human behaviors. When its use is limited to parochial networks of association, euiri blurs the sense of honesty and social justice. A student slipping a tip to his friend, while taking a test, is reprimanded or punished by the school for cheating. But he is atoned, if not upheld as a class hero, by peers for his attempt to help rivals achieve higher marks, rather than let the class suffer from poor results. By the way of justifying his act, he says "I couldn't turn my back on my friend who needed help. I did it because the sense of euri overwhelmed me." Another motive for slipping a tip might be a concern for the pain of being estranged from group members by refusing to cooperate with a group effort to improve achievement for the class. It can be argued that high scores for all is for the good of the harmony of the class. A convict who suffers tortures but never spills the beans which might have tarnished the image of his leader may be hailed as a hero, but the downside of this act is that it numbs his sensitivity to honesty and truth and justifies telling a lie so as to avoid the undermining of group solidarity.

The moral commitment to an old friendship was dramatized in a film entitled "Moreshige" which means a hourglass in which two protagonists appeared. They were class mates who expected their friendship to be life-long, but different family backgrounds set them apart. With unreserved support from parents, one followed a sterling career, becoming a judge of a district court. And the other became a drifter, following what was a patchy education after the untimely death of his parents. Although they were set apart by different paths, they were as close friends as they used to be in childhood. When the latter was brought to the court as a convict accused of murder, the judge agonized over the twist of fate that brought him to deal with the case. His friend might be sentenced to death. After long agony, the judge renounced the job of social envy to avoid determining the fate of his life-long friend. The reason to do so was the sense of euiri which weighed so heavily on his mind. He deserves social acclaim for having been a man of euri. The emotional aspect of his psyche overwhelmed his reasonable judgment about what was good for society. How would his decision have been perceived, if it had happened in the United States? In the absence of an absolute yard stick to measure honesty, an effort to enforce the law is marred by emotional interventions. An excessive concern for human relations hinders the development of civic consciousness: it dulls one's sense of righteousness or social justice in a broad context.

Another meaning of euri is found in a relationship where one has received a favor from another person and come under pressure to pay it back. In this case, euiri finds its equivalent in Japanese giri, though different in meaning, that Japanese make much of. These two words share the same Chinese character, but each has developed along its unique cultural trajectory. The concept of reciprocating favor has developed in Japan to an extent that praises repayment as a virtue. "Giri, defined as a righteous way, is something one does unwillingly to forestall apology to the world" (Benedict Ruth 1946;116). Giri is meant by the term "unwilling" distinct from filial duty or loyalty that appeals to the volition of a performer. One's absolute duty to parents or the ruler is never defined as unwilling, for it is shaped within the immediate circle of his intimate family and in deference to parents or the ruler. Everyone owes his or her parent a boundless gratitude for the gift of birth and rearing. But obligation to repay the parental grace is not considered giri in Japan. Neither is repayment in the display of selfless loyalty considered giri. "Giri arises out of an obligation to a non-related person who has done a favor. Japanese compliance with the duty to repay is unwilling, and virtue comes from the performance of an unwilling duty. Failure to repay constitutes a slur on one's name and an insult to one's honor which may lead even to suicide. Therefore, "Giri denotes one's duty to clear one's reputation of insult or imputation of failure"(Ruth Benedict; 114). Giri to the world is roughly described as the fulfillment of contractual relations. A person fulfills his giri punctiliously, because he must avoid, at all costs, the dreaded condemnation for being "a man who does not know giri."

Jeong

When Koreans speak of jeong, it means a sort of an unbreakable, intimate bond, the fusion of minds to share all, whether good or bad, with others. Jeong is "a kind of glue that holds peoples together in a permanent closeness regardless of situational up and down" (Dian Hoffman 1995;219). Jeong pervades Korean marriage as a process through which two persons become one body and one mind. This explains how the self' is constructed not only in the relationship between male and female but between persons of the same gender. Jeong is an antidote to separateness between persons and brings them into an absolute oneness. Koreans create numerous groups, each fraternized around jeong within a larger group, and it drives Koreans perpetually into a snug and warm corner of a cold room. Although an individual belongs to a large group, he has a high tendency to move to a small group. Jeong is not like a temporary merging of male and female in which both persons maintain readiness to return to a separate individual status and identity. The wife-husband relation at the initial stage of marriage is full of passionate love and intimacy, but there is no guarantee that this passion will remain unabated with the same degree of intensity over time. In later ages when affection begins to dissipate, Jeong binds the couple together, and the marital relationship continues as a substitute for less affection. Old Korean couples rarely show signs of affection, never in public. Westerners wonder how they continue in wedlock without affection. Jeong plays a glue to get them together.

When it comes to divorce in later ages, Korean couples find it very difficult to make decision; their mental functioning becomes more complex as they feel something like a chord built into their relationship. Jeong means the depth of the relationship which refuses to be swayed by whimsical moments. Yang Min-ae defines jeong as a feeling coming from the depth of inter-personal relationship within circles of association in which its members feel firmly entrenched in a niche and developed a "we" feeling (2005.24). Lee Sang-ki sees it as a relationship of mutual dependence where one's disappearance means the end of the other's life, possibly coming from the sharing of a space for long time (2005, 254). Therefore, jeong is not only related to persons but to others including school, home town, a house, a room, and so on. These defined spaces are small and retain some invisible traces of close bonds that make a wayfarer reluctant to depart. Such feelings occur in relation to personal belongings, like furniture one has used, for a sense of attachment develops when a thing has been used for long. The commencement ceremony of a school turns into a sea of tears for those about to depart. Parting causes pain which turns into nostalgia over time. This scene of commencement contrasts that in American schools where students seethe with joy and the thrill of venturing into a new world. Jeong has a touch of retrospection looking into the past. "The psychological definition is a bond of mutual 'resonance' or emotional fusion not only between persons but in relation to an object one has lived with for long" (Lee Sang-ki, 2005, 216).

Jeong follows from a sustained sharing of a space with a person or an object. It deepens with time, and some Koreans rather find it irksome to live with when one hears the reasonable voice of his life to sever the bond. Jeong is a life-long commitment, often too onerous to bear, by compelling one to cast aside an opportunity to start a new life which would have been more beneficial. One is so much attached to a house, hometown and friends that it is hard for a peasant to start a new life somewhere else. Koreans cherish every personal belonging which is "stained by the hand's sweat." Many Korean women are victims to Jeong, since they lose the chance to start a new life after they are widowed, because of an irrational devotion to the dead husband and his family. Jeong aggravates the pain of separation between dispersed families. The seventy years of separation across a tightly sealed borderline left a visceral pain to North Koreans who left their beloved wives and children on a promise to "return in ten days." Jeong saddens Koreans who weep over the fate of a way farer.

The background for the development of such a personality trait is the lop-sided development of the affective domain of human relationship. In cultivating friendship, Koreans accord a greater importance to warmth in the heart, generosity, and tolerance rather than a reason-dominant honesty and reliability. It is indicative of parent-child fusion, particularly a mother-daughter relationship of mutual consonance, which deters the development of an independent and reasonable sensitivity. A man of sympathy with wretched or downtrodden people is glorified as an ideal character. Such a character explains the lack of distinction between "I and others." The sense of egoism and individuality is less developed among Koreans than their Western counterparts.

Han

Koreans, marginalized by giant countries that surround the peninsula, have been traumatized by a succession of tragic events. With the historical traumas came a collective pain of Koreans hidden beneath the surface. Han is the accumulation of the hidden pains, frustrated hopes, helplessness and resentments which could not find outlets. Such a state of mind is an outgrowth of historical beatings the country has suffered over many centuries. The historical trauma of the last century in particular have disturbed the Korean psyche, starting with a collective hostility towards the Japanese and a yearning for reunion between dispersed brethren. Koreans have created none of these pains, but they hold the tragedies as their own destiny through the cognitive or emotional restructuring of the causes. Han is something one has endured and transformed into forbearance and passivity.

With the mutilation of the land, pals from the same school and the same hometown turned into ideological foes. Koreans see themselves as victims of carnages, revenge, and counter-revenge in the course of ideological confrontations. Han finds a ubiquitous presence in ideological confrontation, politics, popular culture, and what not. Koreans are called the people replete with han,(han maneun minjok), because "they are truly a broken-hearted people now desperate to sublimate their pains into a dynamic force for achievement and success"(Michael Breen 1999;35). Han also denotes unfulfilled wishes which Korean individuals carry to their graves. Only a few fulfilled their han. Folklore has a story about a youth who harbored love for a neighbor girl and met an untimely death. The coffin which carried his corpse refused to be lifted off the ground when it came close to the girl's house: presumably his soul didn't want to go on a lonely journey without seeing the girl he loved. After performing a ritual in which his soul was married to the girl, the coffin could be moved. The hapless man finally had his han fulfilled before he went away for good. Korea abounds in soul marriages, that is, most often between the deceased people, which foreigners may find strange. A paratroop soldier died of an accident during an exercise and still married his betrothed spouse who decided to remains celibate with the soul of the beloved.

Among the victims of the downed Korean passenger aircraft in 1982, a pair bonding was made between the unmarried men and women, and soul weddings were performed with their photos looking each other. Soul marriages used to be quite popular when untimely death was endemic. Han has an aspect of an unfulfilled wish which is occasionally hereditary. A father burning with desire to become an attorney, after repeated failures in the fiercely competitive bar examination, passes his unfulfilled wish on to his son. He feels his wish fulfilled when his son or grandson pass the examination. The stage for fulfilling Han is the Koreans' perception of traumas, and this perception transformed their static Han into dynamic Han. Stories of Han explains the hard drive of Koreans to modernize the country in the last few decades.

Gut

A popular way to let go of Han is gut, a ritual performed by shaman. Shamanism is an array of ritual performances to serve various purposes. The shaman concept of the world is an integrated whole of spirits, humans, and nature which gives rise to a range of ritual performances. All pains are on the loose when the equilibrium of the three breaks down. All disasters that mankind suffers is caused by a mismatch of one with the other. The shaman gut is contrived to mediate for the restoration of equilibrium, bring good fortunes, pray for prosperous business, summon a divine hand for help, and the like. Of all shaman rituals, han'purie, literally translated in to "give full vent to the piles of pains" and "let spiritual deities in on them," is dominant, as a means of providing catharsis. It has become a common practice for North Korean refugees to perform a gut to empty the mind of the entangled skein of anger, frustration and yearning. Shamanism in practice is a propitiatory ritual contrived to give solace for the heart-broken souls. Many Koreans wonder how they would have survived an ocean of pain, had it not been for shaman's role in giving comfort and solace. Gut does no longer have a monopoly on the downtrodden but nowadays is ubiquitously practiced, irrespective of social status, by those who wish to put aside the burden of anxiety. Koreans who reject shamanism as a superstition is not immune to a temptation to have a gut performed when it comes to engaging in a risky business or to wishing for a safe journey abroad. It touches a deep recess of human desires to alter or alleviate the life of sufferings which are caused by something other than the self beyond humans' capacity for remedy.

Kibun

In a society where the self is considered in terms of its relatedness to others, one pays attention to what others feels about your behavior. Appreciating the feelings of others offers important clues as to how one should behave. It is important to know that Koreans know the emotional status of a friend, associate or partner. In this connection, another term nun'chi" denotes the ability to sense the feelings of others before one takes an action, and this word is used in referring to someone who is quick to grasp how a situation is unfolding. Koreans consider kibun as extremely important and spend a lot of time sizing up the kibun of someone to meet or talk with in order to catch an opportune time to act, so that they do not incur the wrath of others. When a boss is enraged, for instance, a junior abides by time until he cools down, especially when it comes to reporting unpalatable news. A junior, in an extreme case, will avoid reporting the truth, aware of how the boss will take it, and consider a way to keep him in good kibun as the best strategy. Ambivalence and ambiguity are the hallmark of Koreans' trait due to their tendency to abide his time in reporting to the boss. As a result, Koreans are noted for lacking resolution and blamed for being indecisive or dithering when a matter calls for urgent action.

Indecisiveness often actually denotes prudence or the discreet manners of Koreans, and this trait contradicts the Koreans being impetuous or temperamental. Sensing one's feeling and exercising prudence is one thing, but impetuousness is another trait of Koreans' behavior. Koreans' penchant for harmonious relation underscores the necessity of avoiding kibun-damaging. Koreans are adept at sensing people's mood and at helping one out of a foul temper. But Koreans lose patience when something arises to damage his own kibun. They easily fly into rage and contentious argument over a trifling thing.

Kibun is perhaps best described as that part of us which is deeper than physical appearances. Our inner being or, by analogy, our continental shelf, is not visible. This invisible part of us can be damaged by the loss of face, disrespect, bad news or unhappiness. Koreans' emphasis on kibun eloquently speaks for the Koreans' moral dictum: "one individual being correct is less important than a group being happy." Obviously, Koreans naturally seek harmonious relations of objective truth with goodness. If goodness prevails over objective truth, we can say that a man opts for an affective aspect of inter-personal relationship. Koreans more often owe their success in a career to a good human relationship than their expertise or competency.

With kibun being an important behavioral guide, importance is given to 'timing' and 'feeling right' among Koreans to make decisions. In business dealing. Koreans entertain potential partners to generate good feelings that will establish the right aura. "Such an appeal to emotion at its best energizes the curiosity of potential buyers but, at its worst, blows one's feeling so high as to blurs the sense of rationality or common sense "(Breen 1999;40). "Stick it out" is often the best strategy in negotiation, and this explains part of the reason why Koreans are adept in getting a job done by being "a pain in the neck" to their business partners. In the stick-it-out strategy, reason and common sense are drowned out by hard drive to move them.

Dichotomy and Harmony

A dominant characteristic of oriental thought is the avoidance of controversy and work toward the resolution of contradictions and the reconciliation of conflicts, but not to extirpate them. Note the dichotomous thought entrenched in the Westerners' consciousness, as reflected in their 'either-or' mentality: either man or other species, either good or bad, shuttling between the two extremes. The justice system in the United States, for the most part, tends towards guilty or not guilty. In Korean civil cases, say, an auto collusion, both parties are held responsible, with varying degrees of responsibility apportioned. An Eastern aphorism has it that it is better to be harmonious than right or true. One defends oneself by vague expression or by not talking rather than taking a clear-cut position that may invite confrontation or debate. Logics has no place in Koreans' concern for better human relationship. Foreigners are dismayed by the power of action in unison in particular. A German businessman was struck by the "gold donation campaign" contrived to get South Korea out of the economic downturn in 1997.

"Individual contribution of gold did a miracle for the treatment of economic ills. It was the profession of their patriotism, I knew later. The idea of personal sacrifices for the good of the country is something that does not readily come to mind. Koreans believes in the value of action in unison. When it comes to a company throwing a banquet for its employees, the boss makes a decision on its venue and time and announces it. Everyone accepts it without a word of grievance. For a person who is used to willingly address the concerns of all members in decision-making, this is surely a matter of wonder. Each individual supposedly has his or her earlier engagement. But such a personal thing is willingly discarded, for everyone wants to go with it. Koreans should learn to say 'no to a group decision." (Quanter Reike, Choson Daily Press dated October 18, 2003)

The pursuit of harmony as a conceptual ideal is found in the Korean avoidance of the negative answer built into the linguistic structure. The Westerners are annoyed by Koreans, when they are met with "yes" responses to negatively phrased question. The affirmative answer in this case addresses the intent of a questioner, not the question itself. To a question like "Do you mind my smoking?" a Korean willing to stand it will say reflexively "yes" because his internal urge to go with it has already been expressed by the questioner. On the other hand, the Westerner's "no" speaks for their minds with concern for the literal form of the question raised. To Koreans, 'yes' always carries good connotation. Intuitively, Koreans think that their decision to go with the smoker seems to be a good thing. 'No' answer always sounds intrusive or impolite, without giving much thought to whether the kind of behavior resulting from the answer is good or bad. In other words, Koreans are not so much concerned about the behavior or action resulting from their answers, since it is kind of words that do not hurt the feelings of the persons they are talking with. The Eastern aphorism, "better to be harmonious than right" or "better to bite your tongue" permeates their thought habit. "Why courts a trouble by fussing?" The Confucian legacy of social harmony and care for others in the development of proper human relations lead to the use of communication patterns that preserve the partner's face. The popular attempt at face-saving manifests itself in the suppression of conflict and negativity, that is termed a "non-confrontation" strategy, in which taciturnity and indirect expression are seen as the behaviors most treasured. Indirect expression accounts for, in many occasions, the ambiguity of the language. Koreans are more concerned about the overall affective implications of conversation than specific meanings of the language. Considerateness and kindness are seen as more desirable than the truth as the culture emphasizes the sustenance of social harmony. Behavioral propensity for face-saving complicates the process of communication, when coupled with emotional interactions. For any foreigner coming to grapple with the 'kibun'of Koreans, it is crucially important to know one's state of feeling in communication in order to keep it smooth and inspirational for 'getting things done.' Hurting one's kibun is the last thing for a decent man to do and most undesirable at best. Very often, Koreans encounter occasions where they forsake truth in favor of the kibun of their bosses. All in all, it requires one to go beyond verbal messages in order to arrive at a more precise understanding of Korean communication practices.

Child Adoption

The adoption of a child illustrates another contrast between Korean and Western views. The Korean concept of child adoption is based on the parochial circle of association formed around blood kin. A child is adopted among the siblings who share the same blood with an eye on the male family lineage and inheritance. 'No son' means a dishonorable discontinuation of a family line sanctified by ancestors. Child adoption in Korea commonly happens when a family has no son, but child adoption in the West is based on simple motives, often on a humanitarian concern or to have a child to live with. Adoption across ethnic or cultural borders is hardly conceived by Koreans, since they are all attuned to blood kinship. The notion of social contract, as practiced in Western societies, is a far cry from the Korean emphasis on the thickness of blood ties and the belief that those outside the sphere of kin are non-persons. The Korean concern for blood lineage has allowed many unwanted babies to be adopted by foreigners. Foreign celebrities and professionals, carrying their adopted babies strapped to their chests, one hand holding a bottle of milk and the other a packet of passport and air ticket, became a familiar scene at Korean airports in the 1960s. Such a scene not only put Koreans to shame but made them suspicious of the vaunted warmth of the heart and the concept of family comparable to society. Nationalism in Korea has a strong tone of ethnic centralism, but the irony is that such an ethnic concern left children to be adopted by foreign parents.

Why are Koreans so cold-blooded about compatriots simply because they are not blood siblings? The answer is the questionable performance of filial duty by an adopted child to the adoptive parents when they come of age. Many Koreans are still caught with the idea that nothing is thicker than blood.

The siblings of the same blood are better fit to become a filial son. As adoption shows, the Confucian notion of 'one family' is not free of contradiction. Its emphasis on blood relation breeds partiality and parochialism that contradicts universalism that is unambiguously enshrined in Christianity. The positive side of parochialism is associated with nationalism set against universalism, for parochialism is prone to develop cohesiveness and solidarity within an ethnic group, providing that its members live on shared values. The downside is that it drives Koreans back into the fate of a 'tadpole stuck in a well,' reminiscent of the hermit kingdom where Koreans were invincibly ignorant of the world in the nineteenth century. Sticking to blood relations keeps Koreans in an immovable trench, grating against an open and diverse society. Amid the rising water of universal values, Koreans have still to break loose from their retrogressive outlook on the issue of child adoption. The Korean concept of ethnic identity invites an analogy to an extended family. However, the blood-bound family becomes a drag against expanding one's association to larger groups in which to find new identities.

Tracing the traditional institution of child adoption in Korea shows that adoption was not always limited to blood siblings. Children with no blood association were once the preferred candidates for male heirs to families without son. Mark Peterson traces the Koryô dynasty's practice of child adoption and finds in it a semblance of contemporary Western notion of adoption. Contrary to the practice of the Chosôn dynasty, adoption in Koryô did not require a child to be a boy. Both boy and girl had the higher possibility of being adopted since the majority of adopted children were non-relatives. This indigenous adoption system was wiped out during the Chosôn dynasty (1392-1910) as Neo-Confucianism was made the state's ideology. Viewed from a longer time span, blood siblings are not necessarily the hallmark of adoption practice in Korea.

Korea's obsession with adoption to secure the patriarchal lineage stands in contrast with China and Japan, which continued to practice non-agnatic adoption and the adoption of daughters and sons-in-law. "This important difference probably explains why Japan never experienced a mass migration of children for international adoption after World War Two" (Hubinette Tobias 2005;44-45). Neo-Confucian tradition is reflected in the lethargic inertia of the legal system in changing over time. "It was in 1938 that a legal provision was adopted for the first time in millennia which legalized adoption outside the family" (Ye Son Ok 2001,45). Blood cult is not alone responsible for the Koreans flouting the law. Moral dominance over the rule of law kept Koreans persistently searching for the ideal adoption that adheres to the patriarchal blood line.

Trauma explains part of why Korea became, in the 1960s, the largest supplier of adopted children in the world. Before Japanese colonial rule, the parent-child bond was strong in Korea, and abandoned children were not significant enough in number to strain the state's nerves, because blood relatives adopted the majority of them. The massive migration of up-rooted peasants, beginning with colonial rule, left many children orphaned either by the early death of parents or because of dispersed families. The territorial division and subsequent Korean War turned out millions of orphaned children who were forcibly separated from their parents, if not dead. Some of these children were fathered by American soldiers and sent to their adoptive parents in the United States. "The United States received more than three-quarters of those who went overseas and with annual immigration numbers from Korea exceeding 30,000 between 1974-90"(Chang Edward Taehan 2004, 245). For the poverty-stricken Koreans, these children were enviously looked upon, as they were leaving for an affluent country. It was during this period that Koreans regarded Americans with reverence for their generosity.

Holt International Children Services, symbolic of philanthropy and humanitarianism, was most active in arranging for the adoption of Korean babies orphaned by the Korean War. Just like contemporary Christian fundamentalists who encourage Jews to move to Israel to fulfill the prophecy of Revelation, "Holt, quoting Isaiah 43-5, prophetically conceived international adoption to play a part in a divine scheme for the fulfillment of God's will"(Holt Bertha 1992, 211). To further its philanthropic commitment, Americans became the major adoptive parents of the racially-mixed children who could not make an eternal home for themselves in the ethno-centered Korean society. As traditional networks of family disappeared, international adoption found a new source of adoptable children among the increasing number of abandoned children. They are the crop of unwanted children declared 'foundlings' in the brutal turmoil of rapid industrialization. A fantasy of urban life triggered off a mass migration of the rural population, a majority of whom found jobs in sweat factories. The dreary life of young workers was a grim reminder of the wretched life of industrial workers captured by Karl Marx as the malaise of industrialized Britain. They were tempted to vent their frustrations into moments of pleasure-seeking, and unwanted children were victims to the strictly gendered society.

The Korean parents of the child-born women have not changed a bit in showing a cold-blooded aversion to these unwanted children. Unmarried mothers remain a social anathema condemned to suffer the loss of opportunities for a new life. They are under the merciless glare of relatives and neighbors in tight networks of human relationship. These children found adoptive parents abroad, and South Korea, although a proud member of OECD, was reduced to a child exporting country. The rejection of parentless children by their own people is unexceptionally merciless, although it can be observed in a number of less-developed countries. The phenomena are explained by the Korean loyalty to parochial circles of identity. Koreans have not attuned themselves to an anonymous world which requires them to extend as much concern to strangers as they do to those within the sphere of kinship. The expanding warmth of the heart hit a snag in a society built on blood relations. The naïve belief that adopted children, placed into wealthy adoptive parents, will live a better life was a solace to their biological parents. This expectation conceals the shocking trauma every child experiences when separated from their siblings and relatives, and as they experience rebirth with parents, physically different from their owns, let alone miserable familial backgrounds they may be placed into and mistreatments they suffer by adoptive parents.

"The story of Brian Bauman dramatically raised the awareness, among ordinary Koreans, of the existence of the adopted Koreans, and functioned as a powerful reminder of the genetic bond existing between adopted and domestic Koreans"(Hubinette Tobias 2005;94). Bauman's search for a similar bone marrow enlisted some hundreds thousands of donors in Korea. This tearful response of Koreans is the manifestation of ethnic compassion responding to a particular stimulus. Nonetheless, the sudden upsurge of ethnic romanticism is short lived. The Bauman's case was a rare success story, but it should be noticed that many adopted children who had suffered leukemia perished in the brutal absence of a sustained compassion. Apparently, the Bauman's story served as a wake-up call that galvanized Korean's efforts to increase incentives for domestic adoption and to discourage teenage pregnancies. A self-critical attitude is perceptibly rising among Korean critics who viewed the adopted Koreans as nothing else but victims to the country's face saving culture and patriarchal family system.

Korean parents are, of course, the primary source of affection and help, but the problem is that they try to make themselves necessary by even making their children more helpless and dependent. It seems, though, that the mutual dependence of parents and children remains firm, and is likely to survive many generations. So long as this trend continues, there is no place for parentless children to stand on. In contrast, there are as many parents in Western societies who wish to be relieved of the awful responsibility of being a child's only source of affection and help. There will be a day when no sensible Korean will suppose that love or affection has anything to do with blood. Fostered children and stepchildren are loved as dearly as one's own. Love and affection are psychological and cultural, and blood relationships can be happily forgotten. We notice many cases in which biological parents are deprived of parenthood by a family breakdown and inability to raise them. The family based on blood ties is a product of an ancient form of community, and customs and habits which were thought to be timeless are out of place in a new society.

Courtesy and Propriety

The publicized image of Koreans as courteous people fails many foreign visitors. For new arrivals, Koreans may look apathetic to daily etiquette, uncouth, and unfriendly. In the crowded streets of Seoul, foreigners often encounter pedestrians who pass by without saying a word of apology for stepping on shoes or bumping into their bodies. Many have pointed to Koreans 'impassionate expression in greeting friends. When it comes to foreigners, however, they appear to be unfriendly and coldly impervious. Going further, the poker face with a curious stare jars the nerves of foreigners who are used to smile when meeting the strangers' eyes. Koreans show a revealing contrast with manner-conscious Japanese. Koreans are known for sparing words of appreciation and apology. By contrast, Westerners reflexively utter words like "thank you" for every minor courtesy offered. Words of apology are equally effusive for minor misconduct or a slight mistake, though no harm is done. The proper question to ask is "what is meant by etiquette or courtesy in Korea?" vis-a-vis the Westerners' views. From the normal responses of Westerners in a demanding situation, we can presume that they have greater concern for a specific, visible behaviors, whether ritualized or habituated, and have little to do with intentions.

It appears that Koreans spare words in exhibiting gratitude or apology. From this fact, it is fair to say that Korean etiquette comes from the inner being, whose intention is not necessarily manifest in words or behavior. The intention often remains unexpressed, for its behavioral or verbal expression is doused by the urge of the inner being to show "no verbal response" to every situational demand. Korean behavior is characterized by a temporal gap between intention and verbal or behavioral expression. This momentary diffidence builds an image of Koreans as unconscious of manners or irresolute in a situation that calls for an explicit behavioral or verbal expression. The lack of concern for specific behaviors may have something to do with space consciousness. A more interesting example can be seen in how Westerners and Easterners behave in an elevator. In the small space of an elevator, Westerners, careful not to touch each other, try their best to stand as widely apart as possible, but Easterners do not seem to mind touching others' bodies. In comparison with the North American continent, most Asian countries, so densely populated, cannot afford to be space-conscious. It should be noted, however, that Westerners' habit of keeping proper distance from others came from their increasingly dehumanizing culture. Lee Won-sol asserts that the process of dehumanization starts from the very beginning of one's life in the West, i.e. from the way Western mothers raise their babies without touching them. Considering all factors, it can be said that Koreans nowadays are increasingly conscious of space.

Historically, Koreans are known for their high sense of courtesy, as fondly remembered by their neighbors as 'the people of courtesy.' What is implicated by "courteous" in Korea is not so much a specific behavior or a verbal expression in response to a situational call: rather it is an attitudinal or behavioral pattern that is recurrent and repetitive. A good act that is not repetitious has no place in the Korean concept of courtesy. Courtesy in Western terms is defined as a personal way of acting and doing something in relation to others, and the rightness of a specific act is determined in situational terms. In this respect, the Korean concept of courtesy refers to a set of practices and habits based on the value that emphasizes their congruence with social norms. Courtesy in Korea is coterminous with propriety that encompasses both behavioral and attitudinal patterns, latent or expressive. The Korean definition of courtesy is broader and recurrent, by including the latent aspect of behavior which avoids the eyes of observers. The Western concept is a situation-specific behavior, subject to public attention. In view of its conceptual similarity to propriety, etiquette-conscious Koreans display greater concern for the formalistic and ritualistic aspects of behavior.

Status consciousness plays out its role into face-saving and ostentatious display of the self beyond what one is in actuality. This trend is observed in the presentation of a gift, whose value disconcerts foreign receivers. The value of a gift is determined in terms of what is appropriate to the giver's status rather than a genuine recognition of the receiver's service. For the receiver, the gift itself is the reminder of the giver's status so that he feels perpetually indebted unless it is paid back in another gift of equal value. Self-ostentation is one of the devices to distinguish one from others in regular contacts. In relation to foreigners, an expensive gift is an endless source of dismay and embarrassment, since they feel obligated to reciprocate the offered courtesy, but they often find it beyond their means. But the giver never expects the receiver to reciprocate. Koreans are spendthrift in the ostentatious display of wealth. Kim Young-won, an essayist, well summarizes the fact.

"There was a time, in 1950s and 60s when anyone worth his salt had a Rolex watch. It was a thick, ugly thing with a protruding date window on its crystal. This watch was a bit too large for a Korean slender wrist. ....Then there are those who build inordinately large gates to all too modest houses. These houses are inhabited by disciples of Sydney Smith, who use books as furniture, seldom opening it. Jewelry-bedecked ladies emerge from such houses to attend concerts and discuss Bach, Beethoven and Brahms." (Korea in Transition, 1989, 32)

The large gate to a modest house was a contrived symbol of wealth, for it is imagined to induce all fortunes into the house. To put in an other way, the large gate is a vanity inordinately blown out of what one possess. Luxurious spending on status might have displeased their forefathers who believed in the beauty of simplicity, serenity and humbleness. This trend, of course, is ubiquitous among the upstarts and younger generations from wealthy families. Such a status-conscious manner is an undesirable offshoot of the Confucian value which inhibits the flaunting of one's wealth and the presumption of power or influence. Self-ostentation is the child of Confucian ceremonialism against the grain of those indulging in self-restraint, self effacement and austerity. Choi Hyun-bae, a famous linguistic scholar, was hyper critical of the double standard of Korean behavior. "Formalism is a ritualistic force that binds the thought and behavior of humans to the details of etiquette and mannerism. This, together with the red-tape rigidity of Confucian bureaucracy, has over-emphasized formalities at the risk of substance" (Kim Young-won, 1989, 27). To foreigners, Korean politicians fritter away their energy on what seems to be trivial and of a ritualistic nature. Such a bickering noticeable among law-makers delays decisions on the proposed bills. Many Koreans went on to point to the futility of the parliamentary system, as this institution has become dysfunctional and non-productive as it is frequently involved in debate on ritualistic details.

Koreans are manner-conscious within a sphere of intimates and in the presence of familiar faces. Ethical norms in Korea were confined to the binary relations like father-son, king-subject or husband-wife, but they were not meant for larger units. The Korean sense of courtesy is person-specific vis-a-vis the Westerners' being situation-specific. In relation to outsiders, Koreans are impersonal, and their manner-consciousness dissipates, as they are distanced from the circles of intimates. The Korean concept of courtesy is group and hierarchical-oriented rather than person-to-person relation on an equal basis. Koreans, prone to collective consciousness, separate the world of outsiders from their own and views them with suspicion. In the presence of their intimates, Koreans are assertive and engage in lively talk. In contrast, an individual placed outside the sphere of intimates is extremely shy and repressive of behaviors, as if they felt themselves under the glare of outsiders. They lack the pervasive concept of relationship, and this expresses parochialism in their perception of courtesy.

Collectivism and Factionalism

||||||||||||||||||||||||||||||||||||||||||||||||||||||||||||||||||||||||||||||||||||||||||||||||||||||||||||||||

Collectivism and factionalism contradict each other. Korean society owes its social cohesiveness to dogmatic ideology and ethnic and cultural homogeneity. Such a society is unlikely to descend into contending factions. The juxtaposition of collectivity and factionalism is apparently unique to Korea in that their penchant for a group bows easily to pressure for factional division. The pendulum swings with greater easiness between the two extremes. Obviously, collective society defeats divisive attempts, but an overview of Korean history discloses that a political group, when enlarged into a greater one, crumbled into contending factions, each harboring rancor or hostility against another to continue generation after generation. Factions view rivals as something to be eliminated rather than a partner to talk with to strive for compromise. Confucian emphasis on a harmonious social order contradicts Korean tendencies towards factionalism. Part of the reason for an impossible co-existence of dichotomized tendencies is explained by Samuel Huntington:"Historical experience and sociological analysis show that the absence of an external "other" is likely to undermine unity and breed divisions within a society"(2004, 18).

In the first place, Koreans have a fondness for a strong family tie which centers around a timeless axis of father-son relations built on filial piety. Koreans find blissful contentment within self-contained cell groups that shelter them from incursive forces. Larger groups organized around diverse interests, religious creeds and ideological differences are rarely seen. A large group fraternized around a greater cause, if any, loses its solidarity. Self identity is sought only in a parochial entity - such as family and kinship groups - that feature a strong bond among its members. Koreans feel at ease with the sense of camaraderie they find in a small group. It takes courage or intrepidity, they think, to venture into a larger one.

The Korean linguistic structure also bears witness to the characteristic collectivism. In Korean usage, for example, when one refers to his wife, one rarely say 'my wife'; more often he says 'our' wife (uri manura in Korean), though it is not to be taken literally. The meaning of "our wife " is "my wife" who belongs to 'our family' that means all the 'I's within the family melted into one 'We'(Chung Sun-mok 1980;22-23). 'You', 'they' and 'we' flow into one identity. The term brother (hyung in Korean), is used to address seniors in age without blood ties who come into a regular orbit of association. The same can be said of 'sister' (on'ni in Korean), suggesting that the self is not much differentiated from others.

Collective Society

Yi Kyu-tae, a literary critic, observed. "In the past, individuals were buried in what a group sought to achieve; individual assertiveness was not permitted. They shared group identity equally among the intimates" (1977, 23).The Korean concept of collectivism is based on what is common among equal peers, and such a group is uniquely parochial and cohesive against others. Koreans in this respect lose a horizontal perspective that goes beyond the parochial bound. Absolute loyalty to a group blinds one to what is at stake in a larger group, and this accounts for the Koreans propensity to shy away from strangers in the public realm. One inscrutable aspect that baffles foreigners is that Koreans stare at strangers, notably foreigners, without showing any sign of intimacy. Should this happen to a Westerner, he or she is surely to nod greeting. Sociability finds its place within a group of like-minded members but rarely make part of the public life. Being in the public domain means that one should cross the threshold of a parochial circle. Extraordinary solidarity characterizes small groups bound by emotional needs for solace or comfort rather than by professional or occupational needs. The degree of solidarity has much to do with the place where it is shaped: a rural community boasts solidarity while urbanites rarely organize into such a cohesive group. "Sociability seems to bear an inverse relationship to the density of population" (Allain de Botton 2012;25). Anonymity, therefore, rears its head in urban and industrial culture.

Every group has a set of norms that produces tendencies toward behavioral uniformity among members. An individual feels bound to inscrutable group norms that Korean returnees find it very difficult to acclimatize themselves back after some years of stay abroad. Each group, small and large, retains an ethos or spirit like an unwritten law, and is identified not by class or belief but by the distinctive personality traits of its members. The concept of middle class is strange to Koreans since they are attuned to a steep pyramid-like social structure. Koreans are strong in desire to make themselves distinct from others and to move up along the social ladder. The few on the top of a status ladder are the object of envy. Koreans are never content with remaining middle class, particularly when it embraces a larger proportion of the population. Distinction from the pack provides strong motivation to move upward and excel over others. Few Americans claim themselves to belong to a higher class. Even those who rise to the commanding heights - through wealth or achievement – would have values not different from those of the middle class. The stunning economic growth of Korea failed to build the middle class in a society bound to a hierarchical order. We cannot deny that this proves to be an impediment to the realization of pervasive equality. A middle class society offers the ground for equality to spread. Koreans lose patience with the mediocre and want to rise above the pack and a mediocre or average man is spurred on by avidity to excel over others.

The Western concept of individualism denotes the emancipation of individuals from the state, authority, the Pope, institutions and even family. Koreans, in contrast, sees individualism through the prism of collectivity, and regard it as egoistic and destructive of the fabric of a hierarchical society. The dynamics of change in the West owed much to the emphasis on self assertiveness and individual autonomy as the vehicle for social development. In contrast, group tendencies of non-Europeans, Koreans in particular, are responsible for a stable society and stagnancy. Korean culture has a lot in common with the Japanese in that it produces outcasts within a group, subject to an unendurable pain of being ostracized from the mainstream. Both Koreans and Japanese value the sense of peer camaraderie from which a strong sense of bond derives. It is the collective culture that makes the pain of estrangement unendurable. The outcast is common in the other cultures where there are always a few marginalized from the core of group due to their anomalistic traits. In Korea, a child who stands out in academic performance is rarely considered the object of envy: he or she is more often scoffed at as stuck-up and gradually edged out of the mainstream. Anyone estranged from a core group in the formative stage of their growth suffers an unendurable pain which often leads to suicide. New terms, wangtta (Korean) and ijime (Japanese), were coined for those who fit this marginal category. There is invisible pressure to conform to group norms, and this imposes an enormous burden on repatriates whose life used to alternate between job and family affairs. Contrary to the Western view which stresses individual autonomy, Korean culture defines an individual from the viewpoint of his moral integration into a family or group.

Voices are often heard for "kachi sarayahanda (We should live together). The flip side is that the estranged few are more noticeable in a group where peers are identical and where fellow villagers subordinate their individual grievances to the overriding necessity of living together. Grievances by a few create cracks in a group proud of solidarity. There is what Vincent Brandt calls the "egalitarian community ethic." Egalitarianism views the members of a particular group as "equal for all." The interpretation of this concept varies, depending on the stage of societal development. In a society where most constituents subscribe to a standard norm, what Australians would call the 'tall poppy syndrome' applies. "This label has been taken to refer to a tendency to cut down the tall poppies; that is, to denigrate and humiliate those who achieve excellence, success, fame or honors in any field"(Hugh Mackay 1993,134). Koreans are so obsessed with group solidarity that they cast a suspicious look at anyone who goes ahead, since it implies distancing someone from the pack. The notion of middle class implies a sense of belonging to an enlarged group in a hierarchical society, but the shaky base of middle class inspires Koreans to move upward. Aspirations for social mobility are stronger among the ethno-centric and hierarchy-conscious Koreans in particular. New nation states like the United States, Canada and Australia are strong in the middle-class mentality by embracing the majority of the population. Where economic achievement is coupled with egalitarianism, the boundaries of the middle class are elastic and pervasive, restraining people from wanting to appear flamboyant or too successful. The opposite trend is conspicuously noticed among the Korean nuveau riches.

The Korean concept of collectivism requires individual subordination in favor of group goals. Individual subordination is obviously distinguished from self-sacrifice that the Japanese national ethos once glorified. Self sacrifice embraces a range of different practices, but the extremity of self-sacrifice, as we observed in Imperial Japan during the Pacific War, may have an appeal in some Arab fundamentalist states. Glorifying personal sacrifice for the state would not go over in the industrialized nations where the people claim themselves to be the master of the nation state. Japanese idealism during the Pacific War embraced a mass fantasy or kamikaze, as they were reminded of the Divine Wind that protected Japan from Mongolian invaders. This mass fantasy was resurrected during the Pacific War, convinced that millions of human sacrifices would move the Divine Deity to have compassion and send another divine wind of protection. It in the end turned into fanatic patriotism, with which Japanese were resolved to fight until the last living Japanese had been killled.[8] Japan dramatized collectivism into a fanatic display of patriotism under the Supreme Being to whom subjects paid absolute loyalty.

The concept of the Supreme Being is lacking among Koreans. Single minded loyalty to the Emperor or an organization, it may be argued, blurs one's sense of justice or honesty, that is defined in terms of what is good for society at large. Nonetheless, fanatic commitment to the state is one thing, and the consciousness of moral justice is another. This double standard baffles those immersed in the industrial culture. Masao Miyamoto points to, as a product of collectivism, "the unwillingness of the people to face truth when it is considered to undermine group interest, and this forms the major source of cultural friction with Western countries founded on Christian culture which teaches people to face the truth unflinchingly in all things. The ideality of the Western culture stresses 'even if you have to make trouble with others,' you should not be shaken in belief in truth. Anyone who cannot face truth is a moral weakling" (Masao Miyamoo 1995,28).

To Stay within a Group

Koreans feel comfortable with living among a few equals. Such groups are small, closed, exclusive and repressive. A recent returnee from abroad complained that being in a group required concern for many other engagements in addition to managing job and family. Failure to fit into a group earns one the name of "an outcast" who is estranged from peers. To consolidate group solidarity, Korean companies arrange "self-overcoming" training which, in many respects, resembles a military boot camp. Company orientation programs for new employees exposes them to grueling challenges resembling endurance contests to instill cooperative attitudes and the "company spirit". The group ethos is a familiar idea designed to bond them into an organic teamwork, and the desired outcome of these is "an individual fit to live within a group life." The most familiar catch phrases of business firms or social organizations are "cooperation" and "unity" in contrast to "diversity, creativity and so forth in multi-ethnic societies.

The Korean culture finds virtue in uniformity in an organic network of relations and in harmony. Few Koreans enjoy drinking alone. Drinking is rather a social ritual in which people get together and strengthen their fraternal solidarity. Foreigners are not exempt from drinking together. Therefore, getting together for drink is more often forced on people, and it is difficult to go against the group ethos. By refusing to get together, a person risks being ostracized from the mainstream group. New members of a corporation learn to act in unison and harmony with people taking different roles that accompany their status and competence. By joining a group, Koreans are rarely free to do their own things. Being a member of a group brings social rituals that force greater attention. Some Koreans take pains to attend social gatherings, whether they are for drinking or eating. If one has joined a social gathering, drinking is also forced. Offered a drink, sipping goes against the grain of the ethos; one has to empty the glass in one go, as everyone does. Drinking is a way of ensuring behavioral uniformity among group members. Group drinking after-work hours gives the comfort of appealing to emotions, and group solidarity is reinforced through the flows of emotions.

The moral prescriptions of the five human relationships denote a set of bonds that bind people together into the network of family and socio-economic hierarchy, in which the self is considered in terms of relatedness to others. In a society in which the sense of belonging and human relatedness prevail, one should remain sensitive to what others say before he performs, mindful of the congruence of his behavior with social or group sanctions. In a group-oriented society, questions about personal identity - who you really are or what you are - are less important than your feeling of belonging and connectedness. Normal behaviors are often motivated by shared values rather than an individual assessment of a given situation. Conformity to group norms provides little tolerance for individual behavior within a group and, therefore, deviation from the beaten path is rarely seen. Words such as "exotic" and "outlandish" carry negative connotations by causing viewers to raise their eyebrows. Transvestism and homo-sexuality, products of more self-assertive culture, maintain a low profile in the society wherein the standard rule suppresses an attempt to gain recognition of an abnormal life. There is no or little, if any, room for such weird things to receive social recognition in Korea. A fancy necktie that look far out of the ordinary dark and grey colors may force its wearer to withstand the ruthless glare of group members. It takes genius to look alike within a group but to be different enough to engage others' attention. Many Korean repatriates from abroad complain that they have no giggle time with children; they imagine themselves as Gulliver with feet and hands tied by the Lilliputian threads, enmeshed in the irksome bonds of human and institutional inhibitions.

Group norms are repressive or inhibitive in most cases, leading to a limited range of acceptable behaviors. The sense of connectedness, though, generates a group elan or vigor that allow group members to get jobs done, even works unimaginable by an individual. An individual becomes more daring or feels at ease to do an incredible thing, when he sees his fellows in the same emotional impulse. A momentary grip of such a group elan on their minds does a miracle. A typical example is the marine corps that stirs an individual soldier to heroic acts in battle. The sense of pride in being part of an elite corps dramatizes each potential to serve the group goal. It is not so much for the country they are fighting as for the corps. Groups protect their members, and this notion emboldens them to do prohibited behaviors. Within a group, anything can go, even the most unbridled behavior, because being with the group dulls one's awareness of being exposed to public glare. When one feels safely entrenched within a group, he is less bound by the voice of conscience or social norms and becomes more daring and freewheeling in behavior to an extent that displeases outsiders. Sheltered by the protective hand of a group, one is emboldened to challenge a task that might otherwise have been forbidden. A Korean individual bereft of group's protection is a fish out of water.

Group Egotism

In the highly compact society, grouping is artificial and opportunistic, strong in will to remain distinct from and exclusive against others. Group solidarity rather breeds hostility against other groups, and the aggrandizement of a faction brings the relative shrinkage of another within a political party made up of different factions. The clannish propensity of Koreans is manifest in the creation of informal groups formed around age, the place of birth, hobby, alma mater and the year of employment within the enlarged organization. The result is that an individual is torn between small groups.

Korean society is made up of innumerable cell groups, each intent to expand itself into a more diffusive and powerful one. Fear of losing solidarity forces each group to rarely cross borders, and the only one that crosses borders is a nationwide network of an alumni fraternity. Each university has a nationwide network of alumni, competing to beat others in cohesiveness. A faction with greater solidarity confined to a particular interest is sure to erode the fabric of the nationwide network. While Confucianism is credited with providing ethical and social foundations for solidarity and harmony, it is as much blamed for generating a group egotism that impedes its leap to a more encompassing circle of association. Group egotism is more evident among Korean lawmakers, and vehement bickering is an anomaly by Korean standards. The lawmakers, obsessed with their group interests, are least likely to bring an agreement on a single issue.

Egalitarianism is far from taking root in its true sense in the hierarchically arranged, compact society, regardless of how far its economy advances. Narrow circles of association are hostile to egalitarianism. Absolute loyalty to a parochial circle blinds the members to what is at stake in more diffusive circles. This phenomenon happens in the absence of intermediate values that serves as a link to larger circles. Gregory Henderson's metaphor of Koreans to "atomized citizen" fails to grasp the true nature of Korean society: he regards Korea as made up of sands that slip through the fingers: rather, Korean society is made up of gravels that stay within one's grasp, each comparable to a billiard ball that is hard to crack. This small group solidarity imposes a drag on the elastic circle of intimates to a larger, emotion-neutral entity. The result is an intransigent resistance to compromise with adversaries within the institutions. The same can be said of Japanese in that they show a tendency towards cell groups. "Japanese politicians make up small but well-cohering factions within which loyalty is an unquestioned tenet. But they form alliances with adversaries for a common cause, with the terms of such alliances becoming iron rules" (Kim Young-won 1989,211).

One may question how the so-called Hanahoe, made up of the elite officers from the Military Academy, came to seize political power in the vortex of power transfer after the death of Park Chung-hee. An aggrandized circle destined to clash with a rival, is tempted to enlarge their fraternity as a means for self-defense and survival. Confronted with an arch rival, this circle broke through the top layer of military command hierarchy, eliminated obstacles and founded the Fifth Republic that is viewed as an extension of the military regime. This regime justified its grip on power to override political melee and bring into order the disturbed society. In the hind sight of history, the military seizure of power was condemned as a mutiny, and the two former presidents were imprisoned for having spearheaded the military mutiny. This circle was started as a fraternity of mutual support: if a member is in a privileged position, he is sure to offer favor to other members within the circle. It was through this network that the members enjoyed advantages in promotion with the result of occupying the top echelon of the military command. This group egotism disadvantaged other officers in promotion within the military bureaucracy. Confrontation with foes goaded the circle to win the control of the military establishment, this cycle being repeated by another ambitious circle. Ahn Byung-man refers to it as "a cycle of dominance."Group egotism dims the vision of larger groups..

Factionalism

Theoretically, solidarity is antithetical to a factional trend. Korean society, however, has been pained by the frequent division of civil officials and lawmakers into factions. As Koreans are entrenched in cell groups, they are prone to divisive feuds and trapped into a vicious cycle of factional strife. Ironically, Koreans' penchant for grouping engendered a trend for them to come stuck into contentious factions squabbling over trivial issues. One plausible explanation is reference to the way in which the human psychic works: the more the people look alike, the greater their urge to look different. Ethnic homogeneity, once considered a social blessing playing into the unitary power of people, has become a hotbed for factional seeds to grow.

Much as Confucian values permeate the private domain where intimacy prevails over rationality: man has an instinctual urge to be among equal peers. Group solidarity dissipates as it becomes enlarged and is sure to split apart when it enters the public domain. Confucian virtue, confined within private domain, is outmoded in public life. Few Koreans have an impromptu conversation with unknown persons. Righteousness in the past was a guide to moral decisions associated with public affairs, but it was distorted, when it encountered authoritarian leadership.[9] Factional strife reached a new height when factions were competing for access to power. This may have to do with the Koreans' psychic and social structure in which the 'we-they' or 'in-out' dichotomy is unusually stark and forbidding enough to keep contending factions from crossing the perception gap. A dichotomy mentality remains hidden in relationships among the peers or intimates and rears its head when it enters into the public domain.

In Korean history a political motive for power often led to another cycle of confrontation. Here we see an ideological catalyst at work to make a simple power struggle hereditary over generations. If one was lost in a political game, his unfulfilled idea was passed on to his disciples whose tenacious ideological commitment exhausted the rival faction. The defeated in a political struggle left their ideological seeds to grow in the hotbed of the succeeding generations. Such a factional trend left its sediments to make rival factions intransigently hostile. The adoption of one ideological dogma or one philosophy led power holders to fritter away their energies over doctrinal interpretations, thus leading to a new round of factional strife. Factions used to be formed around doctrinal branches or around those who had studied under one master in the course of preparing for the high civil examination. A strong master-disciple fraternity inspired its members to share all the shifts of fortunes, whether good or bad. If one was hit, the rest were willing to risk scourges, whatever it was. Factional strife was characteristically vehement in the highly centralized power structure.

The brutal obsession of Koreans with an ideological orthodoxy generated "a black and white" mentality to the shrinkage of gray areas for middle roaders to stay in. As we know, moral issues are not by nature divided into black and white dichotomy, but Koreans' obsession with moral supremacy evokes a hostility-ridden debate on behaviors with no end in sight. Where morality is the arbiter of human behavior, argument is carried on to a point where an artificial line is forcibly drawn between 'victor' and 'loser.' In a political confrontation stalemated into an impasse, a person who proposes to make compromise or concessions with the opposite faction is stigmatized as a fickle or a traitor. The family which had its honor smudged by an ancestor traitor was left to struggle with the stigma for generations. This trend is visible among the people who worship and glorify ancestors.

Partisanship in Modern Politics

Far from the tenacious struggle of pre-modern Korea, mostly associated with ideology and creed, ideological divisions are rarely the cause for factional division in the politics of modern Korea. None of the political parties today represent class or ideology, and rather the degree of individual loyalty to the party leader is the key factor for factional association and for one's political fate. Allegiance is not so much to a party or a political ideology as to a person, and this again reflects the Confucian ethos that puts a premium on human relations. To bring reform, a wise person is counted upon to play a vital role with the resulting downplaying of what systems can do. Curiously enough, the party in which loyalty is directed to a person in charge proves to be ephemeral, as demonstrated by the frequent rise and fall of political parties in Korea.

Each party invariably comprises various factions which have been solicited to join or bolt in accordance with the political dictum. In the political party system of Korea that is made up of factions, doctrinal lines are blurred. For all what appears to be a harmonious blending of political factions under an overarching authority, feuds between them remain so strong that they seem ready to split apart any minute. Debate on a political issue keeps a party tenaciously sticking to its guns and one loses the sight of the goal at stake in this case. Any political battle whatsoever involves efforts to save one's face, and the act of making a concession is considered the acknowledgement of weakness likely to bring nothing but defeat. Hence, the contestants lose substantial gains amidst obsession with ritualistic trivialities. This phenomenon is better described by a metaphorical reference to "a dog's tail wags his body." Formalistic and face-saving behaviors are the products of Koreans' penchant for grouping and become a pretext for maintaining solidarity.

Politics itself is an act of expanding social networking, and the prime concern in this case is not so much for issues at hand as who will seize power. Emphasis on human relations, coupled with status or prestige consciousness, beclouds the importance of an issue at stake. It seems that the opposition party finds its reason for existence in opposing whatever comes up for debate: eternal opposition is the surest way to secure popular votes. In such a collective society as Korea, "stakes are low but drama is high." Such a factional struggle, it has been observed, is trendy in other countries, though it varies in pugnacity and intensity. Modern society is replete with variables attendant to its fluidity and structural complexity that blur the transparency of a policy choice. And factional squabbles hobble the rational process of a policy choice. John Steinbeck developed a favorite theme; "the world owes more than it realizes to shared greed." People are held together again by pursuing their common interests in pursuit of secular desires like higher income, power, and status. Nevertheless, a group in Korea and elsewhere, built on a shared greed, is more often divided into factions, each exclusive, if not hostile, against other groups.

Provincial Favoritism

Provincialism cannot be glossed over in explaining collectivism, for it creates an enlarged emotional bloc, strong enough to sway the presidential election in favor of a particular candidate. Provincialism is a kind of obsession with local interests or benefits even at the cost of a greater rational attitude. A political decision is spurred by fondness for regional interest: it involves an aversion or revenge to a particular region. Idealistically, the expandable circle of identity posited by Confucianism is supposed to embrace all individuals and groups into one large "family." Obsession with the anthropocentric family and loyalty to a molecular group explain the absence of glue that holds the people in a larger circle, with the consequent division of individuals into hostile blocs of "us" versus "them."

The premise of the anthropocentric family is that all are members of one extended family in one way or another. A circle of association interpenetrates and joins together individuals of different classes and backgrounds. "A larger circle submerges the differences that individuals might have found among themselves within a smaller inner circle of social categories"(Kim Byung Kuk 1997). The Confucian defense of a straight extrapolation of the family to society is flawed when one considers the difficulty of reconciling groups of conflicting interests. The notion of an extended family might have been at work in the simple, agrarian society. In modern society, an expanding circle hits no hitch in time of national crisis, but it falls apart after the crisis is over. Search for a shared interest engenders a centrifugal force that pushes one to larger circles of association, with a greater concern for what is good for the whole. But it is subject to a gravitational force and bounces back toward a smaller one. Familial solidarity, among others, constitutes the strongest gravitational force working against the expandable circles of association. So far as political acts are concerned, the expandable circle, due to its obsession with regional interest, rarely goes beyond the regional bound. The act of voting based on regional sentiment is delegitimized by the sense of ethnic nationalism that imagines the nation as a community based on consanguineous ties. This depicts provincial favoritisom as ethically unjustifiable.

Ironically, provincialism is the child of a family cult, but it is delegitimized by its own mother. Theoretically, groups organized around blood relatives, school pals, and regional interest are supposed to be stepping stones to larger entities. In actuality, they often worked against the expandable circle, and this paradoxical phenomenon is assumed to be the result of an excessive group solidarity. Provincial favoritisom manifests itself in local interest, associated with environmental and topographical factors. In areas where small-scale peasant farming is prevalent, people live in a network of close relationships which rarely go beyond the bound of genealogy. Thus, they form relatively exclusive networks of trust, strong in the sense of connectedness in a hierarchical structure with retrogressive attachment to the past.

In rural areas, "birth, marriage and death bring forth communized rituals that bound its constituents into an entity of common fate" (Kim Yol-kyu 2001,41). "Thus a sense of locality developed, enabling Korean communities to maintain a degree of isolated stability, but a good degree of contentment with a small group has undermined nation-state on a wider spatial plane" (Yoon Tae-rim 1964;80).

The conventional concept of a rural community has a reference to a clan community where one or two family clans lived in harmony, with a strong attachment to the village bequeathed by ancestors. "A strong community consciousness has resulted in a dichotomy between localities" (Yoon,119). Such a local tie manifested itself in the skewed development program under the authoritarian regime of Park Chung-hee. The military regime had the top notch of the leadership filled by ranking officers from the south-eastern province including the birth place of Park Chung-hee. A coterie group was formed around trust-worthy home town pals to spearhead the country's development with the resulting defense of their regional interests against others. This regional bias was notably intensified against the southwestern province of Korea, which had been an rival in many ways. This province has long been forlorn as a victim in the shadow of rapid development. In presidential elections, voters in this province vented their grievances by giving this province-born favorite candidate, Kim Dae-jung, the majority of votes and astounded Park Chung-hee who was confident of winning, dependent on an extensive network of adherents and popular support of his accomplishments. Kim Dae-jung, branded as a permanent opposition candidate and for all his heroic struggles for democracy, failed in his presidential bid against his formidable rival. In the 1997's presidential election, Kim obtained 98 percent of votes from his province to win the race against the majority party candidate, Lee Hoe-chang. The political activities of the voters, spurred on a frantic fervor to revenge, present a compelling case where localism prevailed over what is at stake for the state. "As such, the political culture of Korea is significantly affected by anthropocentricism which discourages the development of organized class politics within a political system" (Kim Byung Kuk 1977). Political issues are viewed through the prism of local concerns, and provincialism is inevitably imbued by an emotional touch, leaving little room for the reasonable working of the mind.

Korean Women in a New Mirror

Woman's Status

The status of women relative to men in Korea enjoys a robust topic among foreigners, for Korea is allegedly notorious for sexual discrimination, largely against women. Whether this argument is true or not in modern Korea, sexual discrimination is not limited to Korea alone, and it exists in every society, albeit with varying degree of intensity and tone. Debate has warmed up over this issue even in Europe and America which pride themselves on a much longer history of liberal democracy. It was less than a century ago that women were accorded entitlement to political participation in the form of the right to vote in Western Europe. "In 1870 the English Parliament recognized the right of women to control their own finances in the first Married Women's Property Act" (Jeremy Paxman 1998, 218). In 1948, the Constitution of the Republic of Korea was enacted, which declared sexual discrimination unlawful, whether it is in family, education or employment. Theoretically, Korean women were thereafter supposed to enjoy equality before the law. But the Constitution did not ensure equality in every aspect of daily life.

Debate on women's status relative to men brings gender distinction and discrimination into focus, though the two are differentiated. Traditional strict gender distinction is held to have constrained women's public activities and to have perpetuated unequal status. The popular notion of gender distinction overlooks the fact that it had an element of protecting or preserving women's status, reflecting womanly needs based on physiological differences. It was in this context that role expectations were constructed. Gender distinction broadly embraces status, role, treatment, socialization, education, employment, and what not, but not all of these elements have negative connotations. Role distinction is an offshoot of gender distinction, initially contrived to ensure orderly relationship between husbands and wives.

Sexual Discrimination

While gender distinction is a mixture of positive and negative elements, discrimination refers to unfairness, inequality, bias, injustice and mistreatment against a sexual group. Gender distinction initially followed from physiological and genetic differences that did not allow humans to develop themselves into hermaphroditic entities. Neither is it possible nor desirable to establish such a sexual utopia. Informal arrangements were contrived to grant Korean female workers certain privileges over men in certain employment, including, say, extra days off during pregnancy and after child birth, and preferential work scheduling, if they have family responsibilities or if they would have to travel alone at night to get home. In the past, open competition for entrance to the prestigious universities, female candidates were given additional points, and this came from concern for women's competitiveness with male candidates. But it cannot be considered other than the public recognition of women's inferiority.[10]

Giving "extra days off" - due to physiological needs or familial responsibilities - and the arrangement of different working hours for women is undoubtedly considered blatant discrimination by the women of Western societies since it is not in line with the democratic emphasis on principled equality. "For Koreans, however, such preferential treatments are simply regarded as humane or natural, since they reflect a shared understanding of what both men and women consider to be women's needs" (Diane

Hoffman 1995;227). No sensible Korean will deny this practice, simply because it is deleterious to equality-based democracy. Gender distinction and role distinction are the social constructs of the primordial form of belief. These oppose the cosmological view that male and female are not categorically opposed and locked into a dominant-subordinate status, but are, rather, blurred, synthesized or otherwise deconstructed. "Social construct denotes a range of institutional devices for covering up (or even compensating) what constitutes, at a deeper level of consciousness, the undifferentiated categories of gender wherein the sexes are viewed as essentially one, bound together in a deep intimacy that erases their categoricalness and separateness"(Hoffman;219). This explains how the self is culturally experienced or constructed and how male and female aspects of the self are defined.

It is in this matrix that Koreans conceptualize marriage as the process through which two persons with more differences than those in common become one body and one mind. Not only bodies are involved: selves, too, lose their uniqueness, contrasting the Western case of a temporary merging of male and female in which both persons are ready to return to a separate, individual status and identity. In other words, male and female, according to the Asian cosmological view, are subsumed into a greater entity known as the family in which emotion and intimacy are universally binding factors. "The dissolution of the conjugal bond was a social impossibility. The concurrence of the husband's forbearance and the wife's sense of obligation was the ideological basis of marital harmony"(Martina Deuchler 1977;35). Perhaps this is why Korean men and women in marital relations find it less necessary to make gestures of love between them. Korean couples can fight with abandon, and yet not break up, for their oneness (based on the absolute intimacy of the self-other identification) cannot be broken by mere emotional ups and downs. As a result, beneath what may be the surface appearances of aloofness and distance between a married couple lies a certain emotional bond and dependency that most Westerners would find overly close or even suffocating. The concept of bodily fusion that erased individual identities finds expression in the frequent occurrence of family suicide. A father who abandoned himself after business bankruptcy does not want to go alone to the other world. Obviously, the bond, intimacy and warmth act in close social relations as a social glue between people, cementing them in a kind of eternal closeness regardless of their emotional ups and downs, their disagreements, and their personal problems. Breaking a friendly relationship involves pains of emotional explosion as if they were in romantic love.

The Korean persistent adherence to role distinctions raises concerns about social receptivity in role sharing that is widely practiced among young couples in particular. Role sharing is a new phenomenon resulting from changes in family values that paralleled the atomization of the family. Social transformation squeezes the family into a smallest possible entity, where role sharing is unavoidable, particularly when both husband and wife are employed. In other words, role sharing is accepted and practiced by Korean couples as the way it should be, though it does not necessarily reflect what they consider desirable. Amid the retreat of traditional family values, role distinction versus role sharing is a matter of heated debate which illustrate the intergenerational gap. When it comes to "who brings home the bacon," their role consciousness harks back to the past. "The traditional value that defined men as the principal income earner justifies men's authority and dominance in Korean society. The dominant position of men went hand in hand with the normative construction of women as dependent housewives or, at best, as supplementary income earners"(Moon Seung Sook 2002;84).

The concept of marriage has not undergone a structural change; "While marriage has become more a matter of individual choice than in the past, it has largely remained patrilocal and continues to be regarded as a means of sustaining the institution of patrilineal descent" (Moon Seung Sook, 81). The spatial division in the homes of old aristocrats (yangban), sublimated into biased social expectations, set the tone for sexual inequalities in employment and career opportunities. So, many female employees in the public and private sectors are sidetracked from seeking career development and end up with provisionary or dead end jobs. Consequently, they bow to social expectations that force them to find roles at home. This phenomenon was found in gender imbalance expressed in many domains of social practice; we can readily note a significant under-representation of women in all branches of the government and the disadvantages that women suffer when competing with their male counterparts in seeking career jobs. As such, the social expectations of gender role continue to form a matrix within which both men and women shape their perspectives on job, family, marriage and role.

Gender status is constructed through the hierarchical structure of the traditional family: gender hierarchy defines husband not only as the partner in an affectionate relationship but as an authoritarian figure to be respected by family members. Confucian sages envisioned an abiding relationship between husband and wife in which respect combines with affection. This idealistic combination of the two was said to create a force that would enable the family to withstand all problems and difficulties. Nowhere is a woman's yearning for a man of respect and trust more clearly pronounced than when it comes to choosing a potential husband. In general, Korean women pay all but irrational attention to a man's social standing, family background, in-law parents, education, job stability, earnings, and so on, seeing them as a guarantee for a stable wedlock. Selecting a partner used to be a long patient process in which these factors were weighed. Even today, a higher degree of prudence is evident in selecting a spouse: this justifies parents taking a role in assuring that as many conditions as possible are met. Very often, the parental choices run against those favored by the young, but the day has gone when parents forced their choices on children.

Still, the modern concept of partnership struggles with entrenched role expectations. Partnership in its true sense is based on equality both in role and status, and Korean women are in favor of status equality. But they often overlook the fact that it entails sharing responsibility to earn a living. This joint responsibility highlights women's role in sustaining family life, especially when her husband is incapable of earning a livelihood. In a situation that requires both husband and wife to work for a livelihood, the notion of shared responsibility often slips the women's mind, because of a continued obsession with the traditional role distinctions. Status expectations are not necessarily congruous with role expectations, and this inconsistency between the two has become problematic with the partnership concept of family. A husband incapable of serving as a bread earner is the primary cause for divorce among the young couples. The concept of sexual equality has not completely dispelled role distinction frozen in the traditional concept.

Breaking New Ground

Traditional social norms have consistently reinforced male dominance. Confucian norms were untiring in depicting womanly characters and womanly ways of behaving. In old days, a woman with an assortment of the defined womanly virtues – affectionate mother, submissive wife, physical cleanness, taciturnity, chastity and honesty - was a moral paragon representative of idealism and purity. They were regarded as embodying the essential virtues of society and a repository of the moral ideals upon which the entire society is structured. The mother was the citadel of family values guarding against the unwelcome incursion of "low morality" commonly associated with Western evils. Confucianism mandated that a woman should be nurtured within the bound of "home," protected from social evils. The lack of contact with the outside world made a woman extremely shy, sensitive to womanly virtues and repulsive to "unbecoming or unwomanly behaviors" under the glare of society. To befit the idealized profile of women took a lot of pain and self-discipline amid the maze of secular temptations, and the idea behind the strict constraints suggests that women were expected to have unblemished character, shining like a guiding star of morality, while men must live among the dust of the secular life.

The notion of ennobling woman's virtues contradicts Western scholars leaning toward a simplistic understanding of gender relation in Korea in their own conceptual frames which highlights a structured dichotomy between the dominant and moral male and the subordinate and amoral female. This trend reflects the Western bias toward conceptualizing gender relation through the prism of an intrinsically conflict-ridden contest. Role distinction has been constructed in the changing social milieu that parallels the atomization of the family. Through this process, women have made varying degrees of progress in the areas of formal education, marriage and family life in a way that expanded the scope of their role. Released from the demanding paradigm of roles inherent in the extended family, a woman manager of a nuclear family enjoys free hands to expand her role beyond the traditionally defined familial affairs. The modern version of Korean women highlights their dominance not only in family affairs and education but in financial matters. In the highly competitive bar examination, women over-represent those who pass the final screening.

As one Korean husband puts it, "the man is the head, but the woman is the center of the family." The family can function without the head, but it falls apart if there is no center. Women who may appear subservient or deferential to their husbands in public are in fact exceedingly active and aggressive in their almost absolute control over family affairs, including finances. The placid and compliant image of Korean women is no longer valid. There is a lot of masculinity about the way elderly Korean women behave and talk. Their unabashed cackling among the quiet crowd of a subway and shoving their shoulders in the crowd are no longer uncommon sights. The masculinity of women may have to do with their ages or different and additional role they play within the family; the new role of women helped to remove constraints on their public behaviors, allowing them to break a new ground for their role. Hoffman attributes masculinity to the result of desexualization that older women undergo once they are no longer able to bear children. "In a sense, when one's procreative role is lost, there is no longer any need to preserve the structural separation of genders"(Dian Hoffman 1995,222). "There were many heroic stories about young widows who resisted their parents' pressure to remarry and fled to their parents-in-law's house to serve as filial daughters-in-law or cut their hair and became nuns"(Deuchler, 39). Women, bereft of husband's protection at earlier ages, become more boisterous and masculine, for they play additional roles for the family.

Generation Gap

Recent tragedies that had beset Korea left their marks in shaping a new image of Korean women. The women who spent their adulthood through the post liberation and the Korean War have seen kaleidoscopic changes from Japanese colonial rule through stressful years to the recent dynamic growth of the country. Born into the Mars, they feel as if they had traveled to Earth in a blink of the eye. The chaotic pacing of change dispelled *noblesse oblige*, and the women in this age range were called upon to take roles that transgress domestic chores. While the war was in its full swing and during the post-war rehabilitation period, they were thrown into the impersonal arena for survival and toughened by all the problems they encountered while scraping a living between survival and extinction. All sufferings and sacrifices engraved furrows on their foreheads. Strong, self-reliant and selfless mothers in the turbulent age became over-ambitious for their children's education and marriages. Korean mothers were romanticized as an angel, comparable to the women of Victorian values by constructing an asexual and selfless image of womanhood.

But, daughters of these strong and selfless mothers, born in the post-war years, spent their childhood through the stressful rehabilitation period and relished the fruits of economic growth. They witnessed the established norms crumble, giving vent to materialistic ambitions. Imbued with an avid desire to get rich, women no longer sat idle at home, with all social signals beckoning them to pursue income. They displayed their business acumen in real estate dealing and speculative investments and struck a bonanza. Their success in business changed the woman's position from mere dependence on their husbands to uncontested dominance in the financial matters of the family. Millions of salaried husbands were reduced to such a pitiable status of depending on the leniency of their wives to dole out daily pocket money. Behind the success of the "*neveau riches*" class was the unmistakable presence of an exceedingly active and aggressive woman within many, if not most, families that created wealth. Their role in class reproduction and maintenance was vital."For vibrancy, the capacity for self-sacrifice for children and husbands, and the sense of commitment to job, these women have a few equals in the world" (Gregory Henderson 1983:38)

The third generation of daughters form a new cohort which has known only a prosperous and comfortable Korea. Some of them have gone far to "define themselves within a consumer-oriented society where consumption has become an act of identity construction"(Kendall Laurel 2002;17). These daughters are frowned upon in a traditional light that was contemptuous of mercenary craving, lowly appetite and naked ambition. These women not only defied the Confucian injunction to practice balance and moderation in one's daily life but could not escape the watchful eyes of critics for their vulgar snobbery. They assert equality not in kind but in quality. They could have been happier wives, if they had been wise enough to know how to use feminine waywardness to complement macho waywardness. These women may be dismissed away as they constitute an insignificant segment of the female population'; there are millions still laboring away in a manner that might have pleased their mother-in-law. Nonetheless, the influence of this small cohort is becoming more and more pervasive as the consumer-oriented middle class grows. Women who left Korea in the post-war period to seek advanced education and career development in advanced countries were the envy of their friends left at home to struggle through stressful times. Returning after a decade of overseas life, these women find themselves so shabby before the styled, dressed-up women who had once envied them. These upstart wives spend on the sweat of their husbands to display their newly acquired status before the crestfallen returnees.

The women's excessive spending ushered in a new phenomenon epitomized by a neologism, "middle aged men's crisis." For the 'forgotten heroes of economic growth who considered their financial contribution as the single most important family responsibility, failure to provide for the family leads to the loss of respect and authority in the family and, consequently, the loss of masculinity. Since the economic downturn known as the IMF crisis in 1997, TV and print media lavished their attention on "the white-color blues" and "the end of the salary man era" in a nostalgic yearning for the past when they displayed exuberant energy, manly spirit, and paternal authority. Young women these days are increasingly assertive about their individuality. They regard their grandmothers as asexual and selfless motherhood. Their mothers, reactive to the asexual and strong image of motherhood, launched the quest for what was meant by individuality while agonizing over their stand between temptation for deviation and old-fashioned morality. Released from the demanding paradigm of behaviors, the quest for identity directed attention to the part of themselves that have unjustifiably been depressed. Apparently, the compressed industrialization brought the three generations under one dome but the way they think of family, marriage, and gender role speaks for the long distance they have traveled.

So far as their mothers are concerned, they turn to a past that justified the image of asexual and strong mother. The on-going redefinition of gender role, marriage and the family has engendered a flexible definition of what constitutes acceptable social behaviors. Korea is yet far from the stage where alternatives to marriage and family are openly talked about. Role switching is subject to the watchful scrutiny of in-law parents, but these are the topics on which debate is heated. Today's wife will become a noisy mother-in-law, when her son is caught washing dishes while his wife is taking rest.

The Status-Conscious Middle Class

Koreans are highly conscious of status. Homer Hulbert, an early American missionary, noted "a passionate desire to ascend a step on the social ladder, as they tried in every way to move upwards. "The assertion of status has become an important element in both the formation and the definition of its new urban middle class"(Denise P Lett 1998,125). The Confucian view of life as a strenuous effort to realize the highest version of the self generated an insatiable desire for upward move. Koreans are known for their maniac pursuit of education as a means to seek a higher status. Education is highly status-oriented, and this parochial view of education has its influence felt in various aspects of today's education. A strong motive for education, whether for self cultivation or for advancing in social status, has been a driving force behind the development of South Korea. Vertical power structures keep highly motivated persons looking to the summit, constantly sending a sobering call for all to work hard and join in an upward stream. For Koreans attuned to social bifurcation into the ruling elites and the ruled masses, the middle class is not only a strange concept but offers little to envy when engaged in a game of distinction within a kin group. They have little patience with staying in the status quo. The hierarchical view of occupation as being "noble" or "base" (Deuchler Martina1992,378) gives an added spur to a ceaseless struggle for upward mobility, with eyes set on avoiding the stigma of base works. Debasing one in terms of the kind of job is hardly noted in Japan, although its society is as much hierarchically structured.

In the last few years, Koreans have posted the highest suicide among OECD member states, and the reason is their strong hierarchical consciousness; they are not taught to find happiness in the mess of mundane affairs or to appreciate modest successes. They think equality runs against the rule of nature. Repeated failures frustrate the hierarchy-conscious people more deeply than those with a horizontal perspective. Many Koreans suffer status inconsistency that is not considered so serious in other parts of the world. Those who keep their expectations low are amazed at modest successes. But average Koreans are hardly disposed to seek happiness in the routine round of daily life. The present moment is something to be foregone in favor of the future dream. The lack of emotional solace inherent in the dehumanized relationship offers an added spur to frustration, leading to suicide.

The upper class yangban in Korea corresponds to the middle class in Western societies in terms of access to a stable and affluent life. They formed a small elite like frosting on cake, blessed with wealth and cultural capital. Descendants of yangban ancestry but unable to share in the recent economic windfalls emphasize cultural capital as their claim to the inherited upper class. As South Korea modernized and industrialized, the word, middle class (chungsancheung), was frequently heard from the mid 1970s onwards. It was during this period that commoners rose in economic status and began to rival those of yangban ancestry. While the new upper class acquired a higher economic status, "those of yangban find the presence of the new rich as a challenge to their vested access to political resources (Kim Kwang Ok 1992;197) and rely heavily on genealogical and ancestral heritage. Education is an asset in their claim to higher status.

The true measure of the yangban class was the extent to which their lives were guided by Confucian ideals, and financial capital alone was not a sufficient condition for their claim to high status. "Members of the new middle class try to acquire the traditional elite culture in an effort to consolidate their newly earned status within the established cultural community" (Denise P. Lett1998,38). "They retroactively publish genealogies, build ancestor shrines and redecorate ancestors' graves" (Kim Kwang Ok 1992,197-198). Retrospective obsession with the past status was further reinforced by their disdain for the *nouveau riche* for their ostentatious display of wealth, vulgar and gaudy aura that was condemned as "chonmin keun'seong" (the character of the lowborn). They are denounced for the lack of self-restraint, moderation and discipline. The bifurcation of the upper class into the traditional and new ones explains that Korea did not experience a continuing process of social change, and "the historical slate is not wiped clean" (Denise P Lett 1998;1). This leaves ample room for the descendants of yangban ancestry to reassert Confucian virtues as the qualification of the contemporary upper class. The yangban class was neither hereditarily succeeded nor obtained by wealth alone; the status was renegotiated by meeting a set of criteria that consisted of scholastic excellence and moral or manner consciousness. Having been immersed in a vertically arranged status system, Koreans perceive class, consciously or unconsciously, as timeless, once they achieved it.

Another way of status identification is the kind of work one engages in. Confucian norms draw a line between those who labored with their minds and those who worked with their hands or engaging in an unprepossessing labor that is thought to cause the loss of status. The ruling elites obsessed with non-productive literary works relegated productive blue-collar work to the commoners or lowborn. Business, money-lending and commerce were downgraded as a malicious device to secure profits for individuals. Anything short of public concern or a common good was declared "demeaning of the yangban. The discrimination of jobs is used as the weapon of attack on chaebeol, business tycoons, on the assumption that their business involved immoral acts. Confucian disdain for capital accumulation and productive manual labor stunted the growth of business and industry. "A gentleman of the purest blood can engage in farming without soiling his escutcheon, but to be a merchant or manufacturer or broker would be beneath his dignity" (Homers Hulbert 1969;269). The Confucian-imposed dichotomy in works persists, although its intensity faded considerably, and consequently brought forth a severe shortage of manual labor workers.

As South Korea industrialized, business has prospered in the world of anonymity, and many, irrespective of educational attainment, became entrepreneurs. Running a business did not require a college degree, although many entrepreneurs were college educated as well. Education is the determinant of the kind of job one lands and is, therefore, directly linked to the identification of status. A college-educated man may consider himself pertaining to the middle class, even if he did not come from a middle-class family. "When education is inconsistent with low family status, the former takes precedence over the latter. "Construction workers may make more money, but these and other 'dirty jobs' are ones no one wants to do, and those engaging in these jobs are not considered middle class" (Lett;4).

The "New urban middle class" is a direct outgrowth of urbanization and industrialization, representing the white-color employees of government agencies and large business corporations, Their life style is distinguished from that of the old middle class by total dependence on earnings from their jobs. The definition of the new middle class by occupation as 'a salaried man' fits well in with that of the Japanese. "But salaried man does not have the same significance in Korea as in Japan, and there are difficulties inherent in separating the two"(Lett;4). In defining the middle class, major concern is a quantitative criterion which captures two-thirds of the total population, and such a number-centered criterion is subjective by frequently blurring borders between social strata.

Many of the Korean middle class, identified by occupation, were found to be financially dependent on supplementary earnings from the owned lands or other real estate or parents' support in order to maintain a middle class life. Members of a middle class family in dire need of money would turn to their parents or blood kin for support rather than drawing on the bank or other financial systems. The dependence of Korean middle class families on their relatives is in contrast with their Japanese counterparts who are exclusively dependent on their own earnings, unless they are the eldest son entitled to a lion's share of parental property.

A network of trust in Korea includes family members and blood kin to call on for support; they marshal resources necessary to start a joint venture or help each other to find a good job. Unlike Japan which saw the corporate family disappeared in 1945, the extensive family network of Korea forms a corporate entity in which the stem family plays a pivotal role in kin control. This explains that the family system of Korea is still defined in terms of interdependence rather than as a residential unit. While the nuclear family based on the residential unit has become the norm statistically in South Korea (Tsuya and Choe 1991;22), the corporate and stem families continue to exist legally and conceptually, dispelling the possibility of one family independent of another in the extended network of family..

Status consciousness is expressed in class endogamy or marriage within the same class. Marriage was by no means a matter of persons to be espoused. It was as much a lineage affair as it evoked concern of all members of the lineage. Choosing a suitable partner was a primary concern of the family in the hierarchically stratified society, and it was made in such a prudent way that ensured the prestige of the family lineage. It is frequently observed that one who marries a person of lower status put his family in panic and lives a lonely life distanced from his relatives. The collective concern of the extended family system had the advantage of playing a defensive mechanism against marriages that would match with different classes. Parents saw an excuse to intervene to ensure a proper matching. In modern Korea, marriage between different classes is rarely practiced. Class endogamy, inherited from the hierarchically structured society, continues to exist and is employed by the status-conscious upper or middle class as a strategy to maintain or upgrade a family's prestigious status. "This tendency is observed today among major chaebol (business tycoon) families and government elites" (Seoul Business Newspaper 1991), and class endogamy will stay unabated so far as Koreans remain status-conscious.

The history of the United States abounds in the rags-to-riches stories as it befits the country of opportunity. Abraham Lincoln, Andrew Carnegie, Joseph Pulitzer, Jay Gould and many others rose to social eminence, despite their patchy education. President Roh Moon-hyun (2104 -08) was a rose in the ditch, and his ascendency to the summit of power inspired and excited those who bemoaned their lowly status as the product of class consciousness. It takes a heroic struggle to make one an object of envy in the die-hard presence of status consciousness. A nuclear family which rises in social status brings prestige to its entire lineage. Many Koreans live off their status, although impoverished. The yangban family, though impoverished in economic terms, feeds on inherited prestige and Confucian ideals. The popularization of education raised more families of lowborn ancestry to the middle or upper class and the playing field has been leveled considerably, at least in economic terms, making Korean society more egalitarian and fluid. "A few roses from the ditch" broke what seemed to be an impassable barrier by marrying the spouses of the upper class by drawing on high achievement in education and career. Although they land in the privileged social class, they are tacitly disdained for their humble origins. In order to avoid this stigma, they try to emulate the life style of the upper class. Again, cultural capital matters when one claims oneself to higher status.

The yangbanization of Koreans may be comparable to gentrification of Europeans that had taken place two centuries earlier in the sense that their landing on the new class was followed by strenuous efforts to emulate a new life style. However, the former is distinct from the latter by its obsessive attachment to an extended family system. The presence of the extended family system as a network of mutual support in Korea contradicts Goode's theory positing a destruction of traditional extended family systems and a convergence toward a conjugal system as societies industrialize. At a certain point of industrialization, the Korean family, a stronghold of traditional values, resists the pressure of industrialization, and this trend is prominent among upper class families. A conflict between industrialization and family forces produces a paradox – that "the most successful families and family networks in the industrial economy very likely engage in more family-oriented behavior than almost any other stratum" (Goode 1982;190).

Kohyang, More Than Hometown

|||||||||||||||||||||||||||||||||||||||||||||||||||||||||||||||||||||||||||||||||||||||||||||||||||

In connection with provincialism, the Korean concept of kohyang, the English equivalent of home town, is worth mentioning. To English urbanites weary of the roar of traffic and the blight of industrialization, the home town conjures up a return to a pastoral idyll or "green grass home." To Koreans, kohyang evokes powerful emotions and, in this sense, is much more than what hometown means in English terms. It has to do with the warmth of human bonds which Koreans feels with his hometown relatives and pals rather than the pastoral beauty that beckons one to long for. A home town is the place in which one is born and grows up. It was a closely knit human network where all members feel a sense of togetherness as a result of common descent or acquired kinship. Further, kohyang to Koreans is the place where their ancestors are buried: their ancestors' graves on hillsides are as inextricably a familiar part of the local landscape one sees daily on his way from and to school. Life in sight of graves gives a sense of closeness to ancestors, however remote they are in time. The home town is associated with ancestral roots, a place where they lived generation after generation. Leaving one's home town, therefore, brings Koreans the most painful experience, for it means not only departure from a cozy corner filled with comfort and camaraderie but staying away from ancestors. Wayfarers feel the visceral pain of severing the umbilical cord. They invariably visit their ancestors' graves before they depart and affirm their pledge to return. But this pledge occasionally turns out to be an illusion unless one dies of homesick.

The notion of Kohyang affiliated with ancestors, notes Kim Yol-kyu, is reflected in the timber-carved deity that greets visitors at a village entrance. The deity is supposed to protect ancestors who are buried there. One may notice a similar one standing at entrances to Japanese villages. This is the protector of the village from villainous spirits. Koreans associate the deity with ancestors, while Japanese with the village. Frequently, rural folks are cast adrift into impersonal and mindless cities which reduces them into part of the marginalized masses. Released from village constraints, they are free to act, as they want, with less concern for propriety or decency, as dictated by the convenience of living in an inhospitable surrounding. Whenever they are pained by a bitter dose of urban life, they finds themselves haunted by burning desires to go back to their home town where blood relatives and neighbors are expected to open their arms in welcome. Sentimental romances dominate their home sickness, and there are not many to welcome them other than old folks.

Korean songs abound in lyrics about wayfarers bemoaning the fate of drifting far away from hometowns. The wayfarers dream of going back, reliving good old days when they enjoyed the comfort zone shaded by parents and kin. The wayfarers maintain bonds with parents left in home towns like balloons perpetually anchored to a mooring point. "Though time and the unremitting cycle of life and death are beyond the control of man, one can, at least, find constancy in place" (Charles N. Goldberg 1979; 30). Those who suffer bitter urban life long for the day when they will join their ancestors in family graves to be awakened by bustling visits from their descendants."Kohyang, then, is the place of one's ancestors, of one's kin and neighbors; it is the place from which one derives one's identity" (Goldberg;90).

The strong sense of home leads to the negative characterization of people from elsewhere, often in derogatory terms. Cholla people in the southwest sway like willows in spring breezes; Chungcheong people in the middle feign to be demure and gentle but rarely open their hearts. Gyonggi people near Seoul are miserly but discreet about what is right or wrong. Kyeongsang people in the southeast are uncouth and quarrelsome when they talk, but these people assert that they are warm in the heart. North Koreans are divided into Northwestern and Northeastern regions. Northwestern people are fierce like a tiger chasing a prey, but Northeastern people, living in a land filled with rugged mountains, have steely wills, like dogs fighting fiercely in the mud. Negative characterizations rarely stands up to scrutiny but are widely held, even determining whether people are deemed suitable for important posts. Regional characteristics enter the determination of one's eligibility for an important bureaucratic post.

Along with the regional stereotypes, two concepts are juxtaposed, to'bagi (a man of a long residence) and oe'rein (outsider). The former is proud of their ancestral roots and have disdain for or estrange the outsiders. The outsiders who have recently moved in to settle down have difficulty dealing with the clannish village people for some years until they are accepted in as members of the community. Village residents seek their legitimate residency by familiarity with the village people. In many Korean villages before the Korean War, the majority of residents were, typically, all of the same clan. One clan was related to another by marriage, and so some villages had two or three related clans. Such a village is self-contained, and outsiders were not welcome.

Even today, many Koreans seek career or political alliances by using genealogical bonds, and this hinders policies based on unbiased consideration of situational factors. An abiding practice of securing a genealogical bond is sihyang'je, a ritual that brings together all members of one genealogical bond to a village of their ancestral origin to honor their progenitor. On the occasion of celebration or funeral, all villagers are brought together to a feast. A wedding ceremony and funeral of a family becomes a community affair. The community takes a moral cudgel to unethical or unwifely conduct, though their acts are not subject to legal punishment.

An incentive to remain in one's kohyang was very strong in traditional society. Second or third son without an inherited property were more often led to seek a new life away from the hometown. When they left their home town, they lost their identity as members of a reputable family and tended to be reduced into marginalized workers in urbanized regions. A strong 'we-feeling' led to a strong local patriotism which may develop into a counterweight to its neighbor community. The problem arises in the absence of a connecting thread, popularly known as an intermediate value, between a village and a greater political unit. Korea was not immune to the "revolution of rising expectations." In the post-war years, the pull factors of urban life depleted the workers of a village. Rural out-migration has increased at an extraordinary pace. With the influx of mass media and a new sort of culture, the traditional villages lost their lures while they retain the emotional solace of rural communities.

Korean society is very much urbanized. Urbanites accounts for 75 percent of total population, comparable to the reverse when the first economic development was launched in 1962. The Seoul population accounts for one fourth of total population, and a hefty majority of them have local roots, for they have parents or some of their siblings residing in local areas. Now that the first generation of rural migrants to urban areas diminished, a reasonable prediction is that an endless stream of cars heading to home towns, on festive occasions, would no longer be a familiar scene. Far from it, the migrant trend toward home towns remains much the same as decades ago. The passage of time never wears out their passionate longing for their ancestors' graves.

New generations born and grown up in urban areas are deprived of sentimental longing, but they fumble their way to their ancestors' graves on "Chuseok" or the new Lunar Year holiday. Notwithstanding the breathtaking changes in various aspects of human life, Koreans are more home-bound people than other ethnic groups. The chaotic stampede of travelers to train stations, even with a festive day being a couple of months away, remain a unique scene unlikely to abate with time.

A massive drift of Koreans, notably those inhabiting the national border areas, was caused by the ominous fate of their country after the forced signing of the Protectorate Treaty with Japan in 1905. They crossed borders in large numbers and settled in sparsely populated eastern Manchuria, popularly known as "Kando," and Maritime Siberia. These expatriates had been separate from their blood relatives at their home towns for a century or so while the ideological war was raging. Those in Maritime Siberia were forced, on a short notice, to make a daunting journey across freezing Siberia to an unknown destination under the Stalin's reign. Their struggle with an inhospitable environment is the story of a miraculous survival worthwhile to tell others. It was a tragic drama that befell Koreans, when the Soviet regime dreaded that Koreans not far from the borders might be collaborating with infiltrating Japanese agents. Another drift was enforced by Japan in the name of forced labors at the Kurile Islands, and their plaintive longings for kohyang were inscribed on the walls of the mining caves where they met untimely death while dreaming of returning to kohyang. Now that three generations have passed, their descendants pay visit to their ancestors' hometowns, some carrying the chests of ancestors' bone ashes, pursuant to the dead who wished to be buried in their hometown. Despite the free trafficking of the dispersed families across national borders, a tragic drama still saddens the North Koreans who defected to the South prior to or during the Korean War. The forced dispersion of families, estimated at four million, keeps them apart from their blood kin, as well as unable to communicate across the demarcation line. This pain of separation is too visceral for the home-bound Koreans to bear. Their longing for hometowns grows with time and the unfulfilled dreams of family reunions followed them into their graves.

Sentimental romanticism was attached to their departure from hometown by touching the depth of wanderlust under colonial rule, as reflected in songs or poems. They bemoaned the fate of wayfarers, so remorseful of having neglected their filial duties to their parents when they were there. The seemingly timeless dispersion of the family drained the North Korean refugees of a home-bound emotion. The War not only destroyed the fabric of the clan village characteristic of the pre-war Korean society but set millions drifting around. Although they are wretchedly in despair without family reunions or suffer from their baneful existence, having no place to go back adds to their already inflated pains. Urban sprawl drained rural areas of workable youngsters and they are reluctant to return to their home towns to see elderly people around. Their hometowns are empty of industries, cultural amenities and anything that would have captured the dream of youngsters to come back. For the North Korean refugees, the communities they inhabit are an emotional wasteland, no matter how enriched the place may be. They envy those who have a place to return, even a ghost town. So long as they have a place where they claim themselves to be its natives, they are happy. Having no place to go back on festive days, North Korean refugees bemoan their inability to perform filial duties. There set up an altar on the top of a mountain near the demarcation line to perform a sacrificial rite for their supposedly dead parents.

Koreans are noted for their strong tendency to identify themselves with hometowns. The notion of shared ways of life forged around the hometown is most identifiable in politics. A local figure rising to social eminence was based almost exclusively on his personal style and home-based politics rather than political or ideological creed that crosses borders. Obsession with hometowns is the spawning grounds for personality politics. Longing for hometowns is the motivating force for organizing various fraternities of residents in urban areas, dedicated to do good for their hometowns or to help political figures from the same hometown in their bid for a high post. Paradoxically, passion for a hometown causes outsiders to harbor animosity or hostility against home-based people. As much as home town people are homogeneous, they reject people who are declared "outsiders."

Education Mania

Education in Korea has made monumental strides, as reflected in the remarkable quantum growth of educated people. The literacy level is one of the highest in the world surpassing those of industrial countries. In the past, education was status-oriented, with its goal to turn out elite bureaucrats. After the liberation from the colonial yoke, higher education agonized over whether to make skillful lawyers, physicians or engineers or to make capable and cultivated human beings. Education had dual commitments; to teach them to make a living and to teach how to live. As Korea industrialized, educational goals were perceived in the context of human resource development geared to national development at large and economic growth in particular. From this view point, education sits behind Korea's stellar achievement, serving as the vehicle for modernization. Its focus on human resource development calls into question how far education has deviated from its intrinsic goal to nurture an intellectually awakened and morally conscious man. The hierarchical consciousness of Koreans and a high literacy, though, gave rise to pathological problems which are unique to Koreans.

Korean children are disciplined to behave well and be compliant with teachers and parents. Many Koreans who study abroad wonder at the way foreign students challenge their professors or address them without respect and, worse, taunt them. Koreans are more cautious when they engage with seniors, not just in the way they talk, using honorifics and bodily gestures, but maintaining inner posture. Korean children take off sun glasses before seniors. Pointing with fingers to seniors is totally inhibited. The no-holds-barred manners of foreign students strikes many Koreans as uncouth and impolite. Addressing a professor by the first name is something Koreans never get used to.

Many adult Koreans, on the other hand, complain that the new generation behaves like spoiled brats. In classes in elementary school, an increasing number of kids treat their teachers like their peers. They shove teachers who try to teach how to write and are careless about honorifics. Education today has a mass of contradictions, leading educators to hark back to the not-distant past when the large-extended family system prevailed. The large family system disciplined kids, and seniors within the family were mentors admonishing about how to behave. Outright affection between parents and children was hardly observed under the watchful eyes of older members within the family. Self restraint and sobriety hallmarked their behavior. The father was an austere figure, who stayed above petty frays of family routines, and involved himself in guiding and teaching children to correct their behaviors. Mother was a saint whose unreserved affection and devotion to children find few equals in the world. In a freezing winter, a hard-working child broke the ice in his ink bottle and shivered through the morning lesson, while his mother is already up there ready to ply him with a hot breakfast. Learning at school in Korea is indeed a painful experience. Children who prepare for college examination are physically and mentally over-strained by grinding through from eight AM to six PM, followed by a few extra hours of learning before going home. At home, they burn mid-night oil with mother kept vigilant around the clock. Korean high school kids are burdened with prohibitive loads that they are expected to master.[11] Their goal is to enter the prestigious universities of first choice.

Mothers perpetually share all the suffering and are poised to sacrifice to ensure a smooth path for their kids to the universities. A Buddhist mother wouldn't mind going up to a remote temple every day to supplicate godly charity on her pitiful child. On the examination day, huge crowds of over-enthusiastic mothers threaten to smash through the closed gates of the universities, restless with anxiety for their children undergoing the grueling examination. Some sit on their knees for hours of prayer. The untold heroin in one's success is the mother. High achievers never fail to mention the sacrifice of their mothers in their biographies, sometimes with tears in their eyes when recalling what their mothers had done. The nuclear family is a barren land for this sort of education, for elderly family members are stripped of opportunities to partake of it. Nowadays, there is little time for communication, little effort, if any, being made to provide a link between childhood and adulthood. The emotional fusion of parents and children, particularly between mother and child in a nuclear family creates an anomalistic compassion for children undergoing the excruciating experience of school education.

The quality of the education Korean children tortured themselves to receive at school is questionable in many ways. The process of learning is dreary and boring, with cramming knowledge and rote-learning undermining their ability to be creative. Imagine how fanatically verbal their education is, striving for "excellence" by force-feeding children with reading-writing-and-arithmetic from the earliest possible age. The Korean culture is far from valuing diversity: Koreans see virtue in unity, a standard, one path, one race, one system, and so on. The curriculum is what education is all about. A limited range of experiences fosters a mentality prone to the simplification of things into a 'right or wrong,' and debate on grey shades is hardly observed until they become adults. The systems of education prize intellectual ability over integrity, character, courage and honesty.

Unlike the parents of the extended family, today's parents are increasingly permissive, presumably due to their reactive aversion to the repressive family atmosphere they experienced. Another reason consists in the reduced number of children, one boy and one girl typical of the nuclear family, on whom they lavish affection. Children are endlessly indulged and are rarely taught to defer or restrain pleasure. They are impulsive and focused on immediate pleasures. They throw tantrums when they don't get things done in the way that pleases them. This may well be considered a world-wide trend, but what distinguishes Korean children is the degree of dependence on their parents to the point of hindering their maturity. Parents and children are merging into one, clinging together and dependent on each other to erase borders between them. Maturity in its true sense is defined in terms of the degree of independence and autonomy from their parents, a sense of self-initiated action, and readiness to assume what comes out of it. Judging from this standard, Korean children are fish out of water when it comes to making their own living.

High achievement in school is largely attributed to the socio/economic status of their parents, and one's innate talent plays little in the elementary and secondary school, which are the pace setter for further education. This trend is evident from the fact that higher proportions of children from the upper class make a successful landing into the leading universities. The days when children from the needy and poor families outperformed those from wealthy families have passed. A child from a middle or upper class family is groaning under the crushing burden imposed by an ambitious mother. From the pre-school ages, a child is sent to piano lesson, English class, Taekwondo, and what not and savors all bitter tastes of competition from childhood. From the first grade of elementary school, children are tormented by additional special tutoring outside the school, enabling them to land on an island of excellence in a sea of mediocrity. But not all children can become a jack of all trades and a cream of the crop at the same time. High achievers are the filial son in that they meet the mothers' expectations. Mothers provide a strong motivational force to achieve high. They are motivators and the sole source of inspiration for children setting out an Odyssey fraught with pitfalls.

A hefty majority of children are passive learners who manage to muddle through the minimum requirement of study. There is a long column of learners, with the best performers ever widening the gap from those behind. Koreans go about resenting free-spending children from nouveau riche families, not simply because it runs counter to the value which inhibits the flaunting of wealth but because of fear that it may be destructive of social solidarity so much valued by the ethnic nation. Spending on private tutoring by wealthy parents derides the educational policy contrived to equalize the quality of educational programs in all schools. This policy of equalization is contrived to relieve the heat of competition coming from the inequality of education among schools. This hinders the diversification of educational programs supposed to cater to the diverse needs of children and to provide for the earlier eruption of intellectual volcanoes of gifted children. Korean education is trapped between the two imperatives, equality and diversity.

The Confucian tenet is "Man is born to make success in life and leaves his name to be eternally remembered." By self-direction or under the parental pressure, children are perpetually motivated to move towards the highest version of the self. "Grafted on the consciousness of family status, the Confucian motivation for success finds its manifestation in competition between family clans"(Choi Bong Young 1994;34). The status orientation of Korean education is the corollary of the Confucian value which inspired personal success for the honor of the family clan. Given that government offers one of the most preferred avenues to higher status, the civil service examination is an added spur to competition.

Average Koreans hold that nothing is more important than higher status or lucrative job, and education is geared to serving this goal. Such a trend has produced certain categories of preferred employment which have a direct bearing on the content and practice of education. Medical science, law, business management, and life science are popular fields of study in higher education, while philosophy and humanistic studies wither away due to students' apathy. The myopic view of education spawns the feverish pursuit of education, and it is something like chasing a ghost who refuses to be appeased. Impoverished peasants skip their meals to send their kids to colleges in a naive belief that their educated children will realize their blue dream of higher status. Their aspirations to higher status are hereditary and justify parental sacrifice for the honors of the following generations.

Another Confucian legacy is seen in the hierarchical view of schools, that is, to place them in a hierarchical order ranging from the top notch down to mediocrity, less prestigious and least prestigious ones. The vertical arrangement of schools is a common place the world over: Harvard, Yale, and Princeton are on the top of the list of American universities. Oxbridge indisputably towers over a bevy of universities: Grand l'ecoles are the magnet for highest achievers in France. What characterizes the Korean system is that the pecking order resembles a steep pyramid to the point that strangles parallel schools on the same level to death. Failure to enter the university of first choice in the United States leaves one with many alternatives on the same level of the pecking order. But the Korean system rarely leaves an alternative choice to the first one. More problematic is that the pecking order, once established, defies change, in their perception in particular. Any change remarkable enough to alter the ranking order of schools is not likely to bring a radical shift of their established perception of school ranking..

Some educational experts fondly compare the American system to the ever-changing sand surface of a desert where the wind makes new dunes in a matter of a few seconds. In reality, no institute can lay claim to excellence over others in all disciplines. But the notion of 'good school' in Korea is what is listed in the pecking order, with no effort to redefine it with due consideration of the relative strength of disciplines. The fixed pecking order in Korea produces many bigots deadly against a second choice after the aborted attempt at the first choice. Some are caught in a vicious cycle of examination as they fail in a repeated bid for the first choice. Each year sees a new cohort of students spilled over the bottleneck to swell the rank of what we call "repeaters." Many Koreans naively believe that the prestigious university ensures smooth sailing to a promising career; study itself is a distant second to a social or alma mater network. Each university has an alumni tie and there are thousands of seniors or sonbae who have fanned out into prestigious jobs waiting to give their helping hands to the new crops from the same universities."Rush to the best school" heats competition and provides the motivating force for study. Once they have safely landed on a privileged fold, their study loses passion.

There has been an explosive increase in the number of Korean children who study abroad, noticeably in the English-speaking countries. In the past, studying abroad was limited to a few elites. Overseas study was a desirable choice for bright students to further education and develop careers; it offers opportunities to benefit from advanced knowledge and technology. As we notice, those who fail in formal education at their home country seek an alternative education abroad; an increasing number of them are escapists from reality. Education abroad is considered an alternative solution to their own problems at home. Departure from the home country may be considered a natural process of life for a person who seeks an opportunity to develop a professional career in this globalized world, but a blind pursuit of overseas study at an earlier age, irrespective of one's financial means and readiness to manage the rigor of studies and to overcome language and cultural barriers, spawned a new phenomenon that is disruptive of the moral fabric of the family. "A tragic death of a lonely goose dad" headlined in one of the newspapers refreshes our thinking of where the value of family lies. A father who lives alone with his children abroad to study under the care of their mother suffers considerable financial and emotional distress as he struggles to support his children. This tragedy, once a distant echo, is becoming a reality for every one who thinks of a better education for children.

In reality, many Korean parents go crazy about education for their children, with the belief that admission to a prestigious university is the surest way leading to lucrative and prestigious jobs. Chances for the reciprocal contribution of educated children to parental expectations have been reduced drastically. "Despite the enormous financial sacrifice of Korean parents, education shelters their kids from the impersonal competition of the future; education is far from ensuring happiness for the family" (Halm In Hee 2003). Should education seek to bring happiness to the family, this goal is too elusive to allow comprehension. If education is to change children into the frontiers of creative exploration, there is no reason why they should not be content with the given conditions for achievement. A British psychiatrist said that, given the human condition, happiness is an inappropriate and aberrant response which calls for psychiatric treatment. When one does not expect things to turn out well, he should learn to be amazed at modest successes.

The Fast-Changing Society

As Korea industrialized, there was a dramatic turnaround on its people's temperament. Koreans were once known for being continental in character and paid little attention to or dismissed minutiae as unworthy of attention. Korean rulers of the last monarchy were sitting ducks characterized by diplomatic inertia and the lack of alacrity when Western imperialism came knocking the door. They were slow to grasp the unfolding situation of the international milieu and enjoyed blissful isolation from the outside world. Belated attention to the changing world and inability to take timely actions were responsible for the downfall of the last kingdom of Korea. Koreans were notorious for being unpunctual, and their patience with a slow pace of life baffled foreigners. Koreans used to tell the time by where the sun was and were rarely punctual to an appointment. The notion of "appointment" was lacking among Koreans; it was three decades ago that they began to set up an appointment with doctors. Nowadays, Koreans are increasingly impatient, and getting things done in time is a matter of life and death. How dramatic changes have been made in their ways of life.

Changes have been so overwhelming that foreign visitors marvel at new things that Koreans rarely appreciate. Material improvement, as many Koreans enjoy today, is the painful reminder of "spring famine" during which they had to bear until barley came out. Hunger was like a plague that whistled its way through rank and file. With all the changes that dazzle their minds, Koreans feel as if they traveled from Mars to Earth in a blink of the eye. The hectic pace of life hardly offers a breathing spell to be sober and content with daily happenings and appreciate the moment's pleasure. In the hustle and bustle of urban life, Koreans are in haste and rush as if they run after a ghost. Korean repatriates, after decades of stay abroad, say that they never feel at home with things so quickly running away at their home country.

Looking at the past, Koreans' indifference to minute happenings, on the other hand, enabled them to overcome national crises with equanimity. Today Koreans have little patience with the quiet and slow pace of life. The fast turnover of things is congenial to the temperamental urbanites but few realize that it reduces the world of humans into an emotional wasteland. Intellectuals die of boredom if they are not in touch with the fast turnover of new ideas. When it comes to waiting in line to be served, urbanites are increasingly impatient or explode into fury over small delays. Koreans complain about a trifling thing such as a delay in the bus arrival or in the delivery of work which foreigners take for granted. Those in a long queue to draw money at the bank realize how fast their turns come along. Such a hectic pace of life has its own merits, as manifested in rapid growth, but was accompanied by problems tainted by material evils.

Reckless drivers ceaselessly honk at others to give way or curse at slow fellow drivers. For foreign visitors, Koreans appear to be unrestrained in behavior and quarrelsome in contrast to inhibitive and restrained Japanese. Koreans' impatience with the slow pace of life is not attributed to the new life pattern of modern society alone. It has something to do with the survival complex that has been intensified during its rapid development. Human bonds are broken loose, as reflected in the greater frequency with which families break down. Foreigners find living in Seoul exciting in a way, if not displeasing, because they are amazed at new things that happen every minute. Korean repatriates from abroad say that they can hardly hear the clock ticking away. They find themselves as permanent misfits in their mother land. An increasing number of urbanites relish intensive interactions of contrasting tastes and values.

"Bbali,bbali" (hurry up) has become the hallmark of Koreans at home and abroad. The culture of "hurry up" is a byproduct of secular trends that accompany material development, with the consequent lapse of manner consciousness. The whole country was in overdrive, disregarding rules and procedures if necessary, as the government pursued accelerated economic development. Foreigners make the point of mocking Koreans for being impatient if they are not the first to be served. Foreigners wonder at the suddenness with which the former presidents rose to the top of the power ladder and just as quickly fell to a pit of disgrace. Urban sprawl is something Koreans are proud of as the hallmark of fast achievement. The afterglow of rapid growth is quickly dimmed by new problems that put Koreans to shame. Rice paddies and sleepy villages retreat before a ubiquitous vistas of high rise apartments and busy highways bordered by unsightly scene of ghost towns. Economic growth was achieved in half a century while it took forerunner countries some hundred years.

Koreans suffered high infant mortality in the past. The pace of improvement in medical service has been so remarkable that Korea has become an aging society in a matter of 20 years. Korea outpaced other countries in the increase in life expectancy. Koreans, by all accounts, are no longer what they used to be, as perceived by outsiders. They have few equals in aggressiveness, ambition, robustness and self-assertiveness. The rapid achievement bore out positive results on the surface, but modern Koreans suffer from the malaise of spirit and the nightmare of environmental collapse. These are the symptoms that accompany a fast aging society. The society where the people, aged 65 years or above, surpasses seven out of 100 is called "an aging society. If it goes beyond 14, it is called "aged society." 20 out of 100 defines it as "post-aged society. "Transition from the first stage to the last one took France 154 years, England 90 years and Japan 35 years. 26 years lifted South Korea to the post-aged society" (Choson Ilbo dated Dec.14, 2013).

By 2022, the economically active population is projected to diminish into twice as large as the aged population. According to U.N statistics, the number of those countries whose life expectancy averages 80 years or longer is thirty, including South Korea. The low birth rate, presently standing at 1.3, dampens the hopes of Koreans for another economic leap. This is a universal trend not limited to South Korea alone. There are 30 countries whose birth rates are below 1.5, enabling aged people to outpace the birth rate.

The fast aging society is the reminder of the active campaign for birth control in the 1970s, with its catch phrase "boy or girl, stop at two." Its immediate concern was simply more mouths to feed with limited resources and heavy burdens on the working population. Looking back over the past, every Korean rubs his eyes in wonder at the earlier poverty their parents suffered and find it too excruciating for them to bear. In 1950-55, just in time for the Korean War, Korea was not better off than Zimbabwe; the average life-expectancy of Koreans in this particular time was 47.9. Is there any country whose change is so dramatic as South Korea?

A demographic term, "population bonus,"[12] explains what comes after fast change." A greater proportion of the working population, aged from 15 to 64, raises GDP, and this means that the growth of the working population outpaces that of the aged population. Korea, Singapore, Hong Kong, and Taiwan are expected to bring an end to the population bonus in the period 2010-15. "The ending year, 2010, of population bonus found the per capita income of Hong Kong at $32,000 and Singapore at $30,000. South Korea whose population bonus ends in 2015 registers $28,000 in comparison with China ($9,700) and Thailand ($8,700)"(Choson Ilbo, 2013). Fukukawa Yukiko cites an example of Japan's experience as a warning signal against what would befall its fellow Asian countries after the population bonus ends. Although Japan vaunted healthy medical care and new-fangled technologies, it could not avoid bubble economy following the population bonus. South Korea in particular, wrestling with low birth rate, may be hard hit when the population bonus is brought to a halt. The increasing share of working women is supposed to bring birth rate down, and this is exactly what is plaguing South Korea. Koreans are coming up for the price of compressed growth that they have to pay.

Koreans ask why the country – the 13th largest economy in the world – remains as vulnerable to man-made disasters as they used to be. They are no less subject to natural disasters, traffic accidents, pandemics and panics, largely related to industrialization and urbanization, than their medieval forebears. Some point to the process of rapid changes of the '1960s to the '80 that saw Korea rise from the rubbles of the Korean War to become a thriving economy. Following the decades of stability free of major conflicts, Koreans became desensitized to new risks that paralleled technological development. High risk-taking may have to do with an optimistic view of the future based on a messianic belief in the power of science and technology. What do you worry about? Korean proverbial saying has it that unfounded worry courts danger.

The intrepid confrontation of Korea with the Western powers in the nineteenth century was the expression of its heroic acts against the Western powers that had daunted cowardly China and brought Japan to submission. The positive side of intrepidity enabled South Korea to break through what appeared to be impassable barriers. More often, risk-taking does not offer a remedy for problem solving. Scientific and material trajectories have been pointed in an upward direction, but there were setbacks, perhaps more serious than what Koreans had seen. The material development of modern society entails its own problems, occasionally so insurmountable as to cripple our ability to be sober and dwell on who they are and where they are going from here. A man riding on a tiger's back loses his sense of direction.

Elderly Koreans are left to suffer poverty. In comparison with its fast development, the social welfare system was less developed, presumably due to the traditional dependence on the filial duty of their offspring. An increasing number of elderly Koreans have foresworn the filial duties of their offspring, but they more bitterly weep over the fate of being left alone. The poverty of these people is becoming serious. According to a report released by the Korea Labor Institute, the poverty rate among Koreans aged 65 or older was 48.6 percent in 2011, the highest among the 34 members of the Organization for Economic Cooperation and Development. Korea ranks first in the OECD in elderly suicide with 82 out of 100,000. These elderly poverty woes are certain to get more serious as the baby boomers, born in 1955-63, begin retiring from active duty. The working age population – aged 15-64 – will decline and growth potential will suffer a setback.

---

1. Gregory Henderson in "The Vortex of Politics" refers Korea to as mass society made up of atomized entities, related to each other through their relations to state power, This implicates a' direct confrontation between elite group and masses with no intermediate entity capable of mediating. Koreans' propensity to grouping created cell groups formed around family clan, school, and home town to which atomized entities are

lost. Here, he refers atomized entities as "sands that slip through the fingers," a simple aggregation of individuals, devoid of commitment to a goal .His argument is however flawed since Korean society consists of cell groups like gravel which remains after sands are winnowed out. Each group has its goal to achieve and this process leads to the strong fraternity of each group . Some groups exist for the sake of fraternity.

2. Minbon literally denotes "people matter most in the state."What else is more important than the welfare of people? The ruler is defined as a care taker of his own people as he does for his own siblings. This enjoins the ruler to keep his ears to the voices of the people. Listening to their complaints or pleas was a matter of great concern for statecraft. Grasping "where the wind blows" gives clues to a policy that would put the country in solid, harmonious order. This concept finds its resonance in the "nation state" where the people are the master responsible for its destiny. But the Confucian emphasis on unfailing loyalty to the ruler is strident to the defenders of equality and freedom.

3. This narrative emphasizes the heart as a moral motive. Moral sanctions of Koreans were confined within the private domain of life. When a Korean steps out of the private domain, he can hardly see a moral guide to his life, for they lack the consciousness of social justice and righteousness that should guide one's public life. Confucianism overlooked disjuncture between the two domains, a naïve belief that the former automatically extends to the latter. In contrast to Eastern emphasis on the heart as a moral motive, Westerners think that morality is dictated by the head.

4. The constabulary forces of South Korea were improvised in an imminent confrontation with the north. The leadership of the constabulary forces comprised largely those officers who served imperial Japan. This group divides into the volunteers and the forcibly drafted against their wills under colonial rule. It is not fair to denounce categorically all of them as pro-Japan elements. Serving the armed forces was in a way a matter of survival under colonial rule. Few Korean youths could avoid the draft. At the initial stage of military organization, South Korea was in a dire need of veteran soldiers and policemen under an urgent dictum of maintaining order and defending the demarcation line..

5. Neo liberalism claimed itself to be ideologically neutral. But it is far from the truth. Liberalists argued for immediate unification which conceals a scheme to achieve reunification under the communist banner. Neo liberalism epitomizes the resurrection of the leftists' stand for one country in the post-liberation period. Liberalists are barely different from left anarchists. Every society in the state of influx meets with a rebellious mood in the name of liberalists.

6. Koreans regard the Korea-U.S relationship as vertical, seen through the prism of a receiver and donor of support. The flipside of the vertical relationship is the emotional feeling of the one helped where the emotional working of the heart dominated the logic of the head. A vertical relation embodies the emotional bond that easily flies into bursts of rage, when expectations were frustrated.

7. In pre-modern Korea, the measure of morality was flexible. Political foes were destroyed and eliminated, and such human sacrifices, apparently immoral, not to mention its transgression of the law, were justified since it served the great cause of saving the country from falling into the hands of bastards. Victimized people were colored as bad souls. Means were justified by the purpose. There were many instances where the ruler suffered unendurable pains for having siblings and beloved ones stained in blood bath. But he took comfort in the fact that it served the country in good stead. Young Jo (1724-60) had his own son, the heir apparent to the throne, meet an untimely death, on the ground that he was mentally derailed and disqualified for the throne.

8. In 1274 and 1281, Mongolian forces launched attacks on Japan and were defeated not in the hands of foes but the intervention of typhoons. On the part of Japan, they basked in mass fantasy that a Divine Deity was on their side and that their country was under Divine protection. This notion of sanctuary was reinforced by the fact that the insularity of Japan had kept it free of foreign invasions. Mass fantasy enhanced their sense of racial superiority, as a god-chosen people, to others: This fantasy turned into fanatic patriotism during the Pacific War(1943-45).The confrontation of a resource-poor country with a giant country rich in resources was inconceivable by any stretch of imagination, had it not been for mass fantasy. As the war was drawing to a close, Japanese were never resigned, convinced that so many sacrifices will move the Divine Deity to have compassion and send a typhoon. Kamigaze (suicidal attacks by aircrafts) was hastily organized, since it was supposed to cause this typhoon to save the country. Kamigaze itself means "Divine Wind."

9. Righteousness is a social justice that is supposed to guide statecraft. The Korean notion of righteousness is distorted when it applies to a small and cohering group. Unfailing commitment to a group is considered a virtue, and betraying this commitment is condemned as a traitor. When righteousness encountered an authoritarian regime, the authoritarian figure is tempted to deliberately avoid or distort the rule of law. The military regimes were authoritarian to all intents and purposes by justifying its coercive rule, restraining individual freedom, on the ground that it is a passage to an enriched and stable country. Serving a greater good was a moral dictum even if it involves immoral acts, and the legitimacy of means eluded attention in a rush to get the goal achieved. .

10. In the competitive examinations to a top-notch university, female applicants used to be given some points that added to their earned grades in order to level with male competitors. This practice reflected an attempt to induce able women into competition, but its flipside is the recognition that females were innately inferior to their male counterparts. This practice was prevalent in the 1950's and faded out.

11. NBC traced a day's schedule of a Korean high school girl in 1982. Her schedule was started at 5 a.m with breakfast and off to school for additional tutoring before she receive the grueling six hour class teaching and additional private tutoring and return home at 10 p.m. This tight schedule is repeated through the year.

This story was broadcast in the name of "Believe It or Not."The excruciatingly tight schedule was to ensure a smooth pass to the university of first choice. Ending up with a second choice is considered "burning important bridges to the future. This causes unsuccessful students to repeatedly take examinations. They swelled the rank of repeaters, giving rise to the so-called examination hell. Once trapped in this vicious cycle, they find it difficult to escape. Private tutoring institutes are booming, as the repeaters increase in number.

12. The population bonus refers to an increase in birth rate surpassing that of the death rate. As society modernized, more women are employed and the birth rate diminishes. This brings forth a relative increase in life expectancy, resulting in larger percentages of elderly people 65 years of age or above. The aging society casts dark shadows on the prospect for economic growth. Japan was hard hit. Its long economic stagnancy is attributed to a tangible decrease in working population. South Korea, Hong Kong, Singapore, Taiwan, Thailand and Indonesia are bracing up for what will befall upon the termination of population bonus.

Chapter

Five

Youth Culture and Movements

The so-called 'Me Generation' exists in every society as they pass through adolescence and early adulthood.
— *Hugh MacKay*

The Youth Movement in a Global Perspective

The reason to give youth culture one chapter is that the youth movement in Korea sit in a stark contrast with universal tendencies. It was anti-colonial, nationalistic and ideological, while elsewhere it was more commonly cultural, anti-materialistic, and psychological. Amid the global pervasiveness of the Western youth culture, Korean youth had a unique course, remaining aloof from the main stream of youth culture. The popular image of Korea is one of rapid social and economic development. Behind this achievement is the focused efforts of all Koreans unfailingly dedicated to the single goal of national development. Korea is compared to a phoenix rising from the ashes of destruction. Korean youth was an inexhaustible well of anti-government struggle from the 1960s against the military regimes, and this continued through 1990s. The world media focused on police forces battling militant students on tear-gas filled streets. Korea once impressed the world as a country of riots whose pugnacity had no match elsewhere.

Charactering Korean youth different from others requires that we start with the examination of the worldwide trends of youth culture. Common everywhere is the culture of protest, irrespective of region and time. The identification of youth with reformative zeal against the established order and authority is universal. Youngsters throughout the world raise their voices for change against the established order. By and large, they are idealistic, but simplify the world as dichotomized into black or white and right or wrong, rarely seeing a gray zone between them. They are prone to reactionary nationalism, with a touch of genuine naivety, in their view of the world. They want to be identified as something different from their parental generations and endeavor to create a sub-culture by which they are identified. Reference to the universal trend of the youth culture appears to be a plausible approach to shed light on the particular trend of Korean youngsters.

Webster's dictionary defines youth as "the period of life coming between childhood and maturity," synonymous with adolescence, denoting a transitional time from boyhood to manhood. Its interpretation varies as it is viewed through the cultural prism of each country. The old Anglo-Saxon word "geoguthe" carried the connotation of being doughty, brave and valiant. Chinese interpretation is the spring time of one's life-cycle, and Japanese view it as an unripe stage in which dormant energy is almost ready to burst out into action. Youth in Korea denotes a green spring, the prime time of one's life cycle, as its word suggests. They have yet to mature into an adulthood which is slower to come these days than it used to be with the growing complexity of society. They have eyes able to detect truth amid a tangle of social wrongdoings and are determined to fight for what they consider a righteous cause. They rush full pelt, but are easy prey to novelty and burst out their energy. A fully-filled bottle is not so easily swayed as half-filled one. Their sense of righteousness inflames an itch to be different, but it may turn into an action out of the spur of moment which has yet to be tempered by experience and prudence.

Adolescence is seen as the departure from one's comfort zone and entrance to a strange world that tickles one's fancy and curiosity. Everyone at this stage begins to show interest in socially intolerable things and find the self lured into something that one should have been shameful of. In adolescence one finds his or her demands of life rasping with the surrounding world. One belongs to a group and loses the self in group activities and breaking loose from the group requires much courage. The strong sense of curiosity and adventurism turn into rebellion when one's dream does not accord with reality. There is a centrifugal force at work that takes one beyond the comfort zone of life and into a strange world.

The motives of youth vary as much as the stimuli they face in their own cultural or political communities. The students' view of the world is simplistic. The word "simplistic" needs to be qualified in two ways. In the first place, it is considered in terms of self-centeredness. At this stage, one tends to be self-assertive, breeding indifference to others. At a certain stage of development, they begin to listen to others and reconcile their subjective self-concept with what others say about them. At this stage, they develop a new way of looking at themselves and the world and become more tolerant of different views and social malaises. Another interpretation of "simplistic" relates to their intellectual style which is shaped by their encounter with intensive learning experiences focused on the development of a black and white mentality. Naivety of one's thinking means in a way an alternation between the two extremes. The third is the degree of their independence in decision-making and the responsibility to bear the consequence of a behavior.

Korean youngsters rebelled against colonial rule and authoritarian regimes. They were split asunder by ideology. Young people in developing societies yearn for a better life and cannot afford to create a sub-culture under the dominant pressure of older generations. In advanced societies, they are more able to articulate their own identity known as a sub-culture, either counter-cultural or ideological. In 1968, a few students disaffected with crowded classroom at Nanterre University in the suburbs of Paris appeared nothing more than a tiny storm cloud no body expected could become a prairie fire spreading across borders, panicking countries into anarchy. "It is impossible to see how France today could be paralyzed by crisis as she has been in the past," said de Gaulle in his New Year's message. Demonstrations at Berkeley to support French students and oppose de Gaulle turned into two nights of rioting, the fierceness of which brought a curfew and state of emergency on the entire city of Berkeley.

The American engagement in Vietnam War was a detonator for massive anti-war struggles by students and radicals all across the world. Further, the civil right movement in the United States grew to the drumbeat of anti-war demonstrations. New leftism, the sexual revolution, counter-culture, narcissism, Black Panthers, and the assassination of Robert Kennedy occurred in a row, eroding the fabric of the "great society" that Lynden B Johnson envisioned. The young people, sensing their separate identity from the older, developed their own language, speaking among themselves in a cant. The early sign of this drift was evident in the fast tempo of songs and queer clothes and hair styles. They crowded the streets to have their voices heard and some were drawn into political activism and became radical as they waged a sustained bout with suppressive police forces.

The American youth, having lived in an affluent society, saw the limits of material blessings for human happiness. They rebelled against the danger of dehumanization that deterred one's pursuit of freedom and humanity. Influenced by the cult of individual freedom, they reacted against the establishment that produced identical good citizens and against success-oriented values. The Hippies were a typical example of escapists from the establishment, stoned on marijuana and other drugs supposed to help them expand their inner self. As time went by, some, tired of sensual pleasure, began to search for inner peace in religion and many American youth sought their spiritual solace in Oriental religions and mysticisms that calls for the eternal recurrence of birth and death. They tried to find new meaning not so much in the modernistic theological doctrines as in fundamentalist tenets. In Prague and Warsaw, students railed against the repressive communist regimes and marched with a flag chanting "the freedom of the press." In China senior party hacks shuddered before the Cultural Revolution that brought rowdies into power.

Student resistant activisms, though scattered widely across borders, gave the image of being related to one another, as almost simultaneous occurrences converged on 1967 and 1968. The events that took place simultaneously or in a quick succession looked as if they had been orchestrated under one control tower. In reality, however, each of the demonstrations was an instantaneous outgrowth of emotions rooted in the social and political situation. The majority of student demonstrators were anarchists and new leftists dressed in different clothes. Growing up during the cold war, youth rebelled against both the United States and Soviet Union. Their condemnation of U.S military action in Vietnam was not support for communism, but a distaste for a strong empire lording over the world. The enthusiasm of the youth movement abated just as quickly as a typhoon left heaps of wastes to be cleared. The psychic vacuum of the youths was quickly filled by narcissism, "live for oneself," new evangelicalism, and the wisdom of Oriental faiths.

Characterization of Korean Youth

Ideological Commitment

Korean youngsters were ideological, revolutionary, and resistant to the reigning authority, while their contemporaries in wealthy societies tried to find a new meaning of life through retreat into narcissism, hedonism or counter culture. During the colonial period, Korean intellectuals were fascinated by the messianic appeal of communism as a viable alternative to ruinous capitalism. However, their illusion for the promised utopia were shattered by the first armed clash of the global Cold War, to which Korea fell victim. The majority of Koreans in the south thought that communism was villainous enough to be guarded against. Had it not been for the Korean War, the hegemonic expansion of communism might have encountered no obstacle. The on-going ideological confrontation amid the worldwide de-ideological trend explains the volatile Korean politics from which Korean youth cannot remain aloof. South Korean governments have cleverly manipulated anti-communist paranoia. The state circumvented the constitutional protection of free speech and free association. Human rights were sacrificed in the name of unbridled economic development. The state-building efforts of the succeeding military regimes represented the most telling contradiction between democracy and the authoritarian rule. Korean youngsters busied themselves with struggles against the authoritarian regimes. Their obsession with social justice led them to denounce the repressive nature of political leadership. Their anti-government move sprang from a purist view of how to remedy flaws, but offered opportunities for the Northern regime to take advantage of their naivety and seduce them down the road to turn their back against the state to which they owed loyalty.

The dazzling pace of change creates a gaping chasm between generations, and this phenomenon is not confined to Korea alone. The passage of ten years is said to create sufficient change to characterize one generation from another, and this generation gap has been reduced into five years. To be young means to long for a new challenge and impulses to heroism. The so-called "386" generation[1] impressed Koreans as the most radical and militant students, the crop of a particular time when the authoritarian regime reached its apex. One recalls how they disturbed Korean society with their hope of building a unitary state free of ideological conflicts and a land of equality that condemns a few rich preying on the masses.

This particular generation had been born in the 1960's, after the Korean war, and their sensory awareness of reality grew when they entered university in the 1980s, contemporaneous with the advent of the Fifth Republic known for high-handed rule and the suppression of political dissidents. "Three" means that they were most active in political movement in their thirties. Their radicalism was tempered as they came of age, but some of them turned into core radicals ready to turn to populist demagoguery in times of social instability. They took advantage of grievances or dissidences– even of a non-political nature, and lost no time to instigate people to rallies on the streets, going the way they had gone before.

Their rebellious proclivity against authoritarian regimes illustrates a uniquely brutal nature built into the generational gap. Seeds of hatred remain fertile in the climate of ideological confrontation. As one generation enters adulthood, they turned conservative. But a few extremists don new costumes and refuse to abandon their commitment to the utopia built on absolute equality. To the militant students, the new utopia, they conclude, will be realized by overthrowing the existing order and institutions. Each age writes its own history, different from that of the age that preceded and will follow it. Old rules and hierarchies were there for a reason and have worked out for an untold period, though it is not necessarily the best choice. Categorical denial of the existing systems could lead to a blind and unfocussed riot, going beyond the bound of reason. Democracy was once a far-out, subversive notion, condemned by kings and priests. Korean politics saw some of the radicalized activists instated into the institutions and still have their influence felt. It was an age when a radical act carried status or became an object of envy. These ideological bigots are suspicious of the veritable reality, rejecting every evidence that invalidates their creed as a plot to distract their attention from the truth. They regard the cause they are fighting for as a timeless one, for which they are willing to risk their lives.

The First Republic (1948-1960) was heavily toned with authoritarianism, caused by its fierce struggle for survival through the dark ages of the Korean War. Extreme radicals, due to their anti-government movement, were laid vulnerable to the hugging arms of the North Korean regime. The notion of a 'common foe' brought the dissidents and the North Korean regime into a league. The youngsters had little immunity against the seductive pseudo scientific vision of communism. But not all of the radical dissidents could be categorized as tilting to the radical leftists. The word, leftists, cover an elongated spectrum that cannot be placed into one ideological package. The problem with the radicals is that, once driven into a trap, they could never get out of it, if not by death. Unfailing loyalty to a cause is a matter of life and death in a highly disciplined faction.

In reality, authoritarianism is something Koreans cannot do without. A series of military regimes appeared on the stage of politics in South Korea as if it could not tolerate an enfeebled government in their confrontation with North Korea. Crisis awareness in confrontation with its foe made a strong military power the best strategy to ensure national security. Top priority accorded to national security justified a means, whether undemocratic or unethical, to achieve a political goal. Machiavelli's famous passage "Learn how to be good and not to resist evil" permeated the political climate and exalted a goal over means. A moral cudgel substitutes for the rule of law to bring home that authoritarian rule serves the greater good of the country in the long run. It was widely held among the ruling elites that adherence to the rule of law does not always serve the country's best interest.

Both South and North Korea saw eye to eye on the authoritarian rule of the country. South Korea, though known for its repressive rule, has witnessed the shifts of power. A relatively liberal climate allowed people to experience a modicum of freedom, enabling them to air grievances. Ironically, the anti-government movement in South Korea thrived on the draconian rule of the military regimes. The authoritarian regimes brought home the political reality that justified repressive means at the curtailment of civil liberties and rights. Under the hereditary rule of one family in the north, the articulation of political dissidences is completely banned. The regime makes a frantic effort to preserve its polity against surrounding foes, maintaining a semblance of despotism that leaves no room for the paternalistic care of people characteristic of patriarchal authoritarianism.

Authoritarianism nurtures charismatic leaders who are expected to guide the nation. They are ready to burst forth and their leadership is dramatized when the state is going through a stormy sea. Authoritarian leadership put the country on the road to stunning economic growth. Ironically, it was against this authoritarian backdrop that the economic downturn, popularly known as the IMF crisis, dealt a critical blow to Korean pride. A belated response to a persistent plea for value change commands a wide following. The root cause of the economic crisis was allegedly found in the traditional values of Koreans vested in authoritarianism, favoritism, connectedness, inequality, irrationality, and growth fantasy. The old generations were held responsible for the worst scenario of the economic downturn, and all the virtues that had underscored the economic growth were discredited in the eyes of younger generations. An analysis would show that the economic downturn reflected the failure of Koreans to divorce from threadbare values and to heed the call of the new era. .

The renewed call for a value reorientation is alleged to have narrowed the gaping chasm of values between generations. The so-called Me Generation exist in every society as they pass through adolescence and early adulthood" (Hugh Mackay, 1993;140). Aggressive obsession with personal gratification, personal freedom and personal assertiveness are characteristic of this generation. American and European youngsters led others in their departure from the normative ways of life. Lapse into hallucination and intoxication with drugs was a popular way to escape from the demanding commitment of the present. They were determined to create a new world of their own. "Paradoxically, the very generation for whom the term 'generation gap' came into common usage is now experiencing a painful generation gap between themselves and their own offspring" (Mackay, 244)

Korean youngsters were protected from the hardship of the war and the rigors of the post-war rehabilitation. They relished a semblance of liberal democracy and affluence but failed to inherit the cooperative spirit and to surrender to the greater good of an organization or society. Individualistic orientation set them rebellious against the institutions and norms that they perceived to be stuffy and stifling. Their behaviors are more often guided by passion and moment's pleasure. With so many avenues open to life-earning, they are devoid of steely will to make success in life and are less sensitive to what is meant by sweat on the brow. The absence of stilly will paralleled their tendency to downplay self restraint. Some pointed to the negative side of self-restraint in modern Korea, since it is a deterrent to the expression of individualism leading to acquisitive and competitive achievement drives.

King Maker

The youth rebellion in Korea was dramatized in the 2002's presidential election. Roh Moo-hyun's victory in the presidential race meant the triumph of a little known figure. He marched into the center of power and opened up a new era that promised to be dramatically different from its preceding era. As much he was unknown, his victory energized hopes for change that the people longed for. Roh was hailed as a vehicle to steer a new course of innovations that would destroy established values. Roh owed his rise to the support of younger generations riding the tide of anti-American sentiment. Roh himself was branded as an anti-American populist. "The year 2002 generation" was formed in the runner-up to the last presidential campaign to identify themselves as the new master to shape the country's destiny. A message from an anonymous person finds an immediate receptivity among the vast number of citizens on the internet, and this makes it easier to line up supporters for a political cause. They demonstrated an unfailing support for a favored presidential candidate and played a role, with a great fanfare, as the king maker. It was a human drama of Roh Moo Hyun that the election turned out to be, literally, a smashing hit. Formed around a loose and expansive network of information, youngsters saw little need for identification or accountability for the consequences of their acts or words. They were ensconced in a niche hidden away, far removed from the sense of social accountability. Their acts were spontaneous but myopic: momentary zeal was the asset of youngsters but, dazzled by a momentary event, they lost the sight of a sober vision of society.

The electoral system of democracy is flawed because it is unable to do away with emotional interventions that can overwhelm rational decision based on the full grasping of the candidates. Youngsters cry out for direct participation, giving rise to a drift into what borders on mobocracy. Political issues are divided into those subject to compromise and those subject to an absolute "right" or "wrong" nature. Building a social order based on law and justice, defending the country against foes and protecting individual rights and freedom should be absolute dictums, not to be compromised. Basing policy on majority rule runs the risk of trading an immediate interest for what is good for the distant future of the country.

With the revolution of communication technology, youngsters take comfort in the thrill of chatting with unknown persons on the internet and seek a circle of coterie in the world of strangers. "The netizen proportion of total population in Korea surpasses that of the United States and Japan. This trend is ascribed to the growing consciousness of democratic participation, and it is widely held that the internet can bring a direct democracy to reality. In the quest for an opportunity for political participation, the internet offers an alternative to quenching one's thirst for participation"(Song Ho Keun 2003;69). The downside is that a generation increasingly immersed in the simulated worlds of the telecom revolution is at the risk of being less exposed to the kind of authentic real world experiences. In a country, like the United States, people have been attuned to participation in community affairs or a spontaneous organization of groups in a way that minimizes government intervention in solving their problems. This voluntary grouping gives a higher sense of social accountability. In Korea, yet to develop into a civil society, the internet asserts itself as a substitute for satisfying popular desires of participation by way of vitalizing its function in canvassing public opinions. Unlike the voluntary grouping, the on-line community has a fundamental fallacy in developing civil morality; a community of anonymity protects the on-liners from being socially accountable. On the positive side, the internet offers the possibility to overcome the parochial circles of association Koreans are prone to organize and to measure the fathom of public opinions.

Democratic Crusaders

The so-called 386 generation had two faces: they were hailed as democratic crusaders for their heroic struggles against the authoritarian regimes, while they were castigated as troublesome and unruly rowdies. "The term, generation, refers to a group of people in one age bracket who share the same or similar historical and political experience"(Song, 21). The younger generations are characteristically keen to be identified with a land-mark political event. This wishful identification gives them a sense of bond for having accomplished a political feat. High-handed rule galvanized them into a political movement with a specific goal, and they are proud of having accomplished the goal to be remembered in many years to come. Much the same happened in Europe in the 1910s. Their sense of ideological commitment to a social utopia led the deprived class to wage class struggle against their exploiters. This political movement bore fruition in the Russian Revolution in 1917.

The 1960's generation takes pride in having overthrown the First Republic of authoritarian rule and opened a path, though replete with disturbances, to democratic institutions. Having witnessed the downfall of the communist societies, radical youngsters seemed to have lost ideological vigor. As society became increasingly enriched, youngsters were less likely to become politically radical. But this argument proved to be wrong in Korea. Unlike what is happening elsewhere, the Korean peninsula still remains an island of ideological confrontation. Confrontation with North Korea polarizes perspectives into extreme leftists and rightists. Again, older generations remember the bitter experience of the Korean War indelibly built into their consciousness, but this suffering is a distant echo in the minds of the younger generations. Economic euphoria dulled their sensitivity to crisis, and they tend to be oblivious to the fact that the two states of Korea still confront each other in a shaky cease fire. The lack of major conflicts, coupled with a continued economic boom, is mistaken for peace. The 1970s saw a new group of dissidents emerging, those not accessible to the fruits of development. They joined liberal intellectuals and the voiceless minority to organize a joint front against authoritarian rules. The once-voiceless minority became an assertive majority in the name of daejung. They not only questioned the legitimacy and moral justification of the authoritarian regimes but set anti-government struggles in motion.

The progressive view of history regarded these political dissidents as democratic crusaders. Daejung(masses) in its liberal light refers to various groups of people at large who were inaccessible to economic and industrial fruits. These groups, particularly younger generations, face the daunting challenge of constructing a system that brings benefits to all in the name of mass nationalism.[2] And their outcries for the repeal of the national security law and the withdrawal of American troops from the south echo the repeated pleas of North Korea[3]. The triumph of communism in general is the result of instigating the masses against the existing order. Daily concern for survival in this competitive world seems to have reduced ideological fervor among the youngsters. Nevertheless, their emotional nationalism was awakened when North Korea was bashed by America as an "axis of evil." This beating rekindled their ideological fervor into a violent outburst of rage. This ruffled anger again imbued youngsters with a sentimental longing for an alternative society, charmed by a paradise of absolute equality. An attack by a monstrous giant makes an underdog pitiful, evoking sentimental brotherhood. Brothers fight within the walls, but they are allied before an outsider. The youngsters were generations teeming with revolutionary vigor, holding big powers responsible for the unfortunate fate of the country. They accused the United States as the major culprit, an obstacle to the North-proposed reunification model

The radicalization of youngsters is common place worldwide, and the radical students in Korea can find its root in the malignant spin-offs of educational outcomes, unmistakably attributed to a myopic sight as reflected in their secular-oriented educational goals. Having attuned to a black and white dichotomy, Korean children hold a simplistic view of the world, idealizing themselves as embodying good souls. Through their prism, they find the world is far from what they expect it to be. It is fraught with scoundrels, corruption, and wrong doing that contradict what they have imagined it to be. In the eyes of purists, scoundrels are visible to a degree that blinds them to the positive side of their society.

South Korea with a single-minded devotion to anti-communism justified rule by a succession of military regimes. The majority of South Koreans were receptive to the government's argument that a threat to their security necessitated the curtailment of individual freedoms and political rights until the country could become strong enough. Progressive elements, including radicalized students, not content with a given status, continuously search for an alternative to the existing order. They found the political reality of South Korea suffocating enough, and this inflamed their itch to know the true profile of the north. The legal ban on access to information about North Korea was viewed as the government's deliberate attempt to befuddle the true identity of North Korea. But a sense of curiosity demanded free access to information about the northern half, which had been written off as enigmatic and inscrutable. The harder the government tried to block their access to information, the greater was their urge to give North Korea the benefit of doubt.

Student activism traces its root to the Confucian legacy of the Chosôn dynasty where students commonly joined scholars and their mentors in protesting unjust government policies. Through the intermittent flow of memorials and sit-in rallies before the palace, they exhausted the ruler until he surrendered. Since the introduction of modern higher education in the 1890s, all major uprisings against both domestic authorities and foreign powers have involved students. After Korea was liberated from Japan's colonial yoke in 1945, students were driven into ideological squabbles and partook in major incidents that murdered leading politicians. The student uprising in 1960 overthrew the authoritarian regime of Rhee Syngman, and their democratic movements succeeded in ending the military regime in 1987.[4] Popular attitudes toward politically active students range from unreserved support to disgust and contempt. While they are seen by some as the conscience of the nation, they are considered by others as the scourge of national politics.

"It was unmistakably true that the student activists were the most ideologically cohesive and tactically effective force of political opposition to the iron-fisted regimes "(Dong Won Mo 1986). What is unique of Korea is that radical activism thrives on the increasingly determined and high-handed control measures of the government. Perhaps the radicalization of students can best be explained as a reaction to Chun Doo Hwan's seizure of power in the spring of 1980 following the untimely death of Park Chung-hee. The "Spring of Democracy" in that year was a period of renewed hope for democratic government after eighteen years of high-handed rule. Twenty years after General Park Chung-hee wrestled power from a democratic government, General Chun established another authoritarian regime, crushing the popular desire for a constitutional democracy. Chun's seizure of power brought forth an unprecedented massive uprising in Kwangju, the capital of the South-western province. Activist students broke into an outright rebellion against the government and were subjected to a harshest and brutal suppression. In the presence of the repressive riot police and other draconian measures, students became more openly radical, militant, and sophisticated in their tactics. Their ideological orientation added a new dimension to student activism, giving the image of blatantly neo-Marxists. The military regime was stunned by the penetration of student activists into the underground labor movement and high schools which had previously been free from the political influence of university students.

In the spring of l984, Chun's regime adopted a conciliatory policy, loosening its grip on campuses with a rhetoric claim to campus autonomy. "For a while, the university campuses became an oasis of democracy in the desert of military authoritarianism. During this time, those young militants consolidated themselves into nationally organized political groups popularly known as Samintu, Chamintu and Minmintu notorious for vandalism, as demonstrated by their burning of USIS building in Pusan" (Dong Won Mo 1986). Despite the intransigent government, widespread underground political activities did not dissipate. Rather they were further intensified to fuel political demands for the popular election of the president to succeed the Fifth Republic.

The popular presidential election had assiduously been denied by the military regime for fear that it might inspire popular support for the opposition party candidate. At their wit's end, Chun grudgingly accepted the demand by making concessions in favor of popular presidential election. It seemed that the military regime came close to its end, but failure to agree on a single presidential candidate between the opposition parties caused this troubled water to benefit a military-turned candidate, Roh Tae Woo.

The radical pattern of the Korean student activism is largely the function of a gaping chasm between rapid social change and rigid political structures. Activist students were the backbone of the democratic force, and their political role on behalf of the intellectual community, unorganized labor, and deprived farmers gained momentum in the political culture of depression. Even the draconian regime with all possible means of suppressing activist students failed to stem the tide of their democratic aspirations. A sketchy view of student activism in Korea highlights one principle: an urban and industrial Korea cannot maintain its stability and continuing growth without a degree of political institutionalization commensurate with the new level of political awareness among its citizenry.

The perception of the students' movement as a democratic commitment over-simplifies the diverse colors of radicalized students. The leftist group is an elongated column with its front ranks widening a gap from the back. In confrontation with the revolutionary zealots of the north, it would not be easy for the dissident activists to remain aloof from the appeal of communism. Standing against a common foe, the youngsters had a point of contact with the hitherto prohibited ideology and found it difficult to insulate themselves from the resounding appeal of the north's unification strategy. At the same time, their innate curiosity neutralized their ability to be prudent and cautious. Youngsters are simple-minded and easily stirred up. They are rebellious, fearless, eager to fight for a just cause, thirsty for adventure and action.

Marxist leanings of Korean intellectuals served as a harsh reminder of the political turmoil that preceded the Korean War. These radicals represent the extreme end of the ideological spectrum, far distanced from those who were ideologically weak or moderate. "Marxist leanings and nationalism fed off each other, beating its way through the other spheres, as expressed in the native cultural movements that rejected American cultural imperialism. Music clubs, dance troupe, and art groups have turned inward, researching indigenous Korean artistic expression"(Korea Focus 2005 Vol.13 No.4). The anti-government protesters festoon themselves with the banner of democratic crusaders, but few are free of an ideological alignment.

Anti-Americanism

At the dawn of Christianization of Korea in the nineteenth century, American missionaries dedicated their efforts to educational and medical services of which Korea had a dire need. Catering to this compelling needs, Koreans had the image of America as a munificent donor of aid. In their struggle against Japanese imperialism, Koreans made a plea for help from the United States but met its apathy. Theodore Roosevelt regarded Japan as an effective counterweight to the Russian advance. An alternative open for Korea was an alliance with Russia, and the two countries basked, for a short while, in a collaborative attempt to deter Japan's advance. Korea's leaning toward Russia, however, was a detonator for the Russo-Japan War (1904) that was to be ended with Japan's victory. Elated by its victory, Japan began to tighten its grip on Korea. At this time, the United States entered into a full-blown imperialism, starting with its occupation of Philippines, followed by the Taft-Katsura Treaty in which Japan recognized the American occupation of Philippines as quid pro quoa for the American acceptance of Japan's control of Korea. Geopolitics reduced Korea into a pawn in the vortex of imperialistic competition for hegemony in East Asia. At last, Korea gave up the reigns of self-rule and played into the colonial hand of Japan.

The conclusion of the Pacific War made Koreans welcome American soldiers as the liberator and Korea received American attention as a strategic outpost to deter the global expansion of communism. The U.S Military Command occupied the southern half of liberated Korea, pitted against Soviet troops occupying the northern half, but they won the wrath of South Korean leaders for its inability to deal with a widely spread anarchy. Communism was thriving under the nose of the U.S occupation forces, as it declared a neutral policy that pledged to stand above affiliation with any political faction in the south. American apathy shattered the dream of rightists who made pleas for support in their struggle against leftists. The pervasive turmoil of South Korea favored the communist bid for power. As the Korean War broke out, the United States was the first country to come to rescue South Korea. The Korean War brought the two countries into a blood tie that was subsequently congealed into the Korea-U.S Military Defense Treaty

From the 1960s, political turmoil, resulting from the untimely demise of the First Republic, agitated

Korean students to cast doubt about the reliability of the United States as an ally. Their anger leveled against the forthcoming military regimes was a direct conduit to anti-American sentiment. Indignant at the American support for its military stooges, they leveled blame for all bad things on the United States. Nationalistic voices became louder to every drumbeat of violence or crime that accompanied the presence of American forces. Even those less conscious of ideological commitment were annoyed by the recurrence of what they saw and heard as leaving deep scars on national pride. Koreans sought every opportunity to find fault with the United States, smudging its image as a big brother. The more hopes Koreans pin on the big brother, the more they suffered disappointment.

New sprouts of young generations about to enter adolescence were exposed to the loud voices of progressive teachers. Youngsters, particularly in the formative stage of development, were easily persuaded to trust what they were taught, blaming their country as a lackey for America. They were misled about what caused the division of Korea and were suspicious of the legitimacy of the country to which they owed loyalty. Progressive teachers, though few in number, made loud voices, drowning out those of the majority. In an emotion-charged situation, every incidence of violence, misconduct, and arrogance of Americans is brought into magnified relief. The rising pride of Koreans created its own prism through which to view American rudeness. Amid the dominant American perspective, America has become the cynosure of all eyes in the world. The negative view of America was the flip side of envy, admiration and jealousy, for these can easily be transformed into hatred. Anti-Americanism in Korea, therefore, cannot be perceived as being based on a rational attitude but is rather the product of situational episodes. Some of the students gloat over the intrepid confrontation of North Korea with the world power, while fondling memories of the rash confrontation of the Chosôn dynasty, virtually unknown to the world, with the French warships in 1866 and American invaders in 1871. Koreans boasted that they had defeated their enemies. Sympathy goes to an underdog for the display of darning acts, ignorant of the power of its foe. Koreans took pride in standing alone defending the citadel of Asian values, while China and Japan fell on their kneels before the Western imperialists.

The relationship has gone through four major phases. In the first phase, the two countries were brought into a blood tie by American involvement in post-liberation politics, the Korean War and support for the post-war rehabilitation. These remarkable events are considered in the context of the cold war containment policy of the United States. Although the United States and Soviet Union bear major responsibility for the division of Korea, the U.S role as the author of the dividing line is emphasized as a high point that relegates the Soviet role into a minor cause. Bruce Cumings in his controversial book "The Origin of the Korean War" holds the United States as a major culprit in the hierarchy of responsibility for the division of Korea and was instrumental in instigating political dissident against South Korea and America.[5]

The second phase was the military relationship that highlights the U.S-Korea Defense Treaty signed in the wake of the cease fire. South Korea has been home for 40,000 or more U.S. military personnel ever since the Korean War. On the top of direct military participation, the United States has provided various forms of aid and training to South Korean soldiers and elites. The U.S commitment to military aid in particular was of vital importance to its global containment of the expanding communism. The third phase featured trade disputes as the 1980s unfolded. South Korea was the seventh largest trading partner of the United States. As South Korea's economy continued to expand, the U.S began to suffer trade deficits in the 1980s. Frictions over trade in specific industries estranged the two countries. A sudden shift of United States' trade policy toward protectionism exasperated Koreans who expected the U.S to continue its munificent role.

The alliance between the two countries was considered not so much the product of common needs as an emotional bond in which the United States was expected to protect the weaker, while serving its own interest. In the final phase, the United States was concerned with human rights inseparable from the preceding three. The curtailment of human liberties and rights caused the United States under Jimmy Carter to castigate South Korea as an evil state. The relationship between the two turned glacial and dampened Koreans' hope to benefit from a donor country when the Carter administration announced plans for a gradual but complete withdrawal of U.S. ground forces from Korea.

While the United States approved the military regimes, it compiled a record of human right abuses, including arrests, jailing and occasionally torture of political dissidents, and heavy-handed control of the press. The U.S walked precariously on a tight rope between the two dictums, its continuing support for the suppressive regimes and pursuit of its liberal policy against the draconian rule of its partner. The suppressive rule of South Korea was tacitly endorsed, while America was caught in a difficult trade-off between its reputation as a champion of liberal policy and the political stability of its partner. The American commitment to South Korea against expanding communism was steady and fast, though it was half-hearted in support of the authoritarian rule.

On the part of south Korea, burgeoning pride in ground-breaking development is another source of nationalism. South Koreans were elated with a new height of pride upon the successful performance of the world-celebrated events such as the 1988 Seoul Summer Olympics and the 2002 FIFA World Cup Festival. Unmistakably, these events imbued Korean youngsters with a renewed confidence that they could 'do it alone' without dependence on its big brother. The 24th Summer Olympics in Seoul reflected years of painstaking preparation and was supposed to give Korea a moment to bask in its achievements televised to the world, while the communist countries marveled at this dimly perceived part of the world and sent their athletes, despite North Korea's deliberate attempt to deter it. The Summer Olympics was the sweat on their brows, but it turned out into a lapse into a low point in the vicissitude of its relationship with the United States. American media focus on poorly lit sweat shops in the outskirt of Seoul disclosed the dark side of Korea. Their acts might well be justified by feisty media. But a more sensible man should have been careful not to pique Koreans who were stamping their feet for new recognition. South Korea had climbed so high that it thought North Korea would look up to it with envy. To make the situation worse, the American athletes mugged for the television cameras during the opening ceremony, some sitting on the shoulders of their fellow athletes, a revealing contrast with the orderly parade of those from other countries, waving their national flags. An enraged

Korea cabinet minister announced "America had thrown ashes on a perfectly set banquet table." Such unrestrained behaviors might have been taken for granted by liberal Americans who saw little limits to their behavior, but this was perceived by Koreans as outright arrogance.

Anti-American sentiment began rearing its head in tandem with their sympathetic understanding of their northern brethren. At the same time, the Koreans' perception of the United States gave way to negative images - the author of the dividing line and the protector of the military stooges. While the two perceptions of the American role went in parallel, volatile Korean politics, largely resulting from its confrontation with the north, was the major cause for the radicalization of Korean youngsters. The radical students were divided into the National Liberation (NL) and the Proletariat Democracy (PD), each competing for hegemony. The former went one step further in advocating North Korea and tenaciously and openly denied to sing the National Anthem and instead chanted the North Korean mantras, "an immediate reunification under a confederate system" and "immediate withdrawal of American troops." Some of them made a safe landing on the National Assembly and bureaucratic posts under Roh Mo-hyun's regime and have been the object of public glare.

The ideological extremists were estranged from the people. Their volatile activities touched off a paradoxical reactive spurt of deep-seated sentiments to uphold the positive imagery of the United States as the protector and the savior of Korea. The most enthusiastic adherents to the positive view were the older generations, notably those who shed blood to defend this land, and the North Koreans who defected to the south prior to and during the Korean War. But these elderly people diminish in number. At the height of anti-Americanism, even many middle class Koreans cast doubt into the necessity of continuing an alliance with the United States. Occasionally, crass, uneducated and morally depraved American soldiers become an added eyesore that rubbed raw on the emotional wounds of the traumatized Koreans.

American protectionism which was in full swing in early 1980s trade disappointed those who looked to America as a benevolent big brother and resulted in its new portrayal as" a penny pincher" or "a predator bent to exploit a flea's liver." Koreans' penchant for a benevolent big brother was untenable in the ever-shifting frame of reference. The positive imagery of the United States was fixed in time and blinded Koreans to the ever-shifting call for the quest for its own interests. If Koreans had owned any sense of merciless power dynamics, they would not have been so shocked to realize that American actions motivated by self-interest are not extraordinary. The Korean concept of friendship lacks pragmatism and is, therefore, unrealistic. Koreans, once a friendship has been cultivated, expect it to be immutable based on a set of moral obligations. In the eyes of conservatives, an inkling of change in the immutable relationship is provocative enough to incite them into a violent outburst of fury, as if it were a visceral pain to break up a romantic tie. Koreans are not attuned to the dynamics of policy alternating between warm heart and cold head. The Korean perception of its relation with the United States was laden with moral obligations that suggest that the relationship will not change over time. Although the United States is half-hearted in support of the military regimes, it could hardly imagine the discontinuance of its support, as long as it considers itself as the counter-weight to provocative acts to disturb the political stability of the Northeast Asia. The United States has no easy escape from its global commitment.

Anti-Americanism is not a fixed frame of mind. No single view of America is dominant while Korea is moving towards a plural society. Very often, the negative image of America casts doubt about its perpetuity in light of the growing complexity of modern Korean politics. The negative imagery of America is based on episodes, which are still shrouded in a veil of myth. The alleged involvement of American forces in the suppression of the Kwangju uprising in 1980 is a case which has yet to be clarified. Negative guessing, though, is given the benefit of doubt in an uncertain and volatile political culture. When the volatile situation brings a new political issue into focus, debate is rekindled and escalated into an ideological clash. Once an issue has been viewed through an ideological prism, debate continues to annoy Koreans.

The march of the self-styled democratic crusaders into the political hierarchy or officialdom brought anti-American sentiment to a new height, as reflected in the proclaimed diplomatic autonomy and military tactical autonomy against the United States during Roh Moo-hyun's administration. Their seizure of power was morally justified by declaring themselves as a victimized partner of authoritarian rule. Their presence within the institutions, however, strengthened an extremist tone, rendering political compromise virtually improbable. They had their voices heard in debate on sensitive issues. According to a poll published by the Korea Society Opinion Institute, conducted in April, 2005, nearly one in two South Koreans said they would support North Korea if the U.S. launched a military attack without the South's consent. In a poll conducted a year before by Seoul-based Research, 39 percent of respondents said the biggest threat to South Korean national security was the United States, while 33 percent said they dreaded North Korea. The negative view of the United States as a potential threat was based on their fear of U.S provocations likely to rile up a sleeping dog.

For all the anti-American rhetoric, many extremists were charmed by American mass culture. Many of them and their children choose to study in the United States, since it is still considered the most preferred country for achieving one's academic goals or developing professional careers. The emerging countries which had taken hostile attitudes toward the United States tried to emulate the American standards in their quest for democratization and modernization. The positive image of America, nevertheless, does little to change the emotional stand of Korean youngsters. Rather, they are keenly affected by the recurrent misdemeanors of Americans. Should the ruffled emotions be allowed to stay, they will be consolidated into an anti-American posture.

Anti-Americanism is a fitful outburst of indignation at what is perceived as an unjustified involvement of Americans in Korean affairs. It should be noted that anti-Americanism is rarely the result of a long and hard thinking; rather it is an emotional improvisation, spurred by a guess work on the United states' involvement with domestic affairs. As Korea is confident of "going alone," its relationship with the United States will set store by the alliance of partnership rather than dependence on one side. The Korea-U.S Defense Treaty commands a wide following of Koreans, though leftists regard it as a humiliating subjectivity to a foreign power[6]. Anti-Americanism thrives when ethnic nationalism prevails over the sense of alliance. North's provocative activities will be a decisive factor in the balance between the two opposites. New sprouts of younger generations, in the twentieth and thirtieth show the symptoms of change in their ideological commitment. So far as ethnic nationalism remains a potential detonator, however, anti-Americanism will never disappear in its entirety. Neither is it possible to extirpate it at once and for all. As a critic says, "you cannot disown your brother, while you estrange your partner.

"The relationship between husband and wife can never be compared to the tie between son and mother. Wives, sometimes, divorce husbands but mothers never disown sons - at least not in Korea. Why, oh, why do South Koreans seem to like north Korea more than America when Pyeong Yang is so obviously evil? Why would a mother sometimes hinder a police who has come to arrest her killer son who is hiding upstairs? And the boy upstairs is the only one she's got, no matter what he's done or they say he is trying to do."(Herald Tribune dated August15, 2003)

Pragmatism over Ideological

On a superficial level, the ideological fever subsided as South Korea was drawn into the fierce battle against the economic downturn in the late 1997.The economic crisis did much to moderate the loud voices of the radicals, and Kim Dae-jung's government was credited with a peaceful interlude at least in terms of the decline of student radicalism. There is positive speculation that continuous economic growth will do much to constrain the rebellious voices of the younger generations. Social malaise is said to be a leaven for radicalism to rear its head. In other ways, the psychological spinoff of social instability directs their attention away from ideological fever to a greater concern for the means of survival in this competitive world.

With the exception of a few extremists, a study shows that anti-Americanism is not so much a fixed mindset but an event-specific emotional eruption, likely to arouse a romantic brotherhood and compassion for wretched brothers. Volatile as it is, political climate defies an outright hostility of heinous nature - such that is ever-present between religious fundamentalists. In the utter absence of religious dogmatism and in light of South Korea's democracy in place, an overt expression of anti-Americanism is implacably in decline. Students' demonstrations once thrilled the campus with the hopes of revolutionary change. Having reached its peak in the 1980, they stayed strong in the afterglow of the heat and reached a nadir under the two successive left-leaning regimes, Kim Dae-jung's and Roh Moo-hyun's. On a superficial level, one might say that order dispelled chaos. In actuality, realistic needs triumphed over ideological fervor. Riding the tide of pragmatism, students are more concerned with what is immediately needed for survival in the world in which philistinism and utilitarianism prevails. Political radicalism was seemingly sidetracked for a while.

For all the changes that sweep the way of life, a perception gap between generations remains unabated. The older generations labeled the younger as naïve, revolutionary fanatics, easily duped by an ideological seduction, while the younger dismissed the older as stuffy and inept, responsible for social malaise. As the militant students come of age, they are caught in an inter-generation clash. They are now mocked by younger ones as "a wild beast hunted out of every lair." The irony is that they are drawn into an inter-generation gap of which they took advantage in assaulting the older generation and instigating incendiary activities.

Becoming a person means the process of accumulating senses through experiences so that memories of the past beget wisdom capable of making a balanced assessment of self and situation. The increasing diversity of society engenders myriad forces that douse the youth's instinctive impulses to catch straws in the wind. The cause they are fighting for proves to be not worth risking one's life for. Their inexhaustible assault on the institutions lost favor with the people, and this rebellious mood will surrender to the utilitarian and philistine perspective of the world. On the other hand, youngsters fresh from college are often frustrated by the impersonal aura of the job market. The market economy is identified with impersonality and merciless competition, and youngsters intuitively look for a dependent and protective hand of the government. Their discontentment with the reality lies not so much in ideological disputes as the lack of opportunity to work.

We no longer live in the misty age of deities. Neither do we live in the world that favors a massive revolution on a heroic and grandiose scale. Young militants were once spurred by the heroism of fighting for the cause they thought to be right, but this proves to be an illusion. No cause or creed enjoys timelessness. The personality cult goes with revolutionary fanaticism in an alliance with pessimists constantly digging their noses into the dark side of the world. Ideological fanatics, of course, have specific goals to which they pay unfailing loyalty. But ideological dogmatism is losing its ground to stand on. In no way does this mean that radical activism will disappear once and for all. Radical activities were simply reduced into the hard core few ready to be rekindled into more violent activities. After all, a dog barks more fiercely when he is driven into a bay.

Social malaise is leaven for radicalism to thrive. In other societies, leftism is taken for granted as a way of life. But it takes a different meaning in Korea where words of caution beat down on the people's nerves, resounding an outcry "watch out if weeds outgrow the grass in your turf." For all the remarkable changes that overwhelm various aspects of life, a new tide of an ideological clash is looming over the horizon. The backlog of an ideological clash is simmering to be rekindled and remains a standing possibility, as far as the south-north confrontation goes on. But the repeated violations of the cease-fire agreement by North Korea are another factor for the ideological stance of South Koreans. The majority of South Koreans renew their hostility against North Korea on account of the recent sinking of a South Korean naval ship and artillery fire on an island. Repetition of provocative acts by North Korea and its nuclear threat are expected to be deleterious to an emotional sympathy with it.

---

1. Korean politics is familiar with the denomination of a particular generation with numbers. 386 denotes a generation who were 30 years old when they were politically active. Born in 1960, they entered the university in 1980. This generation refers to a particular cohort of population notorious for their extreme stance in political radicalism and, at the same time, their radicalism earned them the title of "the crusaders of democracy." The first number changes to indicate the aging generation. 486 refers to a group of activists who are 40 years old when they are politically active. Ten years are supposed to be sufficient to indicate change that marks a generation from another. This generation gap is being reduced as time passes.

2. Bruce Cumings, a progressive scholar of Korean history, argues that the U.S assumes major responsibility by authoring the 38th parallel. In a hierarchy of responsibility, he writes, the U.S is the major culprit for dividing Korea. His view of the recent history of Korea cannot but be called rather myopic. Interactions between the two powers date back to the time when World War II was in full swing. They go back further into the past when the Russian Empire was thrusting its way through Siberia to Northeast Asia in search of access to non-freezing ports. There were a tangle of events rendering it unfair to trace the cause of division to August 11, 1945, the day the U.S declared the 38th parallel.

3. Mass nationalism involves daejung which literally means a variety of groups denied access to economic fruit. In the ideologically charged climate, it developed to embrace the oppressed against exploiters, intent to wage the class struggle against the established order. Therefore, mass nationalism refers to collective sentiments of those engaged in the eternal flow of the revolutionary movement against the America-supported regimes in the south. Mass nationalism, an outgrowth of students struggles against the authoritarian regimes, is something unique to Korean politics. It denies any government in a divided Korea and its plea for hasty unification is coterminous with the North Korea's Confederate System that brings the two diametrically opposed halves into an overarching apparatus. Will it be possible to orchestrate the antithetical entities into an integrated whole?

4. The ceasefire is a temporary termination of combat. Both are in a shaky balance of power. The ceasefire took effect on July 27, 1953. The presence of American troops in South Korea is justified. as representing the United Nations member countries which fought in Korea, to secure the safety of South Korea when the shaky state of the ceasefire collapses. The cease fire is distinguished from a peace agreement which can do away with the presence of foreign troops.

5. Year 1987 is remembered by the unconditional acceptance, by the Fifth Regime, of political demands by

the young militants who are therefore called democratic crusaders. President Park Chung-hee's reign continued through the third and fourth Republic. Coincident to his inauguration as the fourth President, Park contrived a scheme to perpetuate his rule which goes by the name of Yushin (Reformation) comparable to Japan's Meiji Reformation. On his part, it was an opportunity to reshape the tattered country but it could not be considered other than his plot to perpetuate his rule. The Constitution was amended to institutionalize "an electoral college" patterned after the American's as an assembly to elect the president. With the advent of this institution, the election of the president was changed from direct to indirect system. This system was firmly in place when Chun Doo Hwan took power to start the Fifth Republic. In the middle of the presidential campaign for the Sixth Republic, the public outcry for political reform was reluctantly accepted to open the way to the election of the president by the people. Its concomitants were the immediate release of all political prisoners, free press, and freedom to organize unions of workers. This incidence is regarded as marking a significant departure from the erstwhile high-handed, authoritarian regimes.

6.   South Korea is placed under the nuclear umbrella of the United States, since it is not allowed to develop a nuclear power, in its confrontation with the North. The progressives' argument for strategic independence means that South Korea wants to go it alone without foreign assistance in national defense. The on-going military dependence contradicts their argument for strategic independence. This progressive's stand cannot be viewed as other than the expression of nationalistic sentiment hostile to foreign power.

Chapter

Six

Korean Values in Transition

Man is not a rational animal, will has primacy over reason, and man's emotional and irrational tendencies preclude the following of the dictates of reason.
                                                              — *Saint Augustine*

A Mess of Contradictions

||||||||||||||||||||||||||||||||||||||||||||||||||||||||||||||||||||||||||||||||||

The first thing Korean kids learn in school is how to cooperate with pals and how to harmonize with others or act together to achieve a task. Business enterprises routinely emphasize a cooperative spirit to be instilled in the mind of each new employee so that he becomes an effective member of a team. "Be on the team" or "work in unison" are familiar catchphrases whether in school or concern. Orientation programs for new employees are hard trainings that resemble something one receive at military boot camps. Education itself is a silent pressure for Koreans to fit in with the group norm or ethos, molding them into certain patterns of behavior that a company requires. Koreans see virtue in uniformity, homogeneity and standardization, and these bring forces into play to suppress individual impulses to go beyond the beaten path. Staying within the confines of a system may have a virtue, but this strikes outsiders as unbearable monotony and boredom. Some might prefer the risks of battle to the drab running of mills. Rigid conformity to normative values allows little room for variation of individual behavior. It takes much courage for a Korean to go beyond the trenches they are confined in.

Pluralistic societies enlarge social tolerability for individual behavior. On the contrary, Korean behaviors fit a fixed pattern, due, in large part, to cultural homogeneity and the smallness of the land that leaves little room for regional differences. Nevertheless, value conflicts, resulting from the cohabitation of traditional and new values, do not allow Koreans' traits to be characterized in simple terms. Some may be caught in the grip of traditional values, but others run amok as they strive to achieve individual goals. By and large, Koreans feel a high moral imperative, but are so bent to seek materialistic goals characteristic of a secularized age. The coexistence of different values is not surprising for Koreans, though it is not taken for granted, who have never experienced epoch-making changes. Koreans made few efforts to dispel the darkness of the past to open vista for new possibilities.

Korean values are not clearly bifurcated into traditional and new ones and the result is a mess of contradictions. Dignity, proper etiquette and self-restraint constitute the characteristic quality of a virtuous, educated man. More often, however, foreigners observe the contrasting noisy and excited volatility of Koreans in contrast to the measured tranquility of the Confucian ideal. Over-heated argument and contentious confrontation are frequently observed on the streets. "Free swinging in physical actions and explosive in talk and song, all translating into a new penchant for adventure and risk-taking, pose a severe challenge to the stereotype of placid and compliant Koreans" (Gregory Henderson 1983;15). Self-assertiveness and crude self-aggrandizement have become as much Korean as refinement and impassive dignity. The *nouveau riche* shows an intriguing contrast with the Confucian nobility. Many Koreans display their success through the extravagant consumption of material wealth, while they are trying to imitate traditional upper class life styles, but self restraint and refinement that have become an integral part of the gentleman's way of life are goals that go beyond the reach of the new middle class.

Korean popular culture, Gregory Henderson writes, "has an energetically raw and garish quality and vulgar ostentations bearing affinity to shaman's flourishing pompous robes" (Hendersen;18). Such comment shows one ethnic trait, as perceived through one's cultural prism, and sits at a distance from the Korean self-image. Alternating between cooperative behaviors and factional feuds and between a highly organized discipline and the chaotic pursuit of individual goals contradicts Koreans' professed homogeneity. One might say that a Korean knows his place within the hierarchical society, but this image is far from the reality of modern Korea: they are perpetually dissatisfied with and refuse to stay in a given position or status. Confucianism summons men to rise out of themselves to the highest version of self and to build a society whose leadership they are groomed for. Competition is constantly encouraged among children, and they are locked in "the rational warfare" that Max Weber referred to as the motive for the advance of capitalistic society.

Korea is becoming a pluralistic society. Family values based on inequality and patriarchal authority are giving way to equality and liberalism and the center of family life is shifting from parent-child to conjugal ties. The notion of filial duty withers away among increasingly egoistic youngsters, while they lack the sense of independence by depending financially on their parents even after they get married. This shows that the notion of an extended family network of mutual support still remains strong. A 2010 survey on randomly sampled youngsters aged 15 years or above shows that 78 percent considered their parents as members of the family, even after they get married (Chosôn Daily Press, Jan.20, 2011).

The increasing proportion of aged people dulls their children's sense of filial commitment. A painful burden on adult children was hardly conceivable when the life span of Koreans was shorter. Status inconsistency is another that frustrates old Koreans attuned to the hierarchical society. The recent proliferation of nursing homes suggests that filial obligations are transferred from families to social institutions. The father-son relation based on filial obligations has become looser and some adult sons feel no sting of conscience to abandon their helpless parents. Nowadays, there is a noticeable tendency among educated parents to renounce the filial obligation of their adult children and try to be independent when they are old..

Family fraternity is manifested in parentless children who stick together with their blood siblings, since adoption outside the family means the dispersion of the siblings. They choose to suffer a hard life rather than being split apart. A ten-year old boy takes a fatherly responsibility for his younger siblings. Korean widows selflessly dedicate themselves to children, despite the painful struggle of earning a living alone. Familial fraternity is a holy grail which they see worth defending at all costs.

Equality defines new relations between a husband and wife and between seniors and juniors. The intrusion of equality into Korean society was mediated by Christianity at the turn of the century. Arguing that Western values were the sole vehicle for modernization, however, is the over-simplification of an array of value elements immanent in Koreans. Western values were super-imposed on the nascent urge for change, leading to the secular orientation of Neo-Confucianism and the result is a strong motivation for self-improvement. Discord between offspring and parents is occasionally caused by parental intervention into a matter that determines one's future career. The choice of a right partner for marriage is a grave concern of the family and becomes troublesome when the decision does not suit parents.

Koreans are still in tune with a vertical arrangement of organizational and social structures and find emotional comfort within such hierarchical institutions. The coexistence of antithetical values guards against the package acceptance of Western values. College students in Korea do not want either to follow the Confucian tradition without reservation or to abandon it completely. The 1967 survey on the Koreans' acceptance of individualism concludes "They do not seem to accept the Western version of individualism wholeheartedly; they rather have a tendency to refuse it or at least keep it at a distance in their value consciousness."

Despite being attuned to a standard culture, the word "pluralism" is an appropriate reference to the current variety of religions practiced in Korea. Foreigners who have experienced religious schism and catastrophic wars wonder at members of a Korean family divided into Buddhism, Protestantism and Roman Catholicism. Downtrodden Koreans found a shelter in shamanism from authoritarian rule. A few beleaguered elites persistently attach themselves to onerous Confucian norms. Prayers for the achievement of secular desires have permeated Christianity, and it is often said that a shamanistic orientation dulls the Christian concept of salvation and immortality.

Many church goers worship God with the mental orientation with which they had worshipped the deified natural forces and ancestors. Koreans tend to accept Western culture as representative of Christianity. Ignorant of distinctions between the two, some Koreans became Christians not so much for creeds as for the naive expectation that they would be like any others of Western societies which celebrate advancement and modernization. Intellectually discreet Koreans accept Western mores as desirable and important but balk at the package acceptance of them.

The inexorable move toward a pluralistic society casts doubt over the timelessness of Korean family values. A cautious prediction is that family values will change but at a slow pace. The slow pace of change rules out the possibility that Korean collective consciousness would be replaced by the Western version of individualism in totality. One may wonder how such pre-modern values persistently remain without radical changes in modern and industrial society. A possible answer may be found in the concept of "cultural lag to explain why different sectors of society change at different rates. "There is a lag or temporal gap between change resulting from the application of technology to material culture and corresponding changes in non-material culture" (John Duncan 1997. 52).

By constantly upholding the ideals of educated noblemen and keeping people in sight of exemplary norms, Koreans stoke the fire of Confucianism as a tool for realizing the highest version of the self. Every juvenile crime evokes a knee-jerk reaction crying out for return to the values of the past. Confucian idealism turns off a significant segment of people on account of its demanding paradigm of behavior. One may say that traditional values are implacably dimmed, but it is also true that their grip on the daily behavior of Koreans is much greater than in other countries in the shadow of Confucianism. The Confucian literati, though few in number, imbued with restraint and impassive dignity, persistently defy the temptations of popular culture and pompous stuffed shirts as something that verges on farce.

While any effort to internalize Confucian values requires a great deal of self-discipline and restraint, Shamanism gives free reign to emotional volcanoes, giving rise to unrestrained and volatile characters in verbal and behavioral manifestations. While Confucianism confines individuals into a normative frame of desired behavior, Shamanism is an open field for freewheeling behavior. With the withdrawal of Confucian values, a shamanistic view has come to the fore, claiming itself to represent popular culture. While it is not fair to hold shamanism entirely responsible for scoundrels and Confucianism for good souls, the confusing presence of the idealized and natural patterns of behavior will befuddle Koreans. So long as Confucianism leaves its imprint, albeit much abated, value conflict will accompany social change towards a pluralistic culture.

The notion of a partnership marriage entails status equality which, in turn, means joint responsibility for livelihood. When it comes to a question of "who earns the bread" on behalf of an incompetent husband, Korean women fall back and stand for the merit of feminine virtue. Sexual equality contradicts the notion of feminine virtue. A tight parent-child bond has been transformed into mother-child fusion, as manifested in various aspects of family relations. Children are increasingly rebellious against patriarchal authority but this does not mean that they lose the sense of the hierarchical order in which they position themselves. A trend is evident among the youngsters to break loose from Confucian norms and to increase the latitude of individual behavior. Then, what will happen to the familial solidarity that provides an emotional bond? One of the reasons why street kids are thought to be at particular emotional risk is that they, deprived of familial protection, lack a sense of personal identity which flows almost automatically from being identified with a family. "Being told that you are 'a chip off the old block' is not always flattering, but it provides a reassuring sense of being part of the flow of family generations" (Hugh Mackay, 1993;279)

Particularism and Universalism

From the perspective of globalization, the discourse on value conflicts narrows down to two diametrically opposed elements: parochial values limited to Confucian societies and Korea in particular on one hand and values that lend themselves to universal acceptance. The former concerns the value with its application limited to particular regions or times. Hierarchy, collectivism, nepotism, favoritism, factionalism, ascription, provincialism, nationalism and human bonds are the values particular to Korea and possibly other Confucian societies. All of these values pertain to the private domain of life, the parochial circle of association, whereas universal values are not specific to region or class.

Universalism is, by definition, free of region-specific values and can easily cross geographical and cultural borders. Democracy, equality, individualism, freedom, rationality, and diversity are universally accepted as the normative values within democratic countries. These values represent the universal aspect of the world that papers over all particularistic values. Many argue that universalism results from globalization. Rationalism, in this context, is increasingly regarded as a viable substitute for particular values. Many think that rationalism and globalization are inseparable; they merely wear different clothes, but their roles are identical as substitutes for particular values.

Max Weber developed the concept of 'rationalization' as a cultural force that unleashes a driving force for a rational development in the world. "The concept of rationalization is underpinned by efficiency, calculability, predictability, disenchantment and depersonalization"(cited in de Bary Theodore & JaHyun Kim Haboush 1988;21). Further, Weber regards rationalization as an irreversible power that transforms the world into a more and more rational 'iron cage." Talcott Parsons, a lifetime translator of Max Weber, "developed an analytical tool to define acts at the individual, institutional and social level"(Max Weber 1949;46). Before taking any action, Parsons remarked, actors in a particular situation are confronted with a series of major dilemmas of orientation, which he called "pattern variables." He defined five pattern variables clustered around particularism and universalism.

T. Parsons' Pattern Variables

Particularism	Universalism
Affectivity	Affectivity neutrality
Ascription	Achievement
Diffusion	Specificity
Group egoism	Civic orientation

Affectivity and affectivity neutrality

Treating an individual as an independent being outside a circle of association represents universalism. Treating one as a member of a class or group necessarily entails a relationship imbued with affectivity. A father cannot be free from a paternalistic or emotion-ridden concern for his children. Affectivity is something that characterizes family and intimate relationships. Consider a teacher in a position to assess the achievement of individual students. He is expected to exercise an unbiased judgment when grading a student's work, never allowing personal likes or dislikes to intervene. Universalism, then, represents a process of dehumanization by being free of biases and preoccupations. Modern society sees universalism dominate public life, while particularism persists in private spheres. At the social level, universal criteria, imbued with a tone of impersonal coolness, seem to replace traditional, particularistic forms of affection. Where particularism dominates, its affective links to particulars are instrumental in keeping certain occupations available to a designated few.

Affectivity and affective neutrality points to a relationship between the immediate expression of emotions and the postponement of such an expression in order to achieve some more distant goals. When a doctor treats a patient, he finds himself confronted with a choice - whether he should develop an affective connection or keep a cool aplomb at a distance with patients. Immediate disclosure of a disease, presumably fatal to the patient's life, may sound a wake-up call for greater attention lest the disease run its course. Playing cool in the hope that it will lead to emotional stability may help the patient to recover. Modern society has the value that suggests the desirability of control over an urge for emotional expression even in private spheres.

Ascription and achievement

Let's suppose that you are looking for a person who fits a job vacancy. Your decision alternates between one who is not qualified but happens to be your first cousin and another who fits the bill by any standard but has no such a relationship to you. Recruitment based on the former is the typical case of ascriptive orientation that prevailed in pre-modern societies. Here, an individual is judged not by his competency but by connectedness. As we move toward modern society, an achievement orientation is prevailing over an ascriptive orientation. Associated with ascription are emotionalism, nepotism, connectedness, favoritism and regional bias that blur achievement-based judgment. Achievement orientation, on the other hand, excludes the intervention of such emotions, leaving decisions to be guided by what one can achieve in a system or an organization.

Diffuseness and specificity

A diffused relationship views a person in his or her totality, as practiced in relation to a family member or an intimate friend. A person with warm heart is considered a man who fits the wanted job and to be capable of performing all kinds of tasks, including a complex one. In such a way one element of personal traits is positively related to another in a way that makes no distinction between personal and working relationships. The result is that every Korean worker within an organization is burdened with an undefined range of obligations that cross the line between the personal and public domains. In the world of professionals, however, one is judged in terms of his or her relevancy to a specific work. What counts between fellow workers is only this working relationship with no concern for what happens to their fellow workers outside the sphere of work. Specific job skill assumes a greater importance in modern society. Believing in one's totality based on a demonstrated trait risks the danger of misjudging of one's quality.

Group egoism and civic-orientation

Particularistic orientations are conducive to individual subjugation or loyalty to a group, which likely leads to group egoism. By contrast, a self-centered person is assertive about what he achieves, and an excessive pursuit of personal goal blinds one to what is good for a larger, diffused entity. Egotism, whether personal or group, generates a drag against the expanding circle of identity. What is lacking is the intermediate value, a communitarian spirit that eliminates deterrence to the expansion of a parochial concern to a greater one. Alexis Tocqueville was struck by the communitarian spirit evident among the early settlers of America; he attributed fondly to individual freedom as the underpinning of civic consciousness that exhorts the voluntary participation of the concerned people to achieve a common goal.

The notion of voluntary participation is echoed by Francis Fukuyama's 'spontaneous sociability' that stretches the network of trust beyond molecular groups. Individual initiative and freedom generates an intermediate value, and group egotism is condemned as a barren land for spontaneous sociability. Nevertheless, one cannot deny that one's innate willingness to renounce personal interest in favor of a greater cause is a potential match with a communitarian spirit. The communitarian spirit is nothing but one's will to extend the values of the private domain to the public one. Koreans are less consciousness of distinctions between the private and public domain. Such a trend, according to foreign observers, accounts for Koreans' reluctance to be concerned with what is good for society. In times of crisis, though, Koreans staked out their concern for the country, and this is largely due to their consciousness of ethno-centric nationalism.

"According to the Confucian holistic view, one's self-fulfillment was achieved by creating a state of mind or following a way of conduct that eliminates distinction between self and others" (Parsons, Talcott and Shills 1951;117). The differentiation of self from others is a common way of life, and the ideality of one's character, according to Confucianism, is achieved by eliminating this distinction. History witnessed Koreans renounce their familial responsibility in favor of a greater cause to serve the country in times of crisis. The undeterred expansion of their concern was presumably due to Koreans' unconsciousness of distinctions between the two domains. In a highly homogenized society, it is more likely that the view of society as an extended family plays its role as a catalyst for stretching the domain of concern. Group egotism dissipates when the domain of concern is enlarged to blur the disjunction among social components.

As we have seen here, universalism and particular values form a spectrum of choices. Modernity is a process in which traditional values give way to universalism, emotional neutrality, achievement, specificity and civic orientation. Acts oriented toward these values are guided by the rational working of the head. Rationalization involves an individual in the process of thinking long and hard about what is good or bad in a given situation in consideration of behavior according to social sanctions. In this context, social justice is a relative term, depending on where one stays in the spectrum of family and society. In a particularistic orientation, a person more often has his act determined in the context of what is good for a group or in conformity with external criteria. Particular values cannot be trifled with as useless, since everyone is associated with intimate groups where emotion overwhelms rationality.

A single person is not free from a mix of emotional and rational imperatives. Humans possess two that are not quite congruent. In his own person, he is as quirky as any mad artist. But his profession in the public domain demands of him an emotional-neutral, impersonal and objective grasp of reality. In the private domain, Koreans' behavior, like any other, is largely based on hunches and intuitive knack. In both cases, Koreans' hierarchical and collective consciousness reduces the variation of their behaviors into the easily predictable ones. Of all professional groups, politicians are least advanced toward the universal values, for they have no escape from what is good for their constituents and local interests. Political decisions are made on the basis of family, kinship groups, and shared goals within a regional horizon. When it comes to presidential elections, Koreans find it difficult to go beyond a provincial horizon. Such a parochial concern gives rise to clan politics. Unlike politicians, the cultural domain sees its people advance toward universalism. Search for the right person is based on impartial criteria, and emotional prejudices are neutralized by heightening concern for the performance and quality of work.

Universalism is thought to begin where particularism ends, but the two values defy such a sequential juxtaposition. The inter-state exchange of goods and services among market economies based on the principle of inter-dependence has not dispelled protective nationalism; rather, globalization encountered a renewed upsurge of nationalistic passion as observed among the member states to seek their cultural roots when the overarching Soviet Union and Yugoslavia crumbled. The transformation of society, however, does not follow a straight line, that is, a linear progressivism. The network of Gesellschaft relationships has consistently increased but failed to deal a fatal blow to the existing network of Gemeinschaft relationships, though it carved out its deep bite. The relationship between the two is more often confrontational than mutually reinforcing, and social complexity deters the march of globalization and universalism. Globalization, in a way, reflects the mutual influence of local and global phenomena. Local situations are transformed by becoming part of a wider global arena and processes, while global dimensions are made meaningful in relation to specific local conditions and through the understanding of local actors.

Value Bifurcation and Its Spinoffs

There is regional variation of the value paradigm, dichotomized into the Western and non-western societies. The dichotomized value paradigms neatly divide into gemeinschaft and gesellschaft societies. The Western technological advance, many argue, is in large part attributed to creativity embedded in individual autonomy, and this consequently expanded the latitude of self-directed behavior. Talking about individualism inevitably leads to a debate on collectivism. Against consensus on the contribution of individualism to creativity, a new argument extols the potential of Eastern group dynamism and group competition. A further argument draws attention to the radius of social trust that depends on social behaviors.

Particular values are blamed for the parochial circle of trust, whereas universal values are said to spread trust to enlarged circles of association. Trust is thought to stretch itself where individualism is upheld as a quintessential element of democracy. Strongly entrenched group norms are considered stumbling blocks to the expanding circle of association. When individual assertiveness is carried too far, however, it is likely to impinge upon one's freedom within a group. Given this paradoxical tendency, one is confronted with a choice between group fraternity and individual interest. Group cohesion crumbles as an individual asserts personal interest that falls foul of the interest of others. Anarchism results from liberal extremism when institutions and social inhibitions come to be regarded as irksome to live with.

Family fraternity, once regarded as the citadel of traditional values, is increasingly permeated by universalism. Koreans once proud of family solidarity are losing to a tendency towards frequent breakdown. At a glance, the Korean family is transformed to resemble Western families. As the family becomes smaller in size, conjugal ties become more central, accompanied by less need to live with parents. Taking a closer look, the way in which the Korean family transforms is taking a different path from Western families. A Korean nuclear family is melded into an extended network of mutual support where adult children are kept in a close relationship with their parents, even when not financially dependent on them. At a superficial level, these particular and universal values reveal themselves as opposite beyond a point of reconciliation. But at a deeper level, particular values are not to be completely renounced. Envisioning the post-modern society untainted by urban and industrial excesses, Eastern values, though once labeled as symbols of stagnancy and underdevelopment, may serve as a cure for the ills of materialistic development. Ironically, it may be possible to find a way to remedy some of the material ills spawned in the clashes of the two opposite values just as armed clashes gave rise to dynamism within Western societies. Some intellectuals relish the fast turnover of new ideas and the interactions of contrasting values. A value based on a single culture is not only insipid but unlikely to offer a way of reconciliation, since it extremely limits the choices of behavior.

Individualism and creativity

Individualism is a child of Western culture, resulting from its passage through the Reformation and Enlightenment to the French and Industrial Revolution. In the meantime, non-Western societies have remained in the grip of collectivism. Individualism in the West is said to be the cradle for creative work, regarding mankind as the master of nature. The surrounding world was considered something to be tapped to satisfy human need. "The human-nature dichotomy holds the state in a low profile and places man in the center foreground, exalting, praising, questioning and criticizing him" (Ham Jae-bong 1998;47-48). It gave free reign to the impulse of Westerners to travel into the unknown world to unveil the mysteries of nature.

The Western view of individualism as the source of creativity is challenged by critics who regard individualism as an impediment to creativity. Individualism, as conceptualized in the West, does not necessarily offer impetus to national development in a society that embraces the legacy of "organic relations" (Yang C H 1968,11). When society is organically fashioned, an individual is lost as it is integrated into a group goal. Distance between the West and East has shortened, facilitating a two-way flow of civilization. This means that borders had been effaced, providing opportunities for the two continents to benefit from the two-way traffic of science and culture.

In Confucian-oriented societies, the concept of inter-subjectivity or a single continuum views man as 'being-in-the world' (Ham Jae-bong 1998,80). Given the exchanges of ideas as the source of progressivism, we bring into question Parsons' argument for the "inner isolation of the individual from his fellowmen, including the closest of kin" as the condition needed to foster creative and rational thinking (Ham 88). In the structural absence of religious doctrine, Koreans tend to look for comfort in collective consciousness and dull the cult of individualism.

The Illuminist philosophy in the seventeenth century West exalts man over state authority and encourages the pursuit of individual freedom and wellbeing even to an extent that gives rise to anarchism. Confucian thought humbles man before a collective authority and reconcile individual goals with those of the family or larger entities. "Working for the honor of the family" gives an individual double motivation, since it involves working both for an individual and for a family goal. Individual motivation becomes greater when the private goal is linked to or congruent with a group goal, and this stretches from the family to more expansive entities like the community and state. Individual creativity is not so much the product of speculative thinking by an individual isolated from his fellow workers as what evolves from intermittent flashes of insight through exchanges of ideas with others. Task orientation is an alternative remedy to an individual approach by requiring an individual's immersion in the full swing of team work. Goal sharing among fellowmen creates an aura that supports individual creativity.

"Confucian heroes shape self-identity in the context of connectedness to groups, whereas Westerners are self-assertive and free from customary norms or collective entities" (Ham Jae-bong, 81). Conformity to group norms derives from interactions between group members, but does not necessarily encroach upon one's potential for creativity. Western values sets store by individual spontaneity and initiative as a vessel for the spurt of new ideas. Individualism develops the consciousness of self-responsibility by maximizing the scope of individual autonomy and minimizing state or authority interference. Contrary to the view that collectivistic values constrain individual creativity, development theories attach greater importance to group dynamics for dramatizing one's potential creativity and entrepreneurial prowess. Group dynamics come from a rivalry between egoistic groups. The Eastern concept of collectivism substitutes for individual competition in the West. The "little four dragons" owe much of their economic success to group dynamics.

Morality today is typically based on the logical and rational working of the mind: one must be aware of "one man's right means another's burden." The Korean concept of morality is viewed from the individual's integration into a collective entity, based on what is good for the majority of the members of the entity. When all individuals are permitted to work out their personal preferences, the result may be confusing. This anxiety may prove to be groundless, if one is self autonomous in a combination with civic consciousness. Society is not a mere aggregation of individuals in that it engenders voluntary constraints for the sake of the group. Individuals have developed the sense of authority for his own belief and action within a group.

In a society based on collective consciousness, group norms discipline individuals and constrain autonomy, resulting in a greater dependence on externally imposed norms. Personal attention is limited to circles of intimates, and outsiders are marginalized, subject to impersonal treatment. Group norms, however, do not necessarily reduce the rational working of the mind, since modern society gives more opportunities for individuals to engage with situational decisions. The utter absence of group norms, however, may reduce moral decisions to the point of arbitrary judgment. Tensions and conflicts between an internal motive and an external group norm may drive one to behave in ways that are socially and individually acceptable. A balanced existence of individualism and group consciousness may lead the way to a morally healthy community. Struggles for survival cannot be severed from traditional customs, folklores and law. America did not come from ex nihilo. Had there been nothing, American society would have not developed into a civil society. Kant considers struggle the indispensable accompaniment of progress. If man is free from competition, he would stagnate. "A certain alloy of individualism and competition is required to make the human species survive and grow" (Will Durant 1961,214). This notion is echoed by Henry Adams: "Chaos breeds life and order breeds habit."

Ecological Forebodings

With regard to Western culture, one takes note of its remarkable scientific and industrial advances that spilled over into other parts of the world. The material improvement we enjoy today claims its direct descent from Western science and technology. Western societies have gone through dynamic changes, while Eastern societies were relatively static and orderly. A stagnant society accounts for the lack of epoch-making upheavals. Scientific advance in particular owes much to a messianic belief in reason, a key to open a new vista of possibilities. But the downside of it is that the environment we inhabit is increasingly removed from nature. Historical positivism based on an absolute belief in the infiniteness of reason gave rise to human arrogance and has been under attack for the expanding empire of urban-industrialism. Urban and industrial society shelters humans from crude and untamed nature by making a buffer zone in the name of culture. Artificial culture estranged from nature generates a new force that encroaches back upon nature.

A question arises as to how progress is defined in an artificial culture. The yardstick of progress, notes Theodore Roszak, is "how far we have moved from the original given by nature." The artificiality of the environment we inhabit is symbolic of progress. Individualism, equality, and market were the positive factors that dramatized the turnaround of the West from medieval stagnancy to a dynamic change.

These values had permeated other societies and have become as much the way of life for Koreans in the public domain of life. However, modern society is afflicted by the unwanted child of this historical positivism. Non-Western societies lag behind their Western counterparts in material development, largely attributed to their belated attention to reason and scientific discoveries. Their traditional ways of life, nonetheless, suggest something useful in the way of retarding the pace of transformation to an artificial environment. Koreans owe their material improvement to their acceptance of Western technology, while their traditional values continue to hold sway on their psyches. As Korea moves forward, the distance between material improvement and value consciousness becomes so great that it may have to alter its development trajectory. The iron principle of "industrialization brings development" is no longer tenable in the post-modern society that will befall Korea.

Ecological deterioration is the most salient feature of rapidly growing societies. Korea has its own share of the causes for ecological problems. In addition, the Northwestern seasonal wind carries sands from the Inner Mongolia desert to muddy the air of Korea. The factory chimney was once symbolic of economic growth and prosperity. With the rapid industrialization of China, Korea suffers the immediate influence of chemical pollutants belched out by proliferating Chinese factories. Chinese fishing vessels encroach upon Korean waters in such an overwhelming number that set the Korean coast guards trembling. They threaten to deplete fishes, small and large. Scarce fish in Korean waters become as nimble and slippery as their predators. Should this depletion be left to take its course, the sea will be depleted of its resources.

China used to carry the clout of numbers, and Koreans begin to feel a new "China phobia," not the kind of power that awed Koreans in the past, but a major threat in ecological deterioration. The smallness of the land exposes Korea to collateral damage with its gigantic neighbor. Korea owes its intellectual development to Chinese thought. Nowadays, China is the largest consumer of Korean products, and the fate of the Korean economy depends much on the consuming capacity of the Chinese market. China's rise to a new industrial power poses significant implications for its neighboring countries, both good or bad. Solution to ecological problems, however, requires a dramatic shift of consciousness in favor of a greater sensitivity of common destiny.

Korea has become, to all intents and purposes, an urban industrial society. Before the Korean War broke out, a quarter of the population were urbanites in comparison with three quarters inhabiting rural areas. Recent statistics show the reverse. Three quarters of the population are urbanites sheltered by an urban and industrial culture. Urbanization sprawls at a dazzling speed. Seoul-Inchon has become a mega polis, and another one that links Pusan and Ulsan is under way. It is a matter of time that the land will turn into a network of mega polis connected through busy highways. On the surface, modern Korea is not different from its industrial forerunners. Likewise, urban sprawl will become the subject of hot issue for a balanced development of ecology.

Koreans pay dearly for their belated attention to damages done to humanity and the environment, resulting from "an unrestricted application of the objective mode of consciousness to the whole of the human experience" (Theodore Roszak 1973, 156). Technical expedience outweighs concern for the moral, aesthetic and emotional extensions of technological excrement. For all the remarkable material improvement, though, we are less subject to accidents, pandemics, anxiety and frustration. We should not generalize about the buoyant optimism of the scientific age. A note of caution becomes a frequent refrain in discussions on what the future will be like. A question is raised whether Korea will be like the forerunner countries or have its own version of development.

Natural Continuum

As Korea is headed towards a post-modern society, it is worth to address new problems that plague advanced societies to see what Koreans have to do with the potential merit of the Eastern thought. Apprehension about the negative effects of material development compels greater interest in a possible remedy that maybe gleaned from the Eastern notion of the natural continuum which makes humans inseparable from nature. All components of the universe make one greater whole. In no way do we expect Eastern thought to offer a breakthrough for the problems of unbalanced development. Nevertheless, it foreshadows an opportunity to cure some of the manifested ills.

Our belief in the self-correcting function of the market - that the rational pursuit of personal interests offers a cure-all for social evils – has its own limit. Despite the remarkable material improvement, the complicated and diverse fabrics of modern society are not free from an array of negative effects of development. Koreans are coming up for a headlong collision with "the third wave" to accompany the withdrawal of the industrial society.[1] The cult of science, having the sky as a limit, dazzles our minds at its stellar accomplishments but make us wonder whether it truly holds our future in its hands. In reference to materialistic wealth, Max Weber coined "a cage of iron" which offers no escape, once trapped within it. This term applies to the artificial environment of urban and industrial societies of which humans are prisoners. Humans are enslaved to a wealth-creating machine and excessive avidity, because wealth offers no opportunity for them to be sober and content with the present culmination of history. The dichotomized view of humans as a separate being from nature bred human arrogance as the master over nature and rationalized their brutal destruction of it. Assault on nature is leading the way to ecological deterioration possibly beyond the bounds of recovery. Trapped in a cage of endless avidity, humans have not learned to be a benevolent master of nature. Science is in a way the ostentatious display of human ability, with no attention given to the long-term spin-offs of its development.

The Eastern notion of continuum was submerged by scientific and technological advance and the material development of society. Nowadays the notion of continuum is cautiously sounded out as a remedy for material and technological ills. While continuum allows no difference between humans and other species, it regards nature as something to be awed and keep at a distance. An artificial refashioning of nature was supposed to bring disasters in terms of human sacrifice. Eastern thought may be a counter weight to the human-centered world, the notion of all creatures submissive to humans. Eastern thought humbles humans before the wonders of nature and casts doubt over the omnipotence of reason and intellect. Modern society is supposed to serve as the arbiter of the earlier centuries in terms of blessings or disasters it brought.

"The Buddhist way consists in restraining humans from various kinds of activity which are considered inimical to spiritual progress" (Geoffrey Parrinder 1971, 273). Renunciation of worldly desires fosters the sensibilities of prudence and temperance. The ch'an school (Son in Korean and Zen in Japanese)[2], originating in the Northeast Asian region, is widely used as a psycho therapy in the Western world. Meditation involves the process of cleansing one's mind of prejudices, preoccupations, rancor, preferences, dislikes and bias to make it crystal clear through which one sees his or her own divinity in a deep layer of the inner being. Self-awakening is crucially important as a step toward becoming a person. Confucianism is in essence ascetic by restraining human behaviors from excessive ones. The oriental mystiques take one to a retreat within one's inner being, untainted by social ills and the stressful life of modern society. Taoism enjoins people to live close to nature as a way to control breath, sex and diet.

The materialistic orientation of life, expressed in avidity for possession and merciless competition, stifles our longing to find emotional comfort. In proportion to the human capacity to conquer nature, humans feel themselves reduced into psychic passivity empty of self-dignity and decency by being enslaved to the tools they created to overcome nature. Erich Fromm warned against a 'psychological emptiness' vulnerable to be filled by material possessions and nothing else. The consequent 'self-egoism' creates an emotional wasteland that dims the sense of compassion and human feeling. We observed that material wealth was a reactive conduit of youngsters to forswear all the lures of modern life in favor of a retreat into one's inner being. They are plagued by vague discontents and a sense of inner emptiness at the cost of self-aggrandizement that produced a dynamic force to move forward.

Self-egoism lays fertile in the ethos of individualism. Egoism is often identified with 'self love' but, in its deeper level, the reverse is true. An egoist is indicative of a passionate love for oneself, averse to imagined foes. The downside of egoism is that love of himself, in material terms in particular, rather turns his back against himself. The lack of affection and of a genuine concern for the other parts of the self sets him empty of something more important and mired in a vicious cycle of frustrations after a repeated attempt to satisfy himself. "So far as he tries to fill the empty place with material possessions, he is perpetually lost for the possibility of satisfaction, since he no longer possess a true sense of himself "(Lee Ki-sang, 2009,48). He becomes a lonely being whose life is embittered by the lack of attention by others. We live in an uneasy situation where we deal with a series of balls caroming off one another, resulting in new bounds.

Reason and Secularization

The concomitant effect of the dominance of reason was the secularization of Western values. Ironically, secularization is gaining currency in the region where religious passion once burned bright. Reason defined God as neither the dispenser of providence nor an anthropomorphic God to share pain with us. To draw on Newton's machine metaphor, God endows each creature with its own ability to function. All creatures, notes Darwin, are vested with capacities to prosper their own species. These theories narrow down to the perspective that dismantles the cosmos of its myth-poetic transparency. Koreans earn a reputation for a strange harmony of different religious beliefs even within one family. This phenomenon may be viewed as the lack of religious passion among Koreans. The chaotic presence of different beliefs may be an added spur to secular desires at the cost of their religious piety. Engrossment with the material aspects of contemporary life blinds us to non-material factors that are vital to shaping our future life. Soul searching means not only seeking the immortality of the soul but the variety of non-material life trying to purify one's mind and enhance one's moral consciousness. The rush to grow and acquire blinds us to human dignity, the decency of life and moral values.

The reason-dominant perspective sees civilization as the result of a linear progressiveness. A society devoid of novelty is labeled stragglers to be taken by devils. Eastern thought, by contrast, stands for a cycle of life or the repetition of history. A society, having ascended the pinnacle of prosperity, lapses into low points in its vicissitude. The cycle of life here does not necessarily refer to the repetition of the past, but stands for a march forward though occasionally interrupted by lapses. Eastern thought cries out for leaving nature as it is, while the reason-dominant world is laden with a deliberate attempt to make a new order out of nature that favors the expedience of human living.

The new human habitation is artificial to a degree that it is removed from the nature that our forebears have lived in company with for millennia. It seems that an artificial culture does not favor one's search for inner life. With the secular orientation of values, Western culture is largely based on something that is sensed and appreciated, and their existence owes much to the veritable marvels of nature. Nonetheless, things that touch human senses are not all that exist. There may be a lot more than we can see through our sensory organs. These things stay in the deep recesses of human consciousness, and Hombach calls them "hermetik" in the sense that they avoid exposure and find no verbal expression.

The materialistic orientation of life paradoxically stirs one's dormant longing for the spiritual world, and Eastern thought assumes new importance as a remedy for some of materialistic ills. A major reason for Christianity to win over Judaism and heathens is that it is pessimistic by virtue of its "little ego," as expressed in repentance, piety, and obedience, all deterring the useless quest for earthly happiness. Islam on the contrary is optimistic and materialistic by promising the martyred a heavenly refulgence which they will swim in, a reward that has been denied in this world. Buddhism is profoundest in the philosophical terms of 'little ego' that leads to self-negation: it encourages one to search divinity lying in the deep recesses of consciousness. The so-called counter-culture is nothing more than the search for the solace of the inner being away from materialistic ills. Indian culture, though not free from the ills of fatalism, is considered a response to this challenge by delving into the dark side of earthly existences and becoming a self-professed soul free to move across borders between the earthly and spiritual life. One hardly reads any signs of grief, pain, frustration or anxiety on the faces of those whose days are numbered.

The distance is so great between technological development and cultural change. The change of value consciousness was sluggish as it received belated attention. Although science revolutionized human life,

Koreans are still stubbornly ethno-centric, as if it mocked the cult of technological miracles. One of the great features of the 20th century was the capacity of technology to align with the most benighted form of racist and nationalist megalomania. Nazism and Fascism stand out in this respect. Talking about modern society, there are two main streams, comparable to the flow of a river. Sciences and technologies allow for no regional and cultural variations since their progress has followed a universal, linear trajectory. Culture defies a rational approach based on objectivity, since it has gone an irrational way in the process of formation. The lure of reason was so dazzling that we have been slow to give up on the myth of earth's infinite generosity.

An urban and industrial society defines progress as a degree to which the environment we inhabit is artificial by way of eliminating the original given by nature and controlling natural forces. Humans surround themselves with culture defined as a buffer zone against the untamed nature. Urban and industrial culture separates humans far from nature. Alienation from nature raises the problems that can be solved only by a change in human values or ideas of morality: otherwise, the continuing rational pursuit of human interest at the cost of nature may lead to collective ruin. Our attention is drawn to the moral, aesthetic and psychic extensions of the scientific worldview. The future we envision is an alternation between bright hopes and hidden forces of dehumanization, as Francis Bacon foreshadowed in times of scientific evolution. He saw the bleakest aspect of scientific culture in the malaise of spirit and the nightmare of environmental collapse. In no way does it mean that Eastern societies are free from these concomitants

Low and High Trust Society

The radius of trust is determined by where a pendulum is on the range between particular and universal values. This notion is based on the premise that spontaneous sociability is the major factor for extending circles of trust. The Korean propensity to fraternal solidarity around molecular groups is considered a major impediment to building social trust in a broader social context. Francis Fukuyama draws the world map that classifies the countries the world over into high trust and low trust on the basis of a key cultural characteristic that encourages spontaneous sociability. The apparent lack of spontaneous sociability places Korea among the low-trust societies. Spontaneous sociability has more to do with a social structure or values that allow members of society to trust one another and cooperate in creating new groups and associations.

In this map of the world, Germany, Japan, and the United States are societies with healthy endowments of social capital that fosters sociability in contrast with those with low-trust like Taiwan, Hong Kong, China and Korea. It is worthy of attention, however, that the United States and Japan are placed into the same category, although their social structures are poles apart. Japanese are as much disposed to form groups as Koreans are, giving rise to parochial circles of trust .[3] Given this classification, the radius of trust is not necessarily related to where the pendulum is on the range between individualism and collectivism. The Koreans' circle of trust is more parochial than the

Japanese's, though they have more in common with each other than with other societies. But Koreans are characterized by familial solidarity. A strong familial fraternity in Korea creates small and cohering circles of trust made up of blood kin. This explains a rare case of expanding the clannish leadership of enterprises to embrace professional outsiders. The Japanese circles of association was started with a fiefdom which bounds its constituents to a communal fate in the country where wars between feudal states frequently transpired. At some point in the progression of the circle, spontaneous sociability comes to a halt in Korea, and a parochial network of trust emerges. In contrast, the Emperor in Japan, obviously an earthly being apotheosized to a heavenly being, presides over an undeterred expansion of the circle of trust. Curiously enough, the elastic circle of trust is provided by the Japanese willful belief in the unbelievable.

Spontaneous sociability is invariably weakened by cultures that emphasize crony circles. The radius of social trust is so limited that trust between strangers is rarely observed with Koreans outside the circle of intimates. A stronger sense of individualism, on the other hand, weakens family fraternity and spurs voluntary associations to take the place of families. American society in particular is characterized by a dense network of voluntary organizations, and this art of association is regarded as "a key virtue of American democracy." Social trust beyond the family or blood kinship encourages strangers to cooperate and makes it a lot easier to build corporations of scale.

Another way to distinguish high-trust from low-trust societies, according to Francis Fukuyama, is based on the types of political structures that societies have gone through. China, Korea, and France all went through a period of strong political centralization. By contrast, those societies experiencing a high degree of social trust, such as Japan, Germany and the United States, did not experience a prolonged period of a unitary state power. Germans have relished a central power since 1871 when all German semi-sovereign states were merged into Deutschland. When Germans were divided into princely states, social stability was low. In a unified country, robust social organizations able to generate large-scale organizations could flourish without interference and become the basis for economic cooperation. Low-trust societies feature heavier reliance on a powerful and all-encompassing state to promote economic development. The intervention of state power weakens society's underlying propensity to spontaneous sociability in the long run. Given this premise, it begs a question of whether Japan has more in common with Germany or the United States since the state leadership of Japan was stronger in promoting economic policy.

The feudalistic system of Japan, more or less analogous to that of medieval Germany, was not the major driving force for a high trust society. The long-lingering legacy of feudalism explains the belated advent of a central power that orchestrated different threads of values into a new dynamo for modernization. After the Meiji Reformation, a loose network of fiefdoms was replaced by centralized state power which steered a course of development free from foreign interventions. A centralized power was a powerful vessel for national development. Therefore, reference to the legacy of the pre-modern decentralized structure of power as the factor for trust seems to be irrelevant in this debate. Another question is whether large corporations continue to be an engine for economic growth in the family-centered society.

This debate crosses the threshold, because it involves the role of culture. We cannot argue for or against a particular form of economic structure on abstract grounds. Small, family-centered corporations continue to be the main stay of economic growth in Taiwan and elsewhere; its chances for success depend on the specific cultural, political and historical environment in which they operate. Apparently, the modern state is no longer the major promoter of economic growth. The important factors that affect the real quality of life in modern society lie beyond what the state can do. A civil society, with its intermediate associations rooted in culture, religion, and tradition, will be the key to the success of modern societies in a global economy.

Apart from culture and value, technology appears to be responsible for a short radius of trust. A salient feature of urban and industrial society is that technology is crowding out human interaction. There is actually very little human contact for those hemmed in the non-natural world of technology-centered communication. People, especially young people, spend more and more of their time separated from other humans. Disasters, pain, and even death befalling others do not matter to the people captivated by PC or whatever they use for communication because what they see is images or texts, not genuine human beings.

People enrolled in this non-natural world become insensitive, even callous when confronted with fellow human beings' suffering. Technological means of communication substitutes for human contacts, and there is little spur to expand a network of trust. For those far distanced from genuine human contacts, trust cannot spread. So far as social anonymity permeates modern society, there is no point in classifying societies into high and low trust one. We are headed toward the world of non-human contact.

Family Challenged

The small sized family is divested of its traditional functions. This trend connotes that Korean society approaches an industrialized society where emotion-ridden human relationships are losing out to new tendencies toward impersonality, objectivity and anonymity. Belief in the elastic circle of the family is based on the human instinct to expand circles of trust based on intimacy and familiarity. The key factor to expand the circle of trust is the civic consciousness that embraces more spontaneously organized structures than the abstract notion of familiarity filling the interstice between family and society.

The Confucian belief in the undeterred expansion of familial clannishness to nationhood, however, is flawed by failure to recognize that familial solidarity dissipates in an urban and industrial society that embraces diverse groups and interests. Modern society is marked by the forces that deter a straightforward extrapolation of the familial circle to society. Development theory condemns this clannish trend as an obstacle to civic mindedness. Familial cohesiveness denotes the ideals of traditional society and deters urban and industrial transformation. In the diverse society, the family is losing its role and it may be worthwhile to examine problems spawned in the reduced role of the family in industrial forerunner countries.

The emancipation of individuals from coercive institutions was accompanied by the frequent breakdown of families. This trend is markedly observed in industrial forerunner countries. Idealistically, the family offers parental protection to children, but the breakdown of the family exposes children to the cold-blooded streets. Despite its claim to be the citadel of family value, Korean families frequently break down, largely owing to their failure to achieve the harmonious blend of old and new values. It is not fair to ascribe the frequent breakdown of family to a particular value. It appears to be common place worldwide: it happens even in Islamic fundamental societies.

According to the Chosôn Daily Express' survey, "Among newly married couples, 24.7% divorced within four years. Recent years witnessed the divorce rate of middle-aged couples (longer than 20 years of marriage) rise to 26.4%, surpassing that of young couples" (2015, Oct.22). In the earlier years of marriage, clashes between the two different personalities, largely owing to the husband's inability to earn a family's living, were the major cause for divorce. In the so-called twilight years, divorce reflects much of the wife's desire to be released from the lingering shadow of an authoritarian husband. This fact reveals the fundamental characteristic of the Korean family —that women have endured submissive status for peace at home. Now that the husband has lost authority as the bread earner, the aged wife is no longer financially dependent on her husband and wants to be free of the suppressive atmosphere of the male-dominant family. Her psychic emptiness is filled by her expectation to live with her adult sons. The husband is estranged from the siblings who live with their mothers. The mother and her siblings are bound to a tighter relationship than the father.

Korea is replete with problems, all spawned by rapid urbanization and industrialization. As society grows in complexity, there are more people alienated or isolated and lonely, deprived of familial or institutional protection. Koreans are increasingly self-assertive in favor of cold-blooded calculation of interests over collective sentiment. Homeless children are deprived of emotional and psychological comfort that should be provided by a group or institution instead of families. Solace is found in the emotional comfort of a small circle of trust, if it is not an impediment to enlarged circles of intimacy. The proper question follows; "Can we continue to find an emotional solace in a small group, while expanding the circle of trust in a society composed of anonymous members?"

An individual without a sense of being part of a network is prone to committing crimes, as he or she is not bound by inhibitions that restrain impulsive behaviors. This refreshes our concern for the new role of the family in urban and industrial society, since the family nurtures positive emotion. The road to moral development consists in the growth of those social emotions that bloom in the generous atmosphere of love and the home. The positive emotion deserves attention for its role in refreshing our minds with a new motive or ambition. Familial protection, above all, satisfies the emotional needs of lonely souls in modern society. This conception of the family role contradicts Max Weber's definition of family as an ancient product of history, an irksome institution to live with as it encroaches upon individual freedom. At the same time, we observe a new trend – that an increasing number of Korean youths, male and female, prefer to remain single. Some regard marriage as an irksome institution that binds them to the burden of rearing children. They assert celibate security, presumably attributed to an increasing awareness of egoism and liberty.

All customs and rules that perpetuate the family as an institution are considered outmoded in modern society. Paradoxically, the role of the family gains new importance even against the pervasive notion that the family is no longer an institution all constituents must adhere to. It is worth noting what is happening in the industrially advanced countries, when family lost its protective hand for emotional comfort. "In 2001 about a third of all babies in the United States are born to unmarried women, compared with only 3.8 percent in l940. With so many marriages ending in divorce, formal commitment strikes many people as alien or a bad idea" (Mark Lilla 2001,27). Cohabitating relationships are less stable than marriages but such a fleeting relationship is convenient in coping with factors that work against a steady family. The offspring of single parents are more likely to reject marriage for themselves, perpetuating the pattern of their parents. Although these statistics are out of date, we can imagine that this trend has continued up to this point.

Korea is apparently catching up with the advanced countries, and their problems are no longer a distant echo across borders. Given this fact, familial clannishness enshrined in Korea's particular value system cannot be denounced as an old stuffy thing to be abandoned in its entirety. Contrary to the negative view, there is a new understanding of the family as a gemstone to be constantly polished so that it displays its underlying luster. By and large, many of divorced Koreans are anxious to settle into a new family, and this is the reminder of Korean values that is hostile to those who wish to remain celibate. Widowed people feel as if they were under the glare of neighbors; they are pained by questions getting into their private affairs. The ethos of collectiveness is hostile to one's will to appreciate the expediency of living alone.

Filial duty was the essential element of an extended family system, but it has declined in importance, giving way to the conjugal tie that rules out living with one's parents or in-laws. Despite the social forces that reduce the importance of filial duty, a majority of Koreans understand it as an essential value to be preserved. Even among younger generations whose filial piety is not practiced as expected by their parents, this virtue remains high in importance. This in a way points to the distance between their cognitive understanding of its importance and the internalization in the deeper recesses of their consciousness of this virtue. Any survey of the younger generation on their cognitive understanding of filial piety is misleading because their performance of filial duty is more often based on the cognitive understanding of this virtue rather than their will to perform, cognizant of what it takes to be dutiful to their parents. The awareness that filial duty is an imperative among Koreans serves as a silent pressure for honoring this virtue on a cognitive level. But they are less motivated toward a spontaneous will in comparison with the consciousness of filial duty built into their forebears. Decline in the sense of filial duty has more to do with an increasing number of elderly people. A Korean popular saying has it: one long in life has no filial son.

In reality, some may encounter the case where their filial duty clashes with the dictum of the call of the public realm. "In the pre-modern society, no distinction was made between the public and private realm. Now, we live in an age in which drawing the line properly is quite critical" (Lee Seung-hwan 2000;56). Filial duty is a virtue relevant to the private realm and, projected into the public realm, it becomes irrelevant. A father who stole a cow from a neighbor may be exonerated by his dutiful son, but his behavior is detrimental to order in a legalistic society. The moral issue that most aggrieved the rulers in pre-modern Korea was how to treat demeaning or malicious members of their families; their sacrifices were traded for the greater good of the country. There were many cases where the Korean rulers abandoned paternal affection for their beloved ones in favor of lethal punishment for the sake of dynastic continuity. Korean patriots renounced their responsibility for the care of family in favor of the greater cause of the country under colonial rule. Gangsters renounced their familial responsibility to maintain their unfailing commitment to a group.

As a way of promoting filial duty, "Singapore introduced a tax incentive scheme to benefit those who support their parents and this is supposed to reduce the state's burden to establish a welfare system for elderly people"(Daniel A Bell 1998, 82). This is government-engineered case of inculcating Confucian virtues. Given the global trend toward individualism, such engineering causes apprehension about its negative impact on the role of trust, since every evidence that filial duty has been performed needs to be supported by a voucher or receipt. The performance of filial duty bears the character of transaction. What a difference from earlier years when youngsters tried to emulate the model behavior of the sages! Any means other than those by which a virtue is internalized and imbedded in an integrated whole has a limited effect. There is a persuasive call for a particular form of moral inculcation and its very starting point is the inclusion of virtue in family values. "The process of developing and passing on a system of values is generally unspoken; it happens by example rather than by spelling it out"(Hugh Mackay, 1993;271)

New Identity in Cultural Diversity

Refashioning culture in a way that builds a new tapestry involves the definition of a value system in terms of its role in giving our life new meaning. This process is not to sublimate particular values into universalism, but to achieve an integration of the two. Refashioning our cultural tapestry in a new social context is a continuing work in an ever-shifting frame of reference. Yesterday's virtue has become irksome to live with today. As we are headed toward post-modern society, values should change in response to a new dictum of reality. Value is no longer an independent presence but changes in the unfolding situational context.

The coexistence of particular and universal cultures creates the necessity of choosing value options in complex interplays between the opposite values. Nevertheless, many of them are mutually exclusive. Obviously, value bifurcation makes it difficult to define a cultural or value identity when it needs to be grounded in a particular cultural root. Being of a bicultural identity is not a matter of picking and choosing from the cultures as if to choose items from a *la carte* menu of values. Culture itself is a tapestry whose threads are not interchangeable with other alien ones. Adding a few elements may appear to provide the effect of patch type of remedy, but it actually requires a total restructuring of the tapestry.

Provincialism is an illegitimate by-product of an expanding familial circle to society, but there is no deleting this element alone, since it inevitably leads to the elimination of other elements such as familial solidarity, familial corporation and hierarchy. To do away with authoritarianism is to deny the hierarchical institutions which Koreans have lived in company with over millennia. Provincialism is a necessary accoutrement of a representative system, though blamed for hobbling and distorting it. Provincialism may be redefined in terms of regional representation as a suitable compromise with a greater national interest. One can imagine a bicultural identity in a society where values are polarized into two. A bicultural being is defined as an identity that is forged out of a unique synthesis of different cultural alternatives. A person, located in the middle ground between the two polarities, can move toward either direction. Furthermore, to be bicultural, one has little connection to both cultures in depth but is rather floating in-between the two cultures. Self identity is forged in a unique cultural context, and bi-cultural identity may lead to the loss of self identity by estranging the self from the culture which forged his uniqueness. While the bicultural identity may seem ideal on the conceptual level, it is questionable as to whether or not such an ideal can be achieved in actuality. A natural alignment of ideal and reality is hard to come by. Conceptual recognition may be far from what reality warrants. Rather than conceptualizing a bicultural identity as a synthesized and integrated sense of self, it behooves to accord greater significance to a multi-cultural identity in light of the tendency of each society to approach the global village.

Multicultural identity makes one more flexible and adaptive. Although this flexible version of one's cultural identity offers advantages in adaptation, it is not free from its own contradiction. This situational adaptability, if taken to an extreme, may foster a sense of dissociation and lack of integration of self where a person becomes a chameleon without a stable and cohesive identity of self. Again, such a person, like bicultural identity, is prone to lose his cultural identity. Living in a multi-cultural society, it is necessary to reconceptualize and broaden the notion of self identity and transcend the thinking that has limited our conceptualization to a particular time. Plausible as it may be, a multi-cultural society sees its traditional prejudices and ethnocentrism challenged, as we move toward being part of a global village. There will be the days when Korean society will embrace minority groups who assert their cultural identities and refuse to be acculturated. Changing one's cultural identity is not a matter of a conceptual synthesis of values but of experience with a multicultural environment. Experiences alone offer a unique and valuable opportunity to broaden our perspectives, but this does not increase the range of behaviors in reality. A distinct line is drawn between conceptual understanding and action.

The shift toward a global village begs the question as to whether Korean society will become a multicultural society, a replica of the United States. Multiculturalism materializes in a society where immigrants from various parts of the world live in harmony without a thick frame of shared cultural and historical experience. Multiculturalism cannot be created artificially in a society with an effective linkage to a distant past. Such a society has a built-in defense mechanism against the tide of alien cultures. Korea has its millennia-old history which makes it all but impossible for the people to be alienated from its cultural and historical roots. A multicultural identity elude Koreans so far as they take pride in being part of an inherited cultural legacy.

Liberal Democracy in a New Mirror

The remainder of this chapter analyzes values that have a significant bearing on the feasibility of liberal democracy, the alleged termination of man's experiment with institutional devices to improve conditions for living. Value conflict, as it were, is a common theme in fast developing societies. Korea, burdened with the remains of the past, shakes badly like a vessel breaking through fierce waves. Particular values within the private domain rather reflect the Confucian notion of a built-in tendency towards a communal ideal of harmony and consensus.

For all intents and purposes, equality and freedom, the twin principle of democracy, are effective guides to institutionalize democratic ideals. Nevertheless, particular values still hold their grip on not only the private but public domain and this raises a question about the ability of Koreans to manage democracy. This skepticism sounds a bit absurd to Koreans who have attuned themselves to democracy over the last sixty years. Korean society, as perceived by outsiders, has mellowed into a democratic maturity in terms of the assortment of institutions, but Koreans still display disjuncture between the principles that guide democratic institutions and their value consciousness.

Democratic advancement notwithstanding, equality and liberty have not made their permanent home in Korean consciousness. These democratic principles are clearly expressed in the Constitution but this is far from permeating Koreans' daily life, particularly the domain of private life. Koreans' unconscious rejection of the distinction between the private and public domains connotes a naïve belief in the stretchable circle of familial fraternity towards a communitarian spirit. This projection, however, has proven to be unworkable, due in large part to many variables at work in a vast and anonymous society.

The bifurcation into particular and universal values confronts Koreans with two imperatives: one is to assume that the opposite values have a potential match within a tapestry made up of threads of various colors and sizes and the other is to live with value conflicts, as it were, at the risk of distorting or misguiding the true image of liberal democracy. Value conflicts are unavoidable to live in a fast-changing society, and Korean intellectuals often enjoy interactions between contrasting tastes and values and the thrill of contradictions. Value clashes pose something positive in the way of producing dynamical force. A society devoid of dynamism is, after all, dying of stagnancy.

Contrary to the experimental philosophy that argues for the elastic nature of individualism, the reciprocal virtues of Confucianism foster fraternal solidarity around small units - from family to an extended sphere of blood kinship at most. History has witnessed family fraternity develop into a power bloc - strong enough to overshadow the ruler. Factional strife in pre-modern Korea was largely due to rivalry between family-centered power blocs and ran out of control when they were contesting for power. Rival factions were engaged in an inter-generational struggle that ate up the ruler's patience and a deep factional fraternity did not allow an attempt at reconciliation with others.

The Confucian notion of inequality invites the metaphor of society to a heaven and earth relation and developed into the vertical consciousness of Koreans. This vertical order is a barren land for fostering individual autonomy and creativity. Western values provide for individuality and rationality to feed off each other into civic consciousness. With groundbreaking technological development and owing to the vastness of modern society, the hierarchical and collective consciousness of Koreans inevitably lapses. In this respect, debate is heated over the promises of liberal democracy.

Conditions for Liberal Democracy

Liberty and equality in combination cannot be enjoyed to one's satisfaction. A good measure of equality is made available by limiting liberty to some degree, and liberal democracy therefore requires a skillful balance between the two. Gari Ledyard listed the conditions for liberal democracy to take root in indigenous soil. First, an urban and industrial society creates a favorable climate for liberal democracy since urbanization requires a certain degree of industrialization conducive to the market economy. The market in the modern concept is an arena for competition that rewards those with faculty and creativity. An urban culture also requires a contract-based society of anonymous members and conformity to the rule of law, lauding rationality as an effective guide to individual behavior.

Democracy, first of all, requires rationality and logical reasoning to be the motive for human behavior but this very likely leads to impersonal and dehumanized acts, alien to the emotion-dominant relationships that still persist in Korea. Koreans very often remark "even the rule of law has its own tears." They try to color the impersonal face of society with the warmth of the heart. In atomized societies which see individualism increasingly permeate every aspect of life, rational decisions are equated with the cold calculations of self-interest and indifference to others. Viewed through the prism of the collective consciousness of Koreans, individualism denotes egoism directed toward self-interest that can be destructive of the fabric of an ordered society.

As society grows in complexity, rationality nurtured in the soil of individualism was set free to permeate every aspect of life. Emotion-ridden politics becomes an anathema in a more complex society. The role of statecraft is emphasized to orchestrate conflicting interests into a harmonious interplay. The feasibility of liberal democracy, therefore, depends heavily on the level of urbanization which brings impersonality, anonymity, rationality and objectivity to outshine emotion-ridden human interactions.

Urbanization, accompanied by a great social transformation, rests on an enlarged middle class that provides a counterweight to disruptive social factors.

Economic theorists attribute economic development to the growth of democratic institutions. A certain stage of economic development generates demand for democratic participation. Nonetheless, some factors invalidated this co-relation in the economic take-off stage of South Korea. Economic development was state-driven, imposed from the top down, and it took a good while to energize the masses to follow the development dictum in the absence of an enlarged middle class. Liberal democracy, as demonstrated in the West, rests on the elevation of individual autonomy, resulting from individualism wed to rational thinking. Each individual is a rational being with an instinctive willingness to expand the latitude of self-directed activities with a greater sense of self-responsibility. Liberal democracy also thrives on the privatization of property ownership. Those avid to make success in life are highly motivated to excel over others, and those lagging behind need the spur of their own poverty. Without private ownership, one lacks the desire to be better off than others.

The Bolshevists envisioned a social utopia in which the masses would equally satisfy their basic needs. Human desires, nevertheless, are not content with the equal satisfaction, by all citizens, of their basic needs. Private ownership of property encourages a limitless growth of human desires. Neither Marx nor Lenin envisioned a society where cosmetics, well-styled women's clothes, even automobiles would become the object of mass consumption. Private ownership helps individuals protect their privacy against the intruding authorities like the state. Communism, based on absolute equality in possession but inequality in power and rights, is self contradictory. The law of natural inequality is fertile ground for a class of wealth or excellence to thrive.

In the shadow of professed equality, communism obviously asserts its own image as the champion of the oppressed majority under the disguise of absolute equality. Nevertheless, even a classless society is not immune to the law of natural inequality. In North Korea, for example, a new rich class is created like a frosting on the cake of the masses. Blind pursuit of egalitarianism goes against the laws of nature that a few are winners. Reality is far from what they professed to be, as if the law of nature scoffed at absolute equality. Equality has progressed in an inverse relation to freedom. The complex fabric of modern society fringes upon individual freedom, and excessive equality rips into individual autonomy. Communism is an outgrowth of violent reactions to capitalistic inequality, but its champion of absolute equality was conducive to the enthronement of a coercive and dehumanizing institution. Born from the womb of Western industrialization, communism lives off the fallacies of its own brother, capitalism.

Liberal democracy develops in tandem with globalization. A plural society is made possible when individuals put their fingers on the pulse of the world. Liberalism and globalization in combination eliminate barriers to the free flow of goods and peoples across borders, working toward the creation of a global village. To realize democracy, society should embrace fairness, openness, equality, rationality, transparency, accountability and market dynamics. Failure to make a timely response to these imperatives flung Korea into a disastrous economic downturn, the first symptoms of which were visible in 1997. In the heat of globalization, the frozen lake of particular values melts away. Some are entrenched in their niches and defiant at the call for change. An intriguing question is whether mankind, captivated by universal values, can be totally uprooted from their indigenous cultural fabric. Debate on this issue leads us to address whether some elements of traditional values are compatible with universal values. Rational authoritarianism, for instance, may gain new importance in taming laissez faire into law-abiding citizens in the world.

Hierarchical order and authoritarianism are incompatible with the free will of liberal democracy. Five decades of the Koreans' quest for democratization failed to dispel the hierarchical order and authoritarianism. Leading politicians, despite their life-long commitment to democracy, were never able to divorce their leadership style from authoritarianism. The roots of indigenous culture persistently resist the tide of universal values. When the Soviet Union fell apart, the quest for a root culture paradigm by its member states gained momentum. Nationalism bounced back to restore the identities of people rooted in their culture. Political globalization could not break through cultural nationalism. Liberal democracy broke new ground for its role in relation to globalization, and the global movement does not progress in one direction but alternates between progress and lapse.

For liberal democracy the market is a desideratum. The market in a capitalistic perspective is an arena for rational competition, based on the Illuminist definition of man as a rational being; the ills of the world can be remedied by reason and logic. The Confucian view of morality espouses harmony that is achieved by one's submission to a greater entity. The notion of free competition in the market is rejected by the collective morality of Koreans. In the competition-based market, it is difficult to maintain moral purity free from confrontation, as argued by a collective morality, when a game gives way to a rat race. Morality free from competition rarely finds its place in the push and jostle of the modern world. Where a game is muddied by one's unlimited desires for secular goals, one's triumph means another's defeat.

The perception of liberal democracy as the terminal point is premised on the belief that the system is fixed and the historical process comes to an end with liberal democracy. Nevertheless there is no institutional device that holds its progress in abeyance. Liberal democracy is a process of change, and there is no end to this on-going process. Democracy as a process allows for the dynamics of change, and its strength lies in this respect. Human desire to resort to rules or principles for guidance has been at odds with reality, and no principle has enjoyed absolute truth in its struggle to catch up with changing reality. The concept of the free market based on laissez faire and small government reflects the cult of rationality. The assumption is that if left alone, all problems would work themselves out to be a wholly tolerable solution. Reason is an invisible hand to make it possible. It should be noted, however, that there have been more instances where reality contradicts theory. A benign God was not on the side of free enterprise and the self-correcting function of the market when the Great Depression struck America. Capitalism would not have survived, had it not been for its compromise with reality.

Old Values, Gemstone

Liberal democracy is better able to thrive in a mobile society, for it allows flexibility in human experiment with institutional devices to improve the conditions for living. The expediency of living in a mobile society is a persuasive call for value change. As Korea has taken an irrevocable step toward a pluralistic society, by its own choice or against its will, it has become imperative to locate Koreans in the world. This process may lead to a total rebuilding of a value system from scratch. This does not necessarily mean the total elimination of old elements. Any effort to build a new value tapestry involves wholesale reassessment of value components in terms of potential match with universal ones. Some traditional value components remain gem stone to be honed so that it display their luster in the process of redefinition.

All the great philosophies and religious creeds have, in the hindsight of history, been modified and reinterpreted. Korea has been a haven for Confucianism to tap root and enjoy its millennium existence. Modern Korea has its Constitution based on universal values, but traditional ones constitute the undercurrent of values as a guide to the daily behavior of Koreans. There have been legislative and institutional movements to simplify the grand and financially crippling ritual systems of ancestor worship and to lift the ban on marriage between distant blood siblings. No national campaign has made a significant contribution to de-Confucianizing Koreans. Some people stay stubborn in their position; "why is it necessary to de-Confucinize?" A Korean proverb has it: "trying to catch a rat burns a house." Those who make efforts to de-Confucianize at all are obsessed with the negative side of the ideology. "The Mafia system in Italy may adhere to Christian mores, but no anti-Mafia campaigns in Italy have suggested de-Christianizing the country. The Mafia system is also famous for its family orientation, but the fight against Mafia crime does not affect the family institution as such" (Geir Helgesen 1975,19). A Korean proverbial saying warns against de-Confucianizing at all: "Why do you have to burn a house in order to catch a flea." Centuries of Confucian practices made Koreans subscribe to a system of core values that hold together disparate components of society. "A much more realistic approach is to modernize, rationalize and utilize Confucianism to provide the social context in which democracy takes root. Such an indigenizing effort may result in the development of democracy even beyond the level of the West" (Helgesen,20). The liberal democracy that Koreans seek to realize may not be the mirror image of the western model.

The Confucian defense of a morally-cultivated citizen as a possible substitute for rational beings raises a question about its sustenance in modern society. Obviously, Confucian morality, nurtured in a collective and hierarchical society, is at odds with individual autonomy and market incentives. Koreans are trapped between an irresistible tide of egoistic individualism and the residual force of moral virtues. It comes down to a contest between rational individualism and collective morality or between individual competition and group competition. Korea did not experience a transitional stage leading to democracy; rather change was forced upon the traditional value structure, and the volatile mix of indigenous values and Western ideals peppered the tortuous course of democratic development. Some intellectuals were drawn to the democratic model of advanced countries, since it was symbolic of wealth and modernization. The word of democracy has become vogue in all spheres of life worldwide and even the communized North is not immune to the rhetorical appeal of "democracy" as expressed in the Democratic People's Republic of Korea (DPRK). Communism is concealed behind "Democratic" and the juxtaposition of two words, "democratic" and "communism," notes Brezensky, "is obviously an oxymoron. Koreans subscribe to a society of human relations analogous to the cosmological order" (Yoo Myung Jong 1976;175). A self-cultivated man endeavors to realize self perfection and free will to integrate oneself into a greater entity and he bears the character of civic consciousness. Given moral attempts to eliminate the distinction between the self and others, one may conclude that a morally cultivated Korean can substitute for a rational being idealized by the Illuminists.

The Cult of Equality

The Cult of Equality dims our vision of a new society which sees an ideal match with liberty. Equality means "everybody comes to resemble everybody else." Being equal translates into having something in common, contradicting the iron imperative of modern society to embrace diverse needs. Excessive equality denotes "uniformity or rigid conformity, repressive of individual faculties that thrive on the climate of diversity" (Lee Ki-sang,49). Equality and liberty are complementary to each other leading up to a certain stage of social development but are inherently contradictory when society seeks to achieve both to satisfaction: contentment with one comes at the curtailment of the other. Equality is often identified with absolute equality, a familiar refrain repeated by those who dreamed of a communal utopia. The popular notion of equality is the equality of possessions, susceptible to fierce competition for materialistic acquisition. But equality is not on the purse alone; the quality of life requires the restoration of a total human being, with due recognition of human value and dignity. Social order comes when equality is balanced against liberty and a failure to do so leads o the enthronement of "a free for all" competition and chaos.

The blind pursuit of equality elevates the masses of mediocrity to power and pride, and, hence, the state's authority falls into the hands of secular and anonymous masses. They take the place of men of merit and honor who opt to stay away from the indignities and indecencies of an election. Nietzsche was right to ask "how can a nation become great when its greatest men lie unused, discouraged, perhaps unknown?" His defense of aristocratic rule is echoed by Santayana. "Democracy has its own evils; not merely its corruption and impotence, but worse, its own peculiar tyranny, the worship of uniformity. It blasts every budding novelty and prig of genius with its omnipresent and fierce stupidity" (1905, 239). Imagine a society in which all constituents don equal clothes, and it goes against the law of natural restrictions – that everywhere and every time some are leaders and some are followers. The iron rule is that a few are the winners of the race. This argument for aristocracy has the tone of hereditary aristocracy. Nevertheless, "rule by the best" very likely leads to institutional rigidity, a semblance of hereditary succession, running counter to a tendency to swim with the tide. By propagating equality, modern society builds a climate that favors mass production. As mass production engenders a new trend to standardize goods, massive consumption fits persons into a standard pattern of material life. Paradoxically, a diverse society bears a resemblance to a communal society that favors excessive equality. A standard pattern of life runs afoul of the dictum of the diverse and complicated nature of modern society. By a large group it refers to the constituents who are willing to oblige themselves to common sanctions and cooperate with one another through different roles and status. Social calls for standardization turns off those who refuse to fit in, like alcoholics, drug addicts, and those of bizarre behavior. The standardization of people in terms of a life pattern will produce large numbers of misfits. Equality, when carried too far, is accompanied by 'de-humanized equality to fit them into loyal citizens to serve a state goal. Nazism and fascism are the products of loyal citizens wedded to the most benighted form of politics. The hierarchical and collective consciousness of Koreans is hostile to a pervasive view of equality and the development of public morals, but this traditional consciousness can be an anointed counter-weight to absolute equality and freedom.

The society of equal opportunity allows every man and woman of merit and ability to have an open road to the highest offices in the state. Whatever is said in favor of "rule by all the best," democracy has its own merit because it works better in a plural order by encouraging the spontaneous participation of many people in determining the destiny of the state. Diverse society lives on discriminatory encouragement. Given that society is judged by the measure in which it enhances the life and capacities of its constituent individuals, democracy is a phenomenal improvement over aristocracy. The focus of a political effort is to elevate the quality of citizens, and democracy fits this role by resting on the literacy of its constituents.

The conceptual base of democracy is the "nation state" where the people are the masters of the state, owing their loyalty to the state, not the king. Representative politics and political pluralism are not only an antidote to the exaltation of state or personality cult but generate a superior mechanism for the satisfaction of human needs. Diverse and complex human conditions breed competition and mechanisms that reward creativity. "Competition and creativity feed each other into the evolutionary change of systems toward the betterment of human conditions" (Brezensky Z, 1988,327).

The betterment of an institutional device depends on an evolutionary change based on trial and error, as a scientific discovery is an improvement over the existing stockpile of knowledge. The cause of the earlier downfall of communism consists in the outright denial of the existing system and the loss of patience with evolutionary change. South Korea has seen democratic development condensed into sixty years in comparison with centuries of experience in the forerunner countries. Democracy was distorted by the exaltation of ideological dictum over nationalism that was supposed to create an integrated nation. Particular values were hostile to democratic development. Inequality appears reactionary so far as hierarchical consciousness prevails. It lies fertile in private affairs but is mostly irrelevant when applied to public affairs.

Koreans are often blind to the distinction between the two domains of affairs. Obsession with the particular values - hierarchical and collective – renders Koreans ill-prepared to develop public consciousness rooted in the twin principle of equality and liberty. The soil of inequality hinders the growth of fairness, transparency and accountability. Presumably, the evil of democracy may be inevitable, as Koreans proceed in pursuit of a new institutional device. For all the professed defects, democracy is a process, allowing a new device to be tried out. But frustration with parliamentary impotence gives rise to a voice yearning for rule by the best. This does not mean that aristocracy is a substitute for democracy but a synthesis of the two that opens career to talent.

Collectivism vs. Individualism

Collective consciousness begins with familial relations that are presumably extendable to communities and societies. A manageable territory with stable and clear borders, and a single value system fostered the Koreans tendency to fraternize around small groups, each exclusive of others. Outsiders may be permanent strangers. "In the absence of the causes of cleavages, like those which haunted China and the European continent, Koreans tend to form molecular factions, of which the family is the strongest solidarity" (Ahn Byung Man 2003;20). For all the diminishing influence of Confucian values, discipline, social solidarity and cooperative networks are expected to remain. The Korean notion of a hierarchically structured family is not attributable to Confucianism alone; ecological and environmental factors play their role as shapers of family values.

Self autonomy was a product of expanding individualism in reverse to diminishing state power, while collective consciousness led to the strengthening of an all-embracing government. Individualism and rationality in combination obviously gave the impetus to move towards Weber's Protestant ethics. Weber portrays "Confucianism as most traditional by including elements which hinder capitalistic development" This argument contradicts Ikeman's theory which attributes the recent development of Confucian countries to familism, discipline and morality. "Confucianism, notes Weber, by stressing harmony and cooperation, "leaves no room for "a rational warfare' characteristic of competition and conflict between interest groups." The absence of armed peace was, according to him, a barren land for capitalistic development. Norman F. Cantor noted specific periods of European history when peace and state's leadership led to cultural florescence and industrial productivity. (1963,227-8).

Confucianism endeavors to eliminate feuds and confrontations, and its concern for harmony makes it possible to maintain "industrial peace" and higher productivity. This value is in contrast with the Western stand for confrontations and armed clashes from which to derive a dynamic force. The Korean notion of ethics has kept people ready for cooperative submission to the greater good of a group or society. Prudence in action and austerity in life style, though limited to a few ennobled Koreans, played their share in promoting what resembles Protestant work ethics. Nevertheless, Confucianism lacks the social spontaneity necessary to expand the circle of intimates to larger ones. Weber declares the Confucian society as comprising self-centered families and circles of blood kin and intimates, working against the pervasive nature of trust from one person to another. He further notes "mutual aid in the Confucian society is observed in the private domain and becomes diluted in the public domain."

Koreans are known for their strong solidarity so far as they are among in-group blood siblings or close intimates, and this merit diminishes as the circle of intimates becomes larger. Lee Kwan-yew, former Premiere of Singapore, sees Western societies as composed of self-centered individuals with little compassion for others beyond intimate associates whom they encounter in the daily grind. Confucianism creates an anthropocentric society where each individual is related to another. This explains why, down at the village level, the sense of a common fate remains strong. Lee's argument comes from his failure to admit the parochial nature of compassion confined to a circle of intimates but excluding strangers in Confucian societies.

An individual in a collective society is not separable from society. Theoretically, the notion of one continuum is supposed to keep individuals conscious of their society-mandated roles. Equality in a collective society has a leveling effect on earnings so that the few of wealth, far from something of envy, stick out like a nail to be hammered down. Paradoxically, egalitarianism, as observed in communist countries, strips one of his or her ability to be flexible and creative by demanding the uniformity of possession, resulting in the enthronement of lethargy, apathy and boredom. Communism asserted equality in possession, not equality in rights and power. Voltaire was right: "equality is natural when it is limited to rights, unnatural when it attempts to level goods and powers. Not all citizens can be equally strong, but they can be equally free" (Bill Durant; 1961,86).

In more complicated societies the promise of equality provides a pretext for state intervention and the curtailing of individual activity. A great deal of state control, according to Confucianism, should be exercised to keep society from being split between a few rich and the poor masses. As a social therapy against such an evil effect, it argues that efforts should be made to seek a common good for society and to keep its constituents in sight of what they are pursuing. Such a collective consciousness, by virtue of its standing for something in common, is not necessarily at odds with civic consciousness that endorses "one's right means another's duty"; both share "what is good for an individual is good for the collective entity." Collective consciousness can, then, be considered a cure for capitalistic evils. In opening the door to foreign investment, China's communist regime was scared of capitalistic evils and declared its policy dictum that the "rule of law" should go hand in hand with moral dictum. Morality is the norms of behaviors resulting from having lived in accord with a collective consciousness and is not necessarily consistent with the legal dictum. Exclusive reliance on the rule of law, according to China's projection, may inspire morally-oriented people to ignore or deliberately breach the rule of law without feeling a twinge of guilt or shame for their wrong doings. It depends on how they define morality. Authoritarian regimes were characteristic of Confucian societies that achieved remarkable economic growth. The recent economic growth of the "four little tigers" is attributed to the cultural and spiritual legacy of Confucianism, manifested in a stable family, safe streets, and a strong work ethics. Morality, according to new interpretations of Confucianism, asserts itself as compatible with the rule of law, having its own range of behavior distinct from, but overlapping with a range of law-abiding behavior.

Authoritarianism and Democracy

"A form of paternalistic authoritarianism is rapidly obtaining currency and seems able to challenge liberal democracy" (Francis Fukuyama 2006,3). As remarked earlier, authoritarianism remains strong with

Koreans, albeit considerably abated. Foreign visitors to Korean government agencies are invariably impressed with an aura of authoritarianism. A common scene is that juniors bow and cringe to seniors even when no business is involved. The authoritarian figure silences his subordinates. On the part of subordinates, the best way to behave is to bite one's tongue. Since the birth of the Republic of Korea, there have been eleven regimes, and four of them, responsible for remarkable economic development, were authoritarian to the point of openly flouting the Constitution. No dictator colors his dogmatic acts with injustice. Moral rule is elastic enough to become a tool for the seizure of power. Moral justification of undemocratic acts was the rule rather than exception in Korea. Reference to moral justification enabled the ruler to bend the rule of law. The terminal goal – to realize an enriched and politically stable society - justified putting democratic institutions in abeyance on the road to a democratic society. The so-called five binary relationships are emotional bonds to keep individuals tied to a spider's web. This network of human relations, contrived to ensure social solidarity, had the effect of freezing systems or institutional devices into change-resistant ones.

Political parties in Korea were seldom organized around an ideology, creed or class. A political party, composed of factions, each headed by an authoritarian figure, was temporarily brought under one leadership to serve a particular political goal. Having served this goal or being unable to achieve it, the party was then dissolved, with its member factions free to join other political parties or go it alone. The frequent rise and fall of political parties in Korea belies an underlying group solidarity that endures. The expediency of living within a small group drowns out the cry for getting together in a large group.

The Confucian emphasis on human relations keeps one conscious of a bond with his superior that is maintained by a lavish display of loyalty rather than competency or merit. The downside of group solidarity is the creation of a small circle that is fraternized around a prominent figure. The result is that loyalty to a boss is life-long. Such an unfailing loyalty to a person is an extension of the rock-solid filial commitment to parents. More often than not, a person in charge is insulated by a human barricade of loyalists from the voices of the grassroots. The political climate that encourages unfailing loyalty to a person raises the charismatic appeal of a person which is dramatized into playing a greater role in getting people to rally around a professed cause. Koreans show a high propensity to equate the unfailing loyalty of their subjects with their competencies. Uncritical adulation is a powerful tool for getting a job done, and the triumph of emotion over rationality is characteristic of such a privatized leadership of political party.

Syng-man Rhee, the first President of the Republic of Korea, was a highly authoritarian figure by birth. Although born into a Confucian-oriented family, he spent longer than half his life in the United States and studied at Princeton and George Washington University, working his way up to a Ph.D in political philosophy. No matter how much he was exposed to Western values, his authoritarian character was not diluted by his long stay abroad. His remarkable charisma was instrumental in getting many people to rally around him, but he fell victim to human barriers he built that kept him in mystical remoteness from the people. Such a great politician found himself deluded by the persons he trusted. The downfall of the first Republic was followed by an enfeebled, but democratic regime.

Shaken by a host of problems chaotically sprouting out of ideologically radical groups, this democratic regime was vulnerable to an imagined North Korean aggression. Democratic weakness inherent in its infant stage could hardly withstand social chaos, thus bowing to long established authoritarian politics. The short life span of the Second Republic served as a hiatus leading to the military coup on May 16, 1961. The need for a strong military power justified the illegitimate wrestling of power from an enfeebled, democratic regime; the military regime sought its rationale for political turnover in state-led economic development and the supreme concern to keep the country safe. The Second Republic was akin, by all accounts, to the Weimar Republic, democratic but weak, tittering on the way to Nazism. Democratic effeminacy could not survive troubled waters.

That authoritarianism is an obstacle to liberal democracy is refuted by Lee Kwan Yew who asserted the merit of establishing democracy on the bedrock of Confucianism. In view of Confucian incompatibility with liberal democracy, his interpretation is regarded as "a deliberate, self-serving distortion of Confucianism" as criticized by Fukuyama and Huntington. Liberal democracy was distorted to serve the authoritarian regime, as demonstrated by the political experience of South Korea. The Confucian notion of social harmony is supposed to be feasible when there is no challenge to the ruling authority, and power has to be unitary, free from all potential conflicts and dissidence on which democracy develops. The authoritarian regimes were hasty and daring in performing what has been considered impossible to justify their illegal seizure of power.

For authoritarian politics, liberal democracy appears to thrive on the loud voices of the mediocre majority while great men lie unheeded. Democratic politics are confrontational with rivalry, prone to revenge and counter revenge, alien to harmony-conscious Koreans. Able men are subject to the indignities and indecencies of elections. Nietzsche advocated the merciless nature of his pessimism about democracy, resounding his plea for authoritarian rule by a few able men. "Democracy means drift, permission given to each part of an organism to do just what it pleases, the relapse of coherence and interdependence, and enthronement of liberty and chaos" (1961;324)[4]. His thought, could find resonance among Korean authoritarian leaders. Democracy, nevertheless, is not to blame for all chaos; it is a counter weight to the evils of despotic rule. The flaws of authoritarian rule are made clear when it stands against a liberal democracy capable of managing the complicated issues of modern society. Democracy requires the art of orchestrating different opinions into inter-play and compromise.

After the termination of the military regime, development reached a plateau of stagnation alternating between ups and downs, and the personal leadership of the president was regarded as a key to breakthrough. Authoritarian rule has no institutional buffer that cushions the flaws of personal leadership. It is easy, on the other hand, for such a prominent figure to ride a tide of personal popularity by performing a dashing feat that could hardly be imagined by a consensus-seeking democratic leader. The institutional base of democracy, however, was further consolidated by Koreans' experience with authoritarian rule. Authoritarian leadership gives utmost importance to the moral dominance of personal leadership, and every reshuffle of power makes the new president avow moral refreshment. However, the late years of each regime were smudged by the immoral acts of those surrounding the president. Korean youngsters denounce authoritarianism as the seedbed for corruption. But it cannot be said that corruption is the direct descent of authoritarianism. Rather, corruption is an outgrowth of one party that has monopolized power over many years. Roh Moo-hyun's enthronement to power, despite his radical activist proclivity, owed much to the massive support of youngsters in anticipation of his daring act to dismantle traditional hierarchies and fight against corruption.

Roh's dramatic rise to the presidency owed much to the public expectation of his daring act to fight authoritarianism. His radical approach to reform, defying seniority rule based on age or years of service in the appointment of cabinet members, was aborted and brought about a conservative backlash. This spoke for the depth of seniority rule ingrained in the daily life of Koreans. Authoritarianism is a product of hierarchical consciousness; even the rebellious youngsters who started with reformative zeal, once they have obtained bureaucratic posts, are frozen into inertia and unable to initiate reforms. So far as hierarchical consciousness remains with Koreans, there is little chance for equality in its true sense to permeate Koreans' consciousness. Equality is in an inverse relation to freedom; unrestrained equality brings various forms of pernicious consequences, and laissez faire leads to chaos.

There is no denying that economic development generates outcries for democracy, and this holds true of the development of South Korea, if one looks at process in a longer perspective. But economic growth took off the ground during an authoritarian regime. This regime was credited with a dashing and resolute act to break through chronic problems in the shadow of the residual values. South Korea, Indonesia, Singapore and Taiwan defy "a strong correlation between successful economic development and the growth of democratic institutions" (Francis Fukuyama 2006.344). Korean workers, attuned to a hierarchical order, tend to perform well when they are in company with a competent boss. In addition, Korean workers perform better when inspired by the magnitude of work entrusted to them. Authoritarian leadership and self-directed performance in combination resulted in the phenomenal growth of South Korea.

Personal leadership proves to be effective when it is based on rational authoritarianism. With the activation of an authoritarian role, loyalty breaks ground for new possibilities. The economic success of South Korea is a case where workers' loyalty to a person was converted to loyalty to a system, company or cause, and this is manifested in personal sacrifice for the greater good of a larger entity. Authoritarian rule under a contingency situation served as a catalyst for turning a group potential into stunning accomplishment. A softened authoritarianism is called "rational authoritarianism" which combines a great deal of rationality and a silent forcefulness. The result is that group consensus prevails over individual rights.

A disciplined leadership, wedded to collective consciousness, turned the dormant quality of Koreans into an exceptional work ethic. This work ethics has produced workers dedicated to self improvement. Collective consciousness creates a shared frame of reference which agrees on a common virtue that society seeks to achieve. In contrast to the American emphasis on the rule of law and social contract, the Confucian mind sees an ideal in a community based on consanguineous ties. Great social harmony was the strong point of Confucianism, but factional strife belies the promise of solidarity. Korean society is characterized by an emotional pendulum easily alternating between social harmony and factional fragmentation. This explains the difficulty of achieving appeasement or rapprochement between hostile factions. A self-claimed compromiser, no matter whatsoever his motive, is perpetually stigmatized as a traitor. Authoritarianism divorced from rational thinking offers no promise of individual autonomy. The authoritarian regimes allowed for no rival factions in South Korea: each regime was toppled by another one in the vicious cycle of dominance (Ahn Byung-man, 2003; 108). Social harmony, envisioned by Confucianism, is defined in terms of something free from discord, challenge or threat to the existing order. Such a society is based on the premise that every member should be an educated man with an assortment of probity, austerity, discipline, and asceticism, but a majority of citizens are far from this ideal.

Authoritarian regimes were dismissed as a barren land for civic consciousness. Vincent Brant noted some elements of the communitarian spirit in the rural villages, compatible with liberal democracy. He draws attention to "the communitarian value, generally associated with Confucianism, as the ethical source of participation, presumably related to self sublimation of Koreans to a group, observable down at the village level"(1971, 34). As one moves toward a larger circle of association, however, the communitarian spirit thins out. Koreans' limited identification with others beyond members of their clannish circles keeps their loyalties confined to molecular groups.

Digital Populism

As we have observed, the ideological grip on nationalism in Korea was the primary cause of student activism, and this ideological orientation activated the students' role in political liberalization and struggles against authoritarianism. "The present stage of political liberalization is the result of students-led anti-government struggles wedded to the process of industrialization" (translated from Kwon Tae-joon, 2006;437). Democracy for the masses has taken a new turn as the masses harnessed technological advances. Korea is highly advanced in communication technology, and this had a tremendous amount of influence on politics. The so-called digital politics are gaining currency as the masses are exposed to cyber space such as the internet and twitter, capable of enlarging the circle of shared views in just a few seconds.

One example came in March 2008 with the expression of a public furor over the government's decision to import American beef. The hasty government decision brought hundreds of thousands candle light vigils on the streets in protest, and this shows how even forged or erroneous information circulating on the internet moved the mob to improvise a collective sentiment imbued with hostility. A media focus on a mad cow being slaughtered in the United States rapidly spread through the internet and mass com, inciting angry mothers with their babies to street demonstrations. A fabricated scene panicked the country into chaos. This incidence amply demonstrated the omnipotent power of media and the possibility of putting the populace up to false or fabricated information. Those who consider themselves the down-trodden were the first to agitate the people and took psychological comfort in finding like-minded people. Within cyber space, everyone can enjoy freedom of expression without a sense of social accountability, and some regard digitization as a road to an institutional "utopia" in which direct democracy can be realized by its constituents enjoying equality.

The notion of an institutional utopia is refuted by Albert Razlo Barabashi's Destopia where a few agitators win over the majority; a digital society is a hub dominated by a few, a network that departs significantly from a utopia future. Conditions are ripe for a sensitive issue to be politicized to achieve a goal distinct from what it is intended for. Technological development stirred populism awake to dominate society. Plutarch warned against populism in the Roman era; "running along with the masses ruins politics in the hands of the masses and following the likes of the masses plunges politics into a collateral fall with the masses." Jose Ortega Gasset, the Spanish philosopher, took a step further by declaring "Populism is anathema to culture and reason. The society which vests the masses with power to suppress reason and rationality is bound to go maniac in favor of counter culture." A typical example is readily available; Nazism took advantage of populism with the masses following an extreme rightist nationalism and the "Red Guard" in China followed an extreme leftist nationalism, dulling the sense of righteousness in their maelstrom.

Technological advances fuel debates to take place in the plaza, cyber space, cell phones and even human hearts, whose utility has been demonstrated in gauging the depth of public opinion and mobilizing them into political platforms. While digital politics is commended for its merits, it entails the potential risk of spreading flawed information. It has no screening mesh through which to filter information. The flipside of this phenomenon is the danger of mobilizing the masses into a flawed political cause. It becomes more likely that effects of misinformation, miscalculation or a factual error will magnify into a calamitous result. Popular sentiment fostered around an issue whose topicality is heightened by media coverage, is not necessarily an effective guidepost to political decision. The intractable nature of populism derives from sensational journalism in constructing the emotion of the public sphere.

The triumph of emotion over reason blurs the path to the future, ushering in "mobocracy." The wisdom of modern politics relies heavily on a seasoned political leadership that can see through the scrub of trivia to distant trees. A political movement in favor of mass democracy does not rule out the possibility that the quest for a policy option to serve the best public interest is marred by a misguided or myopic popular sentiment. The mass media finds its potent force in swaying popular sentiment. It is imperative that a policy decision should not be locked in a time-specific frame of reference, if it is to yield a far-sighted vision. A populist movement based on a collective motive, swayed by superficial focus, cannot but be mistaken in a modernized society, since this dulls one's ability to discern "good" from "bad" amid the massive influx of information and presence of so many options. Populism, however, is something to go with democracy, so long as politicians listen to the voices of the people. In order for democracy to embrace populism as a political agenda, it should find a group of supporters who would bring ideas into institutional processes.

Rational reasoning based on a broad base of information is less potent in influencing political decision than the instantaneous reactions of the masses in the digital era. Their reactions are instantaneously improvised by a media focus and, therefore, are prone to sway on the spur of emotions. The speed with which information spreads and rallies like-minded individuals has become the most potent factor to impress people with the truth of a given matter. Technological breakthroughs elevate "digital populism" over rationality or reason, drastically altering the fundamental principle of representative politics which has been considered the terminal point of the human experiment with institutional governance. As observed in various incidents, digital populism has advanced to such an extent that it characterizes today's Korean politics.

Early in 1968, Walter Cronkite, aghast at the globally pervasive impact of a group of French students rebelling against their school systems, drew a disturbing conclusion: "It seemed clear that public demonstrations were being staged for television. Some street demonstrations are good television. You can't put that as the only reason they were in the streets; demonstrations took place before television, but this was an added incitement to demonstration" (Mark Kurlansky,1988;102). A crowd incited to street demonstrations is guided by a truth clothed in populism. Those intoxicated with a sense of accomplishment through street demonstrations are mired in a world improvised by created imagery. Improvised decisions goaded by fellow travelers is something that characterizes the effervescence of youth culture, A cell phone message galvanizes politically indifferent youngsters to create a last minute surge in the polls as they vote for an underdog candidate Roh Moohyun. Some of them take no time to read materials about candidates to make an informed decision about a favorite candidate. Voting patterns under the influence of advanced technology takes a new turn toward emotion-dominant politics.

Digital politics challenges the moral dictum of "freedom entails self-discipline."By hiding within the artificial environment, people feel less need to bear the consequences of their own actions. "Technology," notes Moeller, "is crowding out human interaction, taking us into a world of communication and interaction among humans, but with actually very little human contact." People spend more time on social networks with others they are not familiar with and they become insensitive, even callous, to the sufferings of fellow human beings. This new political phenomenon is also the result of an aggrandized civil society. Civil society has carved out a sizeable domain for itself from the market and state. Rational decision-making in the traditional sense meant the freedom to choose policy options that would serve the best interest of a greater whole. Modern politics is no longer a tug of war between the market on one end and the state on the other. With the addition of civil society, it has become a tripartite competition. Civil chord binds groups of various interests into one, and the most influential of these groups are the dissidents who identify themselves as democratic crusaders. They are antithetical freaks notorious for their sustained challenge to the government.

These democratic crusaders have a strong grip on the sentiment of the masses. It is not fair, though, to categorically dismiss mass sentiment as foolhardy. There is often greater shrewdness and wisdom among the masses when intellectuals and elites become spoiled or are not trusted. Emotional appeals are justified in digital politics. So in the post-modern society, emotional passion is something to be lived with. The exaltation of reason is giving way to emotion in modern politics. When it comes to something vulnerable to public furor, the usual admonition has been "let go of emotion." Since all public furors cannot be justified, we should be able to discern the distinction between private and public furor. A blurred distinction between the two makes the public furor highly susceptible to being privatized so that it serves personal interests. The heart of the matter is how to cool down emotions, and one way is to use an earlier furor as a preventive mechanism against its recurrence. Public furor turns into political passion that very likely fall a prey to a misguided political goal. Stalin and Hitler were extraordinarily skillful in the exploitation of political passion with disciplined organizations.

Nonetheless, there seem to be formidable odds against controlling such a public furor in democracies. As digital politics evoke the masses into political participation – every one fancies himself as a political expert, civil society drifts into a semblance of an amorphous structure, aggravating the difficulty of orchestrating diverse social demands into political programs. The amorphous structure, together with the complexity of social conditions, makes it more difficult to predict what a policy decision leads to; a policy decision has become a risky gambit, something like going blind toward an imagined destination. Statesmanship in modern politics represents an ability to balance popular sentiment, whether blown out of proportion or not, against the rational dictum of reality, and this requires a perspective that transcends the whims and notions of the moment.

Digital populism, coupled with regional loyalties, has an unprecedented amount of influence on popular election. Partisanship in Korea is largely grounded in regional horizon. Regional partisanship is a ubiquitous phenomenon worldwide, but partisanship obsessed with local interests in Korea has an emotional touch. "Regional solidarity is not the product of rational decisions but that of local sentiment. If manipulated with care, it can ensure for party bosses a territorially limited but politically impregnable power base" (Kim Byung-kook, 1995; 10). The party boss resembles a feudal lord of Medieval Europe and this contradicts the Confucian definition of the state as an extended family.

Local-Based Partisanship

Outsiders may wonder at the fact that Korea, proud of its ethnic and cultural homogeneity, has a strong local partisanship. Every circle of association has an instinctive will to stretch its fraternity to larger ones that develop into statehood and nationalism. Centrifugal force is at work pushing the circle of associations outward and bounces back when it comes to a halt. In reality, it rarely goes beyond its regional boundaries when a regional solidarity is firmly entrenched. A political party depends on regional support for its bid for power on the central stage. Local partisanship is, in large measure, not so much the result of regional particulars as a political reaction to discriminatory treatment of a particular region by power elites. And this practice was typical of the military regimes that passionately stood for economic growth. In the discriminated region, a strong political fraternity is shaped to ensure a regional solidarity against other regions and such a trend has more to do with Koreans' proclivity to reliance on personal connections and emotional bonds.

Partisanship is clearly displayed in presidential elections. In the southwestern provinces, for example, 98 percent of votes were cast for the local favorite, Kim Dae-jung, in his 1998 bid for the presidency. The locally-based political party evoked emotional reactions that defied rational explanation. Kim's rise to the presidency was a rare case of success where a strong local solidarity overpowered a nationwide electoral coalition. A small group proud of its solidarity was the winner of the power contest. In view of the strong penchant for a small group, local partisanship is taken for granted.

Another noteworthy feature of Korean politics is "an oligarchic occupation of power, as practiced during the Sixth Republic, based on collusion or compromise between a few factional leaders, and this accounts for a retarded political development in Korea" (Choi Jang-jip and Lim Hyun-jin 2010, 19). No party, organized by a temporary sharing of power for the expedient display of unity, fared long, since party organization was dictated by the urgency of overcoming an pressing problem at hand. Intrinsically, there is no long-term perspective that defines the implications of a political turnaround beyond the whims of the present.

"European regionalism is a mere reflection of simmering religious and class conflict that happen to coincide with territorial zones" (Choi and Lim 2010, 11). The feudal legacy left its marks on the formation of a small sovereign state in a particular region insulated from other societies. Religious and class cleavages divided individuals into hostile blocs of "us" versus "them." Such a region has a clearly defined religious or class belief that favors the formation of a political party in support of an ideological or political platform. Class interest and religious creed feed the party with a political agenda. The fallacy of regional partisanship is made clear by liberal democracy that thrives on the soil of autonomous individualism. Historical progressivism is based on individuals being capable of exercising rationality in pursuit of their interests.

"Each Korean draws numerous concentric circles around the self, expandable to a large one, and these circles are supposed to overlap and join together individuals of different classes and backgrounds" (Kim Byung Kuk 1997,25). It is within the concentric circles that an individual seeks his or her own identity. Humans long to stay with a network of relations, and it may be difficult for the Western concept of individualism to take root in the collective-oriented, spider's web-like society. While Confucianism is blamed for its exclusionary parochialism, it offers a way out of a biased partisanship if Koreans develop a superior state of mind called "jung'yong."[5] Jung Yong calls for a careful synthesis and balancing of practical and moral needs lest one veers toward an extremity. But human nature rarely conforms to this ideal moral dictum, especially when one occupies a powerful position. Jung'yong literally means the "middle way" - standing for moderate character- not given to a volatile temperament. It stands for reconciling extremely opposed forces with a resolute stance for professed goal. Such a state of mind is subject to misinterpretation as being "fickle" or "flappable" in an emotion-charged climate. "Realistic outlook" is a word to fit the character of a moderate man. The emotion-dominant society is culturally inappropriate to make an appeal for the middle way.

Truly, "we live for particular shared historical traditions, religious values and other aspects of shared memory that constitute the common life" (Francis Fukuyama 2006, 343) That modern liberal democracy has its roots in Christian culture begs a question of whether the twin principles of liberty and equality have universal relevance to non-Christian cultures. Samuel Huntington clearly believes that liberty and equality are not universal. He points to "the kind of political system Westerners are familiar with that will never take root beyond the boundaries of that culture." The kind of institution we envision for the future will be the product of our own culture and values. Culture is an irreducible component of society and will assert itself as the major determinant of a political and institutional framework.

Human Bonds Broken Loose

Human bonds are increasingly ephemeral and transient as society ages. Their loosening networks of human bonds break new ground on which individualism thrives. Individualism inherently encroaches upon group solidarity. Youth in particular refuse to be buried by traditional values and tend to pursue something that entertains the senses. New affluence numbs their sensitivity to what is meant by a steady and fast human relationship. They are freewheeling in behaviors, no-holds barred in thought and rebellious against the established order. Many do not appreciate what comes from the sweat of one's brow. Being a salary-man brings a lot one has to endure. Getting up early even in winter, crushing into a commuter train, working late and drinking with superiors ---- they don't want to get on the corporate treadmills. A live-for-the-moment mentality has taken hold of the minds of youngsters. Their thirst for excitement and novelty is not easily satisfied through their ritualized life. Korean workers are conscious of the hierarchy of jobs that are classified into "ennobled vs. base" and "prestigious vs. dirty" and increasingly turn up their noses at the latter. What has become of the self-sacrificing work ethic that made Korea a new focus of the world's lime light? Japan makes no distinction between noble and low jobs: each, whether to be a carpenter or cook, seeks professional perfection, and this probably was the national character that buttressed its economic growth.

Wealth is said to ennoble one's appetite, but, more frequently, it makes one prone to frivolous acts against a long and hard thinking. Ephemeral trends in tandem with liberalism shake up the binary mode of human relationships, permeating all aspects of life. It sets free a new force that splits the binary bond apart between the self and others. Loyalty binds the ruler and subjects with a strong and enduring attachment based on mutual trust. Even such a bond yields animosity between "you and me", when the two are not on the same side.

Paternalism, once dominated by austere authoritarianism, is changing in favor of an affection-dominant intimacy. Depending on the degree of intimacy, parents may simply possess a child or wrap him around their fingers as if he were a perpetually dependent being. But this trend generates a new form of undifferentiated relationships. More often, mother and child are fused into what resembles one body, while husband and wife seem to be dichotomized due to their role distinction. Women in the past more often found themselves fused into the lives of their husbands. Once the relationship goes beyond its pre-ordained boundaries, extending to the people whom they do not consider part of 'us,' it then turns into a tension-ridden relationship, subject to competition or hostility. Koreans rarely nod friendly greetings to strangers. Many foreigners are baffled by Korean eye-to-eye stares that lack facial expression.

With a few exceptions, the tendency is that "the same binary relationship may remain undifferentiated or clearly differentiated, depending on whether the relationship is shaped within the circle of intimates or outside"(Kim Jae Eun 1991;216).The friend-friend relationship sees its depth nestled in a parochial circle of associations but crumbles before the imperative of living in a mobile society where friendship ought to be pervasive and superficial. Reliability in friendship is in decline.

Confucian sages contrived the paradigms of human relations which would help to realize liberal democracy. But parochial circles with a high degree of solidarity dims any vision of larger identities that would obscure ideal relations. The diminished influence of binary relationship gives rise to a tension-ridden relationship between parents and children. Some rowdies – untouched by social inhibitions - treat their parents badly, to say nothing of physical abuse and patricide. What seemed to be a timeless value now struggles against ephemeral or unrestrained tendencies. It is imperative that we re-define and re-interpret the cultural tradition in terms of its compatibility with the alien nature of democracy and individual freedom. Again, Koreans should learn to cross the threshold of the private domain into a larger public domain.

Liberalism and human rights are quintessential elements to democracy. Nevertheless, these two values refuse to stay partners. John Locke stated freedom presupposes self-discipline. Excessive liberalism, according to his argument, leads to the collapse of shared values that hold groups together. The Confucian defense of human bonds is based on the premise of mutual respect, but the bonds are prone to collapse when excessively exposed to liberalism. Restrained liberty reflects a greater concern for the price to be paid by others. Some attribute the rise of liberalism and human rights to Christianity. But "we must remember that the medieval Christian tradition was not so hospitable to either liberalism or human rights thought"(Kang Jung-in 2000;76). Liberalism was a concomitant accompaniment of secularization following the Reformation. Liberalism in the reason-dominant world traces its origin to the French Revolution and Manchester liberalism, with the digressive result of paving the way to new tide of movement to build a socialistic utopia.[6]

The perception of liberalism by Korean enlightened reformists is far distanced from the Illuminist concept of liberalism; rather it reflects the interpretation of Fukuzawa Yukichi (1835-1901), a prominent sage of Post-Meiji Japan[7]. He downplayed the cult of individualism as an impediment to the awareness of individual obligations to the state. The consequent constraining of individual autonomy is in contrast with the Western liberalism that emerged from the state's atrophy. Fukuzawa's skewed view of individual autonomy runs afoul of an individual being the agent of moral practice. The Western view of liberalism vests humans with "an ability to make an informed moral decision, free to expand their association with people in the same ideological chord and to remonstrate unflinchingly with government officials and to burden themselves with fighting for social justice" (Tikhonov Vladmir 2005;280-281). Fukuzawa's notion of individual autonomy needs to be re-fashioned to be reconcilable with the collective value of Koreans. Likewise, family in the context of civil society is not to be treated as an impediment but as a strength that is capable of generating communitarian partnership. "Similarly, the Asian people's attribution of economic development and democracy to their cultural tradition must be interpreted as an effort to re-appropriate and re-interpret their own tradition as something that is compatible with democracy and economic prosperity"(Kang Jung-in 2000;72). A new version of dynamism finds its resonance in the utilitarian interpretation of Confucianism.

Behavioral Constraints in Cultural Homogeneity

Koreans are heading toward the so-called 'cultural pluralism. What society will be like may be glimpsed by looking at multi-ethnic or cultural societies like the United States and Canada, though there is much more to differentiate Korean society from them. American society is no longer a big melting pot but a co-habitation of different cultures popularly termed a "salad-bowl." The United States bears a resemblance, in many respects, to the European continent, a conglomerate of autonomous states made up of distinct but over-lapping cultural layers. What divides the European continent is language, culture and religion, and not its borders or political jurisdictions. There are common networks of historical and cultural identities that cut across all countries, providing a fertile ground for scientific discoveries, counter cultures, fads and other cross-border contamination of ideas.

The citizens of these pluralistic societies are the first to experience new things and flashes of new ideas coming from the cross-fertilization of different cultures. For all the good things about it, society's ostensibly smooth transition was not without bumps in the road toward the integration of conflicting voices. There are a marginalized few who refuse to join the mainstream. During the Vietnam War and immediately thereafter, it seemed that American society was badly shaken by nationwide protests, followed by the counter culture movements. Joyce Carol Oath portrayal of the "emotional wasteland of the American family"[8] was a vivid account of how a middle class family slid on a slippery slope into moral decline. The European continent had gone through the same process of transformation after the early 1960s violent upheaval triggered by the student riots in France.

Despite a tide of new problems that had battered western societies, they survived crises. Feminist militancy has subsided. Homo sexuality today finds itself in a highly tolerant environment without having to make exaggerated claims about their identity. Black panthers reigning in the 1960s have turned into quiet oblivion. Korean society is least tolerable of these quirks. What made it possible to survive crisis? In Western societies, the ballast of the state ship was at work, allowing the center to hold firm and leave more space at the margins for those who don't fit in. Social consensus was hard to come by, but pluralistic societies succeeded in moderating new cultures in the process and wove them into a new fabric with older ones.

Unhindered by the repressive norms and class biases from the outset, Americans are more liberal and free-wheeling than their European counterparts. Their strong suspicion of inherited authority and their almost infinite faith in an individual right to steer his own destiny provides foundation for supporting individual creativity and self-assertiveness. Americans in general are more disposed to try new things, and pragmatism sees cultural changes as a fact of life. At the same time, there is a conservative side to it, which puts a brake on impulsive urges. Cultural pluralism decelerates changes and is the crucible in which such changes are tested over time. Publicized debates over abortion, feminism, identity politics and other contemporary issues seem so bizarre to Koreans who have tiptoed a narrow beaten path. Democracy ensconced in a complicated social fabric - diversified by religion, ethnic identity, and culture - sensitizes these issues and very often elevates them to controversial themes in a presidential election. A hybrid culture enhances the range of human possibilities - even beyond the reach of those who see virtue in one system and uniformity.

In a society where tradition holds firm and fast, its old customs thwart the spread of new ways of life in a way that erodes a society's capability of dealing with new problems. Due to its built-in low tolerance for behavioral diversity, such a society may go bust with a massive influx of absurdities, unless efforts are made to expand the range of human possibilities and tolerance. Social consensus within a group is easy to come by, but it reduces societal capability of dealing with what is way off the beaten path. A sociological principle holds that a society is held together best when it commands a set of shared values that defines the virtues society seeks to uphold, together with a strong commitment to shared purposes and a clear sense of social responsibility. In patrimonial societies, culture and values matter more than ideology or institutions in providing social solidarity. For those who are accustomed to a mono-cultural society, the mosaic society seems to be held together by thin threads of shared values and is liable to fall apart at the seams. What holds these societies together are a common ideological and institutional framework built on genetic-based social behaviors.

Societies based on emotional bonds were built from the top down, whereas those bound by ideological and institutional sharing were built from the bottom up. The social mechanism which draws on ideology and institutions is weak in countering disintegrating forces. By stressing diversity based on institutions but not the cultural elements, society may diminish its already weak and weakening commonalities and face the danger of falling apart. Tocqueville, Weber and many other observers of American society pointed out "America has never resembled a 'sand heap of atomized individuals,' because other factors (such as the sectarian character of American Protestantism) have exerted a powerful counter-veiling pressure in a more group-oriented direction" (Francis Fukuyama 2006,6).

Given this sociological principle, Korean society built on a highly homogenized culture and a deep foundation of shared value is supposed to fare better. Such societies show a greater sense of conformity to customary norms and find it easier to compromise personal goals with the greater good of society. It is thought to make it easier to achieve social consensus from the top down and from the center out to the provinces. Nevertheless, this projection has proved to be wrong. There is a greater need for its members to get out of their cultural limits to cope with diverse social variables. Global trends jolt society out of its entrenchment and put it on the move toward pluralistic society in which transnational migration takes a new meaning but comes with new challenges.

South Korea is mounting the tide of being new "host country" to foreign workers, with an estimated 2,000,000 transnational migrants within its borders. It is fairly clear that the transnational migration of people to South Korea will not only continue, but brings increasingly more significant and extremely contentious issues. The value of transnational labor comes not only from the jobs they fill but the ability of the host society to treat them fairly in accord with native workers. The cultural framework that has held Koreans together is no longer relevant, as society is transformed toward a post-modern society. In a global society in which human rights, social justice and democracy are celebrated, the exploitation and oppression of minority groups as inferior has become less and less tenable. The parochial view of the nation as comprising a people of common descent disqualifies the people who have acquired citizenship by immigration or inter-racial marriage. As Korea has taken an irrevocable move toward a hybrid society, the traditional concept of nationhood will clash with the mandates of a pluralistic society.

No society refuses to change. Once Korea has taken an irrevocable step toward a pluralistic one, there is no returning to the past. Those values that stand for the merits of Confucian societies may become an obstacle to Korea's move toward a pluralistic society. Otherwise, these Confucian values may be drowned out by a tidal surge of individualism, freedom, diversity and democracy. Authoritarianism, for example, is the legacy of the past against which the younger generations are most rebellious. As we observed, however, this traditional value, instead of being replaced, is transformed from a paternalistic to a rational or soft authoritarianism, redefining what it means to be a father or a senior figure. Koreans espouse equality and freedom in public affairs or politics. In the same breath, they apply these values to the family – recasting the traditional hierarchical bond into a partnership relationship. For all the plausible pretensions they present, the concept of partnership rarely finds its foothold in the hierarchical family that is strict about gender or role distinctions. One cannot but wonder. "Is it possible to maintain familial solidarity if it is built on equality and individualism?"; "How to reconcile value inconsistencies between the public and personal domains?" It seems that solidarity is ensured at the cost of equality. Obviously, the blind cult of equality is detrimental to social solidarity.

Diversity within unity and bonded pluralism are new concepts that capture the image of a mosaic society held together by the common frame of ideology and institutions. Unity does not require blending but rather thrives on recognition and appreciation of differences. There is no compelling reason to assimilate diverse values into one indistinguishable blend or to remove all traces of previous ancestry and their cultural hyphens. There will come a time when Afro-Koreans will enjoy their civic rights as much as native Koreans. The sociological trick is to leave some room for the enriching particulars while sustaining the shared values, institutions, and public policies that keep people together.

Traditional values firmly entrenched amidst the legacies of the past is characteristic of a small and homogenized country. The extended family system of Korea refers to an extraordinary obsession with family solidarity. So far as the family is considered in terms of an inter-dependent network to call on, not as a residential unit like a conjugal family, clashes between anthropocentric and anonymous worlds follow. An extended family system is a counter-weight to spontaneous and flexible networks. Many extol the extended family system, but the paradox is that it grows in tandem with traditional values - connectedness, favoritism, authoritarianism and provincialism. Any attempt to battle against authoritarianism, for example, necessarily involves one in struggles against hierarchical and collective consciousness. They are mutually reinforcing and form an invincible whole to resist new values. Nonetheless, a series of catastrophic events, though apart in time, are eating away each of these traits. Traditional values still remain, albeit abated with time. Still they do not allow new values to substitute for old ones on a selective basis.

A transient return to the past was a knee-jerk reaction to cultural imperialism, not a straightforward manifestation of the past, as it were; the past is in the process of being reshaped in an evolving cultural and historical context. In connection with the political domain, the quest for democracy led the way to a series of political movements to assault on authoritarian regimes. Economic growth is supposed to bring new cries for political democratization, but this axiom takes time to bear out in Korea. To say the least, economic growth paralleled authoritarian rule. Koreans have experienced various kinds of clashes between individual and collective norms and between equality and hierarchy. A confusing blend of the two continues to annoy Koreans.

Going Left?

Ideological confrontation stunted Koreans' efforts to realize liberal democracy. Korea, being the first victim of the cold war in the bipolarized world, has much to say about its experience with communism, and an ideological confrontation is still an on-going drama that is not likely to end within the foreseeable sight. To complicate matters, South Korea is confronted with new Marxists growing at home. Given the logic of reunification as a historical dictum, an overriding question is "what will be the political identity of a unified Korea?" This question takes us back to post-liberation Korea mired in endless bickering over the same issue. Ideology is not a matter of "right or wrong" but that of value choice. But the "right-or-wrong dichotomy makes Koreans slog it out until a winner is evident over a loser. The middle roaders lost ground to stand on in a situation of extreme dichotomies.

Communism is an outgrowth of a particular time when the deteriorating conditions of workers evoked an intransigent pessimism about capitalistic society then on a chilly slide into a collective ruin. The concept of workers' utopia had not been tried out on an institutional base when the Soviet Union was born to embody this concept. It was a passionate reaction to what appeared to be a wretched and pitiful state of the downtrodden. Nightmarish experience with capitalistic evils brought an attempt to build a new society divorced from reality. But the time has long since gone when revolutionary zealots thrilled the world with fanatic zeal. Ideology is an organism that goes the cycle of birth, maturity, decline and death. The notion of absolute equality is far from achieving a paradise that entitles everyone to the joy of life. Voltaire was right about the nature of equality. "Those who say that all men are equal speak the greatest truth if they mean that all men have an equal right to liberty, to the possession of their goods, and to the protection of the laws." (Will Durant 1961,186)

The ethnic homogeneity of Koreans is grounded in the history in which they have shared ethnic, cultural and political bonds over a longer period than any other ethnic groups. As a result, there is an accord among ethnic, cultural and political identities that is rarely noticed elsewhere. Their shared experiences and values, however, crumbled before the seductive voice of an ideology they had not heard of. The long-protracted territorial division impresses the world as it is likely to be fixed into a permanent border. What is this ideology all about that produces the visceral pain of the dispersed families? What made Korea experience the unique nature of an ideological struggle, distinct from those of the other divided countries? Does it have something to do with the traits of Koreans?

In light of its millennia-old history as a unitary country, the present demarcation line is rather a blink of the eyes. Reunification of the two Koreas is an absolute dictum, but this stirs awake a sentimental longing to triumph over a realistic assessment of the situation. Nostalgia for the past summons an outcry for a hasty unification, drowning out voices for a rational and cautious approach to a viable order. Younger generations, particularly political activists, are all for a hasty reunification, making a chorus with their Northern partners, but few understand what will come out of hasty unification. The south-north confrontation gave rise to confrontational politics as the order of the day in the south, as seen in the imperviousness of contemporary politicians to reconciliation and compromise. Confrontational politics not only drains Korea of energy for development but misguides people about democracy and morality. The parliamentary function of South Korean government often comes to a halt on account of extreme confrontations.

The leftists at home, most active in the 1980s, changed their stripes to progressives. Some of them turned around in stance as they came of age. Hard core elements, though, are never swayed by the truth of the matter simply because it contradicts the cause they had fought for. Every verifiable argument fails to move them around and to alter their ideological stand, though they were not to mirror communism, as it were, in North Korea. Their ideological passion overwhelms a reasonable conjecture, oblivious of the fact that politics based on a single vision is dehumanizing and coercive. Their stand for an ideological cause finds comfort in their cult of an ethnic bond, bemoaning the tragic separation of beloved ones. And yet ethnic nationalism is not sufficient to explain the on-going confrontation. Neo-Marxists stand pat for a hasty reunification, creating the imagery of them having sympathy with the dispersed families. Nothing is more urgent for the dispersed families to see their beloved ones, and the neo-Marxists are there to placate their bruised souls. But their propitiatory gestures meet the apathy of the dispersed families. The majority of the refugees from the north, particularly those who defected to the south prior to the Korean war, were from wealthy families or highly educated to distinguish them from the pack. They were condemned to hell fire, merely because they were blessed with wealth and cultural capital. By defecting to the south, they chose to be the uneasy masters of their own fates over the blissful ignorance of slaves.

The leftists' yearning for a new utopia is cloaked under their pleas for a peace agreement, beneath which lies an outcry for the withdrawal of foreign troops from Korea. In this move, the younger could not remain aloof from the professed logics of the north-proposed "confederated Korea," the merging of the diametrically opposed parts, each allowed to maintain its unique ideology and institutions, with a federal government created to manage the affairs of common interest. But the outlook for a confederated Korea is murky. The notion of the confederation is predicated on the sharing of democratic principles and institutional commonality. Otherwise, it is a castle built on a sand bank, tottering to extinction.

A headlong move for reunification, however, cost them an opportunity to be sober and smooth the bumpy road to an abiding social order. Unification touches the weak spot of Koreans and this runs the risk of driving them into an ideological cage from which one has no easy escape. The unification should be something that transcends the whims and vagaries of the present. It may take decades to cure the psychological damages even after physical damages are cured. Although time seemed to condemn Marxism, neo-Marxists refuse to be swayed in their stand for a new version of utopia. Their idolatrous faith in the new utopia appears to be out of place in this most dynamic part of the world. Utopia never allows itself to be within human reach, like a shadow eluding human's catch. Man's sense of blissfulness is momentary, as it leads to another desire yet to be met: a true sense of happiness lies in anticipation of it. Hegel is right to say: "life is not made for happiness but for accomplishment." Historical progressivism has long since declared the ideological concept of utopia as anachronistic.

To recent North Korean defectors who risked their lives to seek a new life, South Korea is no longer a dream land. They have their hopes shattered by an exotic land in which they find themselves to be a permanent misfit. They have renounced the tyrannical but protective hand of the communist government and are thrown to a free-for-all competition. A large segment of old Eastern Germans are still said to be retrospective of good old days when they were sheltered by the protective hand of the state, though their life was meager. Mankind has an instinct to paint his past in a rosy color, no matter how bitter it was. With the ever-widening gap in their ways of life between the south and north, South Korea has entered a new phase of the ideological clash with home-bred neo-Marxists.

In the South Korea, a succession of authoritarian regimes was a haven for the leftists to sow their seeds of suspicion to sprout into the self-proclaimed champion of a new version of utopia with an aversion to a few rich preying on the poor masses. Their ideological stand is justified by fighting for the suffering masses. Their struggle against the ruling authority drove them, willingly or unwillingly, playing into the hands of their northern partners. They stay fertile in the dark shadow of rapid growth and vie with their northern partners in a revolutionary zeal for the limelight. Neo-Marxists at home enjoy all the windfalls brought by the economic boom of South Korea, and some of them won secure places within the institutions. The left activists are divided into moderate leftists (Chin-buk, pro-North elements) and radical leftists (Jong-buk, ardent advocates of North Korea). The former, discontent with the repressive regimes in the south, maintains a nodding familiarity with North Korea, likely to tolerate the north's wrongdoings selectively, whereas the latter, still under the spell of a communal utopia, go one step further to ardently champion North Korea's stand on sensitive issues. Different strands of leftists are brought under the dome of a "Progressive Coalition" (Jin'bo yondae). There is an extremist wing which refuses to sing the national anthem and salute the national flag, the routine ritual to be observed at commemorative events. They are politically active by allying themselves with a political party, feeding it with political agenda.

The ideological showdown has penetrated into religious circles. Progressive elements are found in abundance even among young clergymen, who are the crop of the 386 generation nurtured in political activism against the institutions of South Korea in the 1980s. Korean churches were primary sanctuaries of resistance to the dictatorship and stirred the minjung (masses) movement against the authoritarian regimes. The timely encounter of their anti-government stance with Latin American liberation theology energized them to heroic acts for the suffering masses. They embarked, to begin with, on the realization of social justice which they thought to be a sacred mission weighing on their shoulders. By investigating into injustices done by the ruling authorities to political dissidents, they drew public attention to their positive result. As they continued to carry the day, they were increasingly politicized and convinced that their doings conform to what is dictated by justice. But history has never allowed the winner of a game to stay complacent for long. This self-claimed justice trapped them within an ideological cage. By openly denouncing their own regime, some extremists imperceptibly drifted into playing as the mouthpieces of North Korea on sensitive issues - such as reunification, south-north reconciliation, the peace agreement and the withdrawal of American troops. Their disenchantment with the South Korean regime rendered them unprepared for the seductive voice of new utopia.

Whatever their ideological stance may be, we cannot overlook the fallible reasoning of the cause the left-tilted clergymen fought for. In the first place, the ideological creed they endorsed runs afoul of their ecclesiastic mission. Some argue that social malaise justifies ecclesiastical intervention. Given their sacred commitment to the suffering masses, a logical question follows;"what made them close their eyes to a bad guy who strangles religion to death."They weep over the death of democracy in the south, but condone the north for the death of religion. Their ideological obscurity, to say the least, leaves seeds of distrust to grow to befuddle the masses whom they pledge to serve. They are, of course, entitled to the right to air free voices, but the problem arises when they deliberately ignore the nature of theology that is inherently at odds with ideological affiliation. To them South Korea is a more heinous villain than North Korea in the hierarchy of bad guys.

Koreans are still frittering away much of their energy asking questions; "Can the two Koreas become one?"; "how long will the communist regime remain an enclave of extreme austerity and stagnancy in this dynamic region?"; "is there any symptom of change in favor of positive progress?"and "whether South Korea is prepared for possible chaos resulting from unification"? For other countries, such issues are not worthy of a candlelight. Hidden behind the seemingly placid surface, neo-Marxism is stoking the embers of revolutionary fire. Having reached the pinnacle of power in the 1980s, it seemed that time had condemned Marxism to death. Nonetheless, neo-Marxism changed its costume to get rid of the old stigma of "red rebels" and planted its roots among Korean intellectuals and looked firmly entrenched as they were hailed as "democratic crusaders" against authoritarian rules. Some of them went a step further to overtly advocate Kim Il-sung's Jucheism and swear unfailing loyalty to him."They disguise themselves as honest progressives and carve out an important niche in nearly all of South Korea's intellectual circles and redefine nationalism within the framework of neo-Marxism and dependency theory" (Kang Thomas Hosuk, 1973,4-15). Unlike the softened leftists, their political goal is to see the incumbent regime, legitimatized by popular sanction, crumble into widespread anarchy which favors their way to thrive.

The neo-Marxists claim themselves to be the new arbiter of morality and legitimacy. They raise voices for the liberation of their pitiful brethren in the south from the clutch of neo-colonialism. Every anti-government move, even of a non-political nature, finds leftist agitators pulling levers behind the scene. Even a natural disaster offers the pretext for leftists to instigate the afflicted to stand against the government. Then, the issue drifts into an ideology-laden debate which sees no end. The recent sinking of a titanic sightseeing ship with secondary school kids aboard is likely to remain an enigma, so far as it is tinted with an ideological color. The yardstick of morality and legitimacy on their own terms forces every issue through the ideological prism that bypasses honest discourse between progressives and conservatives. Here, radical or extreme leftists should be differentiated from the leftists who are portrayed as true progressives, those of moderate character. Confrontational politics, imbued with a deeply ingrained hatred, go beyond the bound of a debate on "good vs. bad" or "agree vs. disagree." Those who take a middle position between the two extremes in a genuine concern for the country are labeled turncoats or renegades. To the generation fostered in the heat of revolution, concession or strategic retreat means death. Face-saving and formalism are played to obscure reason. The presence of diverse colors within the leftist camp makes it difficult to wrap them into a single ideological package. The progressive coalition is a long caravan, ever widening the gap between radical ideologists in the front and soft-minded progressives in the rear. The latter are honest progressives who stand for social justice, allying themselves flexibly with different groups of ideology.

Ideological passion alone can neither cope with the complexities of modern life nor provide a vessel for progress to meet various social needs. Ideological confrontation has perpetually locked Korean politics into a clash over every trivial issue. Here, political opponents are identified with overarching enemies laden with rancor to live through generations. The radical elements at the end of the spectrum of policy choices do not tolerate any attempt at compromise with their opponents. Ideologically-laden politics is a breeding ground for these activists to occupy places within the institutional establishments in recognition of their having done the lord's work for democracy. The core elements of "386 generation" remain cohesive in the name of "486 generation." They constitute the main stream of the opposition party, a coalition of factions with different political goals. Within the party, it is extremely difficult, due to their hard line, to reach an agreement on a single issue. The party leadership cannot turn its back against the hard-core leftists if it is to win their votes.

The concept of democracy is elastic enough to cover a range of permutations. We often hear the neo-Marxists bemoaning that South Korea is responsible for the lapse of democracy. These people are the radical wing of the progressives and carve out a niche within the Progressives Coalition. Their ideological alignment with the progressive elements posted within the institutions enabled them to feed the political agenda and shape public opinion in their favor on issues of public sensitivity. The records of imprisonment for the breach of the law follow most of the activists into key posts within the institutions: they rather proudly flaunt it as an honorable scar, the symbols of their tortuous careers by which they hope to leave an eternal imprint on time. The honorable scars occasionally give them a vantage ground to draw public attention in seeking elective offices. A scathing defamation of the incumbent President earns the blamer immediate acclaim and increasing popularity. Daring, audacity and rashness mark them as petty heroes. These traits have become an effective tool to win elections. One can imagine the anti-Czar revolutionists who nibbled at the fabric of the invincible Russian Empire and strangled it to extinction. They were more than willing to endure a nomadic exile in Siberia and returned, priding themselves on white beards, symbolic of hard life, to be greeted with a groundswell of ovations. They had no goal other than to have their sacrifice honored and revered by their revolutionary fellows. They lived in an age when rashness of behavior was glorified as the manifestation of heroism.

Should the radical group want to seek a niche in a multi-party political system, the ideological stand needs to be redefined, taking into account differences between the maelstrom of the early 20th century Europe and the confusing complexity of our times. The champions of a new utopia seek hideouts in a large organization. Liberal democracy has the merit of giving the ground for a new ideology to be tried on a new institutional base, blurring the distinction between friends and foes in a frequent debate on issues at stake. In the volatile political climate where friend and foe are dichotomized, however, it is difficult to realize emotion-neutral politics. It is not fair, though, to see all progressive radicals as in favor of North Korea. The hostile confrontation between leftists and rightists is better viewed as a contest between the dominant power and the dominated masses in that some of the latter are simply intransigent in their stance on policy choices. Their diehard opposition deepened the image of perpetual muckrakers standing for the sake of opposition.

The ideal of communism is far distanced from the reality. An institutional device to bring an equal share of possession for all necessarily involves a serious curtailment of individual freedom. The pseudo-scientific vision of communism sees the state as a gigantic machine to be manipulated by social engineering and people reduced into mere cogs. Its concomitant ideological and institutional rigidity leaves no social tolerance or redemption. The utopia envisioned by Lenin was far from an esoteric society where "cloak and dagger" tactics are rampant to dull public sensitivity to reason and justice. The transfer of power entails a massive bloody purge, and the ruling politics, as we see in North Korea, allows no elbow room for any rival or challenge. Politics based on the depoliticized masses features a heavy reliance on the state's propaganda. News are censored and disinformation is fed to make rhetoric triumphant over reason. While the masses are buried in deep layers of fables exalting the ruler as a divinity, the propaganda machine drowns out the voices of reason.

Ideological confrontation finds its manifestation in the on-going debate about the history textbooks in high schools. The debate centers around the legitimacy of the Republic of Korea (ROK) inaugurated on August 15, 1945 as a result of free elections under the U.N auspices. The progressive view of history puts fingers on Syngman Rhee, the midwife for the birth of the ROK, as a collaborator with pro-colonial elements and the surrender to the neo-colonialism of America. The ROK, according to their view, forfeited its sovereignty by failing to liquidate the colonial vestige of Imperial Japan. Its birth in this vein denotes a retreat into colonialism. They seek the legitimacy in the Korea Provisional Government in exile which came after the March First massive resistance in 1919. The government in exile falls short of the state in terms of the assortment of people, land, and sovereignty; rather it deserves due attention as the nationalist front, comparable to the French government in exile during World War II. It is credited with providing the constitutional framework for the birth of the ROK. Further, leftists parted with the KPG, discontent with its strategic impotence, leaving the centralists and rightists to patch the crack and serve as the founding fathers for ROK. Brutal colonial policy goaded Koreans to strengthen ethnic nationalism which still makes a resounding appeal. The anti-colonial prism leaves room for obscuring the state's legitimacy with dogma.

South Koreans say that its confrontation with leftist radicalism takes the wind out of its smooth sail which might otherwise have enabled it to advance further. The leftists stand firm within their niches bashing the south responsible for all problems that deter reunification. So far as confrontation with the new sprouts of Marxism continues, South Korea stands a chance to become another Latin America that is ticking along with generations of misguided leftists. Ideological scars, once engraved in Koreans' consciousness, never allow themselves to disappear into oblivion. A modern and complex society is never free from a rebellious mood of radicals. In one way or another, honest Koreans may have to live with them for good. In retrospect, Koreans were the first to experience communism — even by way of the civil war when a majority of Koreans were ideologically blind. The timing of the experience was a crucial factor, because it gave them an opportunity to be sober enough to make a rational assessment of what communism is all about. What if the war had broken out, contemporaneously with the Vietnam War? The validity of an action is judged in the hind sight of history. Although it appears to be peaceful and stable on the surface, Korean politics remains a smothered volcano.

---

1. Alvin Tofler prophesized the advent of 'the third wave' to befall the post industrial society, foreshadows new challenges that follow the withdrawal of the industrial society . He goes on to say that the post industrial society comes in 300 years after the industrial revolution. We are prisoners of an artificial environment and how to break loose from this cage foreshadows a way to face the post-industrial society. It seems that eastern culture emerges to fill the emotional wasteland of an artificial environment inherent in the urban and industrial society. The post-industrial society we envision lies beyond the artificial environment, awakened from our sick infatuation with progress, productivity, efficiency, and objectivity.

2. Chian in essence teaches that salvation comes from inner enlightenment and that enlightenment comes in an instant flash of insight, as it had to be the Buddha. It is a sudden conversion, obtainable in the routine of daily life. By turning one's gaze inward this can be seen and in one final version it is suddenly revealed. Ch'ian is thus hostile to much that had become traditional in Buddhism. Images and scriptures were viewed with hostility. Metaphysical speculation and theory were discarded for concrete experience. Such a religious experience is emphasized over knowledge and cognitive understanding.

3. The United States and Japan are placed into the high trust society by the elastic bound of the group prone to stake out to a more diffusive one. Individualism is the measure of high trust. It should, however, be noticed that individualism was built into the minds of Americans from the outset of building the nation, whereas Japanese are as much group-oriented as Koreans are. The strong solidarity of a group becomes an impediment to an elastic circle of trust. Fukuyama, despite remarkable differences in social background, attributes Japanese high trust to group-centered tendencies that go against the grain of individualism. Japan had remained feudal through much of its history and carried its legacies up to the Meiji Reformation in 1864. The crucial factor for an undeterred extension of the circle of trust owes much to Shintoism, the absolute reverence of the Emperor. Japan is the only country in the world that give divinity to an earthly being. The supreme being serves as a glue to hold the people together. Japan is much more a solid and collective state than Korea.

4. Part of Nietzsche's quotation reads "Democracy means drift; it means permission given to each part of an organism to do just what it pleases to do; it means the lapse of coherence and inter-dependence, the enthronement of liberty and chaos. It means the worship of mediocrity, and the hatred of excellence....... What is most hated, as a wolf by the dogs, is the free spirit, the enemy of all fetters (Will Durant; 324). His denial of mediocrity leaves ample room for the defense of autocracy.

5. Jung Yong (middle Way) is one of the Four Books, together with Mencius and Great Learning. This dictum teaches how to take a middle and flexible stance between the "excessively many" and the "excessively little."Jung means a middle and Yong for normal behavior that shows a timeless consistency, no matter how long it takes. It refers to a moderate character standing between excessively volatile and excessively inactive, comparable to Aristotle's reasonable behavior overcoming excessive desires. Jung Yong teaches people how to moderate excessive emotions. This ethical dictum stands between Confucian emphasis on reticence, impassiveness, a quiet musing on the one hand and the Shamanistic secular orientation of contemporary life. Such an attitudinal obscurity of the middle way accounts for the failure of many to internalize this virtue into their personality. It explains the absence of a culture that encourages compromise and reconciliation.

6. Both capitalism and communism came out of the same mothering womb, industrialization and capitalism. As industrialization made remarkable progress in material wealth, it was not free from its malignant effects, that is the exploitation of the poor and fattening a few. Communism made a messianic appeal for the world strewn with the wrecks of capitalism and kept the coming generations in the grip of ideological appeal. Communism lives off the fallacies of its sibling.. Communism and capitalism in this sense are blood siblings from one mother, but mutually exclusive. The pseudo scientific view of communism asserts that communism thrives on the ruins of capitalism. It condemns the existing order to extinction and calls for a "start from scratch" in the absence of customs, rites and value inherited from the past that are considered a nightmare.

7. Post Meiji Japan was blessed by a plethora of enlightened thinkers who helped a new state ship sail smoothly clear of imperialist incursions. One of them was Fukuzawa Yukichi, an enlightened reformist who served as a catalyst for the change of Japanese consciousness of nationhood during the post-Meiji Reformation period. He is known for his theory "Datsua-ron" which is translated into "Transcend Asia." According to Dasua-ron,"China and Korea are half-devils to be enlightened, and we cannot wait until they are fully awakened. Japan is fated to lead a backward Asia and deliver Asians from poverty." Japan was no longer part of Asia and should break loose from it in order to rub shoulders with the advanced Western countries. Then, Fukuzawa returned to the "ideal of Asia" and "the shielding of Asia from the imperial incursions." This theory was the spiritual base for Japan's imperialistic advance to establish a Greater Co-prosperity Sphere of Asia.

8. Joyce Carol Oath, author of "Them" published in 1970 captured a middle-class American family falling apart as proof that society was tail-spinning into regression, imbued with hedonism and counter-culture in the aftermath of Vietnam War. This phenomenon was depicted as the corollary of prevailing nihilism and the withdrawal into an inner being among youngsters. Her portrayal of the American home as an emotional wasteland augurs an apocalyptic vision of society on its inevitable path to collapse. John Updike echoed a similar tone in his "Rabbit Run." During this period, young militants laid a claim to Marxist, Leninists, and Maoists, enchanted with something with which they had never had a sensory experience.

The Past, Present and Future

Review of Korea's past conjures not so much a positive as negative imagery of Koreans. Unlike Chinese and Japanese, Koreans have never shouted their existence to the world. They stayed quiet and passive, occasionally losing some of their identity as they suffered from foreign incursions. In 1910, Korea's millennia-old history came to an end by surrendering to the imperialistic ambition of its neighboring country. Nonetheless, the history of Korea marks an exceptionally long existence of a centralized monarchical structure. The monarchical leadership in the nineteenth century, however, was inept and incapable of managing its own fate amid the vortex of imperialistic power struggles. Consequently, the last kingdom of Korea was drifting into the worst scenario of historical tragedy.

One of the most salient features of Koreans is the nation's ethnic and cultural homogeneity. Ethnic homogeneity provided an antidote for the instabilities and uncertainties of society. Despite its claim to a legendary social cohesiveness, Korean society was prone to factional divisions. Korean history attests to the impossible coexistence of social fraternity and division. Factionalism reflects the universal propensity of a people to group together by the same feather. In Korea where one ideology molds people into identical beings, the greater is the urge for one to look different from the pack. In a hierarchical and centralized ruling structure, grouping is artificial and is an opportunistic matter whose tenacity is exceptional when coupled with a competitive bid for power. One culture-dominant society is a fertile ground for rival factions to emerge, and the sense of fealty to a faction blinds one to the importance of a more encompassing community. Group egoism is one of the most prominent feature of Koreans' persona.

Today's Koreans are more self-centered, resulting from a kind of parochial egoism based on the misconception of Western individualism. A mad drive for an insatiable ambition renders Koreans much weaker in the sense of a voluntary commitment to public interests. The ideal side of Confucian tenet is that a man truly serves his self-interests by perceiving self-identity as part of society. The best way to be loved, says Confucius, is to defer others. This Confucian plea no longer makes so a strong appeal as it used to be among the contemporary Koreans.

Nationalism, largely attributed to ethnic homogeneity, was a tinderbox for inflaming the anti-colonial struggle. Claiming itself as the champion of equality and the oppressed majority, communism once enchanted Korean nationalists and intellectuals as the surest way to save the country from the collective ruin of the industrial and capitalistic world. Communism, a violent reaction to the bleak prospects of the capitalistic world, obscured nationalism that could have put forth national interests before ideological concerns. The joy of Koreans' liberation from the colonial yoke was lost in the heat of the ideological war, and their dreams of reshaping their tattered country shattered. Post-liberation Korea was breathless with a succession of world-convulsing events that traumatized a toddler about to walk on his own feet. This was, in large part, due to inhabiting a fringe of the Asian land mass much of which had surrendered to communism by the that time. In the Asian landmass vulnerable to spreading communism, South Korea was a flickering flame before the ideological gust. In this situation, a unitary Korea was most assured of salvation by communism. The first armed clash of the Cold War and territorial division gave way to an abiding sense of grief and frustration among the dispersed families.

In the early 1960s, South Korea made a dramatic turnaround by turning its dormant competency into a new spurt of growth. For the last six decades, changes, starting with an economic spurt, have been so remarkable that Koreans look back with a sense of pride on their past achievement. Trauma theory explains much of the dramatic turnaround, but this is not all there is to explaining Korea's rise. There are other factors that conspire to inflame Koreans' passions for accomplishment. The hierarchical consciousness of Koreans gave rise to a pressure for an upward advance in social order. Educated Koreans are perpetually motivated to improve themselves toward the highest version of the self.

Confucianism still runs so deep among Koreans as the official image of Koreans, though not all Koreans feel the Confucian beating in their pulses. The lofty image of Confucianized Koreans contrasts starkly with the vulgar, crude and lowly aspects of life. Confucianism preaches self-cultivation, self-restraint and deference to others, but its emphasis on hierarchy and group solidarity creates emotion-ridden bonds. Communal solidarity takes precedence over individual autonomy, and vertical consciousness dims horizontal perspectives. The altruistic touch of the Confucian call for "self-perfection and deference to others" find its resonance in Emmanuel Kant's "seek perfection in oneself and happiness in others." Confucian world is not a lonely island to be submerged by the expanding world of universal values. Notwithstanding what appears to be phenomenal differences, the East and West have some of their values in common. Confucianism has merits that need to be refashioned, but this merit is paradoxically obscured by ritualism, face-saving, formalism and mannerism, all coming from stipulating the codes of conduct instead of relying on a voluntary will and internal urges.

Modern Koreans are robust, aggressive and quarrelsome, breaking the stereotype images of submissiveness, compliance and impassive dignity. When these new characters were matched with military efficiency, authoritarian rule radiated its leadership by mocking the rule of law to justify dogmatism. Collective consciousness brings the triumph of the heart over the head. Amidst a widely spread collective consciousness, liberal democracy may have to alter its course pursuant to the particular values. This begs the question about whether Koreans try to mirror the Western democracy or to create its own model.

Koreans find a greater meaning of living in the harmonious blend of antithetical forces, contrary to their Western counterparts who seek dynamism from Max Weber's "armed peace" and confrontation theory. The premise is that progress is possible when one state is pitted against another, for the presence of rivals inspires competition and a dynamic force. By contrast, Koreans maintained a stable order of society that led to a cultural florescence and industrialization. Weber's view of the Protestant ethics as responsible for capitalistic development conceals the ills of capitalism that aggravated people's competitive and individualistic impulses and distanced them from their communities, their traditions and their sympathies with nature. To Koreans, excessive competition is an anathema, for it contradicts a harmonious blend of the opposites. Weber did not see the collective ruin of the capitalistic world that followed excessive competition between the major industrial powers.

By and large, there are four agents of value change; namely, globalization, democratization, scientific and technological development and ideological confrontation. Globalization exposes Koreans to new values, kicking off a chain reaction that shakes society out of its trenches. Easy access to advanced technology across borders has enabled developing countries to catch up with the forerunners, and so Koreans made an impressive headway in the economy to be recognized as a new economic power. Changes are no longer one way, from the developed to less developed countries. In principle, both the developed and developing countries become the beneficiaries of the two-way traffic of technology, capital and ideas.

South Korea was hard hit by the 1997 economic downturn and lost momentum and pride in the rapid growth. Koreans' failure to make timely changes in values is singled out to be responsible for the economic downturn that invited an international agency to bail it out. The economic downturn coincided with political liberalism, as the economic spurt was timed with authoritarian rule. Workers intransigently opposed forced lay-offs, even though it was justified by business difficulties. The forced lay-offs were an anathema to emotion-dominant Koreans who were willing, even at the moment of crisis, to share their last bowls of rice. The communitarian spirit visible down at the village level was supposed to project itself into larger circles of association and society. Confined within a parochial bound of intimacy, Koreans are reluctant to cross the threshold of a village to see the world of strangers. In a situation marked by the lack of an intermediate value, the Korean economy was plagued by the frequent walkouts whose acrimoniousness was comparable to the British railroad strikes in the 1960s and 1970s. South Korea bounced back at a dazzling pace, owing to a rare combination of team work and new leadership. Competition and the rational working of the market redefined the emotional relationship into previously unfamiliar cold calculation of personal interest.

Koreans often look to the past as a mirror to emulate, and their sense of time is endless like the eternal flow of blood through generations. This gives an immediate concern to what happened to their remote forebears and what will happen to their descendants. The contiguity of time contrasts Alexander Tocqueville's view of American dynamism: social conditions severed the tie that formerly united one generation to another. The woof of time is in every instant broken and the traces of generations effaced. Americans were free, at the outset, from feudalistic inhibitions but not from social restraints at all that sculpted rugged individualists into domesticated and law-abiding citizens.

As modernization proceeds, some of the traditional values give way to new ones, but severing ties to the past is unimaginable to Koreans: they try to seek new possibilities within civilized limits. Koreans live with patrimonial values that were once lauded as essential to ethnic and blood continuity. They have a sense of belonging to a succession of generations from a time immemorial to the unknown future. Their prime concern is the endless flow of human relations, comparable to a river that runs eternal. Free move along an endless time corridor erases distinctions between the past and the future, and all generations in the flowing stream are melted into a single identity, stressing the inter-generational responsibility. Confucianism creates a parochial circle of intimates, but this circle loses out in the public domain where cold head prevails over the emotional workings of the heart. Confucianism leaves public life empty to be filled with new, most likely universal values, while Koreans try to mirror the Western notion of democracy. Conflict between particular and universal values comes down to a contest between private and public domains. How to bring the two into a harmonious interplay remains to be answered by those aspirants for democracy.

Koreans' lack of communitarian or a civic spirit owes much to the naïve belief that private familial solidarity can be extrapolated to larger circles of association. Their attachment to molecular values at the cost of intermediate value places Korea among the low-trust societies. Burdened with the weight of the past, they were slow to adopt a value consciousness that matches the hectic pace of technological advance. Change resulting from the application of technology is differentiated from the change of non-material value. Democracy was grafted onto parochial values, and the resulting conflicts and confrontation peppered the tortuous course of democratic development. For all its problems, democracy has made its headway in South Korea, notably in procedural democracy. The promise of democracy ultimately rests on whether Koreans can go beyond the parochial value to internalize intermediate values.

Koreans envision a society that exalts people over the state. Civic consciousness gains new importance as traditional norms decline. In order to become a topnotch official, every Korean must pass muster that scrutinizes the transparency and honesty of one's past performances. Although confined within the hierarchical and collective structures, South Korea owed its quick recovery from the economic downturn to collaboration among all groups and individuals who were dedicated to serve future generations. The long-standing parochial circles of intimates were stretched, at the moments of crisis, so that all responded in a united manner to get the country out of crisis. Personal sacrifice to a common goodness and market competition in combination permeated popular imagination, breaking new ground for greater possibilities. Despite the remarkable changes, the vertical structure of management, clan-centered leadership in particular, defies change. Familial solidarity remains absolute necessity in the hierarchical structure at the cost of the horizontal structure. Industrialization enlarged opportunities for more men and women to engage in productive works, and its concomitant accompaniment is the atomization of the family and the greater frequency of broken families.

Technology not only saves us time but forces us to move fast to catch up with new things. The down side is greater emphasis on surface phenomena, and obsession with the present dulls one's sober vision of the future. Aged people, retrospective of the past, choose to stay in the present, while young people are over-stimulated at novelty and repellent to the tranquility in which solid human bonds flourished. Their obsession with momentary experience fosters a myopic view of the future. There is a welcome sign of digital politics as a direct conveyor belt of public opinions. The rapid spread of contrived or forged information, however, strips Koreans of an ability to make a reasonable and informed decision particularly with regard to topical issues subject to improvised reactions. In the massive rally to oppose the importation of American beef, digital politics fanned anti-American sentiment. The media was crucial in arousing a public fury, and it went even to threaten the representative system of liberal democracy. As demonstrated here, direct participation through the internet brought its own risks to darken the bright side of democracy. Every policy decision, though made in compliance with democratic procedure, is subject to opposition. The loud voices of people often form a chorus of mob mentality that is averse to rationality.

Koreans inhabit a region most vulnerable to uncanny human disasters. Socialist weeds challenge capitalist grass on their turf, and they are keen to see if the weeds outgrow the grass. The ideological trauma Koreans experienced does not flicker and vanish in a flash. The pain stays with the scattered families like a ghost unlikely to be placated. Koreans may have to experience the culture of protest as a matter of life, so far as two Koreas with different conditions for living remain. Gaping chasms between the two halves not only in the quality of life but psychic and emotional make-up do not allow reason to enter their search for a viable way to live together.

Every change partakes of the culture of its time, and ideological passion is time-specific. Ideological obsession results in the over-simplification of so diverse and variable needs of modern society. A country deeply buried in a revolutionary passion dies from institutional rigidity and an invincible ignorance of the outside world. Revolution no longer happens on a heroic and grandiose scale. The time has passed when the mystic invincibility of the Russian Empire crumbled at one Bolshevist stroke. Change may start with a mere accident or random confluence of conditions within itself, and it is not to be forced until it mellows into the will of people. Democracy provides a great degree of subtlety and flexibility in dealing with complicated social issues.

Time brings new needs, but much is left behind as we move along. There are bits and pieces of our past that follow us through life. They appear and reappear in our hearts as connecting threads to the past in our lives that we hope will be enduring. When these legacies of the past are ripe for change, they pulsate with a new spurt of energy that cannot be stopped. Merciless iconoclasm in the heat of revolution, as practiced by North Korea, offers no remedy for value conflicts and no hope to sublimate them into harmonious interplay. In the game of new dynamism, Koreans hark back to the past and revive the utilitarian version of traditional virtues that can serve as the functional equivalent of Max Weber's Protestant ethics. Value conflicts follows us, as long as we balk at the wholesale acceptance of the liberal democracy of an alien nature. The quest for what is workable requires us to examine all aspects of conflicting values and make a new tapestry on a selective basis in due consideration of the historical and cultural context within which Korean society exists.

For Koreans, the tast remains clear that history and culture are the common threads that hold peoples together. In order for Korea to truly recast itself as a responsible power in the region and the world, however, it will have to change its own costume so that it goes beyond its ethnic and cultural restraints. It is imperative that Korea be allied with others not by history and culture but by institutional commonality and shared goal, if it is to become an important partner of this most dynamic region of the world. To explain national identity in terms of past trauma provides little guidance for the policy actions Korea should adopt particularly in relation to its important allies. Stubborn obsession with historical issues provides little cushion when deeper and more important international issues challenge Koreans than "what Japan's textbooks say." Of course, Japan's baffling inability to deal with its past is a haunting ghost to its neighboring countries. However, it is rather Japan not Korea, that has drawn a worldwide criticism.

Brothers in the north summon ethnic nationalism that views reunification in a romantic illusion. Ethnic nationalism lost out since it had served the goal to achieve national independence. Former colonized states dieted on ethnic purity to remain entrenched in its seat. North Korea still adheres to this primordial creed and blames the South for having sullied ethnic purity by colluding with colonialism and imperialism. Globalization does not allow ethnic purity to remain entrenched in its seat. Following World War II, South Korea alone witnessed liberal democracy sprouting through a broken concrete, while all countries freshly liberated from colonial rule were infatuated with communism. Time brings a new historical mandate. South Korea should articulate what it can do by defining itself not necessarily as the North's blood relatives but as an important ally with its neighbors. Ultimately, if South Korea hopes to become a responsible nation in the world, it will have to rethink how it fits into the new world. Defining self-identity involves the process of assessing all virtues and faults of Koreans in terms of their bearings on social change. Changing its national identity is an on-going drama linking the past to the present and future.

Sometime in the future, Korea will become a strong economic power in the world, and a political force in East Asia. On the ideal side, we can imagine the combined economies of North and South, married to such a talented and well educated people. Japanese leaders take a dim view of a united Korea. China will flaunt its clout as a new rival for the world power but will remain a bona fide partner of South Korea so far as it holds cards against an irascible North Korea. But it is never likely that China leaves its bloody ally to fade away. Here is the dilemma that explains the difficulty of reunification. North Korea may be brought closer to asphyxiation under an intense international pressure, but the regime and its system will survive while its people are destined for hell fire. Both the South and North see recalcitrant separatists in place, mostly the beneficiaries of their present systems, reluctant to trade their own interests for the greater cause of a unified country. Reunification, if achieved, will not be free from the abiding scars that are left for uncared.

Bibliographical References

Abelman, Nancy and Lie, John, *Blue Dream*, Cambridge; Harvard University Press, 1976

Acheson Dean, *Present at the Creation*, New American Library, 1969

Ahn, Byung Man, *Elites and Political Power in South Korea*, Edward Elgar Publishing, (London 2003)

Amstrong Karen, *The History of God*, Ballantine Books.(New York 1993)

———, *Fields of Blood*,2015, Anchor Books (New York, 2015)

Arendt Hannah, *The Human Condition*, the University of Chicago Press. 1998

Bary, Theodore de Haboush, JaHyun *The Rise of Neo-Confucianism*, Columbia University Press,1988

Beasely, W.G *The Rise of Modern Japan*, Charles E. Tutle Co. (Tokyo 1990)

Loyalty is defined as an obligation serving masters in a hierarchical order. The warrior (samurai) owe their loyalty to their feudal lords, the feudal lords owe it to the shogun, and the shogun owes owe it to the emperor ruled by prescriptive right, acting "in perfect harmony of thought and feeling with his ancestress, the sun goddess, and by that fact, was entitled to unquestioningobedience. This made the emperor authority independent of the virtue or lack of it.

Bell, Daniel A,*Confucian Democracy, Why and How*, edited by Hahm Chaibong, Hahm Chaihark,David L Hall, *Jeontong kwa Hyundae* (Tradition and Modernity). Seoul 1998)

Benhobib Seyla *The Claims of Culture*: Equality and Diversity in the Global Era, Princeton University Press, 2002

Breen, Michael,*The Koreans*, Orion Business, (Seoul, 1998)

Botton Alain de,*Religion for Atheists*, A Division of Random House, (New York, 2012)

Brand R.S. Vincent, *Korean Village between Farm and Sea*, Harvard East Asian Series (Boston1972)

Brzezinski Zbigniew, T*he Grand Failure*, MacMillan Publishing Company, (New York 1989)

Byun Young Hwa, Doctoral Thesis of Korean Studies, Graduate School of Internal and Area Studies, Hankuk University of Foreign Studies, (Seoul 2014)

Cantor F Norman, *Medieval Europe*, The Macmillan Company, (London 1963).

Carlton Michael, *The Four-Seven Debate*, The State University of New York Press, 1994

Carter Eckert, *Korea Old and New*: A History, Korea Institute, Harvard Univ. Ilchogak Publisher, (Seoul, 1990)

Carriere, Fredericks, quoted from his talk on "The Koreans" in the 1985's summer Korea Studies Program hosted by Korea Research Foundation.

Chang, Edward Taehan, *Korean Kaleidoscope: An Overview of Korean Immigration to theU.S*, Korean and Korean American Studies Bulletin, 2004

Choi, Bong Young, *Hankuk In'eui Sahoejok Seong Kyuk* (The Social Character of Koreans), *Hankuk In'eui Euisik Kujo* (Consciousness Structure of Koreans) II, Seoul; Neutinamu, (Seoul, 1994)

Choi Chang-jip, Jung Ang Daily Press dated January 4, 2010

Choi, Hyun Bae, *Ways to Reform the Korean Nation*, Chong Kum Sa, (Seoul, 1962)

Chang, Jae Shik, "Confucian Reform Movement for Korea's Transformation," *Korea betweenTradition and Modernity* edited by Chang Yoon Shik, Institute for Asian Research, University of British Columbia, (Vancouver, 2000)

Cheong Jae-young, "*Sahoe eh Michienun Gajok Jui Yeong Hyang*" (The Impact of Familism on Society), Sahoe Iron (Social Theory), Korea Society for Theories of Korean Society), (Seoul, 2002)

Cho Kap-je ,"The Legitimacy of the Republic of Korea Stolen to North Korea"*Konkuk eui bal'gyeon* (The Foundation of a New Nation State), Love of the Republic of Korea Press, (Seoul, 2004).

Chung, Sun Mok , *The Image of Man in the Korean Traditional Culture*, Kwang Jang (December Series), Seoul, 1980).

Chung Yak Yong Chong Seo;2 chip (group) 4 kwon (volume)

Creative Art and Critique,*Mirae reul Yoneun Uri eui Sigak eul Chataso* (In search of newperspectives to open the future), Chang Jak kwa Bipyeong Sa (Seoul, 1998)

Cumings Bruce, *The Division of Korea*, A summary paper of the Origins of the Korean War. See Korea's Place in the Sun, W.W Norton and Company, (New York, 1977), pp.185-224

———— Korea's Place in the Sun, W.W. Norton & Company, 1997

Deuchler, Martina, "The Tradition: Women During the Yi Dynasty," In *Virtues in Conflict;Tradition and the Korean Woman Today*, ed. Sandra Matelli, Seoul: Royal Asiatic Society, 1977

———— *The Confucian Transformation of Korea: A Study of Society and Ideology*, Harvard-Yenching Institute Monograph, no.36. Cambridge: Council on East Asian Studies,Harvard University, 1992

Dawson, Christopher, *The Dynamics of World History*, edited by G.G. Mulloy, New York; NewHaven Library, 1966

Dong, Won Mo "University Students in South Korean Politics: Patterns of Radicalization in the1980s." This paper was originally presented at the annual meeting of the American Political Science Association, Washington D.C on 30 August 1986

Doren, Charles Van,*A History of Knowledge*, New York: Ballantine BooksGoode, William J.1963.

Duncan John, Confucian Social Values in Contemporary South Korea, *Religion and Society in Contemporary Korea*, Institute of East Asian Studies, University of California, (Berkeley, 1997)

Durant Will, *The Story of Philosophy*, Simon and Schulster Paperbacks, (New York, 1961)

Elrenreich Barbara, Time Essay Collection'94, Woo Il Munhwa Sa (Publishing Co.) (Seoul, 1995)

Farb Peter, *Man's Rise to Civilization*, Avon Books, (New York, 1968)

Freeman, Alan, The Irish of Asia –Full of Song and Laughter, *Introducing Korea* (edited by Peter

Hyun), Jungwoosa, (Seoul, 1975)

Fukukawa Yukiko, Sociologist and Professor of Waseda University, regular contributor of columns to Choson Daily Press

Fukuyama Francis, *The End of History and the Last Man*, The Division of Simons and Schuster Inc.

———— The Primacy of Culture, *Journal of Democracy*, Vol.6 No.1 Jan.1995

Galbraith J.K, *Economics, Peace and Laughter*, Andre Deutsch Ltd. 1971

Geary J. Patrick, *The Myth of Nations*: The Medieval Origins of Europe, Princeton University Press, 2002

Goldberg, Charles N, Spirits in Place: The Concept of Kohyang, Studies on Korea in Transition, Center for Korean Studies, University of Hawaii, 1979

Hahn Young-woo , *uri eui yoksa* (The History of Korea), Kyung Sewon Publishing Co. (Seoul, 1997)

Halm, Chaibong , *Tal Keundae wa Yukyo* (Post-modernism and Focus Confucianism), Seoul: Nanam Publishing Co.1998

———— 1998 "Confucianism and Politics of Culture" *Korea Focus* 6. No.4

Hahm, Inhee, "Tragic Death of a Lonely Goose Dad," *Korea Focus*, Korea Foundation, Nov.-Dec.Volume11 No.6 This article was carried by Munwha Ilbo date d November 1, 2003

Haldberstam David, *The Best and the Brightests*, A Fawcett Crest Books, 1969

Hannah, Arendt, *The Human Conditions*, Chicago, the University of Chicago Press, 1958

Han Geon-soo, Korea Transforms Itself into a Multicultural Society, *Koreana*, Vol.22, No.2 summer 2008

Hendersen, Gregory, "Grapping with Korean Persona," *Wild Asters*, a report of workshop byWoodrow Wilson International Center for Scholars, 1983

———— *Korea, The Politics of the Vortex*, Harvard University Press, 1968

Hoffman, Dian, "Blurred Genders; The Cultural Construction of Male and Female in Korea and the United States" *The Cultural Roots*, Chicago: North Park College Press, 1995

Holt, Bertha, "Bring My Sons From Afar, The Unfolding of Harry Holt's Dream, Holt International Children Service, 1992

Hong Sah-myung, *Korea and the World*, Hankuk University of Foreign Studies Press,(Seoul, 2008)

Hong Seung Pyo,Social Psychological problems of Koreans and Solution through Asian Thought, *Keimyung Korean StudiesJournal* (Korean Studies Research Center), Keimyung University, (Taegu, 2010)

Horton, Paul B and Hunt, Chester,*Sociology*, MacGraw-Hill Book Co.(New York, 1964)

Hsiao Ching (Hyo Kyung in Korean), Preface

Hubinette, Tobias,*Comforting the Orphaned Nation*, Stockholm University Dept. of OrientalStudies, 2005

Hulbert, Homer B,. *The Passing of Korea*, Seoul: Yonsei University Press, (Seoul, 1969)

Huntington Samuel P. The Clashes of Civilization, Simon & Schuster, 2002

Kang, Shin Pyo, *The Korean Outlook on Life in Korean Culture*, Kwang Jang (Seoul, 1983)

Kang, Jung In, Deconstructing the "Clash of Civilizations" Thesis, *Confucian Democracy, Whyand How* edited by Hahm Chaibong, Hahm Chaihark, David L Hall, Jeontong kwa Hyundae (Tradition and Modernity), 1998.

Karl, E. Rebecca,Can a Post-1919 World History Be Written?, *Sungkyun Journal of East Asian Studies*, Vol.9No.1 (April), The Academy of East Asian Studies, Sungkyunkwan University,(Seoul, 2009)

Kalton C Michael, *Four-Seven Debate*, The State University of New York Press, 1994

Keum Jang-dae, *Confucianism and Korean Thoughts*, Hankuk Haksul Jeong Bo (Korea Science Information), 2006

Kendall, Laurel, *Under Construction. The Gendering of Modernity, Class and Consumptionin the Republic of Korea.* University of Hawaii Press, 2002

————— Korean Shamans and the Spirits of Capitalism, *American Anthropologist* Vol.98, No.3 September, 1996

Kim Hyun,*Imun-hak eui Bburi reul Ik'da* (Read the Roots of Humanities), Iwawoo, Seoul, Korea, 2006

Kim, Jae-eun, *The Koreans: Their Mind and Behavior*, Seoul: Lyobo Book Center, 1991

Kim, Byung Kuk, a paper presented for a symposium jointly held by Korea University and Center for International Affairs, Harvard University in September 20-27, 1997

Kim Byung-uk, Korea Focus Winter, 2009 p.101

Kim, Kwang Ok."Socio-Political Implications of the Resurgence of Ancestor Worship in Contemporary Korea," *Studies in East Asia Society*, Seoul: Center for East Asia Cultural Studies, 1992

Kim Seok-ju, "The Koreans' Perception of Death from the Philosophical Viewpoint," Seoul, *Death and Life of Koreans*, Cholkak kwa Hyunsil (Philosophy and Reality) Co., pp.74-145, 2001

Kim,Tae Gil, "Hyundae Hankuk eui Yunri Sahang" (Status of Morality in Modern Korean Society)*Hyundae Sahoe wa Cholhak* (Modern Society and Philosophy) edited by Kim Tae Gil, Seoul:Munhak kwa Chisung, 1981

Kim Yol Kyu, Death in Modern Korea and Its Relation to Tradition, *Death and Life of Koreans*, Seoul, Cholhak kwa Hyunsil (Philosophy and Reality) Co. 2001,p.148

Kim Young-chan, *Tosan Ahn Chang-ho: A Profile of a Prophetic Patriot*, Tosan Memorial Foundation, (Seoul, 1996)

Kim Young-won, *Korea in Transition*, The Korea Herald, 1989

Kim Yun-shik, Juche wa Jinbo eui Galdeung (Conflict between Subjectivity and Progressivism) in *Hankuk eui Jiseong* (The Wisdom of Korea), Seoul, Munye Publishing Co. 1977

Kingly, Davis,*Human Society*, MacMillan Co. (New York 1969)

Koh Byung-cheol, *Chuch'esong* in Korean Politics, reprinted from Studies in Comparative

Communism. Vol. Nos. 1 and 2, Spring/Summer, 1974

Koh, Young Bok,"Kukje Sahoe Sidae Hankuk In" (The Koreans in the Global Era), *Hyundaesa reul Ottoke Bolgot Inka* (How to View Modern History, Dong Ah Daily Press, 1990

Kurlansky Mark, *The Year that Rocked the World*, Vintage, (London,1988)

Kwak, Baehee "Who Would Dare Cast a Stone upon His Mother?" *Korea Focus*, Seoul: KoreaFoundation Nov-Dec. Vol.11. No.6, 2003

Kwon Tae-joon, *Hankuk eui Segi Ttwionamgi* (Korea to Transcend the Century Horizon), Namam Publishing Co. Inc. (Seoul, 2006)

Lee Eul-ho,*Hankuk Silhak Sasang Gasol* (Overview of Korean Pragmatic Learning); Seoul, Samsung Publishing Co.1976

Lee In,ho, Rhee *Seung-man and National Foundation*, Konkuk eui Bal'gyeon (The Foundation of a New Nation State), Love of the Republic of Korea Press, 2004

Lee Joo-young & Kim Hyong-In, *The Modern History of the United States*, Hwabong Publishing Co. (Seoul, 2003)

Lee, Kang No, "Critical Analysis of Anti-Americanism in Korea", *Korea Focus*, Vol.13, Seoul:Korea Foundation, 2005

Lee, Ki-sang ,,*Jigu Chon Sidae wa Moon Hwa Contents* (Global Village and Culture Contents), Hankuk University of Korean Studies, 2009

Lee Sang-eun, *Yuhak kwa Dongyang Munhwa* (Confucianism and Oriental Thought), Seoul, Bomhak Doseo, 1976

Lee Won-sul, *Reflectionsof a Asian Mind*, Kyung Hee University Press, 1980

Lew, Seokchoon, "Confucianism and the Network Society," *Confucian Democracy, Why andHow* edited by Hahm Chaibong, Hahm Chaihark, David L Hall, Jeongtong kwa Hyundae (Tradition and Modernity), 1998

Lew, Seokchoon, Column entitled "Hahm Byong Choon and Korea's Modernization, Choseon Ilbo dated Nove.17, 2013.

Lee, Sang Eun, *Yuhak kwa Dong Yang Mun Hwa* (Confucianism and Eastern Culture), Seoul: Bomhak Do Seo, 1976

Lee Won Sul, *Gidokyo Sekekwan kwa Yeoksa Baljeon* (Christian View of the World and Historical Development, Seoul: Haeseon Publishing Co.1990

———— Creative Response, Sung Kwang Publishing Co. 1977

Lee Yun-gap, *Hankuk Ryuksahak eui Sarown Gilchat'gi:Minjok Jui Ryuksahak eui Jeon Mang* (A New Approach to Korean History: The Prospect of History based on Nationalism), Keimyung Korean Studies Journal Vol.35, 1977

Lilla, Mark, "Shades of the 60s", *Newsweek*, June 2001

Lin Yu-tang, The Invention of Life, *Life and Living*, Dong Seong Pub. Co. Seoul, 1984

Lun, Yu; Collection of Confucian analects and saying) see the chapter of Politics

Max, Weber, *The Methodology of Social Science* (Edward A. Shills and Henry, ed. and trans.)New York, 1949

————*The Religion of China: Confucianism and Taoism*, edited and translated by Hans H.Gerth, New York: McMillan Co, 1964

———— Confucianism and Taoism, in *Segye Daesasang* (The World's Great Thought, Vol.12, Seojl; Whimun Publishing Co. 1974

McDonald Donald S,*The Koreans; The Contemporary tics and Soceity*, Boulder: WestviewPress, 1990

Mencius Analect, 2A6

Mackay Hugh, *Reinventing Australia*, Angus & Robertson, 1993

Masao, Miyamoto, *Straight Jacket Society*, Tokyo: Kodan International, 1995

Moon, Seong Sook, "The Production and Subvertion of Hegemonic Masculinity: ReconfiguringGender Hierarchy in Contemporary South Korea," *Under Construction: The Gendering of Modernity, Class and Consumption in the Republic of Korea*, University of Hawaii Press, 2002

Mike Binning, "Mother in Nursing Home," Kukje Munye (International Literature), 2011

Morison, Samuel Eliot, *"The Oxford History of the American People,"* New American Library,1942

Novack George, *Democracy and Revolution*, Pathfinder Press Inc. New York, 1971

Park Euikyung, "Voluntary Nationalism with the Idea of Self-Invested Nation: An Aspect of American Exceptionalism,"*International Area Review*, Hankuk University of Foreign Studies (Seoul), 2005 pp.130-145

Parrinder, Jeoffry, *World Relgions*, The Hamlyn Publishing Group Lt. 1971

Parsons, Talcott and Shills A, Edward,*Toward a General Theory of Action: TheoreticalFoundation for Social Sciences*, Cambridge: Harvard University Press, 1951

Parsons, T, *The Structure of Social Action, The Religion of China* ed. by H H Gerth, MacMillan,1964

Prahhavananda, Wami,*The Spiritual Heritage of India*, Doubleday, new York, 1964

Reich Charles A, *The Greening of America*, Random House, Inc.1971

Rietbergen P. Jan, A Short History of the Netherlands, Bekking Publishers Amersfoort, the Netherlands, 2004

Rosaldo, Michelle Zimbalist, Women, Culture and Society: A Theoretical Overview in Women,"*Culture and Society* edited by M.Z Poslado and L. Lamphere, Stanford University Press, 1974

Roszak, Theredore,*Where the Wasteland Ends*, Doubleday & Company. Inc. Garden City, New York, 1974

Ruth, Benedict, *The Chrysanthemun and the Sword*, Tuttle Publishing, 1954

Santayana George,*Reason in Religion* Vol.III, 1905

Shim Jae-ryong, "Bulkyo wa Inkan "(Buddhism and Mankind), *Hyundai Sahoe wa CholhakEdited* by Kim Tae-gil, 1981

Smith Wilfred Cantwell, Belief and History ,Charlottesville, 1985

Song, Ho Keun 2003, *Hankuk Sedae Kaldeung kwa Johwa eui Mihwa* (Inter-generational Conflicts inKorea and the Beauty of Harmony), Samsung Kyung Je Yeonku Sa,(Seoul, 2003)

———— Jung Ang Daily Press Editorial dated 29 December 2009

Song, Young-bae,, *Jegapaka eui* Sa-sang (Thoughts of Ancient Chinese Scholars), Hyun Eum Sa,(Seoul, 1994)

Scruton, Roger,*The West and the Rest*, Intercollegiate Studies Institute, Wilmington, Delaware, 2002

Stump Keith W, The History of Europe and the Church, *The Plain Truth*, 1984

Taussig Michael,*The Devil and Commodity Fetishism in South American*. Chapel Hill, University of North Carolina Press, 1980

Tikhonov Vladmir,*Naneun Pokryok Segi reul Kobalhanda* (I Accuse the Era of Violence), Seoul:Sasang Sa, (Seoul, 2005)

Tsuya Noriko O and Choe Minja Kim, "Changes in Intra-familial Relation Relationships and the Role of Women in Japan and Korea" NUPRI Research Paper Series no.58, 1991

Vos Frits,*Korea*, Schillinger Verlag GmbH, Freiburg, (Germany, 1995)

Wade Nicholas, *A Troublesome Inheritance*, The Penguin Press (New York, 2014)

Won-won, The Term Paper for Graduate Studies entitled "The Globalization of China and the Asian Value," Hankuk University of Foreign Studies, (Seoul, 2009)

Ye, Son Ok, *Urinara Ibyang Jedo Siltae wa Gaeson Bang Hyang,*(Study on Actual Conditions and Improvement Plan of Adoption System for Protection-needed Children in Korea), MA Thesis, Sejong Woman's University, (Seoul, 2001)

Yang, C.H, "Introduction to Max Weber", *The Religion of China* ed. by H H Gerth, McMillan, 1968

Yi, Kyu-tae,*The Structure of Korean Mind*, Vol.1-2, Seoul, Mulli Sa. Read his "Rediscovery of the Koreans published by Mulli Sa, (Seoul, 1977)

Yoon ,Tae-rim,*Hankuk In eui Inseong* (The Personality of Koreans), Seoul: Hyundae Kyo YukChong Seo , (Seoul, 1964)

Yoo, Myung-jong,,*Song Myong Chol Hak* (Sung-Ming Philosophy), Seoul: Hyung Seong Pub.Co. (Seoul,1976)

Who Are Koreans?

초판 1쇄 발행   2017년 11월 20일

지은이   홍사명

펴낸이   김경옥
펴낸곳   도서출판 다웅
마케팅   서정원
디자인,제작   디자인원(031.941.0991)

출판등록번호   제406-2006-000049호
주 소   경기도 파주시 문발로 405, 204호
　　　　서울특별시 마포구 월드컵북로 162-4 1층(편집부)
전 화   031.932.6777(본사) 02.326.4200(편집부)
팩 스   02.336.6738
이메일   aromju@hanmail.net

ISBN   979-11-962237-0-0 13180

이 도서의 국립중앙도서관 출판시도서목록(CIP)은 서지정보유통지원시스템 홈페이지(http://seoji.nl.go.kr)와
국가자료공동목록시스템(http://www.nl.go.kr/kolisnet)에서 이용하실 수 있습니다.(CIP제어번호 : CIP 2017028875)